Radical Tragedy

Religion, Ideology and Power in the Drama of Shakespeare and his Contemporaries

Reissued Third Edition

JONATHAN DOLLIMORE

palgrave
macmillan

First edition published 1984 by Prentice Hall/Harvester Wheatsheaf
Second edition published 1989 by Prentice Hall/Harvester Wheatsheaf
Third edition published 2004 and reissued third edition published 2010 by
PALGRAVE MACMILLAN

Palgrave Macmillan in the UK is an imprint of Macmillan Publishers Limited,
registered in England, company number 785998, of Houndmills, Basingstoke,
Hampshire RG21 6XS.

Palgrave Macmillan in the US is a division of St Martin's Press LLC,
175 Fifth Avenue, New York, NY 10010.

Palgrave Macmillan is the global academic imprint of the above companies
and has companies and representatives throughout the world.

Palgrave® and Macmillan® are registered trademarks in the United States,
the United Kingdom, Europe and other countries.

ISBN 978–0–230–24312–5   hardback
ISBN 978–0–230–24313–2   paperback

This book is printed on paper suitable for recycling and made from fully
managed and sustained forest sources. Logging, pulping and manufacturing
processes are expected to conform to the environmental regulations of the
country of origin.

A catalogue record for this book is available from the British Library.

A catalog record for this book is available from the Library of Congress.

10 9 8 7 6 5 4 3 2 1
19 18 17 16 15 14 13 12 11 10

Printed in China

Contents

Acknowledgements

My thanks to the following who have read all or some of the type-script: John Russell Brown, Paul Brown, Michael Butcher, Inga-Stina Ewbank, R. A. Foakes, Margot Heinemann, Malcolm Kitch, Laurence Lerner, David Morse, Tony Nuttall, Alan Sinfield (to whom I owe a special debt, intellectual and otherwise), Peter Stallybrass, Cedric Watts, Allon White. Sue Roe of Harvester Press gave encouragement for the project in its early stages. Thanks also to the other members of Sussex University Literature Teaching Politics group for stimulating discussion across a wide range of issues: David Forgacs, Frank Gloversmith, Ann Rosalind Jones, Cora Kaplan, Alison Light, Ulrike Meinhof, Alan Sinfield, Peter Stallybrass, Allon White. No one so far mentioned can be held responsible for any shortcomings which remain; all such I cheerfully attribute to my friend, Shelley Twist, in particular to the year he came to stay at the house in London E7.

Brighton, September 1982

The introduction to the second edition was started at the Humanities Research Centre, Canberra, and finished at the National Humanities Center, North Carolina. My gratitude to those who made both trips possible. Dedicated to Shayne and Som, and in recollection of Braidwood, New South Wales, one hot afternoon in March 1988.

Chapel Hill, NC, January 1989

Foreword

by Terry Eagleton

At first glance, the title of this book may seem a contradiction in terms, like 'fascist intellectual' or 'Texan *haute cuisine*'. For tragedy has long been regarded as the most blue-blooded of literary forms, disdainfully aloof from everyday life, a question of the downfall of princes rather than the death of a taxi driver. In the hands of conservative commentators, it has become associated with myth and destiny, ritual and blood sacrifice, jealous gods and hapless victims. For this lineage of criticism, tragic suffering is ennobling rather than appalling: it is through anguish and breakdown that our deepest humanity is affirmed, so that we leave the theatre edified and inspired by scenes of carnage and despair.

In this perverse vision, real-life calamities – an air crash, a famine, an outbreak of genocide – do not count as tragic, since they leave us despondent rather than delighted. Aeschylus is tragic, but Auschwitz is not. If tragedy shows social order being violated, it does so only to demonstrate how ultimately impregnable it is. In its bleak portrayal of human hubris or overreaching, it fosters timorousness, reverence and submission, none of which are exactly radical virtues. Besides, in this view tragedy is a thoroughly virile affair, a matter of heroes, warriors and a very masculine nobility of spirit. It does not chime with the sensibility of a secular, sceptical, democratic age.

This, to be sure, is a highly partial, prejudiced view of tragedy as a whole. There is quite enough in actual tragic art, from Aeschylus to Arthur Miller, to refute these assumptions one by one. Even when it comes to the theory of tragedy, there have been dissenting voices in plenty. It is not as though we had to wait upon the birth of modern-day literary theory to recognise that tragedy does not always meekly buckle down to providence, imagine that the sufferings it represents are timeless, edifying or irreparable, or trade in moral absolutes. Whatever the diversity of tragic art as such, however, a certain consistent *idea* of tragedy has been developed from the German idealist philosophers onward; and what it represents, in effect, is a crypto-religious critique of modernity.

Once religion, discredited by a secularising age, proved progressively unable to perform this critique itself, the idea of tragedy – in fact, a highly edited, tendentious version of the history of the art form itself – was on hand to provide a formidable substitute for it. Like religion, tragedy was a kind of theodicy – which is to say that it could offer some account of why there was suffering in the world, plucking an ultimate meaning from what seemed like senseless destruction. Besides, tragedy was everything that modernity was not: elitist rather than democratic, spiritual rather than scientific, absolute rather than contingent, cosmic rather than earthly, universal rather than culturally specific, a matter of destiny rather than self-determination.

Tragedy served as a kind of aristocratic memory-trace in a middle-class epoch which had less and less use for such high-toned patrician values. If modernity tidied away suffering in its brisk progressivism, tragedy would claim with magnificent perversity that agony and wretchedness were exactly where fundamental human value was most deeply disclosed. If we responded to the torments it presented with fear and horror, this could only be because the human was so unutterably precious to us. For many commentators, then, the form came to represent a golden age of noble spirits whose freedom lay in fearlessly embracing the inevitable – an age which had now yielded ground to a squalid materialism. From this standpoint, it was not as though the men and women of modernity had turned their backs on tragedy for some carnivalesque celebration of everyday life. It was simply that they were not up to it. Tragedy, an art much taken with death, had now expired itself, and along with it a sense of ultimate human value.

It is not least of the virtues of Jonathan Dollimore's pathbreaking study that it rescues tragedy from this sterile ideology, thrusting it firmly back within the complex cross-currents of actual historical life. Reading against the grain of a powerfully tenacious orthodoxy, *Radical Tragedy* shows how Jacobean tragedy – the most astonishing body of tragic art in English history – can be critical rather than conformist, a challenging of authority rather than a confirmation of it. The book takes issue here with so-called new historicism, which repeats the fatalism of traditional tragic theory with a more fashionable twist. Where that theory saw tragic protest as rebuffed by the heavens, some new historicist critics see it as neutralised by the omnipotence of power. In fact, the political power symbolised by the Jacobean state was to be decisively challenged not long after in a bloody civil war. New historicism is much concerned with interpreting the past in the light of the present; but we may need to historicise new historicism itself. It may well be that part of what we have, in this pessimistic sense that protest in Jacobean drama is always nullified, is a reading of it in the light of the bleak situation of present-day radicals in a triumphantly right-wing United States.

It is to the credit of Jonathan Dollimore's boldly original book that, unlike so much radical criticism, it approaches the religious ideologies of Jacobean England with the utmost seriousness. Religion, after all, was what so much of the common life of those times was about; and it is curious that radicals, who are supposed to take popular consciousness seriously, should so often be found skipping embarrassedly over the religious rituals and beliefs which bulked so large in it. No ideology in human history has been more persuasive and persistent than religion, a symbolic form which links the minutiae of everyday conduct to the most ultimate of spiritual realities, and it is hard to see that any ideology ever will be. The radical's nervousness of religion is parochial as well as patronising: religion may not be the driving force in Middlesbrough, but it is in Dacca.

Without accepting for a moment that these turbulent dramas are always decorously orthodox, Dollimore investigates their metaphysical claims, along with their dealings in power and sexuality. The result is a remarkably wide-ranging study, in which John Marston and Bertolt Brecht, Faustus and Foucault, camp and Christianity, are to be found cheek by jowl. Nor is this, as with so much radical criticism, a mere extraction of the usable 'ideas' of literary works, in crass insensitivity to the intricacies of their form. *Radical Tragedy* is vibrant with ideas, but it is also alive to questions of stage realism and naturalism, to the way in which the dislocated, montage-like structure of these extraordinary dramas has much to do with their vision of the world.

Some critical studies are full of insight, but not many of them are *necessary*. *Radical Tragedy* ranks among the necessary critical interventions of our time.

Preface to the reissued Third Edition

A student once asked me why there was nothing on *Othello* in this book. Here's why.

In the momentous year of 1968 I decided to leave my job as a newspaper reporter and try for university. Despite my signing up for an A level course in the meantime, only one university, Keele, offered me an interview. (The university which eventually gave me a job, Sussex, rejected me not once but twice. I mention this by way of encouragement to anyone else trying to get somewhere from the outside.) I wanted to study English with Philosophy. I had a vague but confident belief that philosophy would help me clarify some of the existential confusion which had led me back into education in the first place. But with an interview pending I clearly needed to find out more – specifically, what philosophy at university entailed. So the day before the interview I went to Luton public library to find out. Among the handful of philosophy titles I found one introduction whose dust-jacket blurb went something like this: 'Some people think philosophy is going to answer their questions about the meaning of life. This is a mistake. What philosophy can do, however, is to help you decide whether such questions are themselves meaningful. Quite often they are not.'

I took the book on the train to Keele but never read it. I remember reading Hermann Hesse's *Steppenwolf* instead. I was interviewed late in the day by a woman from English and a man from Philosophy. The man had a pipe. Both looked bored. The man's first question, I now know, is the one you ask when you can't think of anything else to say, or haven't yet read, or can't recall, the student's application form: 'So why do you want to read philosophy?' Suddenly I wished I'd read that library book, but all I had to go on was the blurb. 'Well,' I said gropingly, 'Some people expect it to answer their questions about the meaning of life.' 'And what about you – what do you expect?' he replied suspiciously. 'Me? I . . . I don't expect it to answer questions about the meaning of life.' He began to pay attention. Emboldened by my own duplicity I pressed on: 'Actually,' I said, 'I would hope it might help me to decide whether any of those questions people ask about the meaning of life, are themselves meaningful questions.' 'Interesting,' he said. Warming to my topic, I took a risk and went just a tad beyond the authority of the book blurb: 'In fact,' I said, 'I shouldn't be at all surprised to find out that some of those questions are pretty silly.' 'Excellent!' he cried, and with that wandered off to get some tobacco for his pipe.

That just left the woman from English. She asked me what I thought of *Othello*, the Shakespeare text I was studying for A level. If I'd spoken the truth I would have told her about how this was my first ever encounter with Shakespeare; that I had bought a copy of the play in a Luton bookshop, and sat in a car park in the October gloom, anxiously seeing if I could even understand the language; that I was relieved to find I could understand it, just about, in a halting kind of way, but only with the aid of the notes; that even so, the play seemed frustratingly absurd. And then I'd have told her about how I discovered three months into the course that my girl-friend was having an affair with another boy, which threw me into such a fit of sexual jealousy that I made a very nearly successful suicide attempt, and about how when I was allowed out of hospital and back to college, the theme of sexual jealousy had become so painfully relevant that *Othello* made too much sense – so much so that I could no longer even read it.

Of course I said nothing of all this – only a very shrewd (public/private school?) operator could successfully feed something so humiliating into a formal interview. And anyway hadn't I learned, on the hoof, and only moments earlier, the value of duplicity in the interview? So instead I showed judicious familiarity with the literary criticism of A. C. Bradley and F. R. Leavis (siding cautiously with Leavis against Bradley – like you were supposed to in those days).

Both English and Philosophy were a disappointment to me. I'm speaking only of the formal courses: university itself was life changing. It's probably always been true that you have to find your way through or around formal education in the search for what really matters. You don't have to call it 'the meaning of life' – indeed, after Monty Python's film of that name you'd have to be brave to do so. (But then again, why not?) We might just call it the Big Stuff, although that too is a term already discredited by its own currency. It doesn't matter what we call it: we know what we mean. It's probably true too that this search takes place mostly outside the tutorial or seminar room and is often a lonely and sometimes a frustrating one. And has been so for some time, as John Marston's play *What You Will* (1601) amusingly attests. The character Lampatho laments having wasted so many futile nights in pursuit of wisdom – while his spaniel sleeps in blissful ignorance under the desk. 'Whilst I', he says, 'wasted lamp oil, bated my flesh / Shrunk up my veins . . . still my spaniel slept.' He gets hopelessly lost amidst competing 'Philsosophers / . . . banding factions, all so strongly propped' and eventually declares:

> I staggered, knew not which was firmer part;
> But thought, quoted, read, observed, and pried,
> Stuffed noting-books, and still my spaniel slept.
> At length he waked, and yawned, and by yon sky,
> For aught I know, he knew as much as I.
>
> (II. ii. 866–72)

For me it was a search which led eventually to the writing of this book although not yet to *Othello*: I still hadn't found a way of reconnecting with that play. Eventually I did and it became important for a different way of thinking about literature and philosophy (outlined in the introduction to the third edition, below, pp. xviii–xxxix).[1] To summarise: if the ethical and humane basis of our culture is not to atrophy it must be periodically confronted with its own vital exclusions – that is, it must be exposed to that which makes it possible in the first place; exposed, we could say, to an absent or repressed part of itself. It is a confrontation which can be found definitively in certain kinds of literature and philosophy, but with no prior guarantee that our culture survives the exposure unchanged or unchallenged. To read sensitively isn't necessarily to become a more humane person, as defenders of the humanities sometimes claim.

Indeed, the search for meaning can be deeply disturbing as well as frustrating and lonely. But it can also make one feel more *alive* (Lampatho notwithstanding). Which is why I want to re-dedicate this book to those students who use the opportunity of going to university not as a route into the establishment, but as an opportunity to undertake that search for themselves.

Note

1. It was explored further in *Sexual Dissidence*, Oxford: Oxford University Press, 1991, and *Sex, Literature and Censorship*, Cambridge: Polity, 2001. See also, the afterword to Ewan Fernie (ed.) *Spiritual Shakespeares*, London and New York: Routledge, 2005, and Ewan Fernie, 'Dollimore's Challenge', in *Shakespeare Studies*, vol. XXXV, 2007, pp. 133–57.

Introduction to the Third Edition

September 1914

In September 1914 the novelist Hermann Hesse is agonised at the prospect of war destroying the foundations of Europe's cultural heritage, and thereby the future of civilisation itself. Hesse stands proudly for what he calls a 'supranational' tradition of human culture, intrinsic to which are ideals essentially enlightened and humanitarian: an 'international world of thought, of inner freedom, of intellectual conscience' and a belief in 'an artistic beauty cutting across national boundaries' (*If the War Goes On*, pp. 15–17). Even in the depths of war, insists Hesse, a German should be able to prefer a good English book to a bad German one. Three years later he writes along similar lines to a government minister telling him that he would be a more humane leader in this time of conflict were he to read 'the great authors' and listen to great composers like Beethoven (p. 20).

Much later (1946) Hesse would comment as follows on these and other similar writings of the same war period:

> When I call [them] 'political' it is always in quotes, for there is nothing political about them but the atmosphere in which they came into being. In all other respects they are the opposite of political, because in each one of these essays I strive to guide the reader not into the world theatre with its political problems but into his innermost being, before the judgement seat of his very personal conscience. In this I am at odds with the political thinkers of all trends, and I shall always, incorrigibly, recognize in man, in the individual man and his soul, the existence of realms to which political impulses and forms do not extend. (p. 11)

Here is an uncompromising expression of that spiritual, essentialist individualism which underpinned Hesse's equally uncompromising universal humanism. Here too is the corollary of both the humanism and the individualism – a profound distrust of the political, and a corresponding faith in art. *Radical Tragedy*, first published in 1984, attacked just these ideas: essentialism in relation to subjectivity, universalism in relation to the human, and the belief that there was an ethical/aesthetic realm transcending the political. I'll return to this.

Though not beyond criticism – he was little known outside Germany and so wanted to avoid his own books being banned there – Hesse was implacably opposed to the barbaric nationalism of his own country from around 1914 onwards. He went into self-imposed exile in 1919, and never returned to Germany. He was awarded the Nobel Prize for literature in 1946, but for most of his life remained a struggling, exiled, writer. His books were eventually banned in Germany in 1943, and that was a severe blow. He began his Nobel Prize letter of thanks with the reasons why he could not be present in person: 'the hardships of the National Socialist period, during which my life work was destroyed in Germany and I was burdened day after day with arduous duties, undermined [my health] for good. *Still, my spirit is unbroken* . . .' (*If the War Goes On*, p. 141; my italics).

Wars in the last century compelled artists and intellectuals into rethinking the aesthetic – its scope, its power, its limitations and its dangers.[1] One question becomes paramount: has literature been most compelling when in the service of humane values, or when it has transgressed them? I foreground this question in relation to Hesse – this once celebrated, sometime cult figure, now neglected – because the full significance of an aesthetic humanism becomes apparent in relation to artists like Hesse in a way it doesn't in, say, the squabbles within the English literary critical tradition in the last quarter of the last century. More specifically, the critique of humanism never properly engaged the example of people like Hesse, preferring instead easier targets in academic literary criticism. In other words, within both the humanist tradition, and the theoretical critique of it, the historical conditions of thought matter, and it especially matters that many recent critics of humanism have been formed, and remain, within an education system, from school to university, which is itself the product of relative security and prosperity in the post-war period.

Right now it's especially revealing to reconsider the life, writing and ethical stand of those like Hesse. Since the publication of *Radical Tragedy* the so-called culture wars of our own time have raged around the canon, the western artistic tradition.[2] The case of Hesse shows how this debate is fundamentally dependent upon the fate of what we might call a 'high' European humanism, which includes aesthetic considerations but also goes far beyond them. Humanism was always much more than art, but art was intrinsic to, a necessary aspect of, what it was. I was about to remark the crucial proviso that our lives are not now, as were Hesse's and millions of others at that time, devastated by world war. Indeed they are not, but Britain has been involved in several major wars in the last two decades, and as I write is poised to embark upon another. And although the historical conditions are indeed quite different, we too live in a time of acute distrust, and perhaps despair, of the political realm which Hesse would have understood. Additionally, in Britain there is an increasingly bitter debate about just how integrated with Europe – how 'supranational' – we should become, and nationalism, cultural and economic, remains a potent force, breaking up major political parties and stirring potent if as yet localised racism.

September 2001

After the September 11, 2001 terrorist attacks on New York and Washington, Britain signed up to another type of war, one whose scope and extent was, and remains, uncertain. If the rhetoric is similar – the need to defend western civilisation from barbarism, democracy from fanaticism – the conditions of this war are so different as to be unimaginable for someone like Hesse. A hastily formed international coalition against terrorism proceeds in the name of civilisation but now it does not need – in fact is now embarrassed by – the old humanist universals. This is partly because we are now acutely aware of how arrogant and unheeding western humanism could be in relation to cultural and racial difference, not least within its own colonial and imperialist domains. This in turn is one reason why, in western democracies, a confident humanism has given way to an ethic of the multicultural and the multi-racial; for sure, an uncertain assumption of underlying similarites is not entirely absent, but it is subordinate to an equally uncertain embrace of cultural and racial difference. Nothing could be more indicative of this change than the fact that Britain's Prime Minister, as he commuted the world in October 2001, shoring up support for the coalition against terrorism, allowed it to be known that, as he travelled, he read translations of the Koran.

What has become truly supranational is, of course, the very capitalism which Hesse and others saw as yet another enemy of humanism. At one level global capitalism needs and nurtures the multiculturalism which has superseded humanism; at another it promotes a cultural imperialism more arrogant than humanism ever was and underpinned by popular rather than high culture – Hollywood and MacDonald's rather than Shakespeare and Claridge's. I just described it as cultural imperialism; it is also of course an aggressive economic and military imperialism which exacerbates cultural antagonisms. And that means that the multicultural can shift very quickly from being the imagined resolution of those antagonisms, to being the ground where they intensify. Bluntly, terrorism may thrive in relation to the multicultural; a certain kind of terrorism may even presuppose it. The United Kingdom is desperate to show that these new wars are not being waged against Islam precisely because there are many Muslims, including many residing in Britain, who regard them as being so, or at least as a conflict between irreconcilable cultures and religions.

So what has all this got to do with the aesthetic, with literature – indeed with Renaissance drama? For a start, so much contemporary literature is about racial, political, sexual and cultural conflicts experienced at the level of identity. Certainly, for the most part, these are conflicts which seem incapable of aesthetic resolution. Notoriously, Salman Rushdie's *Satanic Verses* both expressed and incited such conflicts. And the awkward truth (voiced by Rushdie himself) that bad times produce good books, can no longer be obscured by the mystifying belief that good books can prevent bad times or at least compensate for them. Just as it seemed as if those conflicts were being fudged into history, they erupted again on September 11th with a terrible ferocity. For the humanist the most traumatic fact about the Rushdie affair was that a work of literature provoked rather than transcended those antagonisms. Does anyone really now believe that good books can prevent bad times?

Without proposing a facile continuity between the early modern and the modern it must be obvious that much of what has just been remarked about conflict in contemporary literature is applicable also to the circumstances of the Elizabethan and Jacobean stage (see below, p. lii). One difference is that, whereas today we witness the demise of the humanist aesthetic, in the early modern period it was still centuries away.

Whereas in September 1914 Hesse passionately affirms the humanist aesthetic as an answer to war, in September 2001 it was as if such a vision had simply been forgotten: one listened in vain for significant voices promoting art as an articulation of civilised values transcending cultural, racial and religious conflicts. What precipitated the decline in Humanist faith? Well, all four aspects of Hesse's cultural philosophy – its universal humanism, essentialist (spiritual) individualism, its distrust of the political and a corresponding faith in art – all these were the object of fierce criticism by almost all the strands of literary, cultural and critical theory in the last 25 years or so, and with a degree of success which helped generate the so-called culture wars. Again, this was the context of the writing of *Radical Tragedy*. Culture became 'politicised' as never before, often around the issue of who was excluded from the humanist universe in terms of that holy trinity, race, class and gender. Some academics and politicians trying to cling to the humanist tradition blamed 'theory', and the books it spawned, including *Radical Tragedy*, for its demise. This was too easy and often plain diversionary: the problem goes much deeper, and back much further. Quite apart from the growing antipathy to western humanism from other cultures and world religions, of the kind already mentioned, there were deep misgivings from within the tradition itself.

September 1939

As an example of what I mean, let us go back to the outbreak of yet another war, and yet another September. W. H. Auden's poem '1st September 1939' – widely invoked in relation to September 11th[3] – offers a response to the impending Second World War reminiscent of Hesse's to the First:

> Defenceless under the night
> Our world in stupor lies;
> Yet, dotted everywhere,
> Ironic points of light
> Flash out wherever the Just
> Exchange their messages:
> May I, composed like them,
> Of Eros and of dust,
> Beleaguered by the same
> Negation and despair,
> Show an affirming flame.

Reminiscent indeed – but so different. To begin with there is the speaker's poignant hesitancy: beleaguered by negation and despair, can he – can we – ever be strong enough to sustain the affirming flame? In this poem we are composed not of spirit and dust but of Eros and dust; no mention here then of that fierce spiritual flame which once fortified us against both dust and injustice – and against Eros, for that matter. (Remember Hesse: 'my spirit is unbroken', above, p. xix). Unlike spirit, which eventually escapes mortality, Eros is the catalyst of mortality. The early moderns would have understood: 'Leave me O Love, which reachest but to dust' (below, p. 94). And now the communication between the civilised is furtive; Hesse's image of a brave supranational humanism reaching out in overground unity, across and above the strife, is replaced here by one suggesting an underground hiding from it; erratic, clandestine communications occur at night between the fragmented and the dispersed. And then there's the description of these very communications as 'ironic': perhaps nothing was more indicative of the diminishing faith in the humanist salvation of the world than the turn to irony. Irony becomes part confession of, part defence against, the failures of the humanist vision. Together with its near cousin ambiguity, irony becomes the crutch of 'late' humanism, at once guarantee of its sophistication, and confession of its uncertainty; irony provided the intellectual with a rationale for non-commitment, and enabled the academic critic to contain anything which disturbed, by putting it in an imaginary, neutralising tension or balance with what didn't. Yeats saw through this kind of irony, which is why it's almost obligatory now to cite him: the best lack all conviction while the worst are full of a passionate intensity. No surprise then, Auden's subsequent down-playing of the importance of art and the artist; 'we live in a new age', he wrote a decade later, and the artist today, unlike his Romantic pre-cursors, 'neither can have . . . a unique heroic importance nor believes in the Art-God enough to desire it' (*The Enchafèd Flood*, p. 150). Later still Auden came to regard even that last stanza of 'September 1st, 1939' as too full of self-congratulation; in fact he came to so dislike this poem he wanted to prevent its being reprinted in his life-time. So the loss of faith in the artist as 'legislator' (Shelley), is voiced here not by a hard-core anti-humanist 'theorist', but arguably the greatest poet of the last century.

Though Hesse's own faith in the redemptive power of art never faltered, by the end of the Second World War it was tempered. In his acceptance message for the Nobel Prize, as well as the one for the Goethe Prize, also awarded in 1946, he affirms again the belief that 'culture is supranational and international', but speaks too of a 'deathly sick Europe' and his own temptation to abandon European culture altogether and turn to the wisdom of the Orient. It's a temp-tation resisted, but the influence of the Orient is indeed central to his new realisation that the fundamental message of mankind's greatest teachers is stoicism. In these final years there is an even greater insistence on the individual soul as the touchstone of integrity, perhaps now at the expense of the humanism (pp. 123–4, 145, 149). Here he anticipates a development of the latter half of the twentieth century.

For others the Second World War confirmed the bankruptcy of European humanism. And now we are talking not just of its inability to prevent barbarism, but its complicity with it. Theodor Adorno and others in the Frankfurt School detected in Enlightenment humanism the seeds of the very evil which Hesse imagined it to save us from.[4] Adorno declared the worthlessness of 'traditional culture', coming as it now does 'neutralized and ready made', adding, famously, that 'to write poetry after Auschwitz is barbaric' (*Prisms*, p. 34). Later Baudrillard would take this critique to its limit:

> the 'Human' is from the outset the institution of its structural double, the 'Inhuman'. This is all it is: the progress of Humanity and Culture are simply the chain of discriminations with which to brand 'Others' with inhumanity and therefore with nullity. (*Symbolic Exchange and Death*, p. 125)

Even as a thumb-nail sketch of western humanism this is crudely distorting; indeed, that assertion – 'this is all it is . . . simply the chain of discriminations' etc. – is crassly reductive.

Today's anti-intellectual guardians of high culture love to tell us that Marxism is obsolete, and heavy-duty continental theory just nonsense. For the moment I want to bypass that particular culture-wars stand-off by not relying on dubious theorists like Baudrillard, or even great ones like Adorno; I invoke instead George Steiner's passionate and seminal essays of the 1960s collected as *Literature and Silence*. Steiner gives a blunt, untheoretical elaboration of Adorno's argument: not only did the Nazis destroy 'central European humanism', but the barbarism of the twentieth century 'prevailed on the very ground of Christian humanism, of Renaissance culture and classic rationalism'. Remember that in 1917 Hesse could confidently advise a politician that he would be a more humane leader if he immersed himself in high culture. Compare that with this, from Steiner, in 1966:

> We know now that a man can read Goethe or Rilke in the evening, that he can play Bach and Schubert, and go to his day's work at Auschwitz in the morning. To say that he has read them without understanding, or that his ear is gross, is cant.

Steiner asks a compelling question – 'What are the links, as yet scarcely understood, between the mental, psychological habits of high literacy, and the temptations of the inhuman?' (p. ix). At the very least high literacy and humanism no longer imply each other, and quite probably there is an historical connection between them. Post-Second Word War, we are dealing with two related issues: the loss of faith in aesthetic humanism and the potential inhumanity within high literacy.

Art and Humanism

Today then it is not just Hesse's idea that salvation might lie in a reaffirmation of a universal, spiritual, and ethical humanism that rings hollow; so too does his underlying premise, namely that art humanises. And yet our culture industry and our humanities education system still rest upon that premise. The centrality of the arts within the humanities, most especially of English literature, has always rested on the claim that they have a civilising influence, promoting national if not transnational humanitarian values.[5] This is Sir Claus Moser, speaking in October 2000: 'I speak with a passionate belief in the enriching force of the arts in the life of each one of us and of society as a whole.' Complaining of those philistines in today's society, some in high places, 'who fail to appreciate . . . what the arts bring to a civilised society, to our quality of life . . . [and] that a civilised society demands fine culture at its core', Moser endorses President Kennedy's belief that 'the life of the arts . . . is a test of a nation's civilisation'.[6] For Hesse and numerous others in earlier generations, the humanist aesthetic was a liberating expression of profoundly civilising sympathies; I don't know if it ever, as Hesse hoped, humanised the powerful, but it certainly empowered the dispossessed.[7] In short, I have deep respect for Hesse's advocacy of humanism in 1917; but I can't but regard Moser, writing in 2000, as deeply complacent. Far from being liberating, the humanist aesthetic has become a way of standing still amidst the obsolete, complacent and self-serving clichés of the heritage culture industry, the Arts establishment, and a market-driven humanities education system. The aesthetic has become an anaesthetic. And this even more so now than when *Radical Tragedy* first appeared in 1984. The humanist aesthetic has become like an edifice which is still standing, but on rotten foundations, taken over and propped up by vested interests.

However, my argument is not just that Hesse's humanism is untenable and unpersuasive now, 'after Auschwitz', or after the capitulation of culture and education to market forces, but that it was already so at the time in which he proposed it. In fact, I believe it hardly survived the insight of autobiographical works of his own like *Steppenwolf* (in retrospect the terrorist fantasies of that work are especially arresting in this regard). Without doubting Hesse's sincerity, it's surely obvious that some artists have paid lip service to the humanist defence of art in order to license an aesthetic vision which they knew contravened it. The ethical defence of art has been deployed politically, at least by some. Consider aesthetic didacticism in earlier periods, especially when state censorship prevailed: was it really complict with that censorship, or a tendentious way around it? In *Radical Tragedy* I argued that such didacticism, far from foreclosing on subversive thought, was often its precondition. In the mid-twentieth century a generation of critics of early modern drama tried to convince themselves that this didactic closure effectively discredits or at least neutralises the subversive questioning and thought which preceded it. However, from a creative, a theatrical and an intellectual perspective, the didactic dénouement does not so much close off that questioning as enable it: it subscribes to the law's letter precisely in order to violate its spirit; far from foreclosing on it, a conforming framework actually licenses a subversive content via the aesthetics of lip-service.

Another, contrasting example: nothing could be more removed from didacticism than the creed of art for art's sake, not least because it evolved as a direct repudiation of the moral demand made of literature. Which makes it the more ironic, and significant, that artists exploited it as tendentiously as they did didacticism. This is Oscar Wilde in 1890: 'No artist has ethical sympathies . . . There is no such thing as a moral or an immoral book. Books are well written, or badly written. That is all' ('The Preface', *The Picture of Dorian Gray*, p. 5). Many take this to be not just anti-didactic but a definitive statement of the non-referential theory of art for art's sake: art is not *about* anything; it exists in and for itself, as pure form. In fact,

Wilde's decadent creed of art for art's sake was always cunningly ten-dentious, rhetorically and politically: it expresses not an indifference to content, but a determination to incorporate a great deal of barely disguised illicit content, and a clear invitation to the initiated to recognise exactly that. By liberating art from morality it was also lib-erating illicit experiences and desires for art. It's to the credit of Oscar Wilde that he knew this and wore the deceptions of for-malism on his sleeve. (And, incidentally, 'good writing' had little to do with it: the writing of *Dorian Gray* is variable to say the least.)

I make this point about the tendentious objectives of didacticism and the creed of art for art's sake because they are just two (con-trasting) instances of ways in which the aesthetic I'm exploring is already old; I'm advocating a departure which is also a return. Steiner struggles to redeem something of the humanist aesthetic from its ruins in the twentieth century; in contrast I have wanted to abandon that aesthetic in favour of another, one which becomes visible within those ruins because it was always there. It is the aes-thetic where dangerous knowledge crosses with dissident desire, and may well exacerbate conflict rather than transcend it. One might promote this as a manifesto – as a demand for what art should be now. I wish it were. More appropriately in this context, one could show this aesthetic as already existing in disreputable kinds of writing like pornography, or the semi-respectable, like gothic fiction, the literature of sexual dissidence, or Jacobean tragedy. Along with others, I have tried to do that in books like *Radical Tragedy* and *Sexual Dissidence*. Most recently, in *Sex, Literature and Censorship*, I went further, arguing that this aesthetic is alive and thriving even at the heart of the canon, though misrecognised as such. Here, my objective is different again: I argue that it has always been latent within western aesthetic concepts. My case for saying that literature all the time violates the humanist imperative could proceed by invoking the views of those who have wanted to censor art, from Plato, through the anti-theatrical prejudices, to advocates of modern state censorship. But again I justify this aesthetic not with reference to the enemies of art (though I do argue that they are not as philis-tine as some would claim) but from within its practice and its defence. First, though, another contrast which is also a similarity.

Humanism and Materialism

I mentioned just now that the core premise of the humanist aesthetic, namely that art is a profoundly humanising force, continues to underpin the humanities education system and the culture industries. More surprising perhaps is that critics of humanism also adhere to it, albeit in a radicalised form. The stand-off here is not so much one between the humanists and the anti-humanists, as between a conservative and a progressive humanism. Consider one of the most confrontational examples of all, namely the cultural-materialist critique of literature.[8] At first sight it opposes the humanist project in every respect. Certainly beleaguered academic humanists see it that way. For example, John M. Ellis, writing in 1997, laments the threat to a humanist education posed by this critique's obsession with gender, race and class. Ellis pines for a humanities education which enabled students to become 'enlightened citizens'; which produced a society of people educated 'for full and intelligent participation in a modern democracy'; which helped us 'develop a richer understanding of human life and to train the mind'; which taught us to enjoy and to love literature, not least because it 'delighted and instructed' (*Literature Lost*, pp. 3–4, 33, 49, 51). Those like Ellis are right to this extent: the materialist critique resolutely rejects all three of the tenets I've attributed to Hesse (universal humanism, essentialist individualism, an aesthetic realm standing above the political); instead it might see art as either appropriable for the oppressed and exploited, be they defined in terms of class, and/or sex and/or race, or as an instrument of their oppression, or as a merging of both positions. In so doing it clearly retains humanitarian ideals albeit under another name, with changed terms and constituencies, and a scepticism about how art, *as currently conceived*, contributes to those ideals. The argument now is whether or not, or to what extent, aesthetic discourse has a 'democratic and radical potential' (Armstrong, *The Radical Aesthetic*, p. 2).

But there's a sense in which these arch-enemies, the humanist and the materialist, are competing for the same ethical high ground. To invoke Ellis again, both humanists and materialists would endorse the idea of a society of people educated 'for full and intelligent participation in a modern democracy', while disagreeing about (i) what such a society looks like; (ii) the proximity of actual existing societies to that ideal; (iii) the part that canonical artworks, and an education based on ideas of the aesthetic as conventionally understood, actually play in promoting democracy and participation. Additionally, from the example of a latter-day humanist like Richard A. Etlin, we can see how the humanist has already conceded ground to the political/ethical agenda of the materialist. Etlin defends nineteenth-century novelists against Edward Said's claim that they were complicit with imperialism. But far from saying, as his predecessors might have done, that such political considerations are irrelevant to aesthetic ones, Etlin not only marshals those novelists' own anti-imperialist and antislavery sentiments, but reads their novels for evidence of the same (*In Defence of Humanism*, pp. 114–22). He thereby implicitly extends the humanist agenda to partially accord with that of his opponents, even while trying to discredit their arguments.[9] It's difficult not to conclude that the materialists have already won the high ground, although only by extending its terrain. At the very least, the old argument that such political considerations are irrelevant to the aesthetic vision has gone for good: while Etlin refuses to accept Said's uncompromising assertion that politics and culture, far from being different spheres, are 'ultimately the same', he can only counter it with an evasive generalisation: the humanist refuses to conflate the two spheres 'in all times and in all respects' (*In Defence of Humanism*, p. 114). The irony of all this is that the survival of humanism may well depend on its critics rather than its adherents; in its conservative form as defended by Ellis and Etlin, it's a tired convention; in its radical – that is, its appropriated form, on the extended terrain of the materialists – it's still alive.

Returns

From within the same materialist critique something else was emerging more germane to my purpose than this struggle for the ethical high ground, something which redirects us to the power of literature to convey dissident ideas, desires and knowledges. As the constituencies of the oppressed were refined and enlarged, and the operations of power understood in all their (often counter-intuitive) complexity, so attention turned from the 'conscious', manifest, and apparently unified project of the artwork, to a consideration of its latent tendencies, or in Fredric Jameson's phrase, its 'political unconscious'. One read not for unity, that archetypal aesthetic category, nor even for explicit content, so much as for internal *dis*unity, the text's tensions, conflicts and contradictions – for what it did not say, yet maybe half revealed. This was part of a significant change in ways of reading culture more generally, and in particular of understanding what Derrida was to call its 'violent hierarchies' (*Positions*, p. 41): the centre came to be understood in relation to its margins, the 'other' in relation to the 'same', the dominant in relation to the subordinate, the sane in relation to the insane, the heterosexual in relation to the homosexual, and so on. This way of reading explored that paradoxical dialectic apparent in history itself whereby 'in opposition to' became strangely 'implicated with' and even 'dependent upon'. Inside the violent hierarchies strange dependencies were discovered to exist, and, in time, strange reversals occurred: for example, charges of hysteria, pathology and inadequacy shifted from the homosexual to the homophobe, from the racial other to the racist, from woman to misogynist. It was also a violent dialectic whereby the repressed and the oppressed returned to haunt and terrorise the identity and well-being of their dominant others, perhaps even striking at the literal and symbolic centre of their being: binary opposites fusing in violence.

The violent dialectic between the dominant and the subordinate was something which humanism could not comprehend – hence, in part, the so-called 'anti-humanism' of the critique which explored it. Nor could some humanists accept that to be critical of humanism did not entail being inhumane or anti-humanitarian. It also became apparent from this critique that certain types of literature had always contained their own imaginative or darker understanding of this violent dialectic, and, if only implicitly, contradicted the very humanism which sought to appropriate them. At the very least, many of the canonical works of literature claimed by and for the humanist vision so obviously threaten rather than confirm it: put too simply, those works reveal too much. And so a new challenge emerges, one importantly different from the materialist challenge to aesthetic humanism's blindness to the fact of exclusion, and the way its supposed 'universality' was not universal at all. Again, that's an important argument in the culture wars but one which doesn't concern me now. The challenge now is to understand the tension between the aesthetic and the humane as commonly understood; to understand that the aesthetic vision has been most captivating precisely when it exceeds and maybe violates the humanitarian one. Captivating, and by the same token potentially dangerous: there can be no guarantee that (for instance) the imaginative exploration of the return of the repressed will be conducive to the health of either the individual or the society; only the utterly naive can believe that all repression/suppression is bad. Arguably everything that distinguishes us as human – I should say everything that distinguishes us as humane – involves repression, suppression and exclusion.

Art-lovers generally refuse to recognise this challenge. For them great art is always on the side of civilised life because it is nothing less than its most exalted expression. They insist that such art and the high culture it serves can only enhance the lives of those who truly appreciate it; that such art, unlike say, propaganda, popular culture or pornography, is incapable of damaging or 'corrupting' us. Such an attitude not only fails to take art seriously enough, but rests on a prior process of pro-art censorship more effective than anti-art state censorship. Their defence *of* art is more often than not a defence *against* art, and an exaggerated respect for it becomes a way of not engaging with it. Those who love art the most also censor it the most. To approach literature insisting on an alignment of the ethical conscience and the creative imagination is to be blind to the fact that some of the most compelling writing is about the tension between, if not the incompatibility of, these two things. Far from denying the aesthetic, I want to privilege it, perhaps to a dangerous degree.[10]

We know that the aesthetic vision can challenge reactionary social agendas. Indeed, for most defenders of art today, though by no means all, that's welcome enough because theirs is a moderately liberal agenda. But art can also challenge progressive and humanely responsible social agendas. For that reason, to take art seriously is to recognise that there are some reasonable (i.e. rational) grounds for wanting to control it, although I say this as someone with a libertarian hatred of censorship. I'm not claiming that art is inhumane in the sense that it insidiously legitimates the interests of the powerful at the expense of the dispossessed, exploited, etc., although there are indeed some canonical works which have been plausibly read in such terms. Nor is my argument a transhistorical one about all art, or even all literature. It is obviously more applicable to some genres, periods and movements where what is central is a dangerous knowledge of the dissident desires which threaten rather than what confirms psychic and social equilibrium, and prevailing notions of civilised life – e.g. Greek Tragedy, the drama of the English Renaissance (including Shakespeare's), the epics of that same period (especially those of Spenser and Milton), and countless nineteenth- and twentieth-century texts.

Again, a disquieting half-realisation of this has been apparent within conservative aesthetic perspectives. We can detect it in the most basic and apparently reassuring category of the humanist aesthetic, that of 'character'. We know where we are with individual characters: they help us make ethical sense of the world, and of the work. Or do they? Time and again, and across centuries if not millennia, the most compelling individual creations are the ethically confusing ones: the vice figures in medieval moralities had a destructive vitality and anarchic wit on their side; the malcontents in Elizabethan and Jacobean tragedy are charismatic anti-heroes whose deep insight into corruption derives from their willing complicity with it; Milton's Satan in *Paradise Lost* has a perverse integrity in evil which, at the very least problematises, and for some readers discredits, the didactic project of the entire epic. In *Paradise Lost* the devil may indeed be in the detail, but he's also sure as hell in its structure too.

This kind of writing is not necessarily the consequence of a consciously radical agenda, as Shelley suggested of Milton, or conversely, an unconscious one, as Blake implied (Milton being of the devil's party without knowing it). It may in fact have unlikely sources, including theological ones. Consider, for example, the affinity between this aesthetic identification with the daemonic and the theological and ethical impulse to exact a full look at the worst. What we encounter in the epics of Spenser and Milton may be the courage – or arrogance, and perhaps paranoia – of the most formidable kind of theology, that which believes it can most effectively overcome what threatens it only by knowing or rehearsing it to the full. To comprehend something thoroughly enough is to move closer to it and to thereby risk entering its thrall; a knowing identification *of* becomes an imaginative identification *with*. In crucial respects this is exactly the condition of some of the knights in Spenser's epic *The Faerie Queene*. As guardians of civilisation those knights struggle to uphold the repressions, the disavowals and moralities which bind civilisation into its fragile, competing unities. In the process they are beleaguered by all the primaeval, daemonic forces which would destroy them, and it is in the imagining of these forces that the writing is at its most powerful. *The Faerie Queene* is a sprawling, unfinished allegory of civilisation, in which the official project is constantly overwhelmed by what it seeks to exclude and repress. And the fact that its creator, Edmund Spenser, was personally involved in the barbaric attempt to 'civilise' Ireland, makes his epic of greater, not lesser, significance.[11] Are such imaginative identifications with the daemonic and the inhumane ultimately contained, placed or neutralised by some over-arching ethical vision or structural closure within the literary work? If a minority of critics have argued this to be so, a majority of readers have thought otherwise.

Knowledge and Desire

My argument entails a view of aesthetic appreciation as in certain respects cognitive, that is, possessing a truth- or knowledge-content. Such an account is associated most immediately with Adorno but again, has a longer, conventional history both as working assumption and as theory: we find it in Aristotle, Horace, Tasso, Sidney, Pope, Johnson, Keats, Shelley, and others. In the early modern period, one of the reasons why those in authority feared the theatre was because it imparted ideas and information which they, the authorities, regarded as threatening to social order. That's also why, in defences of literature, both then and later, *knowledge* was often tied restrictively to the idea of *instruction*, this being another dimension of the didacticism mentioned earlier. In other words, 'instruction' censors the scope of 'knowledge'. My project, beginning with *Radical Tragedy*, has been to prise those two apart and to show that in the writing of literature they have never been that close anyway. To see art as cognitive does not preclude it having specific and even unique formal properties (language, style, genre and so on), nor does it diminish their importance. But it does challenge claims that such aesthetic qualities render the cognitive element of a work secondary or even irrelevant. And since such claims are quite recent,[12] the onus of proof is on those who make them.

In proverb and myth, in theology and philosophy, one human discourse after another insists that there are things we should not know. This forbidding of certain kinds of knowledge as harmful has always been a feature of human cultures, conceptualised most obviously in taboo and heresy.[13] But such concepts also indicate that such knowledge becomes most dangerous when it is crossed with, or driven by, dissident desire. Milton's Adam and Eve are told: 'know to know no more' (*Paradise Lost*, IV, 775). They disobey, and their transgressive desire for forbidden knowledge brings death and disintegration into the world, into desire. In other words, transgressive desire is inseparable from forbidden knowledge and together they kick-start history and become the driving forces of tragedy.

For some this is not a matter of regret: we are most ourselves when we are in this destructive, dangerous and suffering state of freedom, violating the restraints of the very history which has produced us. This was Nietzsche's view, which he attributed to Shakespeare. The rationalist might regard the accumulation of knowledge as a progressive and irreversible consolidation of civilisation. But Nietzsche is speaking of another kind of knowledge, one which does not consolidate civilisation, but threatens it. It is the knowledge that civilisation itself is at heart illusory. 'Illusory' here refers not to residual superstitions, soon to be swept away by the march of rational progress, but to the very structure of civilisation; anticipating Freud, Nietzsche believed that human civilisation

requires illusion (what Freud would call repression, disavowal and
sublimation) in order to be what it is. Knowing this to be the case
makes one an outcast from society, understanding too much from a
position 'beyond good and evil'. This is Nietzsche's reading of
Hamlet – he has 'seen through' the illusions by which his culture
maintains itself; inaction derives not from confusion and doubt, but
too much certainty.[14] Likewise with Macbeth, but with him it is also
about affirming what has been repressed – of desublimating the life
force itself, of holding it up against civilised morality, and even celebrating its destructive power. So it's a mistake, says Nietzsche, to
think that Shakespeare's theatre was aiming for moral effects. In this
regard *Macbeth* does not warn against hubris and ambition; on the
contrary it affirms their attraction. And the fact that Macbeth 'perishes by his passions' is part of his 'demonic attraction'. By 'demonic'
[*dämonisch*] Nietzsche means 'in defiance *against* life and advantage
for the sake of a drive and idea' [*Gedankens und Triebes*]. He adds
'Do you suppose that Tristan and Isolde are preaching *against* adultery when they both perish by it? This would be to stand the poets
on their head: they, and especially Shakespeare, are enamoured of
the passions as such and not least of their *death-welcoming* moods.'
Shakespeare, like other tragic poets, 'speaks . . . out of a restless, vig-
orous age which is half-drunk and stupefied by its excess of blood
and energy – out of a wickeder age than ours is'. But the guardians
of high culture in our own day disavow this: they seek to '*adjust* and
justify the goal of a Shakespearean drama' precisely in order that they
(and we) 'not understand it' (*Daybreak*, pp. 140–1). Thus
Shakespeare and his guardians fall on opposite sides of Nietzsche's
great divide between those who affirm the life-force and those who
turn away from it: between, in other words, the daemonic and the
humanitarian. In *The Gay Science* this distinction is expressed in
terms of two distinct kinds of sufferer – those who suffer from a
superabundance of life and those who suffer from an impoverishment of life. The former 'want a Dionysian art as well as a tragic
outlook and insight into life', and willingly confront 'the terrible and
questionable . . . every luxury of destruction, decomposition, negation'; while the latter need 'mildness, peacefulness, goodness in
thought and in deed . . . a certain warm, fear-averting confinement

and enclosure within optimistic horizons' (*The Gay Science*, p. 234). All this is to the point, although Nietzsche wilfully misconstrues *Macbeth*. This play is indeed a profound exploration of the daemonic, but its *tragedy* is the deep and recalcitrant conflict between the daemonic and the humane, between the Macbeths' 'black and deep desires' and the 'milk of human kindness' (I. iv. 52, I. v. 16). And if this type of conflict is the focus of many of the most memorable tragedies, it is also embedded in the history of human civilisation, and one reason why tragedy is widely regarded as the most profound of all literary genres.[15] But Nietzsche's view of the artist and philosopher as knowing too much, of seeing through, demystifying and maybe undermining the ideological, religious and cultural 'fictions' of society, and thereby 'de-repressing' subversive desires – all this is clearly relevant to the drama of the early modern period, whose own heroes, anti-heroes, lovers and malcontents are already doing something similar. Similar but with even darker implications: if Nietzsche revels in the idea that Macbeth 'perishes by his passions', these plays dramatise the agony, the violence and the psychological conflict generated by destructive and illicit desire. If Macbeth is an obvious case in point there are many others, less well-known but no less compelling, like Tamyra from George Chapman's *Bussy D'Ambois*:

> . . . Fear, fear and hope
> Of one thing, at one instant fight in me:
> I love what most I loathe, and cannot live
> Unless I compass that which holds my death
>
> (II. ii. 168ff)

To observe the injunction not to know (or, more accurately, for *some* people, often the majority, not to know) has been regarded as a precondition of social and psychological well-being, and the survival of civilisation itself – again implicit in the very idea of censorship. Against that, the breaking of the injunction has been regarded as profoundly liberating, although the liberation often leads to violence and tragedy. Straddling that opposition are some of the great transgressive figures of myth and literature, including Eve, Prometheus, Faust/us, Mary Shelley's Frankenstein, Flaubert's Madame Bovary, Thomas Mann's Aschenbach, and Joseph Conrad's Kurtz. Others, like Robert Louis Stevenson's Jekyll/Hyde, suggest that knowledge of evil derives from genius rather than barbarism, while those like Shakespeare's Macbeth and Dostoyevsky's Raskolnikov confirm Pascal's observation (anticipating Nietzsche) that there is a kind of evil which often passes for good because 'it takes as much extraordinary greatness of soul to attain such evil, as to attain good' (*Pensées*, p. 215). Dangerous knowledge indeed.

If most of the foregoing tragic protagonists carry a sense of the dangerous as well as the liberatory potential of the forbidden knowledge, this is because the knowledge that is forbidden so often reveals the alarming, underlying proximities of evil to good. Once again, where we thought there was a clear opposition we find a mutual implication. Long before Derrida, Freud has a disturbing explanation of this:

> [T]he objects to which men give most preference, their ideals, proceed from the same perceptions and experiences as the objects which they most abhor, and . . . they were originally only distinguished from one another through slight modifications. . . . Indeed . . . it is possible for the original instinctual representative to be split in two, one part undergoing repression, while the remainder, *precisely on account of this intimate connection* undergoes idealization. ('On Repression', p. 150; my emphasis)

Dangerous knowledge indeed.

To take art seriously is to know it comes without the humanitarian guarantees which currently smother it. Again, if bad times produce great books it does not follow that great books compensate for, let alone alleviate, bad times. Let us say at the very least that the ethical and the humane, in order not to atrophy, must be constantly exposed to their own vital exclusions – exposed, that is, to what allows them to be what they are. But without any guarantee that they can survive that exposure. That is the promise and the danger of art.

We may agree that the suppression of 'truth' is harmful socially and ethically, while remembering that it happens in all cultures, including 'democracies'. 'Why do they hate us so much?' was the bewildered, anguished response of some Americans to September 11, 2001, seemingly unaware of so much: unaware that their country was indeed hated with a vengeance of the kind wreaked on that day; unaware that they were vulnerable to such an attack; unaware even of who their enemies actually were. In such cases we grieve for the ignorance as well as the loss of life, because if more people had been better informed, history might, just might, have been different. However, it does not follow that a hypothetically adequate knowledge is always socially and ethically beneficial. To believe it is must be one of the few remaining naiveties of Enlightenment humanism. In the last century we acquired the knowledge to wipe our own species (and most others) off the face of the earth. In this century we will acquire genetic knowledge which threatens our most basic categories of the human. Knowledge destroys as well as empowers. Rebels against the established order know the knowledge they use against it is reflexively dangerous for them too. In *The Birth of Tragedy*, Nietzsche remarks, in relation to *Hamlet*, that 'Understanding kills action, for in order to act we require the veil of illusion' (p. 51). To be fully knowing *and* commit to praxis becomes almost a contradiction – hence Gramsci's tragic maxim, coined from Romain Rolland: 'pessimism of the intelligence, optimism of the will' (*Selections from Prison Notebooks*, p. 175). If ignorance is bliss, it's only realised as such after knowledge – that is, when ignorance is no longer possible. Hence that other tragic maxim, or knowing question: after such knowledge, what forgiveness? Under such circumstances, the radical political project does not render tragedy obsolete so much as assume some responsibility for it.

Jonathan Dollimore
March 20, 2003

Notes

1. In this connection see also Tate, *Modernism*, and Atkin, *A War of Individuals*.
2. The following collection of essays on the drama of Shakespeare and his contemporaries are helpful in this and other respects: Kastan and Stallybrass, *Staging the Renaissance*; Sinfield, *Macbeth*; Drakakis,

Antony and Cleopatra; Loomba and Orkin, *Post-Colonial Shakespeares*; Simkin, *Revenge Tragedy*.

3. Daniel Swift, 'Letter From New York', *Times Literary Supplement*, October 5, 2001, pp. 17–18. See too the letter from Peter M. Oppenheimer in the *TLS* for October 26, 2001, p. 17, describing 'September 1st, 1939' as 'an aberrant piece of junk [to] be consigned to the scrap heap', and that defending the poem from Derek Roper, *TLS*, November 2, 2001, p. 21.

4. I'm thinking here of not only Adorno and Horkheimer's seminal *Dialectic of Enlightenment*, but also of Herbert Marcuse's important collection *Negations*.

5. Witness the title of a recent book by one of humanism's most strident contemporary advocates: Harold Bloom's *Shakespeare: the Invention of the Human*.

6. Lecture delivered to the Royal Society of the Arts, October 23, 2000; printed in an abridged form in the *Independent* (Wednesday Review, p. 4), October 25, 2000.

7. The appropriation of the humanist aesthetic by and for those traditionally excluded from it is an important aspect of its history – see especially Jonathan Rose, *The Intellectual Life of the British Working Class*. This appropriation was also a transformation which threatens some of humanism's founding principles.

8. See Dollimore and Sinfield, *Political Shakespeare*; Sinfield, *Faultlines*; Brannigan, *New Historicism and Cultural Materialism*; and Healy, *New Latitudes*.

9. Generally, I find Etlin's beautifully produced book devoid of insight into the arts in proportion to its tasteful appreciation of them.

10. If I allude again to *Sex, Literature and Censorship*, it's simply because I only now have time to sketch and develop the argument outlined more fully there.

11. Writing on Spenser and Ireland is considerable – see especially appendix 3, 'Guide to further reading', in Spenser, *A View of the State of Ireland*, ed. Hadfield and Maley, and most recently, Patricia Palmer, *Language and Conquest*. On Shakespeare and Ireland, see Christopher Highley, *Shakespeare, Spenser, and the Crisis in Ireland*.

12. See especially J. M. Bernstein, *The Fate of Art*: 'The experience of art *as aesthetical* is the experience of art as having lost or been deprived of its power to speak the truth. . . . This loss . . . I shall call "aesthetic alienation"; it denominates art's alienation from truth which is caused by art's *becoming* aesthetical, a becoming that has been fully consum-

mated only in modern societies' (p. 4; emphasis original). For recent engagements with the cognitive view, see Bowie, 'Aesthetic Autonomy', and 'Confessions of a "new aesthete"', John Joughin, 'Shakespeare, Modernity and the Aesthetic', and James O. Young, *Art and Knowledge*.

13. Shattuck, *Forbidden Knowledge*; Ziolkowski, *The Sin of Knowledge*.
14. On Nietzsche and *Hamlet*, see Leonid Shtremel, *The Tragedy of Hamlet as 'The Dionysian Man': An Application of Nietzsche's Reading of* Hamlet', MA thesis, University of Haifa, Israel, August 2001.
15. On tragedy, see especially Drakakis, *Shakespearean Tragedy*; Drakakis and Lieber, *Tragedy*; and most recently, Nuttall, *Why Does Tragedy Give Pleasure?* and Eagleton, *Sweet Violence*.

Bibliography

Adorno, Theodor W., *Prisms*, trans. Samuel and Shierry Weber, London: Neville Spearman, 1967.

———, and Horkheimer, Max, *Dialectic of Enlightenment*, trans. John Cumming, New York: Seabury Press, 1972.

Armstrong, Isobel, *The Radical Aesthetic*, Oxford: Blackwell, 2000.

Atkin, Jonathan, *A War of Individuals: Bloomsbury Attitudes to the Great War*, Manchester: Manchester University Press, 2002.

Auden, W. H., *The Enchafèd Flood or the Romantic Iconography of the Sea* [1950], London: Faber, 1967.

Baudrillard, Jean, *Symbolic Exchange and Death* [1976], trans. Iain Hamilton Grant, with an introduction by Mike Gain, London: Sage Publications, 1993.

Bernstein, J. M., *The Fate of Art: Aesthetic Alienation from Kant to Derrida and Adorno*, Cambridge: Polity, 1992.

Bloom, Harold, *Shakespeare: the Invention of the Human*, London: Fourth Estate, 1999.

Bowie, Andrew, 'Aesthetic Autonomy', in D. Cooper et al., eds, *A Companion to Aesthetics*, Oxford: Blackwell, 1992.

———, 'Confessions of a "New Aesthete": a Response to the "New Philistines"', *New Left Review*, 225 (1997), 105–26.

Brannigan, John, *New Historicism and Cultural Materialism*, London: Macmillan, 1998.

Chapman, George, *Bussy D'Ambois*, ed. N. S. Brooke, Manchester: Manchester University Press, 1964.

Clark, Michael P., *The Revenge of the Aesthetic: The Place of Literature in Theory Today*, ed. Michael P. Clark, Berkeley: University of California Press, 2000.

Derrida, Jacques, *Positions* [1972], trans. Alan Bass, London: Athlone, 1981.

Dollimore, Jonathan, and Sinfield, Alan, *Political Shakespeare: Essays in Cultural Materialism* [1985], second edition with additional chapter, Manchester: Manchester University Press, 1994.

Dollimore, Jonathan, *Sex, Literature and Censorship*, Cambridge: Polity, 2001.

Drakakis, John, ed. and introduction, *Shakespearean Tragedy*, London: Longman, 1992.

——, ed., *Antony and Cleopatra*, London: Macmillan, 1994.

——, *Alternative Shakespeares* (second edition), London: Routledge, 2002.

Drakakis, J., and Lieber, N. C., *Tragedy*, London: Longman, 1998.

Eagleton, Terry, *Sweet Violence: the Idea of the Tragic*, London: Blackwell, 2002.

Ellis, John M., *Literature Lost: Social Agendas and the Corruption of the Humanities*, New Haven and London: Yale University Press, 1997.

Etlin, Richard A., *In Defence of Humanism: Value in Arts and Letters*, Cambridge: Cambridge University Press, 1996.

Freud, Sigmund, 'On Repression', in Pelican Freud Library, vol. 11, *On Metapsychology: the Theory of Psychoanalysis*, trans. J. Strachey, ed. A. Richards, Harmondsworth: Penguin, 1984.

Gramsci, Antonio, *Selections from Prison Notebooks*, ed. and trans. Q. Hoare and G. Nowell Smith, London: Lawrence and Wishart, 1971.

Healy, Thomas, *New Latitudes: Theory and English Renaissance Literature*, London: Arnold, 1992.

Hesse, Hermann, *If the War Goes On: Reflections on War and Politics* [1946], trans. Ralph Manheim, London: Pan Books, 1974.

Hickmann, Hannah, *Robert Musil and the Culture of Vienna*, London and Sydney: Croom Helm, 1984.

Highley, Christopher, *Shakespeare, Spenser, and the Crisis in Ireland*, Cambridge: Cambridge University Press, 1997.

Jameson, Fredric, *The Political Unconscious: Narrative as a Socially Symbolic Act*, London: Methuen, 1981.

Jarvis, Simon, *Adorno: A Critical Introduction*, Cambridge: Polity, 1998.

Jay, Martin, '"The Aesthetic Ideology" as Ideology: Or What Does it Mean to Aestheticize Politics?', in *Force Fields: Between Intellectual History and Cultural Critique*, London: Routledge, 1993.

Joughin, John J., 'Shakespeare, Modernity and the Aesthetic: Art, Truth and Judgement in *The Winter's Tale*', in *Shakespeare and Modernity: Early Modern to Millennium*, ed. Hugh Grady, London: Routledge, 2000.

Kastan, David Scott, and Stallybrass, Peter, *Staging the Renaissance*, London: Routledge, 1991.

Korsmeyer, Carolyn, ed., *Aesthetics: the Big Questions*, Oxford: Blackwell, 1998.

Loomba, A., and Orkin, M., *Post-Colonial Shakespeares*, London: Routledge, 1998.

Luft, David S., *Robert Musil and the Crisis of European Culture 1880–1942*, Berkeley: University of California Press, 1980.

Marcuse, Herbert, *Negations: Essays in Critical Theory*, trans. Jeremy J. Shapiro, Harmondsworth: Penguin, 1968.

Nietzsche, Friedrich, *The Gay Science* [1882/1887], ed. B.Williams, trans. J. Nauckhoff, Cambridge: Cambridge University Press, 2001.

——, *The Birth of Tragedy* [1870–71], trans. Francis Goffing, New York: Doubleday, 1956.

——, *Daybreak: Thoughts on the Prejudices of Morality* [1881], trans. R. J. Hollingdale, intro. by Michael Tanner, Cambridge: Cambridge University Press, 1982.

——, *Werke in Drei Bänden, Erster Band*, Munich: Carl Hanser, 1958.

Nuttall, A. D., *Why Does Tragedy Give Pleasure?*, Oxford: Oxford University Press, 2001.

Palmer, Patricia, *Language and Conquest in Early Modern Ireland: English Renaissance Literature and Elizabethan Imperial Expansion*, Cambridge: Cambridge University Press, 2001.

Pascal, Blaise, *Pensées* [1669], trans with intro. by A. J. Krailsheimer, Harmondsworth: Penguin, 1966.

Rose, Jonathan, *The Intellectual Life of the British Working Class*, New Haven: Yale University Press, 2001.

Shattuck, Roger, *Forbidden Knowledge: from Prometheus to Pornography*, New York: St Martin's Press, 1996.

Simkin, Stevie, ed., *Revenge Tragedy: Contemporary Critical Essays*, Basingstoke: Palgrave Macmillan, 2001.

Sinfield, Alan, *Faultlines: Cultural Materialism and the Politics of Dissident Reading*, Oxford: Clarendon, 1992.

——, ed., *Macbeth: Contemporary Critical Essays*, London: Macmillan, 1992.

Spenser, Edmund, *A View of the State of Ireland*, ed. Andrew Hadfield and Willy Maley, London: Blackwell, 1997.

Steiner, George, *Language and Silence: Essays on Language, Literature and the Inhuman*, New York: Athenæum, 1977.

Tate, Trudi, *Modernism, History and the First World War*, Manchester: Manchester University Press, 1998.

Wilde, Oscar, 'Pen, Pencil and Poison', in *Intentions* [1891], London: Methuen, 1925.

——, *The Picture of Dorian Gray* [1890/91], Harmondsworth: Penguin, 1949.

Wilson, R., and Dutton, R., eds, *New Historicism and Renaissance Drama*, London: Longman, 1992.

Young, James O., *Art and Knowledge*, London: Routledge, 2001.

Ziolkowski, Theodore, *The Sin of Knowledge: Ancient Themes and Modern Variations*, Princeton and Oxford: Princeton University Press, 2000.

Introduction to the Second Edition

Why did I write this book? There were several reasons for writing *a* book, the main one being a naive aspiration simply 'to write' which had helped keep me going on an arduous and damaging journey from being a miserable 15-year-old school-leaver chained to a lathe in a car factory to becoming – well, someone else. The aspiration to write was tied up with a restless dissatisfaction, a desire for – well, something else. Naive, yes, but if eventually it was made apparent to me that such aspirations are so widespread as to be banal, 'adolescent' even, I think none the worse of them for that, either in myself or others.

But this book? I first read Jacobean drama while studying English at university, some way along that journey. There was a perversity about it which attracted me and which resisted the staid and narrow attitude with which literature was usually taught at that university. This drama seemed to cross conventional boundaries, or require that I did so in reading it. For example, the individual versus society dichotomy had to go; everything about the Jacobean hero/ine or malcontent was already social, and in an obviously political way. Later, as I became more familiar with literary criticism of this drama, I realised that much of it tended to normalise, moralise and suppress exactly whatever it was I found attractive. In literary terms anyway, the wish for something else was finding a certain direction.

After only a short time as a graduate student I arrived at Sussex University, to teach, in 1976. It was a revelation. I encountered there for the first time what was usually called 'theory': new ideas; controversy; intellectual excitement; new ways of understanding literature in relation to culture and politics. Arriving at the same time as me were other new faculty including Jacqueline Rose and, later, David Forgacs, Allon White and Homi Bhabha. Those already there and participating in these debates included Tony Nuttall, Alan Sinfield,

Laurence Lerner, David Morse, Frank Gloversmith, Cora Kaplan and Peter Stallybrass. If Sussex has become known for such work it is not only because a younger generation is doing it; it is also because Sussex, from its inception, had a strong commitment to interdisciplinary work in the humanities, and theory is nothing if not interdisciplinary. It was that base which helped make new work possible.

At Sussex then the desire for something else found an intellectual direction. Critical and cultural theory enabled me to make political sense of my own past; it also enabled me to articulate and explore what 1 found challenging in Jacobean drama as well as clarifying the reasons why traditional literary criticism seemed inadequate – for me personally, and, as I soon found out, for others too. I abandoned the PhD thesis I had begun two years earlier as a graduate student at London University, and started to write *Radical Tragedy*.

It was completed in 1982 and published in 1984. I asked London University if I could submit a copy of this book instead of the thesis. Committees met, and after some months I was told that yes, I could, but that its covers would have to be removed and somehow replaced with others of regulation size. This was to make it look more like a real thesis. I expressed unwillingness to do this: the book was at that time available only in hardback at an exorbitant price and I was loath to butcher even one copy. (Reviewers would be doing that anyway.) Some months later, after the appropriate committee(s) had once again met, I was told to arrange with a bookbinder to have a cardboard box made up which was the exact size and colour of the regulation thesis. In the back there was to be a compartment to take the book, while on the side of the box (corresponding to the spine of a thesis) the title was to be embossed, just as with the real item. All this was accomplished, with the result that somewhere in the University of London library there is a copy of *Radical Tragedy* disguised as a PhD thesis; only in the unlikely event of it being removed from the shelf and its hidden compartment explored will the deception become apparent.

I like the irony of this. Supposing the project to have taken a normal course, first being completed as a thesis, then revised as a book – and I'm not confident that the thesis let alone the book *would* have materialised if I had continued on that road – whatever eventually did appear between hard covers would have been very different from *Radical Tragedy*. Bypassing the thesis helped make this an arrogant book, one which not only reads Jacobean tragedy differently, but presumes to challenge a politically conservative way of doing criticism; a book which claims to be interdisciplinary, oppositional, intellectually challenging rather than academically stifling, politically engaged rather than spuriously impartial. How, I now wonder, could I have been so naive as to be put out in discovering there were those who disliked it (and me)? Arrogance *or* naivety, but surely not both.

Charles Marowitz is a director famous not only for his radical productions of Shakespeare's plays, but also for his rewriting of them. Why does he do this? Well, he gives one reason in a recent article in *Shakespeare Quarterly*:

> I have to say, quite frankly, that some of the most contemptible people I have ever known have loved Shakespeare, and I have found that very hard to take. It's like sharing your bed with bigots and junkies. For many of them, Shakespeare is a confirmation of their world view. The Christian Universe is memorialized in his work, and, from his sentiments, they can easily justify their bourgeois smugness, their conventionality, and their pompous morality. For them, it is as if Shakespeare wrote only so that they could quote his aphorisms on their calendars.[1]

I confess to having harboured such ungracious thoughts myself, especially at the inception of this book, and then again when some of the people Marowitz describes reviewed it (or so they seemed to me). This apart, and despite some shared enemies, I suspect that politically Marowitz and I would find it hard to fall into step. But there are two points on which we might agree: first, a current, political engagement with Shakespeare is inseparable from what others have already made Shakespeare mean; the rewriting is as much a critique of existing interpretations as it is a production of new ones. Second, what those others have done with Shakespeare is as political as what Marowitz is doing. Often, interpretation is most biased, most timebound, when it claims to be most impartial. Such at least was where *Radical Tragedy* started from.

A new introduction like this is of course a unique opportunity to answer one's critics back, not so much those who did not like it and said so, but those who could express their dislike of the book only through misrepresenting it, intentionally or otherwise. Perhaps the greatest naivety of all in the aspiring writer, especially if she or he seeks controversy, is to expect that reviewers, whether they like you or not, will accurately represent what you are saying or trying to say. Now this really is naive, and is where I quite lose sympathy for my earlier self, not least since I have done my share of misrepresenting others (intentionally or otherwise). So it is through no especially virtuous motives that I have decided against slinging back the mud that did or did not stick; instead I shall engage with some of the work that has appeared subsequent to *Radical Tragedy* and which, to my mind, advances some shared concerns. As well as outlining work which is helping to transform our understanding of the theatre of Shakespeare and his contemporaries, and the practice of English Studies, I shall try to exemplify the procedures and aims of a materialist criticism.

Many of the controversial changes in literary criticism derive from the influence of a range of intellectual developments in post-war Europe and North America, including anthropology, Frankfurt School critical theory, Marxism, post-structuralism, deconstruction, psychoanalysis, feminism and gender critique, and cultural studies.[2]

To make this essay manageable, but also because I consider them to be the most interesting and important in this context, I shall be concerned mainly (not exclusively) with feminism and gender critique and a perspective in cultural studies known as cultural materialism;[3] they draw selectively on the other perspectives while also developing their own forms of cultural theory and critical practice, in significant cases doing this in studies of the Renaissance period and of Shakespeare.[4] For the perspective I am outlining there is no question of simply describing some new readings of English drama in the narrow sense typical of conventional literary criticism. Here are three reasons why not. First, some of the most challenging work has originated in a wider context and often has not even been by those primarily identified as 'Shakespeareans' or critics of Renaissance drama. Second, this work is often interdisciplinary, and rather than focussing exclusively on dramatic texts, it seeks to inter-relate the theatre with other aspects of culture. Third, materialist studies of the reproduction of 'Shakespeare' have shown him/it to be a powerful cultural institution. More is at stake in the cultural struggle over what he represents and embodies than for any other figure in literature and maybe within the humanities more generally. There was a time when it was thought bad form for critics to write on other critics rather than on the authors themselves. Now, however, traditions of criticism are seen as significant aspects of cultural history, and worth attending to for that reason; they not only register, but help to make, that history (I shall return to this). It follows that the student of literature can learn much by studying these traditions as well as the canon – asking, for example, which traditions actually constructed the canon and why. Materialist criticism relates both the literary canon and changing interpretations of it to the cultural formations which produce(d) them, and which those interpretations in turn reproduce, or help to change. In the process it attends to non-canonical texts and offers different conceptions of (for instance) human identity, cultural, social and historical process, as well as the activity of criticism itself.

Such an approach is premised on the belief that behind every substantial literary-critical disagreement can be found a substantial cultural and political difference rooted in the society of its time. This is perhaps nowhere more so than in the controversies surrounding the genre of tragedy. As Raymond Williams observes:

> Tragic experience, because of its central importance, commonly attracts the fundamental beliefs and tensions of a period, and tragic theory is interesting mainly in this sense, that through it the shape and set of a particular culture is often deeply realised. (*Modern Tragedy*, p. 45)

For this reason, and before outlining more recent critical developments, I want to return to a fundamental disagreement on the nature of tragedy which preceded this book and partly inspired it.

Tragedy and Politics[5]

Literary criticism has often been explicitly Christian in perspective. And, even where it has drawn back from the doctrinal certainties of Christianity, or been actively sceptical or even anti-Christian, its language has often remained religiose, especially in the acceptance of suffering as inescapable yet mysteriously ennobling, even redemptive. In 1961 in *The Death of Tragedy*, George Steiner gave this account of the truly tragic:

> In the very excess of his suffering lies man's claim to dignity. Powerless and broken . . . he assumes a new grandeur. Man is ennobled by the vengeful spite or injustice of the gods. . . . Hence there is in the final moments of great tragedy, whether Greek, or Shakespearean, or neoclassic, a fusion of grief and joy, of lament over the fall of man and of rejoicing in the resurrection of his spirit. No other poetic form achieves this mysterious effect; it makes of *Oedipus*, *King Lear*, and *Phèdre* the noblest yet wrought by the mind.[6]

This view can be traced to A. C. Bradley's *Shakespearean Tragedy* (pp. 260–1) (see below, pp. 53–6), a classic working out of the idealist theory which consciously but cautiously broke with the Christian metaphysic. Steiner breaks with it much more emphatically: Christianity believes in an ultimate justice and, says Steiner, where there is justice there cannot be tragedy (pp. 6, 324, 331). Even so, the idealist reading of tragedy, including Steiner's, remains inherently religious, and we can therefore find its most cogent expression not in literary criticism (for which literature has often served as a substitute or compromise theology) but in the work of those who are more aware of, and who remain confidently committed to, its metaphysical origins. I have in mind especially *Beyond Tragedy* (1938), by the protestant theologian Reinhold Niebuhr. In a chapter entitled 'Christianity and Tragedy' he gives a bold summary of the idealist preoccupation with integrity, subjectivity and suffering:

> In true tragedy the hero defies malignant power to assert the integrity of his soul. . . . The really tragic hero of warfare is not the soldier who makes the greatest sacrifice but the occasional discerning spirit who

plunges into the chaos of war with a full understanding of its dark, unconscious sources in the human psyche and an equal resolution, either to defy these forces or to submit himself as their tool and victim in recognition of his common humanity with those who are unconscious victims.[7]

Even those advocates of the tragic vision who argue that Christianity is incompatible with it would probably go this far with Niebuhr. So while there are significant differences between Niebuhr and Steiner, they share an important perception of tragedy as focussing profound and ennobling truths about the human condition in the suffering integrity of the unique individual. Both books are written with an enhancing moral passion; yet even as they invoke the human spirit as in some sense beyond the historically contingent, they are both pressured by the tragedies of their own historical moment: Niebuhr in the passage cited uses the example of warfare; his book was published twenty years after the First World War, at the end of the Spanish Civil War and on the eve of a second World War in whose shadow Steiner is consciously writing his book in 1961 (see especially the conclusion). For both, the history of recent warfare profoundly affected their vision of the tragic.

Writing in 1971, just a decade after Steiner but in a very different political, intellectual and cultural climate, J. W. Lever largely broke with this influential account of tragedy. He sees the protagonists of Jacobean drama very differently:

> We are not greatly concerned with the characters as individuals. . . . In Jacobean tragedy it is not primarily the conduct of the individual, but of the society which assails him, that stands condemned.[8]

He says of the White Devil in John Webster's play of the same name that it 'is not Vittoria Corombona but Renaissance Europe' (86); of the malcontent in *The Duchess of Malfi*, he says 'Neither villain nor hero, Bosola typifies the plight of the intellectual in the world of state, at once its agent and victim' (94). Lever's argument here is most immediately with those literary critics who saw the plays as growing out of the morality tradition and working as exemplary warnings of God's retribution on those who transgress. But

Lever is also offering a materialist alternative to the more searching, anguished, tragic vision of those like Niebuhr and Steiner.[9] Many of the differences between the idealist and the materialist perspectives centre, as here, on opposed conceptions of individuality and subjectivity. I shall return to this. Lever retains a concern for suffering integrity, especially when it occurs in the form of stoic rationality, which he sees as a strong influence on the drama (see, for example, pp. 10 and 94, and below, p. 194). At the same time he believes that a play which shows the defeat and destruction of human integrity does not thereby cease to be tragic (p. 10; something which Williams explores at greater length in *Modern Tragedy*).

What, then, is the relationship of the social and the political to the tragic; in effect, what counts as tragic? Steiner is emphatic:

> The tragic personage is broken by forces which can neither be fully understood nor overcome by rational prudence. This again is crucial. Where the causes of disaster are temporal, where the conflict can be resolved through technical or social means, we may have serious drama, but not tragedy. . . . The distinction should be borne sharply in mind. Tragedy is irreparable. (p. 8)

In a sense then, Lever's 'tragedy of state' is what Steiner says tragedy cannot be. It isn't that Lever sees Jacobean tragedy as politically optimistic; rather that, in contradistinction to Steiner, he sees the causes of suffering and conflict in these tragedies as contingent rather than necessary, the effect of social and historical forces focussed in state power. Though terrifyingly destructive, these forces are not irresistible in the sense of being cosmically or divinely destined.[10]

The decade which separated Steiner's and Lever's books was notoriously eventful, not least with respect to the political radicalism of many young people. It is hard to believe that any intellectual (or even academic) could have remained unaffected by the radicalism of that decade, even if only to oppose it (though the work of some literary critics suggests that they did). Lever's book originated not as a monograph for other scholars and critics but as a series of lectures for students. Not surprisingly then, he begins with a question which the student radicalism of the previous few years had made more or less unavoidable (whatever one's answer to it): the question of relevance. He has an unambiguous answer:

> In the present-day world, alienated in poverty and affluence, dehumanised by state bureaucracies and military machines, the most urgent study of mankind would seem to be not the eternal human condition, but the prospect of survival in the face of impersonal power drives. (p. 1)

Lever here registers an intellectual and political commitment rare for academic critics at that time. One response of the teacher to the question about relevance was simply to dismiss it as irrelevant to the study of literature; another was to see that question as the consequence of narrowminded ignorance which only impartial teaching would rectify.

The patronising review of Lever's *The Tragedy of State* in the *Times Literary Supplement* of 17 December 1971 says a great deal:

> It seems unfortunate that this constant and often unavailing search for 'relevance' should occupy so many pages of this study since, when Mr Lever can escape from its entanglements he shows himself a sound and often subtle expositor. His treatment of theme and character is penetrating, and we must regret that his preoccupation with real or supposed political features causes him at times to neglect the play's dramatic qualities. (p. 1583; unsigned, according to the convention at that time)

To reject the terms and values of this review is not necessarily to remain uncritical of the concept of relevance. Like many other indispensable concepts it is ambiguous and open to different and conflicting interpretations. Historically – which is to say at that time and in relation to the institutions within which it was made – the student demand for relevance was a political demand; and, for the materialist perspective being outlined here, a progressive one also. Even so it could be used in the name of a disregard of cultural difference, both in the past and in the present. And yet it was the very demand for relevance which helped produce the recognition of the limitations of the demand itself and the need to address questions of cultural and historical difference. This very tension (between relevance and difference) itself helped shift English Studies in the direction of a wider-ranging cultural politics and interdisciplinary intellectual concern, with implications at once methodological, political and ethical.

Containment/Subversion

Not for Lever then the ahistorical universality of Steiner's human condition, nor its instantiation, that 'treatment of theme and character' which the *TLS* reviewer wished he'd stuck to. Lever advocates a criticism which explores the Jacobean dramatists' own concern with state power in a period of 'intellectual ferment and spiritual upheaval which preceded the first great European revolution' (p. vii). This particular aspect of Lever's project has found confirmation outside of literary criticism. In two recent articles Christopher Hill offers a persuasive synthesis of the evidence for seeing the drama as not only concerned with contemporary politics, but having wider implications for understanding subsequent history. Writers of literature, especially drama, were, says Hill, 'not dealing with "the human condition", with "man", but with specific problems which confronted rulers and their subjects in a specific historical situation – problems which were bloodily resolved in the sixteen-forties'.[11]

Clearly not all Elizabethan and Jacobean drama can be usefully discussed in these terms. It depends on the dramatist, the play and the issues involved. A particular play might offer a radical critique of providentialist ideology while being inherently conservative in other respects. Recent critics have divided over Lever's claims for the oppositional nature of the theatre. Is it more conservative than challenging, or vice versa? In particular – and the point is recorded here somewhat simply for the sake of brevity – did these plays reinforce the dominant order, or do they interrogate it to the point of subversion? According to a rough and ready division, US critics known as new historicists have inclined to the first view. UK cultural materialists to the second, while feminism and gender critique, as I shall show shortly, has operated in both categories.[12]

Historicist critics like Stephen Greenblatt and Steven Mullancy have read Shakespeare's *Henry IV* and *Henry V* plays in relation to a process identifiable in both the theatre and its wider culture whereby potentially subversive social elements are *contained* in the process of being *rehearsed*.[13] In contrast, *Radical Tragedy* finds in this theatre a substantial challenge; not a vision of political freedom so much as a subversive knowledge of political domination, a knowledge which interrogated prevailing beliefs, submitted them to a kind of intellectual vandalism; radical in the sense of going to their roots and even pulling them up (below, p. 22, and note 17, p. 274). It is true that some of the most intriguing plays of the period do indeed rehearse threats in order to contain them. But to contain a threat by rehearsing it one must first give it a voice, a part, a presence – in the theatre, as in the culture. Through this process the very condition of something's containment may constitute the terms of its challenge: opportunities for resistance become apparent, especially on the stage and even as the threat is being disempowered.[14]

In sketching the radical/conservative debate I have oversimplified: there is no complete alignment of new historicist critics on one side and materialist critics on the other; also, the arguments for subversion as well as those for containment register a complexity in text and history often missed by commentators.[15] Moreover, both perspectives cross between categories; materialism might, for example, contrast the challenge offered by these plays on the Jacobean stage with the often highly conservative appropriation of them in subsequent criticism and theatre productions. Conversely a critic like Louis Montrose, involved in new historicism from the outset and playing an influential (and critical) role in its development, has always been sensitive to the instabilities of containment – especially when considering issues of gender.[16] Finally, in a materialist critique of the notion of containment Alan Sinfield describes a way of approaching texts which shows them not so much as *either* conservative or subversive, but as sites of struggle.[17]

Reading Contradictions

One shrinks from describing a critical perspective with neat formulae, or even giving it a name. Such things live to hauntingly mis-
represent. But it has been said that whereas traditional criticism reads
for coherence, materialist criticism begins by reading for incoherence
or, as it might better be called, *discoherence*, a term I invoke in its
now obsolete seventeenth-century sense of incongruity verging on
contradiction. The *OED* cites Hooker: 'An opinion of discoherence
. . . between the justice of God and the state of men in this world'. A
materialist reading, though it would reject idealist concepts of coherence, does not thereby subscribe to the (residually idealist) notion
that all is ultimately incoherent, random, arbitrary or whatever (see
below, pp. 5–8, 59–69). From a social, political and historical point
of view, the discoherent is always meaning-full; always readable.[18]

In response to an article on *Measure for Measure* by L. C. Knights,
F. R. Leavis vehemently denied that Shakespeare shows himself 'the
victim of unresolved contradictions, of mental conflict or of uncertainty'; he adds:

> Complexity of attitude isn't necessarily conflict or contradiction; and,
> it may be added . . . some degree of complexity of attitude is involved
> in all social living. It is Shakespeare's great triumph in *Measure for
> Measure* to have achieved so inclusive and delicate a complexity, and
> to have shown us complexity distinguished from contradiction, con-
> flict and uncertainty, with so sure and subtle a touch.[19] (p. 166)

This view indicates a difficulty experienced not only by Leavis but
many other critics in conceiving contradiction and conflict as anything but psychic disability or aesthetic failure, the latter often being
seen as a reflection of the former. *Radical Tragedy* takes a different
approach to conflict and contradiction, arguing that Jacobean
theatre interrogated structures of belief which legitimated prevailing
power relations, and that it often did this by seizing upon, intensifying and exposing those contradictions in the prevailing social order
which it is one of the effects of ideology to efface (see below, chapters 1 and 3, especially p. 8).

Franco Moretti similarly invests the disturbance of Jacobean tragedy – what earlier critics might have called its 'chaotic vision' – with a historical significance. He makes Elizabethan and Jacobean tragedy a major exception to his general theory of literature itself as a conservative form, one which tends to secure consent to (because it is an ideological legitimation of) the existing order. But not so this tragedy, argues Moretti; on the contrary, this tragedy 'contributed, more radically than any other cultural phenomenon of the same period, to discrediting the values of absolute monarchy, thereby paving the way, with wholly destructive means, for the English Revolution'. With wholly destructive means: Moretti here stresses the revolutionary potential of negation: tragedy, in this period, was 'an unrivalled instrument of criticism and dissent'; Shakespeare 'may announce the dawn of bourgeois civilisation, but not by prefiguring it. On the contrary, he demonstrates inexorably how, obeying the old rules, which are the only ones he knows, the world can only fall apart.'[20]

But what happens when this kind of challenge begins to have its effect and prevailing power structures are indeed partially 'delegitimated'? At this stage those in power typically make violent and punitive bids for relegitimation, finding scapegoats in the process. I can illustrate what I mean here by sketching a different reading of *Measure for Measure* from Leavis's.[21]

That play begins with, and is about, a crisis of authority. Society is presented as unstable enough for it to be expedient for the Duke temporarily to abdicate. Before he leaves he sanctions a policy of authoritarian repression. Low life, prostitution and lechery are identified as the causes of crisis, yet we learn increasingly of a corruption more political than sexual. The Duke himself describes it in terms of insurrection:

> Liberty plucks justice by the nose,
> The baby beats the nurse, and quite athwart
> Goes all decorum.
>
> (I. iii. 29–31)

This is the world turned upside down, and hierarchy itself is under threat. For his part Escalus fears dissident factions within the state, while low-life characters point out that the actual sources of disorder are within the law itself, or practices sanctioned by law. Elbow's confusion of terms tells us that maybe the respected *should* be suspected. Arguably then, the play shows corruption to be less the effect of anarchic desire than of the power structure seeking to recontrol it, and this policing of sexuality is surely both a relegitimation of the state, and the downward displacement of a more fundamental political instability within the state, the two things being inseparable.

The process is neatly focussed in the fact that the desire which Angelo seeks to police erupts within himself. And this is not just desire which seeks to escape the law that commands virtue, but desire rooted in a wish to pervert and corrupt that law; as Angelo says, he desires Isabella 'foully for those things that make her good'; he desires to 'raze the sanctuary'.

So the 'disorder' which, in terms of the binary rulers/ruled, is supposed to characterise those designated by the inferior term, the ruled, actually erupts from within the dominant term, the rulers. Despite all the propaganda to the contrary, it was quite possible for people to see that disorder was often generated from the top down rather than from the bottom up. Shakespeare's *Coriolanus* dramatises just this perception, while Machiavelli theorises it in the *Discourses* (see below, chapter 14).

Marginality (1)

Mention of the prostitutes in *Measure* (to which I shall return) reflects a particular concern of materialist theory and criticism with the oppression and exploitation of the marginal, the subordinate and the excluded. It is not of course that the awareness of such things has only just occurred or that subordination relates only to minorities; consider the case of the subordinate classes, of women or of Third World countries subjected to imperialist domination. At this point the *TLS* reviewer of Lever's book might object that this has nothing to do with Jacobean drama, that once again we have drifted into the misguided preoccupation with relevance. The reply is that, on the contrary, issues of class, sexuality, imperialist and colonial exploitation have everything to do with Jacobean drama, as recent studies have made abundantly clear.[22] At the same time, the concern with marginality has to be more than a moralistic declaration of the obvious or the easy rhetoric of oppression.

It will help to proceed through a specific example and contrast. Kenneth Muir, discussing the supernatural elements in *Macbeth* (he is speaking specifically of Lady Macbeth's sleep-walking scene), remarks:

> The fact that we no longer believe in demons, and that Shakespeare's audience mostly did, does not diminish the dramatic effect for us; for with the fading of belief in the objective existence of devils, they and their operations can yet symbolize the workings of evil in the hearts of men . . . The changes in custom and belief do not seriously detract from the universality of the tragedy.[23]

Contrast this with Terry Eagleton in *William Shakespeare*, speaking of the witches in *Macbeth*:

> The witches are the heroines of the piece . . . they . . . by releasing ambitious thoughts in Macbeth, expose [the] hierarchical social order for what it is . . . the pious self-deception of a society based on routine oppression and incessant warfare . . . Their riddling, ambiguous speech . . . promises to subvert this structure: their teasing word-play infiltrates and undermines Macbeth from within, revealing in him a lack which hollows his being into desire. The witches signify a realm of non-meaning and poetic play which hovers at the work's margins . . . [They] catalyse this region of otherness and desire within [Macbeth] so that by the end of the play it has flooded up from within him to shatter and engulf his previously assured identity . . . The witches figure as the 'unconscious' of the drama, that which must be exiled and repressed as dangerous but which is always likely to return with a vengeance . . . The witches inhabit an anarchic, richly ambiguous zone both in and out of official society . . . But official society can only ever imagine its radical 'other' as chaos rather than creativity . . . Foulness – a political order which thrives on bloodshed – believes itself fair, whereas the witches do not so much invert this opposition as deconstruct it.[24]

I have chosen these two critics because each is deservedly respected by, and representative of, his own critical context and, to a large extent, his generation.

For Muir the demons constitute an awkward aspect of Shakespeare; we don't believe in them, and if it turns out that Shakespeare did then his universal appeal might be diminished. He will become too much of his time in a way which compromises his reputation as the greatest playwright; dependent on that idea is his transcending his time. Reconstituting the demons as symbols of evil saves Shakespeare. Note that Muir does not say Shakespeare believed in demons, only that his audience mostly did. But the implication is that even if he did, he and/or we could also see a deeper truth behind the surface superstition. I say and/or we because, to be fair to Muir, he is rather scrupulous in this passage, not actually attributing the symbolic view to Shakespeare either; that 'can yet' includes what it does not actually specify. However, the overall effect is to dissolve an awkward piece of history, via an appeal to symbolism, into a transhistorical truth.

What Muir seeks to remove, Eagleton seizes upon and stresses. I have quoted him at length because the passage represents something important in recent work which Eagleton is here voicing though not directly specifying: a concern with the subordinate, the marginal and the displaced. In that work these individuals, groups or sub-cultures are seen as being (i) of importance in their own right – histories which literary criticism and official history have ignored or repressed; (ii) of further importance for understanding the society which has rendered them marginal (for example, the dominant defines itself *over* and *against* its deviants); and (iii) sources of a potential or actual instability and subversion in that society. So, for Eagleton, the witches are fascinatingly deviant, but they also reveal much about, and subvert, the social order which demonises them. Here then we can see the process which has preoccupied cultural anthropologists – in the words of Barbara Babcock (recalling Muir's), 'What is socially peripheral is often symbolically central.'[25] Though in quite different ways, this is so both in the society of early modern England that demonised them, and in the contemporary criticism which foregrounds and appropriates them. But this is a very different kind of symbolism from Muir's symbolic dissolution of the witches into 'the hearts of men' – although as we shall see, there is a sense in which witchcraft might indeed be said to originate in the hearts of men (see below, pp. lxxiv–lxxvi).

The paradoxically central significance of marginality is taken up by contributors to *Political Shakespeare*,[26] with the difference that here an attempt is made to give the subordinate more of a history: two essays analyse English colonialism in the New World and Ireland in relation to Shakespeare's history plays and *The Tempest*; other essays consider the prostitutes in *Measure for Measure*, and the representation of women's subordination in this same play, together with *King Lear*, and in early modern England.[27]

Subjectivity or Writing of/f the Unitary Self

Materialist theory, and it is by no means unique in this, argues that those areas of human life commonly thought to be antithetical to and independent of the political realm – for example subjectivity, personal identity, gender identity, the privacy of the home, the intimacy of the family, aesthetics – in fact actually include, and often actively reproduce, the exploitation, repression and oppression visible in that larger public realm. And some of the forms of that oppression – patriarchy, phallocentrism and misogyny for example – are of course internalised psychically as well as working institutionally and legally.[28] This has considerable importance for the drama, not just because patriarchy and misogyny pervade it, but because this is a drama in which we see these things operating at all levels simultaneously – the psychic, the private, the familial, the public.

So materialist theory rejects those ideologies which sustain the belief in an ultimate separation between the political, historical and social on the one hand, and the subjective and spiritual on the other. In particular it rejects – as indeed do virtually all the post-war intellectual developments mentioned earlier – the humanist belief in a unified, autonomous self (see below, chapters 10 and 16). Materialist and feminist critics draw on such theory, working out its implications for the view of the Renaissance as the supposed origin of modern 'man'. There are differences here: Barker in *The Tremulous Private Body* offers a critique of the subjectivity produced in and by bourgeois culture, Belsey in *The Subject of Tragedy* of an equally large historical development which she categorises as 'liberal humanism';[29] in this book I speak more specifically of 'essentialist humanism'.[30] But all three challenge central assumptions of the traditional reading of character, human nature and individual identity as they are found in studies of Shakespeare, of Renaissance literature and, more generally still, in the practice of English Studies.

They proceed via a twofold analysis – a critique of the way literary critics have reproduced Renaissance drama in terms of a modern depoliticised subjectivity, and an attempt to recover a more adequate history of subjectivity, especially in the early modern period. Belsey begins with the proposition that 'Man is the subject of liberal humanism. Woman has meaning in relation to man. And yet the instability which is the result of this asymmetry is the ground of protest, resistance, feminism' (p. ix). She reads the drama in relation to the development within liberal humanism of a distinction between public and private, man and woman; Webster's *The Duchess of Malfi* (1613–14) is seen as 'a perfect fable of emergent liberalism' (p. 197). Barker points out how successive generations of critics, especially Romantics but also others since, have attempted to discover the essence of Hamlet, finding in him (for example) the 'alienated modern individual dejected in the market place of inauthentic values' (p. 38). But for Barker, 'at the centre of Hamlet, in the interior of his mystery, there is, in short, nothing' (p. 37); at this time the modern forms of bourgeois subjectivity are only – could only be – gestured towards; they were incipient, not yet formed. In relation to Milton's *Areopagitica* he proposes a Foucauldian account of the way 'the state succeeds in penetrating to the very heart of the subject, or more accurately, in pre-constituting the subject as one which is already internally disciplined, censored, and thus an effective support of the emergent pattern of domination' (p. 47). Such studies show that psychic disorder always signifies more than personal breakdown, and cultural conflict more than social breakdown.

God and Man

Of one thing we can be fairly certain: in the Renaissance God was in trouble; 'he' was being subjected to sceptical interrogation, not least in the theatre. I say God, but mean a larger metaphysical scheme of things of which he is only a part, including providentialist theology and providentialist legitimation of the social order. Jacobean plays provoke by revealing as social, political and historical what prevailing authorities would legitimate metaphysically.

But if God was in trouble, so was 'man' (on my use of this term see note 16, p. 274 below). In Christianity, identity is metaphysically constituted – i.e. it derives from, and is dependent upon, divine and natural law. At its simplest, man is an effect of God; God not only created him but did so in accordance with a certain plan whose most fundamental laws regulate both nature and human nature, and not only externally but internally: following biblical precedent, it was a Renaissance commonplace that divine law was written in the hearts of men.

In modern parlance, we could say that this drama 'deconstructed' providential legitimation. And because of the way that 'man' was conceptualised as a dependent creation of God, to deconstruct providence was also, necessarily and inevitably, to 'decentre' man (see below, chapter 10). Such is a principal argument of this book, and where it parts company with a straightforwardly secularist or humanist reading of the Renaissance as the origin of modern man. Hiram Haydn, in *The Counter-Renaissance*, found in western philosophy during the Renaissance 'the ultimate desertion of the universal for the particular' (see below, p. 159); the humanist might say 'the desertion of God by man for man'. To reiterate a point made in this book, it has always been notoriously difficult to make the particular (essence) signify independently of the universal. Nowhere is this more so than with human subjectivity. It is an error of idealist culture to assume that, with the displacement of God, man, and more particularly the individual, is foregrounded in all of 'his' intrinsic uniqueness. Such is the idea behind the view of Renaissance man throwing off his medieval constraint as the prisoner might throw off his or her shackles.

But to deconstruct God is to decentre man; in metaphysics the particular is a fundamental effect of the universal, and to destabilise the latter is to do the same to the former. In practice – in the drama – instability in the constituting structure of necessity feeds into the constituted subject. And vice versa: psychic dislocation pressured by that instability is fed back 'outwards', in the form of scepticism, metaphysical doubt and so forth. In plainer terms, in subverting the idea of a divinely ordered universe, these playwrights also subverted its corollary: the unified human subject supposedly positioned at the centre of that universe. Hence, I argue, the Jacobean anti-hero: malcontented, dispossessed, satirical and vengeful; both agent and victim of social corruption; inconsistent and contradictory in ways which are incapable of being understood in terms of individuality alone, and which turn our attention outwards to the conditions of the protagonists' social existence. The Jacobean malcontent appears as the bearer of a subjectivity which is not the antithesis of social process but its focus (see below, p. 50). It was said that man was at the centre of the cosmos; sometimes it was also said that he was a microcosm of the whole, meaning that man was a microcosmic reflection of all other parts of the structure, even incorporating all of them within him. This invests man with a strange signifying power, especially when the structure is in dissolution; he ceases to be an integral part of the whole and becomes instead a focus for the contradictions and instabilities of the whole. Hence again, the contradictory, decentred subject of Jacobean tragedy.

Eventually Enlightenment humanism will develop a conception of man as his own universal. The individual subject is autonomous, unique and so on; but scratch 'him' and you will find underneath that he is an instantiation of man or human nature. The individual carries his own universal with him or, more accurately, within himself. We may indeed see the origins of this development in the Renaissance, but let us be suspicious if we seem to recognise ourselves in that moment. We are in all likelihood reading back into that moment a complex and/or partial *subsequent* history. What remains powerfully active in the literature and culture of early modern England – a description of the period with less assumptions than 'Renaissance' – is the sense of identity as *constituted*, as an effect of what pre-exists it. To that extent perhaps we can say that post-structuralism rediscovered what the Renaissance already knew: identity is powerfully – one might say essentially – informed by what it is not. And what partly enabled post-structuralism to make that redis-covery was its critique of the humanist conceptions of identity which are the product of histories which intervene between us and the Renaissance, including the Enlightenment, Romanticism and Modernism.

So if on the Renaissance stage the idea that divine and/or natural law informs identity is being interrogated, the result is not man released from medieval shackles, but subjects caught up in a messy, conflictual displacement of the metaphysical (divine/natural law) by the social. The contradictions of history flood the space vacated by metaphysics. Correspondingly the metaphysically constituted subject becomes a decentred, contradictory subjectivity. In the fate of Antony, Coriolanus, Vittoria or Flamineo, we 'read' not the working of Fate or God, but a contemporary reality which both creates and destroys them; a reality which asks to be identified in materialist terms – it is manifestly historical, social and political – even though it cannot be exhaustively described by them.

Literary critics have not been unaware of this, though they have interpreted it in very different ways, especially where problematic characters like Vindice, the perverse malcontented anti-hero of *The Revenger's Tragedy*, are concerned. Some have followed the didactic view of Renaissance moralists in seeing psychic disorientation as one predicted consequence, and perhaps punishment, of succumbing to passion. Others have sought to foreclose on the problematic excess of that particular play by interpreting it as the deficient creation of a disordered personality.[31] Bridget Lyons gave us a more revealing per-spective on such protagonists when she pointed out that 'dissatisfac-tion with self, with family authority, and with political authority were seen to be intimately connected; all were subsumed in the word "malcontent"';[32] repeatedly the malcontent shows that to be dislo-cated socially was to be dislocated psychically.

Much has already been written on subjectivity. Nevertheless I suspect it will remain an issue in Rennaissance studies, as well as in literary theory and cultural analysis more generally. This is an

understandable consequence of the fact that constructions of subjectivity are central to the literature and history of western culture, and
are being foregrounded, now, at a time when they are in process of
change. Moreover there is a pleasure as well as a politics in disman-
tling repressive notions of self-hood, especially those which dress up
individual conformity and political quiescence in the jargon of
authenticity.[33] However, just as there is a form of atheism which
remained preoccupied with the non-existence of God, thereby
forever occupying a God-shaped space, so there is a form of modern
criticism inexhaustibly preoccupied with the supposed non-existence
of the essential unified self. So the question needs to be put more
often: what exactly is the purpose of drawing attention to, or critically provoking, a decentring of the subject? Here is one of the
answers argued for in this book: if essentialist humanism involves a
fundamental misrepresentation of literature and history, it does so in
part with an ideology of a transhistorical human nature and an
autonomous subjectivity, the second being an instantiation of the
first; in short, a metaphysics of identity occludes historical and social
process. A critique of essentialism is about making history visible
both within the subjectivity it informs, and beyond subjectivity, by,
as it were, restoring individuals to history.[34]

Feminism, Sexualities and Gender Critique[35]

Of the differences distinguishing recent critical practices from their
traditional counterparts, attention to gender is one of the most
important. There are two contrasts to be noted here. The first is
between the traditional and the new work, the second between different emphases within the latter.

Nothing dates conventional Shakespearean criticism so much as
its attitude to sexualities and gender. It has been ready to reproduce
the most tired and oppressive clichés about female 'virtue' and
female 'vice', and either deny the existence of the sexually unconven-
tional (especially where it is an embarrassment to canonical dignity)
or endorse punitive attitudes towards it (e.g. sexual nonconformity
as a metaphor for evil). Conservative literary critics have sometimes

felt superior to prevailing social norms, contrasting their own culti-
vated values with those of the vulgar. I cannot say whether this has
ever been justified; as regards their attitudes to gender and sexualities
I am sure it is not: these attitudes often reveal critics to be up-market
moral hacks, giving academic respectability to conventional 'wisdom'
indistinguishable from bigotry. Linda Woodbridge's critique of male
critics writing about *Antony and Cleopatra* is especially telling.[36]

The second contrast is within recent work, and has already been
addressed in more general terms; it is between those who would see
the drama as conservative in its representation of gender and those
who would see some plays at least (though in historically relative
terms) as challenging.[37]

In 1975 Juliet Dusinberre published *Shakespeare and the Nature of
Women*, a pioneering and still inspiring study which argues that 'the
drama from 1590 to 1625 is feminist in sympathy', and relates this
to the development of more positive views of marriage within
protestantism and puritanism. This book, and an influential collection of feminist essays on Shakespeare which appeared five years
later,[38] have constituted points of departure for much feminist criticism.[39] Often, though not invariably, this 'first generation' of feminist critics of the drama read it (especially Shakespeare) for positive
identifications of women. Subsequent feminist work has examined
instead the ways in which these plays are implicated in the patriarchal values of the period, and in particular how women are represented in relation to social crisis and change. Thus Lisa Jardine
argues that the strong interest in women shown on the Elizabethan
and Jacobean stage does not reflect an increasing liberty for women
at that time, but 'is related to the patriarchy's unexpressed worry
about the great social changes which characterise the period'. Jardine
shows how such fears were focussed in terms of the 'disorderly'
woman (on and off the stage).[40]

Likewise Kathleen McLuskie dissents from what she calls the
'liberal feminism' which would co-opt Shakespeare:

> Feminist criticism need not restrict itself to privileging the woman's
> part or to special pleading on behalf of female characters. It can be
> equally well served by making a text reveal the conditions in which a

particular ideology of femininity functions and by both revealing and subverting the hold which such an ideology has for readers both female and male.[41]

Her study of *King Lear* exemplifies an important trend in feminist criticism, one which connects with other kinds of gender analysis:

> The misogyny of King Lear, both the play and its hero, is constructed out of an ascetic tradition which presents women as the source of the primal sin of lust, combining with concerns about the threat to the family posed by female insubordination. However the text also drama-tises the material conditions which lie behind assertions of power within the family, even as it expresses deep anxieties about the chaos which can ensue when the balance of power is altered. (p. 106)

Jardine and McLuskie show that gender is implicated in the entire social domain: arguably gender, like writing, will be found to dis-close the complexities which its ideological representation must disavow. Certainly it cannot be studied in isolation.

In a study of Gertrude in *Hamlet* and Isabella in *Measure for Measure* Jacqueline Rose shows how sexuality is also implicated in issues of aesthetic form. Drawing on a psychoanalytic perspective she shows how in these plays and in criticism of them the woman is made a focus 'for a set of ills which the drama shows as exceeding the woman *at the same time* as it makes of her their cause'.[42] In 'Transgression and Surveillance in *Measure for Measure*', I offer a comparable approach, showing how social crisis is displaced on to the prostitutes of the play. They are indeed made 'symbolically central' even while remaining utterly marginal: everything in the play presupposes them, yet they have no voice or presence. Those who speak on their behalf do so as exploitatively as those who want to destroy them. The prostitutes are precisely 'spoken for'. The con-dition of their being made central is that they actually be marginal, and of their demonising that they be powerless.[43]

These essays show that though gender is indeed central to the social order, it cannot be isolated *as such*. However, Carol Neely has argued that the three essays just mentioned (among many others) tend to silence or marginalise women or treat gender in a way that turns it into something else, or makes it cease to matter.[44] These three essays do indeed attend to the complex ways in which women are marginalised and silenced. They attend also to the way social anxieties are displaced on to sexuality, and to the interconnections between women's subordination and other kinds of subordination; but it does not follow, as Neely seems to imply, that by describing these processes the critic is somehow complicit with them. I shall return to this.

Arguably, the greater challenge of gender in this drama derives not from 'positive' representations of women unproblematically located within a patriarchal order, but from representations of disreputable women who disrupt the scheme of (hetero)sexual difference. A case in point is cross-dressing in the drama and in Jacobean England. the subject of a number of recent articles and books,[45] and one of the most interesting and important aspects of gender currently being reconsidered. Orthodoxy at that time insisted that differences in dress were not merely conventional but a reflection of one of God's most fundamental principles of order in the world: sexual difference. Cross-dressing spelt 'confusion' in the far-reaching, devastating, religious sense of the word. Intense anxieties about social change and its unsettling of gender and class hierarchies (see Jardine, especially chapters 1 and 5) were punitively displaced, in dramatic as well as non-dramatic literature, on to the issue of dress violation, especially women dressing in men's clothes. Conversely, in some plays and tracts cross-dressing is used to challenge traditional evaluations of women's inferior status. In these texts cross-dressing is a specific and fascinating instance of something already explored: in this drama metaphysical legitimations of the social order are interrogated and displaced by the recognition that it is custom, not nature or divine law, that arranges things as they are; and that the laws of custom are also the laws of privilege and domination.

Of course the theatre had a particular investment in dress violation – not only were female parts played by boys, but actors who played the parts of those from superior classes also violated the dress codes of class. So the very devices of theatre itself – artifice, cross-dressing, disguise, roleplaying – facilitated exploration of the cultural construction of gender, its contradictions and discriminations. The

artifice of theatre reveals the artifice of gender – the fact that it is a
social construction and not a natural or biological fact. And it sometimes suggests a creative perversity of desire itself; this theatre rev-
elled in what Ray Davies rediscovered in 'Lola': in the sphere of the
social, boys will be girls and girls will be boys.

One implication of the articles on cross-dressing by Mary Beth
Rose and Jean Howard is that Shakespeare's treatment of gender may
be more conservative than that of some of his contemporaries. A
case in point is Shakespeare's *The Taming of the Shrew*, whose
apparent misogyny makes it, for a modern audience, one of
Shakespeare's most problematic treatments of gender. Thompson
observes in the introduction to her New Cambridge edition of the
play: 'Since the late nineteenth century the movement for the liberation of women has done for [this play] what reaction to the anti-
semitism of our time has done for *The Merchant of Venice*: turned it
into a problem play.'[46] But even *The Shrew* can be read, in feminism, as challenging. Karen Newman argues that its 'patriarchal
master narrative' is subverted by being exposed 'as neither natural
nor divinely ordained, but culturally constructed'.[47]

There recurs in the numerous tracts attacking the theatre and its
dress and gender transgressions a fear that men dressing as women
will lead to an erosion of masculinity itself. Laura Levine, in an
interesting article on this subject (see note 45), shows that these
tracts, even as they confidently sermonise on the fixed nature of
identity, especially gender identity as prescribed by God and signified through dress difference, display a deep anxiety that identity is
not fixed; that, underneath, the self is really nothing at all (pp. 126
and 128). Further, they fear that 'doing' what a woman does (on the
stage and in women's clothes) leads to 'being' what a woman is; the
most unmanageable anxiety is that there is no essentially masculine
self (p. 136), and cross-dressing in women's clothes can lead to a
man 'turning into' a woman. The frequent charge that the theatre
encouraged sodomy enters the discourse of the anti-theatricalists as
the focus for this fear that gender difference is ever under threat of
breakdown and, more generally, the fear that 'under the costume
there is really nothing there or, alternatively, that what is there is
something foreign, something terrifying and essentially other' (p.

135). My own analysis differs from Levine's, but her argument shows clearly how the preoccupation with sodomy is inseparable from the preoccupation with gender and, through gender, with human identity and the ordering of society. But what exactly was sodomy in the Renaissance?

The question is not as odd as it might appear, since historians have argued that modern notions of sexuality are inappropriate for early modern England, when the category of the 'homosexual' did not exist, and sodomy had a very different meaning. Michel Foucault, in an oft cited and increasingly challenged passage, has described how the homosexual identity was created in the nineteenth century. Before that individuals were regarded as performing deviant sexual *acts*, but an intrinsic *identity* was not attributed to, or assumed by, them: 'The sodomite had been a temporary aberration; the homosexual was now [in the nineteenth century] a species.'[48] Alan Bray's *Homosexuality in Renaissance England*[49] presents evidence for this argument, as do Jeffrey Weeks' indispensable wider studies, though not without qualification of Foucault's account.[50]

In any event, the 'homosexual' in the modern sense did not exist in early modern England. He or (less often) she is partly a creation of modern discourse, medical, sexological and psychological. The word homosexual was coined in 1869: neither it nor the sexual sense of perversion appeared in the *OED* until its 1933 Supplement. The nearest concepts to it in the Renaissance were probably those of sodomy and buggery. But as Bray and Weeks point out, even the meanings of these terms were very different from ours. Sodomy was associated with witches, demons, werewolves, basilisks, foreigners and, of course, papists; and it might signify a wide range of practices including prostitution, under-age sex, coitus interruptus and female transvestism. Socially, sodomy was repeatedly equated with heresy and political treason; metaphysically, it was conceived as a 'force of anarchic disorder set against divine Creation', not a part of the created order but an aspect of its dissolution. Moreover it existed as 'a potential for confusion and disorder in one undivided sexuality', not to be identified in terms of homosexuality in its modern sense but rather 'sexual confusion in whatever form'.[51] Sodomy was not thought to originate in a pathological subjectivity (the modern pervert); rather, the deviant was the vehicle of sexual confusion, the point of entry into civilisation for the unnatural and the abhorrent, the wilderness of disorder which beleaguered all civilisation. As such the sodomite was the supreme instance of the demonised other. But so extreme was the sodomite's construction that most of those actually engaging in 'homosexuality' did not identify themselves with it; not only did they not have our modern categories, but the prevailing categories were so far removed from how they saw themselves that apparently the connection was just not made. Nor were they so identified by the authorities – except in times of political and social crisis, the eruption of class hatred, religious and political persecution.[52]

Most critics, including some feminists, have tended to overlook the issue of 'homosexuality' or relied on customary assumptions about it, making recent writing on the subject all the more necessary, especially in relation to the question of homosexuality and Shakespeare's *Sonnets*. 'And' rather than 'in' because again, the point here is not the notorious anxiety about Shakespeare's 'homosexuality' so much as a questioning of the category itself. The foregoing account of sodomy in the Renaissance will not directly assist in a reading of homosexuality 'in' the *Sonnets*; hopefully it will hinder such a reading. What it does help us to understand – as Levine's article shows – is the part sodomy plays in the construction of (hetero)sexual difference in the period, the anxieties attendant upon it, and its relation to identity, subjectivity and social ordering. It also tells us that we cannot simply invoke the modern sense of homosexuality in a discussion of these poems. Unfortunately this is, more or less, what Joseph Pequigney does in *Such Is My Love*, the most sustained argument ever for the homosexual basis of Shakespeare's *Sonnets*: the sequence is read as not only 'extraordinary amatory verse, but the great masterpiece of homoerotic poetry'.[53] Commendably, this book addresses aspects of gender and sexuality that have been suppressed in Shakespeare criticism. But its account of homosexuality is anachronistic: the concept is not historicised and, worse, Freudian theories are used to 'explain' it as it allegedly figures in the *Sonnets*.[54]

Pequigney's analysis of these poems proceeds via close textual analysis. Contrary to what is sometimes assumed, materialist criticism does not object to close textual analysis, nor to analysis of form and genre;[55] it objects rather to the ahistorical (and antihistorical) ways in which it has traditionally been done. As the history of homosexuality suggests, what is left out in such readings is not just a historical context which might illuminate (without fundamentally changing the reading), but a history which transforms it.

Eve Kosofsky Sedgwick changes the terms of the debate in her book *Between Men* (published, like Pequigney's, in 1985). In her chapter on the *Sonnets*, Sedgwick sees them not so much homosexual as 'homosocial'.[56] In an article called 'A Poem Is Being Written', highly recommended to all Shakespeareans, she defines 'the male-homosocial structure' as that 'whereby men's "heterosexual desire" for women serves as a more or less perfunctory detour on the way to a closer, but homophobically proscribed, bonding with another man'.[57] Sedgwick's category of the homosocial is subtly developed, encouraging us to take apart modern and reductive psychosexual categories and rethink the history of sexuality in Shakespeare and the Renaissance. It does not so much answer old questions (are the *Sonnets*/was Shakespeare homosexual?) as show the inadequacy of those questions and the old answers given to them. Discussing Sonnets 136 and 137, she says:

> My point is . . . again not that we are here in the presence of homo-sexuality (which would he anachronistic) but rather (risking anachronism) that we are in the presence of male heterosexual desire, in the form of a desire to consolidate partnership with authoritative males in and through the bodies of females. (*Between Men*, p. 38)

This distinction offers new ways of understanding heterosexuality – over and against which homosexuality was and is constructed;[58] the homosocial illuminates heterosexual male-bonding in a way that does not simply conclude that such bonding is 'really' homosexual.

Given that homosexuals have typically either been banished to the margins of society, or been dragged and demonised centre-stage and there made the objects of displaced social fears, anxieties and repressions, it is axiomatic for studies of homosexuality that one cannot simply recover its history as something authentic and untouched by this banishment, demonising and displacement; indeed, they are precisely what one has to begin with. But in showing those processes, and the dominant culture's investments in them, one begins to track back, as it were, to the dominant culture itself, disclosing in and through its others what it cannot acknowledge about itself. As with the example of witchcraft, assumptions about the deviant may be read in a way which illuminates the dominant culture making them: patriarchy, heterosexuality and sexual difference are read *in* and *through* the deviance which they are constituted *over and against.*[59] Therefore the question of homosexuality is implicated in all aspects of gender discussed here.[60]

The Return to History: Marginality (2)

It follows that a historical perspective on deviance is as important for witchcraft as for homosexuality. Enjoyably different as it is from Muir's account, Eagleton's celebration of the witches in *Macbeth* (see above, p. lix) shares something in common with it: both fail to supply such a perspective. Eagleton, like Muir, appropriates the witches as symbols, except that instead of the tired cliché about evil in the hearts of men, they become symbols of an anarchic, decentred desire, occupying a radically ambiguous zone, a subversive, knowing marginality. Additionally, Eagleton engagingly 'rereads' the witches as prototype literary theorists, remarkable not least for the breadth of their theoretical sophistication: glance at the quote again and it becomes apparent that they are at once Marxist, Lacanian and deconstructionist; not a little Eagletonian in fact. But – and how can this be said without sounding gauche? – to become eclectic literary theorists was not the fate of most 'witches' in Renaissance Europe.

We need to address the history of witchcraft, and do so in a cultural analysis more inclusive and interdisciplinary than some conventional history and most literary criticism. Recently critics have learned much from historians exploring similar areas. Stuart Clark's dense but informative 'Inversion, Misrule and the Meaning of Witchcraft' (discussed below in another context, pp. 26–7) indicates how witchcraft was conceived in the context of a 'vocabulary of misrule' (p. 100), an inversion of right order, an antithetical component in a world view which was also a legitimation of 'ordered' relations. Examining *Macbeth* from this perspective, Peter Stallybrass shows the way the play associates witchcraft with a whole range of inversions and disorders – rebellion, the world upside down, female rule and the overthrowing of patriarchal authority. Again, the marginal becomes symbolically central, thoroughly implicated in both the structure and the instabilities of rule.[61] Addressing similar issues but now from a psychoanalytic perspective, Janet Adelman has argued that *Macbeth* fantasises a destructive maternal power and then displaces this with another fantasy: an escape by men from this power. By the end of the play 'the problem of masculinity' is solved by eliminating the female: 'in *Macbeth*, maternal power is given its most virulent sway and then abolished; at the end of the play we are in a purely male realm'.[62] Witchcraft belief facilitates the creation of these fantasies and the displacement of one by the other. Adelman reminds us that the evil attributed to witches in England was not as virulent as that attributed to their continental counterparts. Generally, the things which the latter were supposed to do – the ritual murder and eating of infants, attacking male genitals, engaging in sexual perversity with demons – the former were not. But, argues Adelman, the extreme evil associated with continental witches does figure in the play and is identified with Lady Macbeth.

Reading such work, we begin to see that witchcraft beliefs were inseparable from gender beliefs, and that the important connections are not always the obvious ones. Catherine Belsey, in *The Subject of Tragedy*, sees the witchcraft craze as coterminous with a crisis in the 'definition of women and the meaning of the family'. Reminding us that 'Of the witches executed in England, 93% were women,' she explores the relation between witchcraft and women speaking out of turn: 'These women, at the extreme edges of the social body, old, poor and often beggars . . . broke silence and found an unauthorized voice, but the social body required that they paid a high price for the privilege of being heard' (pp. 188–91). Moreover: 'The supreme opportunity to speak, was the moment of execution' (p. 190). On this same issue of women's insubordinate speech, D. E.

Underdown[63] sees witchcraft as part of the crisis in gender relations. He remarks that the period of public anxiety about scolding women and witches is roughly similar, and paralleled by the chronology of a third category of rebellious women, the 'woman on top' (p. 121).[64]

Such then would be a materialist approach to *Macbeth*: attending to rather than suppressing the problematic presence of the witches, the inquiry opens out into a historical study which is necessarily also theoretical, and vice versa; which asks questions about gender, language and social order from an interdisciplinary perspective, and does so because it wants to do much more than simply provide a persuasive modern interpretation of *Macbeth*.

The example of witchcraft is important for two further reasons. First, by exploring its history we are led to reject the view that the marginal are usually or easily the source of subversion. Witches no more fell into that category than did prostitutes.[65] Secondly, witch-hunting has been extremely difficult to explain adequately; no single, and certainly no simple, explanation is adequate to the historical reality. Like other forms of discrimination and demonising – misogyny, racism, homophobia, for example – witchcraft seems to work at different though interrelated levels. If a psychological explanation ignoring the material conditions which foster the demonising of minorities is inadequate, so too would be a sociological argument which presented witchcraft as simply functional for the prevailing social order.[66] What is required is an interdisciplinary analysis, by which I mean not just a loose combination of perspectives but a conjunction which provokes each into transgressing disciplinary boundaries, the tension between incompatible methodologies itself becoming a source of insight rather than confusion.

Not everyone working within a materialist perspective would agree with this last point. A recent study by Walter Cohen[67] integrates diligent historical research into an ambitious theoretical and political perspective, but in a different way, insisting on the necessity of a totalising aspect, one which attends more to large-scale historical changes than to issues of subjectivity, marginality and gender (see especially pp. 21–2). This is a book with a substantial historical thesis written by an author with the intellectual integrity and confidence to state it clearly:

The entire study pursues a single and simple hypothesis: that the absolutist state, by its inherent dynamism and contradictions, first fostered and then undermined the public theatre. More precisely, the similarities between Spanish and English absolutism help account for the parallels between the two dramatic traditions, while the divergent courses of economic and religious development in England and Spain begin to explain the differences. (pp. 191–20)

But if Cohen's language and argument are accessible, and his perspective coherent, his is by no means a simplistic approach. He explores a process which is at once evolutionary and revolutionary, marked by contradiction and uneven development. His framework is eclectically Marxist, deriving from a spectrum of contemporary Marxist historiography and cultural theory. On these grounds alone this book should be compulsory reading for those literary critics, humanist and otherwise, who legitimate their own political bad-faith by castigating the allegedly reductive premises of that paradigm of political commitment and coherent methodology, Marxism. This book is one of many which currently indicate that contemporary Marxist criticism has as complex and dynamic a relation to the writings of Marx as does contemporary psychoanalysis to Freud, or Christianity to the Old and New Testaments. This is usually allowed in the case of Christianity, sometimes in the case of psychoanalysis, rarely in the case of Marxism. Perhaps it is allowed inversely to the ability of each to challenge.

The work I have been considering here can usefully be seen in the context of what David Simpson calls the return to history.[68] In recent years, especially in the United States, about which Simpson is principally writing, literary theorists influenced by Jacques Derrida and Paul de Man (among others) have viewed 'history' as a kind of 'fiction in disguise' or, in more rigorous terms, claimed that 'all analysis of cultural and historical forms is limited by the same impasses of textuality as characterize the formal dimensions of literature' (p. 725). Such indeed was one trajectory of deconstruction. Now, however, there is a wish to get back to history. While clearly supporting it, Simpson wonders whether it is not just another stage in the academy's endless quest for innovation. He also sets out ways

in which certain kinds of 'history' end up complicit with the history-
as-text view they seek to replace, and points out that to do history in
any significant way requires hard work. Doing 'real' history may well
be arduous, and coming up with a definition that might be accept-
able to both historians and literary critics even more so.[69] The issues
are important, and unamenable to facile formulae asserting either
the brute facticity of the past, or its textuality. Without the space to
do justice to these issues, I am prompted instead to note three paradoxes, hopefully enabling rather than otherwise.

First: Brecht was an avowed Marxist. As their ignorant enemies
never tire of declaring, you can never trust Marxists on history since
they always rewrite it according to prevailing party policy. Brecht
was more outrageous still, committing the ultimate act of sacrilege
by actually rewriting Shakespeare. But that rewriting helped to
produce real historical insight into Shakespeare's plays and his culture
(see below, pp. 223–6).[70] Brecht appropriates the past for the
present while remaining committed to the past as different. He once
wrote: 'If I choose to see Richard III I don't want to feel myself to be
Richard III, but to glimpse this phenomenon in all its strangeness
and incomprehensibility.' He criticised the theatre of his own time
for its tendency to 'annihilate distance, fill in the gap, gloss over the
differences. But what comes then of our delight in comparisons, in
distance, in dissimilarity – which is at the same time a delight in
what is close and proper to ourselves?'[71] For Brecht the sense of a
deeply inadequate present historical moment combines with a non-
nostalgic wish to know rather than relive the difference of the past,
learning from it being a precondition for understanding and being
able to change the present.

Second: whereas Simpson, as a teacher of literature, says we have
not even begun to do any history yet – 'Let us above all refuse the
consolation of a "return" to history, and ponder instead all the
reasons why we have not yet been there' (p. 747) – Christopher Hill,
a historian, remarks that for years now the best history of the seventeenth century has been written by literary critics.[72]

Third: rather than seeking to arrive at a 'theoretically correct' way
of reading history, let us reverse the procedure and, at the risk of
assuming what we should be demonstrating, use history, no matter

how provisionally conceived, to read theory. What we thereby assume (history) will no more remain constant than what we question (theory).

History Reading Theory

I remarked earlier, somewhat provocatively, that post-structuralism rediscovered what the Renaissance already knew. It is a way of stressing a particular development. Cultural and critical theory has been invaluable in breaking new ground in Renaissance studies. Equally important though, the taking of theory to this major historical period has led to a significant rethinking of some of the orthodoxies of theory itself. In the United Kingdom this was partly because Renaissance studies were among the first areas to benefit from a growing feeling that theory itself had reached a level of sophistication which required historical engagement as its next stage, meaning by this not *just* a rereading of past literature through theoretical lenses, but a historical exploration of theory – hence using history to 'read' theory as well as vice versa.[73] I have space to consider a single example only, chosen because it relates closely to the earlier discussion of subjectivity.

In *Discipline and Punish* Foucault speaks of a crucial change taking place in western culture towards punishment:

> The expiation that once rained down upon the body must be replaced by a punishment that acts in depth on the heart, the thoughts, the will, the inclinations. Mably formulated the principle once and for all: 'Punishment, if I may so put it, should strike the soul rather than the body' . . . A new character came on the scene, masked. It was the end of a certain kind of tragedy; comedy began, with shadow play, faceless voices, impalpable entities.[74]

Foucault is writing an ambitious study and doing so in pursuit of far-reaching changes in western culture that have produced some of the prevailing structures of our own time. This particular change he locates as occurring in the second half of the eighteenth century, and while he concedes that in our own time punishment is not merely a matter of 'converting a soul', he argues that the effect of Mably's principle 'can be felt throughout modern penality' (p. 17).

As elsewhere in Foucault's work, the distinction he offers us is indeed important for understanding western culture, but historically it is too narrowly located. His own formulation of the principle – 'converting a soul' – indicates the religious antecedents of the process. It may be true that the idea of a punishment working internally, on and in the very terms of subjectivity itself, is new in penal theory, but it is not new as a disciplinary strategy. At the very least the earlier history of this process modifies the implications of Foucault's argument. In the sixteenth century William Perkins actually compared God with a jailer who targets the soul and conscience rather than the body:

> God doth watch over all men by a special providence. The master of a prison is knowne by this to have care over his prisoners; if he send keepers with them to watch them and to bring them home againe in time convenient: and so Gods care to man is manifested in this, that when he created man and placed him in the world, he gave him conscience to be his keeper, to follow him alwaies at his heeles, and to dogge him (as we say) and to prie into his actions, and to beare witnesse of them all.

Perkins continues:

> Conscience is like to a judge that holdeth an assise, & takes notice of indictments, and causeth the most notorious malefactour that is, to hold up his hand at the barre of his judgement. Nay it is (as it were) a little God sitting in the middle of men[s] hearts, arraigning them in this life as they shal be arraigned for their offences at the tribunall seat of the everliving God in the day of judgement. Wherefore the temporarie judgement that is given by the conscience is nothing els but a beginning or a fore-runner of the last judgement.[75]

I have quoted these passages at length because they show explicitly the internalisation of law, or subjectivity as subjection.[76] In *Measure for Measure* the Duke, disguised[77] as a cleric and thereby embodying both ecclesiastical and state law, rehearses this kind of strategy with several imprisoned subjects, two of whom also face the threat of execution. He is unsuccessful with Barnadine, partly successful with Claudio, and most successful of all with Mariana. In a sense the play enacts the transition Foucault describes, from a punishment targeting the body (incarceration and the threat of execution) to one targeting the soul. Though only partially successful, this process of reincorporating subjects in and through their subjectivities is shown in this play to be indispensable in the task of upholding the legitimacy of rule.

If the history of this period suggests a modification of Foucault's argument, that argument in turn shifts our perception of the period. In particular we are led to question the view of the Renaissance as the origin of modern man. The Renaissance, far from producing the internally autonomous subject of idealist criticism, might more accurately be seen to contribute to new forms of subjection as well as an emerging humanist sense of freedom. And in retrospect the two things – subjection and humanist freedom – look to be more closely connected than we once thought.

Reproducing Shakespeare

It has been a commonplace of literary criticism that every age interprets Shakespeare for itself. The implication of this is that Shakespeare is only, ever, what we make of him. Or it might be, were this commonplace not generally harnessed within another: in each age we discover new ways of perceiving the eternal verities perceived by the genius who was Shakespeare and embodied in his plays. So an interpretation or production 'for our time' is not so much changing the meaning of the play as making an unchanging meaning accessible to a (changed) modern audience. An emphasis in materialist criticism involves not just the rejection of these commonplaces, but an account of the actual political uses to which Shakespeare has been put within and by *institutions*: separate chapters of part two of *Political Shakespeare* explore the way his plays have been reproduced by the Royal Shakespeare Company, in education, the cinema and television. *The Shakespeare Myth*[78] extends this kind of analysis: it includes examples of how Shakespeare has been used to sustain delusions of social unity and subjective freedom in what is in fact a divided, strife-ridden culture.[79]

The influence of Shakespeare extends unpredictably; in a fascinating essay which exemplifies the connection between materialist and feminist perspectives, Elaine Showalter explores the cultural refiguring of Ophelia not only in the arts but also in 'reality', showing among other things how illustrations of Ophelia have played a major role in the theoretical construction of female insanity.[80]

Other studies of the reproduction of Shakespeare include Terence Hawkes' intriguing account of connections between polities – for example colonialism and nationalism – and the development of Shakespeare criticism. This is a witty analysis of major figures, including A. C. Bradley, Sir Walter Raleigh, T. S. Eliot and John Dover Wilson. By exploring the influence on these critics of large-scale ideological formations as well as specific historical events, Hawkes shows how thoroughly, often alarmingly so, criticism is of its time.[81]

Stephen Orgel shows how the same can be true of traditions of textual and editorial scholarship, notwithstanding their aura of judicious scholarship and impartial scrutiny of the evidence. Orgel begins with a consideration of the controversy over whether or not the recently 'discovered' poem 'Shall I Die?' was indeed penned by Shakespeare. Little that has been written on the in/authenticity of the poem is as informative as this discussion by Orgel, largely because he addresses not the tedious issue of whether Shakespeare did or didn't write it, but the assumptions behind the dispute itself, for example the assumption that a bad poem cannot be by Shakespeare.[82] Orgel shows how the issue of authenticity involves doctrinal and political elements; authenticity itself is shown to be something bestowed, not inherent.[83] The implication of this and other work on the history of texts suggests how even to talk of 'Shakespeare's plays' makes unwarranted assumptions.

Clearly such questions about the reproduction of Shakespeare are important for precise issues of authorship and textuality as well as more general ones concerning institutions like theatre and education. But they can be usefully pursued at a more general level still, even in relation to the state itself, not least because those other institutions will have some relationship to the state.

Shakespeare and Statecraft

In December 1987 I attended a conference on Shakespeare in Moscow at which most of the papers were conservative. They were delivered in an institute for the arts, not a stone's throw from the Kremlin. Listening to respected Shakespeareans intoning clichés about how the human condition and the poetic genius of Shakespeare transcended the merely political, it was hard not to let one's attention wander; who was in those black limousines sliding in and out of the Kremlin that we had seen earlier?; whose fate was being decided today: 'rebels' in Afghanistan, internal dissidents in the USSR, the fate of all of us *vis-à-vis* a new initiative on nuclear disarmament? There was a seeming incongruity between *what* was being said and *where* it was being said. Actually it would seem incongruous in any socio-political context, but in *this* case my wandering thoughts were clearly overlaid by a cold-war rhetoric which, I realised only then, had spanned my entire life. Though repudiating that rhetoric, from both sides (or so I thought), there was its residue informing my 'spontaneous' images of the USSR as an insidious scheming power. Not that it was not and cannot be again, only that western cold-war propaganda displaced on to the USSR a political identity which it shared with it, not least in its use of such rhetoric to 'persuade' populations in the West to line up behind their own governments for protection against the Russian threat. Could Shakespeare figure in such a strategy? If that seems just too absurd to contemplate, consider a more cautious formulation of the same question: what is the relation between high culture and state power? One hesitates to put the question in even that form because it invites a misleading impression of the state as a homogeneous conspiratorial block. In fact states are typically made up of competing factions, while culture works in terms of, in relation to and through many other kinds of authority.

The misleading form of the question is perhaps confirmed by the inadequacy of one answer to it: high culture is always in the service of state power. Margot Heinemann cites what has now become a rather notorious instance of this: Nigel Lawson, Chancellor of the Exchequer in the UK Conservative Government, invoking Shakespeare in support of his own political philosophy. Arguing that egalitarianism is not only unworkable but 'wholly destructive', he quotes Ulysses' 'degree' speech from *Troilus and Cressida* ('Take but degree away, untune that string,/And hark what discord follows'). He concludes: 'Shakespeare was a Tory, without any doubt.' Heinemann comments: 'To hear Shakespeare cited directly in the context of cutting the health service and reducing taxation on the well-to-do is unnerving.'[84] But, she goes on to argue, the cynical answer to the effect that high culture is always merely the instrument of such power is just wrong. For one thing, even if intellectually that trip to Moscow was something of a charade, we nevertheless wanted to be there if it meant making even the most slender contribution to East/West relations. Probably we didn't – I certainly didn't – but in principle cultural events can and do affect the prevailing power relations which in other respects they also serve. Second, we should recall that Shakespeare is tremendously popular in Russia,[85] one focus of a passionate humanist commitment which in the recent history of that country, far from always being co-opted by the state, has sometimes been oppositional to it, and the subject of its repression.

Inadequate as it might be, the question kept posing itself in the context of a curiosity about what was really going on at the conference in Moscow. It was part of a cultural exchange organised from the UK end by the British Council. It became apparent that its success really did not depend on our respective lectures, or indeed on anything particular we might say about Shakespeare. If, listening to each other's papers we learned little or nothing about each other, this, paradoxically, was probably a condition of the trip's success. A simultaneous translation of each paper into the others' language was hardly a communicative success, but perhaps that did not matter either since Shakespeare stood for something that transcended political differences even though no one could exactly identify what it was. Maybe that was just it: the trip's success depended on our *not* identifying what it was; the 'universality' of Shakespeare which the trip presupposed would not stand up to scrutiny if it were to succeed. If so, that trip was just one more indication of the contemporary malaise of high culture as epitomised by official Shakespeare. It is ironic but not surprising that the conservative tendencies which share much of the responsibility for intellectually bankrupting high culture are also the ones sapping whatever potential is left to it.

A dream fragment. Arriving in Moscow's Red Square I saw something unremarkable: before Lenin's tomb stood two soldiers, on guard, at attention, expressionless, immobile, facing each other. Such soldiers might be seen anywhere. So why that night did I have a dream in which those soldiers had become Shakespeare? Actually, *two* Shakespeares, identical to, and facing, each other. They too seemed to be on guard, but with a difference: both were laughing – quietly, gleefully, intimately.

Six months after the Moscow trip I went to the Folger Shakespeare Library in Washington. There was a certain symmetry: here was an institute of learning, located in the capital of the other superpower, and in similar proximity to the Capitol. So similar questions about high culture and state power posed themselves but, significantly, not with the same urgency; initially at least cultural familiarity kept them muted. Which only means that in this case (cultural) familiarity breeds (political) blindness; it is from within and against familiarity that such questions most need to be asked, especially since the United Kingdom is fast becoming a satellite of the United States, and for other reasons that might best be represented geographically: the 'familiar' Washington is about seven hours' flying time from England, the 'alien' Moscow about half that. At the Folger, reading an article given to me there by Louis Montrose, I came across the following passage:

> Fortunately, about the time the forces of immigration became a menace to the preservation of our long-established English civilization, there was initiated throughout the country [USA] a system of free and compulsory education for youth . . . In our fixed plan of

elementary schooling, [Shakespeare] was made the cornerstone of cultural discipline . . . Shakespeare was made the chief object of [pupils'] study and veneration [which] did not stop with the grammar and high schools; it was carried into the colleges and universities, and there pursued with still more intensity.[86]

The year was 1932, the speaker Joseph Quincy Adams, a Shakespeare scholar, and the occasion? – the dedication of the Folger Shakespeare Library. Without qualification, Adams celebrates the centrality of Shakespeare in a history of colonisation and cultural imperialism – first in the British settlement of the colonies, 'when the foundations of our racial stock and of our American culture were laid'; second, in 'the period of territorial expansion, when frontier conditions came to modify [sic] the character of our nation as a whole', and 'Shakespeare, bearing the sceptre of cultivation, moved in the dusty trail of the pioneers'; third, the period of foreign immigration, to which the above passage refers (pp. 213, 229 and 230).

Louis Montrose cites Adams in his criticism of those who are currently arguing that higher education in the United States has failed because it no longer advances the modern equivalent of Adams' project; who see the country once again threatened with cultural fragmentation, and the 'western tradition' falling prey to those in the universities who give too much attention to minority cultures and teach in a politically aware way. This has become a hotly disputed issue in the United States,[87] suggesting a degree of political engagement which, not long before, would have been seen to characterise UK rather than US criticism. Once again, the state has an interest: among those Montrose quotes are the US Secretary for Education, who has criticised the attention given to minorities in humanities courses in a way which recalls Lawson's use of Shakespeare to denigrate egalitarianism.[88]

Shortly after returning, and on the same day, I came across two further accounts of political controversy involving Shakespeare at the national level. The first was an article by Phillip Brockbank in which he described the anger surrounding South Africa's participation in the Shakespeare Birthday Celebrations at Stratford-upon-Avon in 1986, which continued into the following year when the Birthday

Celebrations Committee decided not to invite South Africa to send representatives. The controversy provoked 'virulent differences of opinion [and] transformed a once inconsequential and delightful festival into a local as well as a national Political forum'. It also prompted Brockbank to reflect in this article on the forms Shakespeare assumes in South Africa:

> Of the South African Shakespeareans I myself have had the privilege of teaching, some are in exile and some have been imprisoned, but the majority are at work in schools and universities (white and black) convinced that access to Shakespeare, taught and played in a more-or-less English tradition, should be a universal inheritance.[89]

The second instance was a copy of the *Kenya Times* for Monday 11 June 1988 in which President Moi is reported as having asked the Ministry of Education to reinstate Shakespeare's plays in the school syllabus on the grounds that he was an 'international figure'. The report continues: 'Shakespeare's plays were dropped from the "A" and "O" level syllabus in 1981 in what the curriculum makers described as "getting rid of the colonial hangover in independent Kenya".'

Moscow, Washington, Stratford-upon-Avon, South Africa, Kenya: episodes in cultural politics with their own diverse cultural histories, awareness of which, I would suggest, must at the very least figure more prominently in our critical practice; we should learn to 'read' these histories with the sensitivity once reserved for canonical literary texts. In such a reading we discover how and why Shakespeare is always already political, always already appropriated. Those who still dream of recovering the authentic Shakespeare untainted by politics will not only have to go *through* these multiple appropriations and incarnations to get at him, and many more besides, but will also have to try to disentangle him from them. I would not like to prejudge the outcome of such a heroic task, but I suggest that what will be revealed in the attempt is that there is no authentic Shakespeare to be recovered. The appropriations and the incarnations are inextricably a part of Shakespeare, which is not to say that 'he' can be reduced to them. This is true even of what may seem to be crass appropriations. There are those to whom Nigel Lawson's co-option of Shakespeare as a Tory will seem ludicrous but, as Margot Heinemann says, it needs to be taken seriously – 'for as the right knows if the left does not, Shakespeare is *there*, deeply embedded in the culture, the language, the media and the educational system of Britain' (pp. 203–4) – and, we might add, often in a form which, for some, would render Lawson's appropriation more than plausible. Nor is this a problem for critics alone. As Alan Sinfield has argued, virtually all serious work in the theatre may entail, at some point, a confrontation with the Shakespeare myth; it is a myth which has to be negotiated and in a range of ways which may include the rewriting of his plays. It is a question of having to *make* cultural space, as opposed to discovering an empty space.[90]

For this reason I want to end this introduction with two oppositional studies of Shakespeare, both of which consider the way he has been embedded in racist, imperialist and colonialist forms of education, and how he is or might be read oppositionally in those same contexts. Writing from within South Africa, Martin Orkin points out that, whereas much South African drama has been marginalised or banned, Shakespeare continues to figure centrally in a racially organised education system.[91] He sees this as predominantly an idealist Shakespeare concerned with the suffering and integrity of the individual, and with supposedly transhistorical truths about human nature. Orkin reads Shakespeare differently, *against* apartheid. There are those who will say he is 'forcing' the plays; he might justly reply that they have always been forced. For my part, I might be accused of an easy moralism in invoking the South African situation. This might be warranted if I thought that our own culture was innocent of complicity with what is happening there. Manifestly it is not, and I do not mean in economic terms alone: the origins of South Africa's Shakespeare are in Europe and the United States. Moreover, the same essentially conservative and often reactionary use of Shakespeare continues in both places.

The use of a materialist perspective to counter racist and postcolonial forms of education, and Shakespeare's roles therein, is taken in new directions by Ania Loomba in *Gender, Race, Renaissance Drama*.[92] Loomba observes that, even though much has been written on the history of English Studies, a crucial aspect, the teaching of English as it developed in colonised countries, has largely been ignored. Her book is challenging because it considers this history in and through a study of gender and race in Renaissance drama. Loomba argues that 'the study of racial difference is useful beyond analysing the representation of blacks; it also allows for a more complex perspective on the question of authority itself, even where colour differentiation either appears to be, or actually is, absent'. Loomba locates the teaching of Renaissance drama in India in the context of colonialism, English literature being a 'crucial component in establishing the ideological hegemony of the British Empire in Asia and Africa', the means of 'imposing a culture, a cluster of ideologies, a way of being and seeing, of which the literary text became the privileged signifier'.[93] She remarks that her position as a teacher of English literature at Delhi University is shared with more than 700 others, an 'indication of the massive presence of the subject in colonial education and its tenacity in the post-colonial situation'. Also indicative of that presence is the likelihood that more students read *Othello* at Delhi University every year than in all British universities combined. But Loomba insists that to see this situation only and exclusively as one of blanket domination by and through a colonial language is wrong. The situation is more complex, for English language and literature have been appropriated in complex ways – for example, on behalf of emergent nationalism or, after independence, by the Indian bourgeoisie in consolidating its power. Further, 'the transcendental nature of the literary text continued to be useful in containing the tensions of a society that was not rendered homogeneous by expelling its colonial masters'. As one writer in India put it seventeen years after independence, 'the England of trade, commerce, imperialism and the penal code has not endured but the imperishable empire of Shakespeare will always be with us' (quoted by Loomba).

An imperishable empire: the political disavowed with a political metaphor. The same happens in education, as Loomba shows. There is, she remarks, a startling similarity between the violence repeatedly committed on the female body in Renaissance tragedy, and that directed at women in India now. But in the classroom this is often ignored, such violence in the plays being interpreted as an aspect of 'the much vaunted theory of the spiritual chaos of Jacobean drama'. Drawing on materialist and feminist work, Loomba offers readings of Shakespeare and his contemporaries which contest that approach and challenge us all to extend our critical awareness in ways that can and should be described as political.

I end with the studies by Orkin and Loomba because they above all make it clear that there are some critical perspectives on Elizabethan and Jacobean drama which are important not only for the theatre, but also for an understanding of the wider culture of early modern England and the subsequent histories, our own and others', in which that theatre refigures. Such studies generate not only new readings, but participate in historical and cultural debates extending beyond Shakespeare and his contemporaries and beyond contemporary English Studies as well.

Notes

1. 'Shakespeare Recycled', *Shakespeare Quarterly*, 38 (1987), 467–78 (pp. 467–8).
2. For accounts of these and other developments in English Studies see Terry Eagleton, *Literary Theory: An Introduction*, Oxford: Blackwell, 1983; and Raman Selden, *A Reader's Guide to Contemporary Literary Theory*, Brighton: Harvester, 1985. More specific in their concerns but equally accessible are Terence Hawkes, *Structuralism and Semiotics*, London: Methuen, 1977; and Catherine Belsey, *Critical Practice*, London: Methuen, 1980.
3. Perhaps the best introduction to cultural materialism is the interviews with Raymond Williams collected as *Politics and Letters*, London: New Left Books, 1979.
4. Even within this self-imposed limitation, and its obvious bias, this introduction is not comprehensive. I have tried to cite writing which constitutes valuable points of access or departure – work with which to begin, to return to, to contest.
5. This section is a revised version of an introduction written for the 1987 reprint of J. W. Lever's *The Tragedy of State*, London: Methuen.
6. *The Death of Tragedy*, London: Faber (1961), 1963, pp. 9–10.

7. *Beyond Tragedy: Essays on the Christian Interpretation of History*, London: Nisbet, 1938, pp. 156, 158. Historically speaking the part played by religion in the Renaissance was quite different from anything Bradley, Niebuhr or Steiner imagine; see Alan Sinfield, *Literature in Protestant England, 1360–1660*, London: Croom Helm, 1983.

8. *The Tragedy of State*, London: Methuen, 1971, reprinted 1987 (pp. 10, 12; cf. p. 13).

9. Another study which can be read as a sustained refutation of Steiner's position is Raymond Williams' *Modern Tragedy*. In the afterword to the revised 1979 edition (London: Verso), Williams offers a moving, prophetic account of the political tragedy of contemporary society. When I first began writing *Radical Tragedy* I assumed or hoped the idealist vision had been effectively displaced. But, as Williams makes clear, the social and political conditions which have sustained that vision in the past are now re-emerging.

10. Compare Steiner: 'In Greek tragedy, as in Shakespeare, mortal actions are encompassed by forces which transcend man' (p. 193); 'authentic tragedy' presupposes hell (p. 128).

11. Christopher Hill, 'The Pre-Revolutionary Decades' in *Collected Essays: Vol 1: Writing and Revolution in Seventeenth Century England*, Brighton: Harvester, 1985, p. 24; see also Hill's 'Literature and the English Revolution' in *The Seventeenth Century Journal*, vol. 1, no. 1, 1986, 15–30; Walter Cohen's study, *Drama of a Nation: Public Theatre in Renaissance England and Spain*, Ithaca and London: Cornell University Press, 1985; and Franco Moretti's *Signs Taken for Wonders*, both discussed below. On literature and politics more generally, as well as the specific issue of literature and the Civil War, see Martin Butler, *Theatre and Crisis: 1632–42*, Cambridge University Press, 1984; David Norbrook, *Poetry and Politics in the English Renaissance*, London: Routledge, 1984; Gary Waller, *English Poetry of the Sixteenth Century*, London: Longman, 1986; *Reviving the English Revolution: Reflections and Elaborations on the Work of Christopher Hill*, ed. G. Eley and William Hunt, London: Verso, 1988, especially the introduction by Eley.

12. For a summary of the subversion/containment debate see the introduction to *Political Shakespeare: New Essays in Cultural Materialism*, ed. Jonathan Dollimore and Alan Sinfield, Manchester University Press, 1985.

13. Stephen Greenblatt, 'Invisible Bullets: Renaissance Authority and its

Subversion, *Henry IV and Henry V*' in *Political Shakespeare*, pp. 18–47; and Steven Mullaney, 'Strange Things, Gross Terms, Curious Customs: the Rehearsal of Cultures in the Late Renaissance' in *Representing the English Renaissance*, ed. Stephen Greenblatt, Berkeley: University of California Press, 1988, reprinted as chapter 3 of Mullaney's *The Place of the Stage: Licence, Play and Power in Renaissance England*, University of Chicago Press, 1988.

14.   For a development of this argument, see Jonathan Dollimore and Alan Sinfield, 'History and Ideology: The Instance of Henry V' in *Alternative Shakespeares*, ed. John Drakakis, London: Methuen, 1985; Alan Sinfield, 'Macbeth: History, Ideology and Intellectuals' in *Futures for English*, ed. Colin MacCabe, Manchester University Press, 1988; Jonathan Dollimore, 'Subjectivity, Sexuality and Transgression: The Jacobean Connection' in *Renaissance Drama*, new series, XVII (1986), 53–81.

15.   Especially misrepresentative of its subject is Edward Pechter's 'The New Historicism and its Discontents: Politicizing Renaissance Drama', *PMLA*, 102 (1987), 292–303. Carolyn Porter identifies the limitations of Pechter's argument in 'Are We Being Historical Yet?', *The South Atlantic Quarterly*, 87 (1988), 743–86, as does Louis Montrose in 'Professing the Renaissance: the Poetics and Politics of Culture', in *The New Historicism*, ed. H. A. Veeser, New York and London: Routledge, 1989.

16.   In one essay, for example, Montrose explores the problems created for Elizabethan patriarchal culture by having a woman as monarch. He identifies these problems in terms of male fantasies of dependence and domination. In Shakespeare's *A Midsummer Night's Dream* he finds 'a fantasy of male dependency upon women . . . expressed and contained within a fantasy of male control over women'. Alert to the dialectical, political and often unstable aspects of cultural representations, Montrose also shows how the Elizabethan regime generated tensions which threatened its fragile stability; how strategies of containment in *Dream* intermittently undermine themselves. '*A Midsummer Night's Dream* and the Shaping Fantasies of Elizabethan Culture: Gender, Power, Form' in *Rewriting the Renaissance*, pp. 65–87.

17.   'Power and Ideology: An Outline Theory and Sidney's *Arcadia*', *ELH*, Summer 1985, 259–77.

18.   See the introduction to *Political Shakespeare* for a fuller account of cultural materialism in relation to the Elizabethan/Jacobean period.

As we began to put that book together in 1982, Alan Sinfield and I thought that, despite obvious differences, there was sufficient convergence between UK cultural materialism and the then just-named new historicism in the US to bring the two together in a collection of essays. *Political Shakespeare* appeared in 1985. There were those in the US who did not like, or found themselves unable to endorse, the political inflections of the UK work. Since then there have been interesting discussions of the ways UK and US work converge and diverge. US critics often remark that British criticism is more politically engaged. Sometimes this is accompanied by intelligent analysis as to why this might be so. For the ways they identify, in the US context, the cultural and political issues at stake in the emergence of these critical movements, I especially recommend Walter Cohen's 'Political Criticism of Shakespeare' and Don E. Wayne's 'Power, Politics, and the Shakespearean Text: Recent Criticism in England and the United States', both of which are in *Shakespeare Reproduced: The Text in History and Ideology*, ed. Jean Howard and Marion F. O'Connor (New York and London: Routledge, 1987); and Louis Montrose's 'Professing the Renaissance: The Poetics and Politics of Culture'; Montrose's article is also important for the way it identifies the political imperatives implicit in recent reactions within the US academy against these critical positions; in the US as well as the UK, important cultural-political debates are surfacing in and around Renaissance Studies.

19. In *The Common Pursuit* (1952), London: Chatto, 1972, pp. 160–72. See also Jacqueline Rose's reading of this passage in 'Sexuality in the Reading of Shakespeare: *Hamlet* and *Measure for Measure*' in John Drakakis, ed., *Alternative Shakespeares*, London: Methuen, 1985.

20. Franco Moretti, *Signs Taken for Wonders: Essays in the Sociology of Literary Forms*, trans. Susan Fischer and others, London: New Left Books and Verso, 1983, pp. 27–41 and 68.

21. I develop the argument more fully in 'Transgression and Surveillance in *Measure for Measure*' in *Political Shakespeare*.

22. Most of the following works have a scope much wider than the subject headings they are included under here, although these subjects do constitute a major focus; several books indicate how the three subjects themselves relate inextricably.
(i) On class see Lucy De Bruyn, *Mob Rule and Riots: The Present Mirrored in the Past*, London and New York: Regency Press, 1981; Margot Heinemann, *Puritanism and Theatre: Thomas Middleton and*

Opposition Drama Under the Early Stuarts, Cambridge University Press, 1980; Walter Cohen, *Drama of a Nation* (see note 11).

(ii) On sexuality and gender see below, 'Feminism, Sexualities and Gender Critique', pp. lxvi–lxxiv.

(iii) On imperialism and colonialism see Stephen Greenblatt, *Renaissance Self-Fashioning: From More to Shakespeare*, Chicago University Press, 1980; Stephen Greenblatt, 'Invisible Bullets: Renaissance Authority and its Subversion', and Paul Brown, 'This Thing of Darkness I Acknowledge Mine: *The Tempest* and the Discourse of Colonialism', both in *Political Shakespeare* (see note 21); Peter Hulme, *Colonial Encounters: Europe and the Native Caribbean: 1492–1797*, London and New York: Methuen, 1986.

23. Kenneth Muir (ed.), *Macbeth* (The Arden Shakespeare), London: Methuen, 1964, p. lxx.

24. Terry Eagleton, *William Shakespeare* (Rereading Literature Series), Oxford: Blackwell, 1986, pp. 2–3.

25. *The Reversible World: Symbolic Inversion in Art and Society*, Ithaca: Cornell University Press, 1978; for an insightful development of this perspective see Peter Stallybrass and Allon White, *The Politics and Poetics of Transgression*, London: Methuen, 1986, especially the introduction.

26. Of other recent collections of essays which concentrate on Shakespeare, three should be mentioned: *Alternative Shakespeares*, ed. John Drakakis, London: Methuen, 1985; *Shakespeare and the Question of Theory*, ed. Patricia Parker and Geoffrey Hartman, London: Methuen, 1985; and *Shakespeare Reproduced: The Text in History and Ideology*, ed. Jean H. Howard and Marion F. O'Connor. The first two exemplify the variety of the alternative perspectives now available.

27. A concern with the subordinate and the marginal is likewise apparent in *Rewriting the Renaissance: The Discourses of Sexual Difference in Early Modern Europe* (ed. M. Ferguson *et al.*), one of the best recent collections on the period. I have in mind especially Peter Stallybrass's 'Patriarchal Territories: The Body Enclosed', which includes a discussion of *Othello*, Coppélia Kahn's 'The Absent Mother in *King Lear*', Stephen Orgel's 'Prospero's Wife', Louis Montrose's study of gender, power and form *vis-à-vis A Midsummer Night's Dream*, and Ann Rosalind Jones's study of sixteenth-century women poets and their audiences. This collection is a persuasive reminder that some of the most innovative recent work has been interdisciplinary and con-

cerned with the period as a whole rather than a single author. This is also the case with Walter Cohen's *Drama of a Nation* (see note 11), an important cross-cultural study which I discuss below.

28. See for example Sheila Rowbotham, *Women's Consciousness, Man's World*, Harmondsworth: Penguin, 1973, especially pp. 28–9 and 111; Michelle Barrett, *Women's Oppression Today*, London: New Left Books and Verso, 1980; Michelle Barrett and Mary McIntosh, *The Anti-Social Family*, London: New Left Books and Verso, 1982; Jeffrey Weeks, *Coming Out: Homosexual Politics in Britain, from the Nineteenth Century to the Present*, London: Quartet Books, 1977.

29. Francis Barker, *The Tremulous Private Body: Essays on Subjection*, London: Methuen, 1984; Catherine Belsey, *The Subject of Tragedy: Identity and Difference in Renaissance Drama*, London: Methuen, 1985.

30. See entry for this concept in the Index of Subjects (below, p. 312).

31. On these and other critical disputes surrounding this play see R. G. Foakes' introduction to his Revels edition of *The Revenger's Tragedy*, especially pp. xix–xlv, and below, chapter 9. See also Peter Stallybrass, 'Reading the Body: *The Revenger's Tragedy* and the Jacobean Theatre of Consumption', *Renaissance Drama*, n.s. vol. XIII (1987), 121–48.

32. *Voices of Melancholy: Studies in Literary Treatments of Melancholy in England*, London: Routledge, 1971, p. 18.

33. The phrase is a title of a book by Adorno (cited below, p. 288, note 2). See also Adorno's terse, insightful essay 'Monad' in his *Minima Moralia: Reflections from Damaged Life*, trans. E. F. N. Jephcott, London: New Left Books, 1974, pp. 148–50. The Frankfurt School's critique of essentialist theories of subjectivity is especially illuminating when understood in relation to the historical pressures producing it: the need to understand Fascism and Nazism. In the case of Adorno and Marcuse, it led to them seeking the origins of these movements in exactly the place where others had complacently discerned man's freedom (see below, pp. 250–1).

34. At the same time, as I have argued elsewhere and in relation to a different period, it is crucial to realise how essentialist theories of subjectivity have been put to radical use, especially when appropriated by subordinate cultures. See 'Different Desires: Subjectivity and Transgression' in Wilde and Gide, *Textual Practice*, vol. 1, no. 1 (1987), and 'The Dominant and the Deviant: A Violent Dialectic' in *Futures for English*, ed. Colin MacCabe, Manchester University Press, 1988.

35. I include a wide range of work under this sub-heading, a shorthand
     way of indicating not so much separate perspectives as several over-
     lapping ones. The analysis of gender from feminist, lesbian, gay and
     materialist perspectives – to name but four – will typically interrelate.
     At the same time there may be important areas of dispute or, at the
     very least, different histories and diverse objectives which it is impor-
     tant to recognise; certainly not all analysis of gender and sexual differ-
     ence can or should be described as feminist. Also, the very concept of
     gender itself requires critique since it is usually used in a way which
     takes no account of sexual orientation, or of class and race with which
     it interrelates. Nevertheless, I believe that some of the most illumi-
     nating discussions of gender and sexuality are at the points of connec-
     tion between the varying perspectives.

36. Linda Woodbridge [L. T. Fitz], 'Egyptian Queens and Male
     Reviewers: Sexist Attitudes in *Antony and Cleopatra* Criticism',
     Shakespeare Quarterly, 28 (1977), 297–316.

37. Even those who have felt that, when all is said and done, these plays
     relocate desire and gender within the conservative confines of patri-
     archy and family, as ordained by the metaphysic of nature and divine
     law, would probably agree that, somewhere on the way, the patriar-
     chal view is questioned, perhaps even subverted temporarily.

38. Carolyn Lenz, Gayle Greene and Carol Neely, eds, *The Woman's
     Part: Feminist Criticism of Shakespeare*, Urbana: University of Illinois
     Press, 1980. A further significant influence in the development of a
     feminist perspective on Shakespeare in the US has been the psycho-
     analytic work of (for example) Janet Adelman, especially her essay on
     masculinity in *Coriolanus* ('Anger's My Meat: Feeding, Dependency,
     and Aggression in *Coriolanus*' in *Representing Shakespeare: New
     Psychoanalytic Essays*, ed. Murray M. Schwartz and Coppélia Kahn,
     Baltimore: Johns Hopkins University Press, 1980, pp. 129–49; and
     Coppélia Kahn's study, *Man's Estate: Masculine Identity in
     Shakespeare*, Berkeley and Los Angeles: University of California Press,
     1981.

39. A book which gives a good introduction to some of the controversies
     around gender as they figured in literature is Linda Woodbridge's
     *Women and the English Renaissance: Literature and the Nature of
     Womankind, 1540–1620*, Brighton: Harvester, 1984. At once schol-
     arly, comprehensive and readable, this is an invaluable resource, espe-
     cially for students. For an article-length survey of recent feminist
     work see Ann Thompson, ' "The Warrant of Womanhood":

Shakespeare and Feminist Criticism' in *The Shakespeare Myth*, ed. Graham Holderness, Manchester University Press, 1988, pp. 74–88.

40. Lisa Jardine, *Still Harping on Daughters: Women and Drama in the Age of Shakespeare*, Brighton: Harvester, 1983, esp. ch. 5.

41. 'The Patriarchal Bard: Feminist Criticism and Shakespeare: *King Lear* and *Measure for Measure*' in *Political Shakespeare*, pp. 88–108 (p. 106).

42. 'Sexuality in the Reading of Shakespeare: *Hamlet* and *Measure for Measure*' in John Drakakis, ed., *Alternative Shakespeares*, London: Methuen, 1985, pp. 95–118.

43. 'Transgression and Surveillance in *Measure for Measure*' in *Political Shakespeare*, pp. 72–87.

44. Carol Thomas Neely, 'Constructing the Subject: Feminist Practice and the New Renaissance Discourses', *English Literary Renaissance*, 18, no. 1 (1988), 5–48 (pp. 10–11). For another critique of recent work in this respect see Lynda E. Boose, 'The Family in Shakespeare Studies; or – Studies in the Family of Shakespeareans; or – The Politics of Politics', *Renaissance Quarterly*, 40 (1987), 707–42.

45. Juliet Dusinberre, *Shakespeare and the Nature of Women*, London: Macmillan, 1975, esp. pp. 231–305; Simon Shepherd, *Amazons and Warrior Women: Varieties of Feminism in Seventeenth-Century Drama*, Brighton: Harvester, 1981, esp. ch. 6; Lisa Jardine, *Still Harping on Daughters: Women and Drama in the Age of Shakespeare*, Brighton: Harvester, 1983, esp. ch. 5; Linda Woodbridge, *Women and the English Renaissance: Literature and the Nature of Womankind, 1540–1620*, Brighton: Harvester, 1984, esp. part II; Mary Beth Rose, 'Women in Men's Clothing: Apparel and Social Stability in The Roaring Girl' in *English Literary Renaissance*, vol. 14, no. 3 (1984), pp. 367–91; Sandra Clark, 'Hic Mulier, Haec Vir, and the Controversy over Masculine Women', *Studies in Philology*, vol. LXXXII, no. 2 (Spring 1985), pp. 157–83; Catherine Belsey, 'Disrupting Sexual Difference: Meaning and Gender in the Comedies' in *Alternative Shakespeares*, ed. John Drakakis, London: Methuen, 1985, pp. 166–90; Laura Levine, 'Men in Women's Clothing: Anti-theatricality and Effeminization from 1579 to 1642', *Criticism* (1986), 28, 121–43; Jonathan Dollimore, 'Sexuality, Subjectivity and Transgression: The Jacobean Connection', *Renaissance Drama*, n.s. 17 (1986), 53–81; Kathleen McLuskie, 'The Act, the Role, and the Actor: Boy Actresses on the Elizabethan Stage', *New Theatre Quarterly*, 3 (1987), 120–30; Phyllis Rackin, 'Androgyny, Mimesis, and the Marriage of the Boy

Heroine on the English Renaissance Stage', *PMLA*, 102 (1987), 29–41; Jean E. Howard, 'Crossdressing, the Theatre, and Gender Struggle in Early Modern England', *Shakespeare Quarterly*, 39 (1988), 418–40; Stephen Orgel, 'Nobody's Perfect, or Why Did the English Stage Take Boys for Women', forthcoming in *The South Atlantic Quarterly*, Winter 1989, special issue, 'Displacing Homophobia'.

46. *The Taming of the Shrew* (The New Cambridge Shakespeare), Cambridge University Press, 1984.

47. Karen Newman, 'Renaissance Family Politics and Shakespeare's *The Taming of the Shrew*' in *English Literary Renaissance*, 16 (1986), 86–100 (p. 100).

48. *The History of Sexuality*, vol. 1: An Introduction, p. 43.

49. London: Gay Men's Press, 1982.

50. See especially Weeks' *Sex, Politics and Society: The Regulation of Sexuality Since 1800*, London: Longman, 1981, pp. 1–11; and David F. Greenberg, *The Construction of Homosexuality*, Chicago University Press, 1988.

51. Bray, pp. 14, 19, 25, 68, 103, 112; Greenberg, esp. pp. 20, 275, 279; see also Weeks, *Coming Out*, pp. 11–14, and Jonathan Goldberg, 'Sodomy and Society: The Case of Christopher Marlowe', *Southwest Review*, Autumn 1984, 371–8.

52. Greenberg, pp. 298 and 323; Bray, p. 71.

53. Joseph Pequigney, *Such Is My Love: A Study of Shakespeare's Sonnets*, Chicago and London: University of Chicago Press, 1985.

54. However, Pequigney's reading should be clearly distinguished from those modern critics whose acceptance of the modern, pejorative notions of homosexuality leads not only to anachronistic readings of Renaissance literature, but also shows their critical discourse to be of its time in a specially narrow way. Simon Shepherd, in his book on Marlowe and his essay on Shakespeare's *Sonnets*, indicates how the assumptions of such critics are not only culturally specific, but often confused and hypocritical. Simon Shepherd, *Marlowe and the Politics of Elizabethan Theatre*, Brighton: Harvester, 1986, esp. pp. xii–xiv and 198–9, and 'Shakespeare's Private Drawer: Shakespeare and Homosexuality' in *The Shakespeare Myth*, ed. Holderness.

55. What a materialist analysis can achieve through a close analysis of language which is at once historically aware and textually sensitive is exemplified in John Barrell's fine chapter on Sonnet 29 in his *Poetry Language and Politics*, Manchester University Press, 1988. Patronage, whether possessed or lacked, was a crucial factor in the production

(or not) of Renaissance poetry; Barrell explores its relation to, and its representation in, Sonnet 29, right down to crucial issues of punctuation and editing. In the process he shows how the pathos of this poem is 'inextricably a function of how it represents the specificity of the historical moment it produces and which produced it: a pathos which arises from the narrator's attempt to claim a transcendence he cannot achieve' (p. 42).

56. Eve Kosofsky Sedgwick, *Between Men: English Literature and Male Homosocial Desire* (*Gender and Culture Series*), New York: Columbia University Press, 1985.

57. 'A Poem Is Being Written', *Representations*, 17 (1987), 110–43, (pp. 129–30).

58. See Greenberg, *The Construction of Homosexuality* (see note 50), esp. pp. 482ff. Greenberg, while defending the view that homosexuality has been differently defined in different historical periods, rightly contests the extreme 'constructionist' view, namely the idea that the homosexual as a distinct species originated only about a hundred years ago (p. 485). Simon Shepherd qualifies Bray's view of the Renaissance in arguing that same-gender sexuality was associated with certain socially identified types of person. 'What's so Funny about Ladies' Tailors?: A Survey of Some Male (Homo)sexual Types in the Renaissance', forthcoming.

59. Neely argues, as we have seen, that studies which explore the interconnectedness of gender with other forms of power, and the construction of women's subordination within and by those other forms, end up marginalising or silencing women. That this is not necessarily the implication of this work is suggested by the analogous (though not identical) approach taken here to 'the homosexual question'. However, this is an analogy which Neely does not apparently accept (p. 10 of her article).

60. Shepherd, in *Marlowe and the Politics of Elizabethan Theatre*, discusses sodomy in connection with the representation of women and in relation to the construction of masculinity. He sees Marlowe as problematising the Renaissance ideology of gender difference, especially the part played within it by the ideal of manliness.

61. Peter Stallybrass, 'Macbeth and Witchcraft', *Focus on Macbeth*, ed. John Russell Brown, London: Routledge & Kegan Paul, 1982, pp. 189–209. For a fuller account of some of the issues addressed in this essay, but across a much wider period, see Peter Stallybrass and Allon White, *The Politics and Poetics of Transgression* (see note 25).

62. Janet Adelman, '"Born of Woman": Fantasies of Maternal Power in *Macbeth*', *Cannibals, Witches, and Divorce: Estranging the Renaissance*, ed. Marjorie Garber, Baltimore and London: Johns Hopkins University Press, 1987, pp. 90–121 (p. 111).

63. D. E. Underdown, 'The Taming of the Scold: The Enforcement of Patriarchal Authority in Early Modern England', in *Order and Disorder in Early Modern England*, ed. Anthony Fletcher and John Stevenson, Cambridge University Press, 1985, pp. 116–36. For two other studies relevant to issues of order, social control and cultural resistance see Underdown's *Revel, Riot and Rebellion: Popular Politics and Culture in England 1603–1660*, Oxford University Press, 1987; and Derek Hirst, *Authority and Conflict: England 1603–1658*, Harvard University Press, 1986. Lawrence Stone has a useful review essay of these three books and other related work in *The New York Review of Books*, February 26, 1987, pp. 38–43. Stone describes England between 1580 and 1640 as pervaded by change: 'It was characterized by turmoil, anxiety, suspicion, and discord, provoked by demographic growth, price inflation, poor harvests, enclosure of open fields, changes in agriculture that augured further productivity increases, and a widening gap between rich and poor. It was a disorder that was just barely kept under control . . . ' (p. 43).

64. For a discussion of women in Webster's *The White Devil* in relation to the woman on top, see below, pp. 239–42. For further material on witchcraft see Christina Larner, *Witchcraft and Religion: The Politics of Popular Belief*, Oxford: Blackwell, 1984; Alan Macfarlane, *The Culture of Capitalism*, Oxford: Blackwell, 1987, pp. 107–11; *Witchcraft in Tudor and Stuart England*, London: Routledge, 1970; and Maria Mies, *Patriarchy and Accumulation on a World Scale: Women in the International Division of Labour*, London: Zed Books, 1986, esp. p. 87.

65. Above, pp. lvii–lviii; and lxviii. For a more general critique of the marginal as a source of easy politics see John Carlos Rowe, '"To Live Outside the Law You Must be Honest": The Authority of the Margin in Contemporary Theory' in *Cultural Critique*, no. 2 (Winter 1985–6), 35–68.

66. In another review essay, this one on the history of sexuality, Lawrence Stone observes that we still have no adequate account of why certain periods produce an intensification of social control and repression. He is talking in particular of the emergence of sexual asceticism in the late Roman period, and the renewed and intense repression of

deviants of all kinds in the thirteenth, sixteenth and late eighteenth centuries. Comparing these periods of active repression he does confirm that characteristics familiar in early modern England and the twentieth century are common to all:

> They have usually included attacks on most forms of deviance, whether racial/religious (Jews or Arabs), or exclusively religious (heretics), or magical (witches), or occupational (usurers), or political (traitors), or sexual (homosexuals or fornicators). All are driven by moral panic, a great fear.
>
> *The History of Sex,* two parts, *The National Times,* July 19–August 1, 1985, pp. 9–14 (9–12); quotation from part 2, p. 12.

67. *Drama of a Nation: Public Theatre in Renaissance England and Spain,* Ithaca and London: Cornell University Press, 1985.

68. 'Literary Criticism and the Return to "History"', *Critical Inquiry,* 14 (Summer 1988), 721–47. See also Howard Horovitz, '"I Can't Remember": Skepticism, Synthetic Histories, Critical Action' in *The South Atlantic Quarterly,* 87, no. 4 (1988), 787–820.

69. *The New Historicism,* ed. H. A. Veeser, London: Routledge, 1989, contains essays on the difficulty of reconciling post-structuralist theory with historical inquiry, with strong arguments for the necessity of the latter.

70. For Brecht's adaptation of *Coriolanus* see *Collected Plays,* vol. 9, New York: Vintage Books, 1973, pp. 57–146 and 374–400.

71. *Brecht on Theatre: The Development of an Aesthetic,* ed. and trans. John Willett, New York: Hill and Wang, 1964, pp. 27 and 276; quoted from Alan Sinfield, 'Against Appropriation', *Essays and Criticism,* 31 (1981), 181–95 (pp. 194–5). There is a fuller account of Brecht's theories, and their significance for Jacobean drama, below (pp. 35–6, 63–9, 153–4).

72. *Times Literary Supplement,* 1–7 January 1988, p. 17. Carolyn Porter, 'Are We Being Historical Yet?' (see note 15), is more appreciative of the historical work already undertaken by culturalist critics in the UK, and within US literary studies, women's studies, ethnic studies and Afro-American studies. The same is true of gay studies, both in the UK and the US.

73. It should be added that there were those, like Raymond Williams, who never subscribed to anything else.

74. Michel Foucault, *Discipline and Punish: The Birth of the Prison,* trans. Alan Sheridan, New York: Pantheon, 1977, pp. 16–17.

75.   *William Perkins 1558–1602: English Puritanist: His Pioneer Works on Casuistry: 'A Discourse of Conscience' and 'The Whole Treatise of Case of Conscience'*, ed. with intro. by Thomas F. Merrill, B. De Graf, Nieuwkoop, 1966, p. 9.

76.   Discussed in more detail below, pp. 11–13.

77.   Cf. Foucault (cited above): 'A new character came on the scene, masked. It was the end of a certain kind of tragedy; comedy began, with shadow play, faceless voices, impalpable entities'.

78.   Ed. Graham Holderness, Manchester University Press, 1988.

79.   *The Shakespeare Myth* also has sections on education, popular culture, ideology, the theatre, sexual politics and broadcasting; a helpful feature of this collection is the juxtaposition of critical essays with interviews with prominent cultural practitioners of Shakespeare in education, the theatre and television. The frequency with which theatre directors reiterate the clichés of idealist criticism is revealing, as Terry Eagleton remarks in his Afterword.

80.   Elaine Showalter, 'Representing Ophelia: Women, Madness, and the Responsibilities of Feminist Criticism' in *Shakespeare and the Question of Theory*, ed. Parker and Hartman.

81.   Terence Hawkes, *That Shakespeherian Rag: Essays on a Critical Process*, London and New York: Methuen, 1986.

82.   The extraordinary amount of scholarly energy devoted to the question of whether what was generally agreed to be an indifferent poem was actually written by Shakespeare, resembled a religious dispute about the authenticity of a relic. If there was something absurd in this, magnified by the international news coverage it received, it is also true that the enormous vested interests of the Shakespeare industry were never more apparent than during that dispute.

83.   Stephen Orgel, 'The Authentic Shakespeare', *Representations*, 21 (1988), 1–26.

84.   Margot Heinemann, 'How Brecht Read Shakespeare', in *Political Shakespeare*, pp. 202–3.

85.   See *Shakespeare in the Soviet Union*, translated from the Russian by Avril Pyman, Moscow: Progress Publishers, 1966. This collection of essays covers the study of Shakespeare as literature, and in the theatre.

86.   The passage is cited by Stephen J. Brown in 'The Uses of Shakespeare in America: A Study in Class Domination' in *Shakespeare: Pattern of Excelling Nature*, ed. David Bevington and Jay L. Halio, Newark: University of Delaware Press, 1978. It was brought to my attention by Louis Montrose, who cites it in his article 'Professing the

Renaissance', p. 27. See also Don E. Wayne, 'Power, Politics and the Shakespearean Text: Recent Criticism in England and the United States' in *Shakespeare Reproduced*, eds Howard and O'Connor, pp. 47–67, especially pp. 64–5. Adams' lecture, entitled 'Shakespeare and American Culture', was printed in *The Spinning Wheel: A Magazine of National and International Scope*, vol. 12, nos 9–10 (1932), 212–31.

87. See the Occasional Paper, No. 7, 'Speaking for the Humanities' from the American Council of Learned Societies, New York, 1989; and Barbara Herrnstein Smith's presidential address to the MLA, 'Limelight: Reflections on a Public Year' in *PMLA*, vol. 104, no. 3 (May 1989).

88. See also two books recently published in the US, both best sellers: Allan Bloom, *The Closing of the American Mind: How Higher Education Has Failed Democracy and Impoverished the Souls of Today's Students*, New York: Simon and Schuster, 1987; and E. D. Hirsch, *Cultural Literacy: What Every American Needs to Know*, Boston: Houghton Mifflin, 1987.

89. 'Shakespeare's Stratford and South Africa', *Shakespeare Quarterly*, 38 (1987), 479–81 (p. 479).

90. 'Making Space: Appropriation and Confrontation in Recent British Plays' in *The Shakespeare Myth*. Sinfield discusses Stoppard's *Rosencrantz and Guildenstern*, Marowitz's *Collage Hamlet* and *Measure for Measure*, Wesker's *The Merchant*, and Bond's *Lear*.

91. Martin Orkin, *Shakespeare Against Apartheid*, Craighall: Ad. Donker, 1987. See also his study of drama in South Africa, forthcoming with Manchester University Press, 1989.

92. Forthcoming with Manchester University Press, 1989. All quotations from manuscript.

93. This is addressed also by Gauri Viswanathan in 'The Beginnings of English Literary Study in British India' in *Oxford Literary Review* (*OLR*), vol. 9, nos 1–2 (1987), 2–26.

Examine carefully the behaviour of these people:
Find it surprising though not unusual
Inexplicable though normal
Incomprehensible though it is the rule.
Consider even the most insignificant, seemingly simple
Action with distrust. Ask yourselves whether it is necessary
Especially if it is usual.
We ask you expressly to discover
That what happens all the time is not natural.
For to say that something is natural
In such times of bloody confusion
Of ordained disorder, of systematic arbitrariness
Of inhuman inhumanity is to
Regard it as unchangeable.

Bertolt Brecht, The Exception and the Rule

This our age swims within him . . .

The Revenger's Tragedy

For several: Mother, Jolan, Percival, and Alan

The third edition is dedicated to Rachel, and to Helena and Louisa Dollimore. 'The woodthrush singing through the fog/What images return'.

Chapel Cross, East Sussex, June 2003

RADICAL DRAMA: ITS CONTEXTS AND EMERGENCE

1

Contexts

Writing of Jean Genet, Antonin Artaud and Bertolt Brecht – major exponents of what he calls 'critical theatre' – Jean-Paul Sartre declares: 'these authors . . . far from being afraid of creating a scandal, want to provoke one as strongly as possible, because scandal must bring with it a certain disarray'. Theirs, adds Sartre, is a theatre of *refusal* (*Politics and Literature*, pp. 39, 65, 66). The disarray generated in and by Jacobean tragedy has likewise scandalised, then and subsequently. Few writers have provoked as much critical disagreement as, say, John Webster, who has been acutely problematic for a critical tradition which has wanted to keep alive all the conservative imperatives associated with 'order', 'tradition', the 'human condition' and 'character'.[1]

It is no accident that Artaud and, to a much greater extent, Brecht were indebted to Jacobean drama. Brecht in fact figures prominently in my argument to the effect that a significant sequence of Jacobean tragedies,[2] including the majority of Shakespeare's, were more radical than has hitherto been allowed. Subsequent chapters will show how the radicalism of these plays needs to be seen in the wider context of that diverse body of writing which has been called 'the greatest intellectual revolution the Western world has ever seen'[3] and also identified as 'the intellectual origins' of that actual revolution in the English state in 1642.[4] Some forty years before this event, as Raymond Williams has reminded us, we find in Elizabethan and Jacobean drama 'a form of total crisis': in the 'formal qualities of the dramatic mode . . . real social relations were specifically disclosed' (*Culture*, pp. 159, 158). Is it too ambitious to see such a relationship between the drama and the English revolution? Analysing the causes of the latter, Lawrence Stone insists that the crucial question is not war breaking out in 1642 but why 'most of the established institutions of State and Church – Crown, Court, central administration, army, and episcopacy – collapsed so ignominiously two years before' (*The Causes of the English Revolution, 1529–1642*, p. 48).[5] If the causes of that collapse can be discerned in the previous decades then, at the very least, we might postulate a connection in the early seventeenth century between the undermining of these institutions and a theatre in which they and their ideological legitimation were subjected to sceptical, interrogative and subversive representations.

In the hundred years up to 1629, Stone identifies the four most salient elements in the manifold preconditions of the war: first, the failure of the Crown to acquire two key instruments of power – a standing army and a paid, reliable local bureaucracy; second, a decline of the aristocracy and a corresponding rise of the gentry; third, a puritanism which generated a sense of the need for change in church and state; fourth, a crisis of confidence in the integrity of those in power, whether courtiers, nobles, bishops, judges or kings (*Causes*, p. 116). Each precondition constitutes a social and political reality addressed by Jacobean drama. The lack of such things as a standing army rendered effective ideological control the more imperative – and its interrogation the more challenging (interestingly, Althusser's rather crude distinction between repressive and ideological state apparatuses seems to be a more tenable one under such conditions).[6] The crisis of confidence in those holding power is addressed in play after play. Moreover, the corrupt court is, of course, a recurrent setting for the drama; far from being (as is sometimes suggested) a transhistorical symbol of human depravity, this setting is an historically specific focus for a contemporary critique of power relations.[7]

In recent years it has become increasingly apparent that this was a drama which undermined religious orthodoxy. My aim is to show that its challenge in this respect generates other, equally important subversive preoccupations – namely a critique of ideology, the demystification of political and power relations and the decentring of 'man'. Emerging from the interaction between these concerns was a radical social and political realism characterising plays as diverse as Shakespeare's *Coriolanus* and Webster's *The White Devil.*

I draw selectively on recent advances in historical methodology and critical theory which, having significantly illuminated the nature of ideology and literature's relationship to it, are especially relevant to Elizabethan and Jacobean drama.[8] Additionally, they have established new criteria for exploring the relationship of litera-ture to its historical context, and for understanding the importance of literary structure in this respect. In this introduction I indicate the significance of these advances for this study, summarise in the process its main themes, and set out some of the important histor-ical and ideological parameters of the Jacobean theatre.

Literary Criticism: Order versus History

The main tradition in Anglo-American literary criticism has been preoccupied, aesthetically and ideologically, with what Raymond Williams has called (quite simply) 'a problem of *order*' and John Fekete (with more complexity) 'a *telos* of harmonic integration' (*The Critical Twilight*, pp. xii and 195). It is, adds Williams, a pre-occupation deriving from a social and cultural crisis 'in which the limits of current religion and science, but also the probable disinte-gration of an inherited social and cultural order, were being sharply experienced'. This preoccupation has been particularly distorting for Jacobean tragedy. The reason is not difficult to see: that drama emerged from a sense of crisis similar to that which Williams here describes in relation to the modern period. However, unlike the influential movements in recent literary criticism, the response of the drama to crisis was not a retreat into aesthetic and ideological conceptions of order, integration, equilibrium and so on; on the contrary, it confronted and articulated that crisis, indeed it actually helped precipitate it. Every major theme of the plays which I explore in this book transgresses or challenges the Elizabethan equivalent of the modern obsession with a *telos* of harmonic inte-gration.

The result was a dramatic structure which has been notoriously controversial. T. S. Eliot, in a now famous essay, disapproved of the Elizabethan dramatists 'impure art', their attempt 'to attain complete realism without surrendering . . . unrealistic conventions'. It is a confusion which for Eliot makes for 'faults of inconsistency, faults of incoherency' (*Selected Essays*, pp. 111, 114, 116). But Bertolt Brecht, himself much influenced by Elizabethan and Jacobean drama, *approved* this impurity, particularly its elements of experiment, and 'sacrilege', and its dialectic potential (*The Messingkauf Dialogues*, p. 60). Eliot's formalist views were tremendously influential in constituting the subsequent critical tradition, but Brecht's dialectical conception of theatre provides much the more illuminating perspective. Brecht recognised in Jacobean theatre a prototype of his own epic theatre, one where the refusal and disarray of which Sartre speaks involves a positive rejection of 'order' – in the universe, society and the human subject – as ideological misrepresentation. What is at stake here, as we shall see, is nothing less than opposing conceptions of reality and, even, of rationality.

The view that Shakespeare and his contemporaries adhered to the tenets of the so-called Elizabethan World Picture has long been discredited. Yet we still do not possess an adequate conception of their actual relationship to it. In the rest of this section I want to explore aspects of that relationship which have hitherto been ignored or oversimplified.

The ideology of the Elizabethan World Picture was built around the central tenet of teleological design: the divine plan informed the universe generally and society particularly, being manifested in both as Order and Degree; further, identity and purpose were inextricably related, with both deriving from the person's (or any thing's) place in the design. Critics who have rightly repudiated the claim that this world picture was unquestioned orthodoxy have tended also to give the misleading impression that it survived, if at all, only as a medieval anachronism clearly perceived as such by all Elizabethans. In fact, it survived in significant and complex ways – that is, as an amalgam of religious belief, aesthetic idealism and ideological myth. Thus *at the same time* that it was unthinkingly (and perhaps sincerely) invoked by the preacher it was being exploited by the state as a 'creed of absolutism [serving] chiefly to bolster up a precarious monarchy which lacked a standing army or an efficient police force' (J. W. Lever, *The Tragedy of State*, p. 5).

To understand how this could be we need the kind of nonreductive approach to historical process advocated by, for example, E. P. Thompson. History is not a unilinear development; on the contrary, at any historical moment 'there will be found contradictions and liaisons, dominant and subordinate elements, declining or ascending energies. [That] moment is both a result of prior process and an index towards the direction of its future flow' (*The Poverty of Theory*, p. 239). Raymond Williams, with specific reference to literature, has analysed the same complex historical process in terms of the *residual, dominant,* and *emergent* elements which coexist at any cultural moment (*Marxism and Literature*, pp. 121–7). The residual is not to be confused with the 'archaic' (elements of past culture which survive but are obsolete nevertheless); it denotes instead experiences, meanings and values which have been formed in the past, which cannot be expressed in terms of the dominant culture and may even be in opposition to it, yet are still active. Emergent culture involves the finding of new forms, in the process of which there occurs 'Pre-emergence', that is, an expression which is 'active and pressing but not yet fully articulated' (p. 126). If we further recognise that there also exist subordinate and repressed cultures, then we see very clearly that culture itself is not a unitary phenomenon; non-dominant elements interact with the dominant forms, sometimes coexisting with, or being absorbed or even destroyed by them, but also challenging, modifying or even displacing them.

An historical perspective like that advocated by Thompson and Williams further avoids the naive error, common in literary studies, of describing the inception of a particular movement in terms of its subsequent historical development; that is, of telescoping the development back into its inception and reading it off as already contained ('encoded') there, and, simultaneously, ignoring elements contemporary to the inception which were working against, perhaps even contradicting it. So, in resisting the view that Elizabethan/Jacobean drama simply conforms to the Elizabethan World Picture – itself a blend of the dominant and residual cultural elements – we need also to resist the temptation to align it reductively with the emergent. To take a simple example: it is wrong to represent the (emergent) Marlovian atheist repudiating (dominant) religious orthodoxy from a position of atheistic independence and modernity. Sometimes the subversiveness of Jacobean tragedy does work in terms of outright rejection. Generally, however, this procedure was, apart from anything else, thwarted by the censorship which I discuss later in this chapter. More often, Jacobean tragedy discloses ideology as misrepresentation; it interrogates ideology from within, seizing on and exposing its contradictions and inconsistencies and offering alternative ways of understanding social and political process. This is not a transcendent awareness; the drama may incorporate the contradictions it explores. It is, then, a tragedy which violates those cherished *aesthetic* principles which legislate that the ultimate aim of art is to order discordant elements; to explore conflict in order ultimately to resolve it; to explore suffering in order ultimately to transcend it. All three principles tend to eliminate from literature its sociopolitical context (and content), finding instead supposedly timeless values which become the *universal* counterpart of man's *essential* nature – the underlying human essence. Measured against such criteria much Elizabethan and Jacobean drama does indeed lack aesthetic completeness and ethical/metaphysical resolution. But perhaps it has to be seen to lack these things in order to then be seen to possess real (i.e. historical) significance.

According to Albert Camus, tragedy is generated by a particular kind of historical transition: 'Tragedy is born in the west each time that the pendulum of civilisation is halfway between a sacred society and a society built around man' (*Selected Essays and Notebooks*, p. 199). The operative word here is 'halfway' – man 'frees himself from an older form of civilisation and finds that he has broken away from it without having found a new form which satisfies him' (p. 194). To modify Camus' argument somewhat, certain Jacobean tragedies disclose the very process of historical transition which brings them into being.[9] An understanding of that transition requires a preliminary account of ideology.

Ideology, Religion and Renaissance Scepticism

To investigate the confusing history of the concept of ideology is to discover its indispensability as well as the notorious difficulties surrounding it.[10] In its most direct sense it refers to a system of illusory beliefs held in the state of so-called false-consciousness, beliefs which serve to perpetuate a particular social formation or power structure; typically this power structure is itself represented by that ideology as *eternally* or *naturally given* – i.e. as inevitable, immutable. Strikingly, this is the sense implicit in Christopher Marlowe's reputed blasphemy to the effect that 'the first beginning of Religion was only to keep men in awe' (an idea which compares of course with Marx's own declaration that 'religion . . . is the opium of the people').[11] This, roughly, is the view of ideology as a process of conspiracy on the part of the rulers and misrecognition on the part of the ruled (for convenience I call it the cognitive view). In recent years its inadequacy has been insisted on by those who have in turn stressed the extent to which ideology has a material existence; that is, ideology exists in, and as, the social practices which constitute people's lives. If this is so then (it is argued) we must 'reject the view that ideology has its basis in some sort of defective perception of clearly perceptible facts' (John Mepham, 'The Theory of Ideology in *Capital*', p. 167). Ideology becomes not a set of false beliefs capable of correction by perceiving properly, but the very terms in which we perceive the world, almost – and the Kantian emphasis is important here – the condition and grounds of consciousness itself. Additionally, if the beliefs which constitute ideology are understood as eternally true or naturally given, they are never likely to be consciously questioned. In short, our consciousness is in-formed by ideology and although we may experience ourselves as autonomous individuals within, yet essentially independent of, the social order, in truth that order is within us.

Louis Althusser's has been the most influential (and, now, notorious) version of this theory; it has been described by Terry Eagleton as 'an emphatic, irreversible shift in Marxist thinking on the matter – a shift that may truly be described as "epochal"' ('Ideology, Fiction, Narrative', p. 62). It is, however, also a shift which has rendered the distinction between the ideological and the non-ideological difficult to sustain. Indeed, some post-Althusserians have abandoned the distinction preferring instead a theory which constitutes the world as a series of 'discursive practices'. This has in turn prompted a re-emphasis on certain aspects of the cognitive view of ideology. Terry Lovell for example has offered an uncompromising critique of Althusserianism and in the process argued that ideology should be understood as 'the production and dissemination of erroneous beliefs whose inadequacies are socially motivated' (*Pictures of Reality*, p. 51). And Anthony Giddens insists that '*The chief usefulness of the concept of ideology concerns the critique of domination* . . . To analyse the ideological aspects of symbolic orders . . . is to examine *how structures of signification are mobilised to legitimate the sectional interests of hegemonic groups*' (*Central Problems in Social Theory*, p. 187). Both Lovell and Giddens unambiguously reinstate the crucial relation between ideology and power.

In fact, neither the cognitive nor the materialist conceptions of ideology are adequate in themselves, especially when applied trans-historically. Yet each is indispensable for understanding the Elizabethan/Jacobean period, not only because it is then that they emerge into prominence, but also because they were, at that time, inextricably related. This is, I want to suggest, a fascinating but largely ignored aspect of the period. Those who simply dismiss the cognitive conception of ideology (for example Althusser in *Lenin and Philosophy*, p. 153) ignore not only its historical importance in earlier periods but also the way in which it was indispensable in giving access (again historically) to the more complex material formulations.

Bacon articulates the cognitive view of ideology when elaborating his famous doctrine of the idols; man's mind, he said, is full of 'fallacies . . . superstition and imposture, if it be not delivered and reduced'.[12] One of the most notable fallacies was that whereby 'The human understanding is of its own nature prone to suppose the existence of more order and regularity in the world than it finds. . . . Hence the fiction that all celestial bodies move in perfect circles.' Other fallacies concern the confused use of language and erroneous philosophical systems which, says Bacon, 'by tradition, credulity, and negligence have come to be received' (*Works*, pp. 118, 265). Bacon's conjunction of 'tradition' with 'credulity and negligence' at least suggests the way that the cognitive and materialist notions of the ideological could then be thought simultaneously; tradition, or what was more often called 'custom', becomes the basis of the latter – what was in effect a quite sophisticated view of the power of social practice in maintaining social order. Thus in an essay entitled, significantly, 'Of Custom and Education' Bacon observes: '[Machiavelli's] rule holdeth still, that nature, nor the engagement of words, are not so forcible as custom'; men behave, adds Bacon, 'as if they were dead images and engines moved only by the wheels of custom' (*Essays*, p. 119).

When epistemological and ethical truth was recognised to be relative to custom and social practice, then ideological considerations were inevitably foregrounded. Machiavelli, Montaigne and Hobbes all testify unambiguously to such recognition. Truth and falsity, says Hobbes in *Leviathan*, are 'attributes of speech, not of things. And where speech is not, there is neither *truth* nor *falsehood*' (chapter 4). Even more contentiously: 'good' and 'evil' are concepts only 'ever used with relation to the person that useth them: there being nothing simply and absolutely so [i.e. good or evil] nor any common rule of good and evil, to be taken from the nature of the objects themselves' (chapter 6).

This period's developing awareness of ideology in both its cognitive and material forms can best be seen by looking further at the growing concern with religion itself as an ideological practice. Calvin had conceded that '*in order to hold Men's minds in greater subjection,* clever men have devised many things in religion by which to inspire the common folk with reverence and strike them with terror' (*Institutes,* I. iii. 2; my italics). Here, crucially, 'subjection' involves an ideological operation at the level of subjectivity itself. But such exploitation could only take place, Calvin assures us, because God had already imprinted true religion in the minds of men. But the problem then becomes one of distinguishing 'true' from 'false', the authentic divine imprint from its ideological surrogate. Further, in the struggle to so distinguish, Calvin's criteria for identifying the false would be both supplemented and cross-applied.

Sir John Davies entertains (though only to reject) the same atheistical idea:

> though vaine it is,
> To thinke our Soules to heaven or hell do go,
> *Politique* men, have thought it not amisse,
> To spread this *lye*, to make men
> Vertuous so.
>
> (*Nosce Teipsum*, ll. 1805–8)

Davies' source, de La Primaudaye in *The French Academy*, shows an anxious awareness of just how disturbing such an idea could be; after outlining it, he adds, 'Is not this, a very proper means to call all trueth into question, and to trample *all* vertue under foote? (pp. 566–7; my italics). Shakespeare's Richard III asserts that 'conscience' – a word which, in this context, suggests the *internalisation* of ethical and religious norms – 'is but a word that cowards use,/Devis'd at first to keep the strong in awe' (*Richard III*, V. iii. 309–10).

The view of religion as a political expedient was an old one. We find it for example in Pliny's *Natural History*, Holland's translation of which appeared in 1601. But for the Elizabethans the recent and most contentious source of the idea was of course Machiavelli who argues in *The Discourses* that religion (which he often equates with superstition) was not only an instrument of power but an indispensable one. Felix Raab has established at some length Machiavelli's considerable and disturbing influence on the Elizabethans (*The English Face of Machiavelli*, especially chapters 2 and 3). By prising history free of providentialist ideology and conceiving it instead as radically contingent, Machiavelli intensified the conflict in this period between religion and 'policy'.

From all the English writers who hated, approved or simply mentioned Machiavelli, it is worth selecting Richard Hooker who, even while he is opposing him, offers a succinct account of Machiavelli's view of religion as ideology:

> A politic use of religion they see there is, and by it they would also gather that religion itself is a mere politic device, forged purposely to

serve for that use. Men fearing God are thereby a great deal more effectually than by positive laws restrained from doing evil; inasmuch as those laws have no farther power than over our outward actions only, whereas unto men's inward cogitations, unto the privy intents and motions of their hearts, religion serveth for a bridle. (*Of the Laws of Ecclesiastical Polity*, II, 19)

The ideological function of religion is referred to even more precisely by Hooker when, a little later, he speaks of 'politic devisers, able to create God in man by art' (p. 21).

Politicians, says Robert Burton in *The Anatomy of Melancholy*, 'make religion mere policy, a cloak, a human invention; *nihil aeque valet ad regendos vulgi animos ac superstitio* [nothing is so effective for keeping the masses under control as superstition]'. He cites 'Captain Machiavel' as one such and also quotes Sabellicus: '"A man without a religion is like a horse without a bridle". No way better to curb than superstition, to terrify men's consciences, and keep them in awe' (III, 328–9). Hobbes, in *Leviathan*, gives a detailed account of Hooker's 'Politic devisers'. The first legislators of commonwealths, 'whose ends were only to keep the people in obedience, and peace', took care to achieve three things, says Hobbes. First, they 'imprinted' in the minds of the people the erroneous belief that religious precepts came not from them (the legislators) but the gods. Second, they ensured that 'the same things were displeasing to the gods, which were forbidden by the laws'. Third, they prescribed rituals and sacrifices to appease the gods, and led the people to believe that both general misfortune (e.g. the loss of a war) and private misery were the result of the gods' anger. 'By these, and such other institutions' says Hobbes, 'the common people . . . were the less apt to mutiny against their governors' and 'needed nothing else but bread to keep them from discontent, murmuring, and commotion against the state' (chapter 12). This account of religion (or rather superstition) is just one aspect of Hobbes' own philosophical radicalism; he urgently wanted to demystify politics, to show that pragmatism and expediency rather than divine prescription was the basis of political obedience and the justification of state power.[13]

One important factor stimulating the ideology/religion controversy was the unintentionally subversive effect of controversy itself.

Protestants had questioned the authority of tradition while catholics rejected the protestants' exclusive emphasis on biblical authority; by each eroding the ideological basis of the other's position they were also undermining their own, since protestants needed tradition and catholics needed biblical authority. Consequently there occurred, according to Montaigne, an indirect and unintended liberation of 'the vulgar' in whom 'awfull reverence' gives way to rebellion precisely because religious conflict undermines the 'grounded authoritie' of religion itself: 'Some articles of their religion . . . made doubtfull and questionable, they will soone and easily admit an equall uncertainty in all other parts of their beleefe' (II, 126–7; once again Bacon concurs: see 'Of Unity in Religion', *Essays*, pp. 8–12). This, presumably, is one reason why protestant divines came to contradict their own principle of the priority of conscience and, in practice, ruthlessly repress religious dissent.

If ideology typically legitimates the social order by representing it as a spurious unity, metaphysically ordained, and thereby forestalls knowledge of the contradictions which in fact constitute that order (such knowledge being a precondition for the recognition that change is possible), then this analysis of Montaigne's suggests how far-reaching could be the consequences of that unity being ruptured. Jacobean theatre prompts the release from *within* religious discourses of contradictions already made the more visible by the power struggle *between* them.

Historically, the idea that religion was invented by the powerful to keep other men in subjection is untrue. Religion, like any other ideological formation, had an inception much more complex. Nevertheless, that it has historically served to legitimate systems of power and subjection is indubitable, and what was happening in the Elizabethan period was of the utmost historical importance: religion was increasingly being perceived in terms of such legitimation. The Machiavelli who delivers the prologue of Marlowe's *The Jew of Malta* is a comic caricature, yet despite that he still carries subversive potential, what Gramsci saw as the 'essentially revolutionary character' of Machiavellianism (*Selections From Prison Notebooks*, p. 136): he counts 'religion but a childish toy' and insists that 'Might', not divine right, 'first made kings' (II, 14, 20).

What Machiavelli did for religion, Montaigne did, with equally devastating effect, for law: 'Lawes are . . . maintained in credit, not because they are essentially just, but because they are lawes. *It is the mysticall foundation of their authority; they have none other*; which availes them much: they are often made by fooles; *more often by men, who in hatred of equality, have want of equity.* . . . There is nothing so grossly and largely offending, nor so ordinarily wronging as the Lawes' (*Essays*, III, 331; my italics). Montaigne was already controversial in Elizabethan England, and one of the most important single influences on Jacobean drama (Florio's translation of his *Essays* was published in 1603 and circulated in manuscript several years before that). Even where direct influence is in question, a similarity in perspective is not. Thus, for example, in Daniel's *Philotas* a Persian asks a Grecian why Philotas is being put on trial since his accusers have already decided on his guilt. To the Grecian's answer – 'it satisfies the world, and we/Think that well done which done by law we see' – the Persian retorts 'And yet your law serves but your private ends.'[14] And in Jonson's *Sejanus* Silius tells the Consul which is 'framing' him:

> This boast of law, and law, is but a form,
> A net of Vulcan's filing, a mere engine,
> To take that life by a pretext of justice,
> Which you pursue in malice
>
> (III. 1. 243–7)

Both *Philotas* and *Sejanus* were found seditious and their authors summoned before the Privy Council.

What is happening here to both religion and law is a process of demystification whose basis is a radical relativism. '*Diversity is the most universall quality*' says Montaigne (II, 523), thus robbing the universal of its ideological power to reduce diversity to unity, the particular to its form, development to its origin, and so on. Diversity for Montaigne simply refutes the belief 'that there be some [laws] firme, perpetuall and immoveable, which they call naturall, and by the condition of their proper essence, are imprinted in mankind'; it does this because there is not one of these so-called laws which is not 'impugned or disallowed, not by one nation, but by many' (II, 297). Consequently 'the lawes of conscience, which we say to proceed from nature, rise and proceed of custome' (I. 114) or, in the words of Francis Bacon, 'moral virtues are in the mind of man by habit and not by nature' (*Works*, p. 133). One effect of this is to reveal the belief in 'universall law' to be an ideological misrecognition of 'municipall law' (Montaigne, *Essays*, II, 229) – that is, 'the law of a particular state' (*OED*).[15] Cultural relativism had been of course the impetus for that earlier and notable instance of law demystified, Sir Thomas More's *Utopia* (1516; English translation 1551). Raphael, the narrator, possessed of a wisdom stemming from an incomparable knowledge of 'strange and unknown peoples, and countries' (p. 79), concludes his story of Utopia by declaring that in all contemporary commonwealths there exists a:

> conspiracy of rich men procuring their own commodities under the name and title of the commonwealth. They invent and devise all means and crafts, first how to keep safely, without fear of losing, that they have unjustly gathered together, and next how to hire and abuse the work and labour of the poor for as little money as may be. These devices, when the rich men have decreed to be kept and observed under colour of the commonalty, that is to say, also of the poor people, then they be made laws. (p. 190; this is the passage which Nashe enthusiastically paraphrases in his reference to Utopia and 'the merry Sir Thomas More' in *The Unfortunate Traveller*, 1594, pp. 290–1)

To recognise that law and morality have their origins in custom rather than with an eternal order of things (God or nature or both) is to put the ideological process into reverse. The radical implications of this can be seen from another remark of Montaigne's: 'wee may easily discerne, that only custom makes that seem impossible unto us, which is not so' (I, 239). That Montaigne opposed radical change (see for example 'Of Vanitie') does not cancel those implications, and may even be explained by a recognition and fear of them.

What is especially interesting is the way that so many of these writers are aware of what approximates to the notion of false-consciousness – that is, the powerful internalisation of false belief which keeps individuals in 'awe' and unaware of the contradictions in their lives. Thus Hooker in the passage earlier quoted describes the view that human law merely restrains people externally whereas religion reaches and bridles their 'inward cognitations . . . the privy intents and motions of their heart'. Such awareness leads to the decentring of 'man'.[16]

Ideology and the Decentring of Man

Althusser's account of ideology has been important for the development of modern theories of the decentred human subject (see chapter 16). It is, therefore, all the more striking to find Montaigne defining 'custom' in an almost identical way – striking because he too is concerned to decentre man. Compare the following quotations from Althusser and Montaigne:

1 (a)   It is clear that ideology . . . is indispensable in any society if men are to be formed, transformed and equipped to respond to the demands of their conditions of existence.

(Althusser, *For Marx*, p. 235)

1 (b)   It is by the [mediation] of custome, that every man is contented with the place where nature hath settled him.

(Montaigne, *Essays*, I, 230)

2 (a)   When we speak of ideology we should know that ideology slides into all human activity, that it is identical with the lived experience of human existence itself . . .

(Althusser, *Lenin and Philosophy*, p. 204)

2 (b)   The lawes of conscience, which we say to proceed from nature, rise and proceed of custome . . . the chiefest effect of [which] is to seize upon us, and so entangle us, that it shall hardly lie in us, to free our selves . . . to discourse and reason of her ordinances; . . . custom doth so bleare us that we cannot distinguish the true visage of things.

(Montaigne, *Essays*, I, 114–15)

3 (a)   Men 'live' their ideologies as the Cartesian 'saw' or did not see – if he was not looking at it – the moon two hundred paces away.

(Althusser, *For Marx*, p. 233)

3 (b)   Nothing is so firmly beleeved, as that which a man knoweth least.

(Montaigne, *Essays*, I, 230)

Both Althusser and Montaigne see ideology (or custom) as so powerfully internalised in consciousness that it results in misrecognition;

we understand it (insofar as we 'see' it at all) as eternally or naturally given instead of socially generated and contingent.

But how does this arise? Again, Althusser and Montaigne have similar answers. For Althusser it is because ideology has a material existence – that is, the system of beliefs which constitutes ideology is built into cultural practices and social institutions. Tony Bennett summarises Althusser as follows: 'The celebration of communion might thus be regarded as quintessentially ideological. It consists of a practice of signification which, inscribed in ritual form and housed within the ideological apparatus of the church, produces the consciousness of the communicant: that is, produces him/her as, precisely, the subject of a religious consciousness' (*Formalism and Marxism*, p. 113). Compare Robert Burton, who in 1621 asks: 'What devices, traditions, ceremonies, have [priests] not invented in all ages to keep men in obedience . . .' (*Anatomy*, III, 331). Montaigne likewise presents custom as embedded in social practices, institutions and rituals. He lists numerous examples. And this is what makes for its power: in engaging in those practices we internalise the customs which structure them. Bacon concurs: 'it must be confessed that it is not possible to divorce ourselves from these fallacies and false appearances, because they are inseparable from our nature and condition of life' (*Works*, p. 120).

Of course the analogy between Montaigne and Althusser would break down if pushed, as it would with any two philosophers so historically distant from each other. I make the comparison here as a way of insisting first, that the Renaissance possessed a sophisticated concept of ideology if not the word; second, that Renaissance writers like those discussed here were actively engaged in challenging ideology; third (and incidentally) that the originality of Althusser has been overestimated, not least by some Althusserians with an inadequate philosophical and historical perspective.

As I have already indicated, and argue more fully in chapter 10, Montaigne's scepticism, like the materialist conception of ideology, involves the decentring of man. To begin with, both are anti-essentialist: they reject the belief that we possess some given, unalterable essence or nature in virtue of which we are human. As we shall see, this relates directly to that other preoccupation of

Jacobean theatre, its interrogation of providentialism: hitherto man had been understood in terms of his privileged position at the centre (actual and metaphysical) of the cosmic plan; to repudiate that plan was, inevitably, also to decentre man (actually and ideologically). More specifically, in subverting the purposive and teleologically integrated universe envisioned by providentialists, these playwrights necessarily subverted its corollary: the unitary subject integrated internally as a consequence of being integrated into the cosmic design. In their interrelation these two levels of subversion constitute, first, a devastating attack on the two basic tenets of Christian humanism and second, the starting point of this tragedy's political and social realism. As with Brecht's *Mother Courage*, it is a realism which, even as it shows the powerlessness of individuals, demystifies the power structure and the social order which constitute and destroy them. Jacobean tragedy inscribes social process in – or rather as – subjective identity.

Secularism versus Nihilism

The secularisation of this period undoubtedly contributed to, and was in turn influenced by, the process of demystification which I have been describing. However, the analysis of the preceding sections should indicate that this was not, and could not have been, a simple, unilinear transition whereby scientific secularism displaced religion. Christopher Hill and others have explored the intellectual aspects of an emergent secularism which, by allowing unto God what was properly His, was able to appropriate the world for its own not so humble ends. Thus: 'Bacon separated science from theology by pushing God upstairs after he had established the laws of motion for the universe . . . Raleigh secularised history not by denying God the first cause, but by concentrating on secondary causes and insisting that they are sufficient in themselves for historical explanation' (*Intellectual Origins of the English Revolution*, p. 181). But we must be careful here not to represent the period simply in terms of an optimistic rush for the empirical. There is ample evidence to suggest that this was, as it were, a reluctant rather than an optimistic empiricism. For Montaigne (at least in the 'Apologie') empiricism was inseparable from a nihilistic scepticism which led finally to a retreat into fideism. The anxiety of writers over the 'new philosophy' which, according to Donne, called 'all in doubt' has been well documented, while the obsession in the period with the appearance–reality dichotomy reminds us of just how insecure their empiricism could be.

The point, I think, is that certain ideological and metaphysical categories were no longer adequate to explain reality and reality became, as a result, *more* not less problematic. Christianity, like any ideology, is characterised by contradictions, points at which it falters and the dogma(tic) is specially and crucially reinforced by faith; in effect, the contradiction is dissolved in and by the paradox of faith. The Elizabethan period was one in which that shift from contradiction to faithful resolution became, for many, too difficult.

Taken on its own terms any ideology may appear internally coherent. When, however, its deep structure is examined it is often discovered to be a synthesis of contradictory elements. Alternatively (or additionally) in the course of its historical development it may generate contradictions within itself. According to Nietzsche this is what happened to Christianity: it developed a sense of truthfulness which was self-destructive; it became 'nauseated by the falseness and mendaciousness of all Christian interpretations of the world and of history' (*The Will to Power*, p. 7). As he puts it elsewhere: 'After drawing a whole series of conclusions, Christian truthfulness must now draw its strongest conclusion, the one by which it shall do away with itself' (*The Genealogy of Morals*, p. 297). Moreover, 'scepticism regarding morality is what is decisive. The end of the moral interpretation of the world . . . leads to nihilism' (*The Will to Power*, p. 7). Now Montaigne's scepticism does indeed lead perilously close to nihilism, at least in 'An Apologie of Raymond Sebond'. He avoids it finally by embracing a form of fideism which is an intriguing mutation of earlier faith – one working, it may seem in retrospect, to cope with Nietzsche's contradiction. It does so by advancing a faith whose intensity is in inverse proportion to the empirical 'truthfulness' which contradicts it (see especially *Essays*, II, pp. 325–6). Arguably, this is a contradiction which fideism can, as it were, absorb but not dissolve. It is interesting to compare with Montaigne Bacon's famous declaration of fideistic belief: 'the more discordant and incredible [*absonum and incredibile*] any divine mystery is, the greater the honour we do to God in believing it; and so much the more noble the victory of faith' (*Works*, p. 631). Are we to take this 'straight', or are we to read behind it a political discretion laced with irony, a scepticism being officially allayed but in language which actually alerts it? It is difficult to know. (The Bohn edition of *De Augmentis* translates '*absonum*' as 'absurd', not 'discordant'.)

Montaigne's scepticism is central to Jacobean tragedy whereas his fideism is not. Further, that tragedy's involvement with nihilism is also different from his. It takes the form of an extreme stultification felt to be working at the very heart of existence. As I show in Chapter 5, this is an idea associated with the Elizabethan/Jacobean fears of cosmic decay. The dramatists exploit this idea as a way of destabilising providentialism. Time and again we encounter the idea of individuals and society being destroyed from *within*. The declaration in *King Lear* that 'humanity must perforce prey on itself' (IV. ii. 49) is just one instance of an idea which, in some plays, becomes a principle of their very structure. Often this involves a regressive pessimism which resembles the familiar tradition of *contemptus mundi*; now however it seems more desperate and characterised by *anomie* because lacking that tradition's compensating faith in the eternal. Thus even as the emergent culture is displacing the dominant, an aspect of the residual is powerfully reactivated. Significantly, in the later tragedies the idea diminishes considerably; contradiction comes to be understood not in terms of metaphysical condition but, rather, social process. But the paradoxical coexistence of residual and emergent elements in the earlier drama will illustrate an important point: writers fall prey to a certain aspect of an ideological configuration which they themselves, in other crucial respects, have discredited. In fact, it may be the case that they fall prey to the one precisely because they have discredited the other.

Censorship

In one place Montaigne can sceptically undermine the ideological basis of law, in another warn against the dangers of change. This suggests why it would be wrong to categorise him as radical in the sense of embracing 'advanced political views of a democratic kind' (*OED*). But it also explains why his ideas were radical in another sense also cited in the *OED*: 'affecting the foundation, going to the root'.[17] Montaigne's warning against change may itself testify to the radical *implications* of his writing, implications which he may have been unwilling to allow politically but which others were not. We need to recognise then how a writer can be intellectually radical without necessarily being politically so. In the individual writer or text subversive thought and political conservatism may seem to be harmonised in a way which belies the fact that historically the two things relate dialectically: the former relates to the latter in ways which are initially integral to it yet eventually contradict it. Bacon's reconciliation of empiricism and religion might be a case in point, as indeed might Machiavelli's political theory: the latter demystifies power in order that the powerful may rule more effectively yet he has the effect of undermining the very basis of power itself. I say 'might' only because, according to Gramsci, Machiavelli actually intended this effect; his ideas were not, says Gramsci, 'the monopoly of isolated thinkers, a secret memorandum circulated among the initiated'. In fact, far from telling the rulers how to be more effectively tyrannical Machiavelli was revealing to 'those who are not in the know' the truth about how tyranny operates, especially at the level of ideological legitimation (*Prison Notebooks*, p. 134). Historically accurate or not, Gramsci's argument suggests something of fundamental importance: what makes an idea subversive is not so much what is intrinsic to it or the mere thinking of it, but the context of its articulation – to whom, and to how many and in what circumstances it is said or written. That the theatres in early seventeenth-century England were a potentially subversive context is evidenced by the fact of their censorship. (But the significance of censorship for this study also lies in the fact that by being aware of its existence we better understand the strategies whereby the drama evades it.)

The authorities feared the theatre. Time and again it was alleged that the theatre was a breeding ground for irreligion, corruption and riots. Glynne Wickham, in *Early English Stages*, confirms that riots occurred often enough to cause anxiety to officials (II. 86). Philip Stubbes, writing in 1583, declared that in the theatre 'you will learn to contemn God and all His laws, to care neither for Heaven nor Hell' (*Anatomie of Abuses*, p. 145). Significantly, the later objections of William Prynne include very precise political anxieties; in his eyes at least the theatre was successfully demystifying religion and state: 'there is nothing more dangerous in a state than for the Stage and Poet to describe sin . . . because it causeth magistrates, ministers and statesmen to lose their reputation, and sin to be less feared' (*Histriomastix*, p. 491). In 1605 Samuel Calvert had written that the players were performing 'the whole course of the present Time, not sparing either King, State or Religion, in so great Absurdity, and with such Liberty, that any would be afraid to hear them'.[18] Four years before, the Earl of Essex had tried unsuccessfully to lead an uprising; the conspirators persuaded the Lord Chamberlain's men to stage what seems to have been Shakespeare's *Richard II* in the hope that the play, especially the abdication scene, would encourage rebellion. (They failed and Essex was executed.) The abdication scene was cut from the first Quarto (1597) and not restored until after Elizabeth's death. Some months after the uprising Elizabeth was reported to have said 'I am Richard II. know ye not that?' (*Richard II*, ed. P. Ure, p. lix).

Not surprisingly then, censorship was considerable. What began as a simple policing of the auditorium quickly extended to direct censorship of the plays themselves: 'The most topical of all subject matter, the relationship between Church, state and individual human being . . . was the very subject matter which the whole machinery of censorship and control had been devised to license and suppress' (Wickham, II, 94). This suppression was actively ideological in the sense that it went far beyond simply forbidding the performance of controversial material; it was also designed to predetermine the nature of all drama. In order to get beyond the hostility of the City government, playhouses were built in the suburbs, areas which, interestingly enough, were noted for discontent, rioting and opposition to authority generally (see Valerie Pearl: *London and the Outbreak of the Puritan Revolution*, pp. 40–1). Henry Chettle, in 1591, describes the suburbs as 'no other but dark dens for adulterers, thieves, murderers and every mischief worker' (quoted in Pearl, p. 38). The Orders of the Privy Council present a similar picture of the theatres themselves; one, of 1600, asserts that plays were: '[the] dailie occasion of idle riotous and dissolute livinge of great numbers of people [who] leavinge all such honest and painefull Course of life, as they should followe, [meet at plays] and many particular abuses and disorders . . . doe thereupon ensue' (Chambers, *The Elizabethan Stage*, IV, 330). The authorities expressed particular anxiety when stage plays become an alternative to the church. There was here a double threat: not only were people abandoning what was then thought to be the principal institution of social discipline and control, they were frequenting instead an alternative which contradicted and challenged much of what it stood for.[19] Apprentices were often cited as a group most likely to be incited to seditious behaviour by play-going. One reason for this might be that they and servants were the two socio-economic groups most prone to vagrancy, a problem which increased massively in London between 1560 and 1625 (A. L. Beier, 'Social Problems in Elizabethan London', pp. 204, 214). The apprentices were indeed well known for their political activism and notorious for their rioting; according to Ann Jennalie Cook they rebelled at 'strangers who undercut the guild system, at farmers who charged exorbitant prices in hard times, at warders who imprisoned their fellows, at seats of privilege like the Inns of Court, at centres of costly pleasures like the brothels' (*The Privileged Playgoers of Shakespeare's London 1576–1642*, p. 258).[20]

Lastly, we should remember that the dramatists were actually imprisoned and otherwise harrassed by the State for staging plays thought to be seditious. *Pace* Astrophil, these writers wrote looking not into their hearts but over their shoulders. There is also evidence to the effect that the dramatists fell foul of the law outside as well as inside the theatre; sedition, atheism, homosexuality and espionage are among the charges made against them (Buckley, *Atheism in the English Renaissance*; Bray, *Homosexuality in Renaissance England*, especially pp. 54–7).

Given the censorship, it is not surprising that we find in the drama not simple denunciation of religious and political orthodoxy (though there is that too) so much as underlying subversion. As I shall show, this takes many forms including parody, dislocation and structural disjunction. Lest it be thought that all this is too abstract to be realised in the theatre, I will conclude with an example to indicate otherwise.[21]

Inversion and Misrule

In Jacobean tragedy court life is savage to an extent which outrageously contradicts its self-image as the 'fountain' of civility (*Duchess of Malfi*, I. i. 12). A remark of Flamineo's in *The White Devil* catches exactly what is involved: 'I visited the court, whence I return'd/More courteous, more lecherous by far' (I. ii. 315–16). Though divergent in meaning, 'lecherous' and 'courteous' are forced together through parallel syntax and ironic tonal control; formal balance and symmetry heighten rather than diminish the disjunction, the point being of course that the 'courteous' ideal is not just the cover for 'lecherous' practice but an inextricable part of it. A famous passage from Nashe's *The Unfortunate Traveller* provides an interesting comparison and a likely source:

> Italy, the paradise of the earth and the epicure's heaven, how doth it form our young master? . . . From thence he brings the art of atheism, the art of epicurising, the art of whoring, the art of poisoning, the art of sodomitry. The only probable good thing they have to keep us from utterly condemning it is that it maketh a man an excellent courtier, a curious carpet knight; which is, by interpretation, a fine close lecher, a glorious hypocrite. (p. 345)

Nashe elicits from the language an ironic quality in meaning similar to Webster's, and his way of qualifying 'courtier' with 'lecher' sufficiently resembles Webster's 'more-courteous, more lecherous' to be yet another instance of the latter's borrowing. (But if it is, it is also another instance of the way Webster transforms his sources; where Nashe's irony is pondered, Webster's is startlingly incisive.) Throughout Jacobean tragedy words like 'courteous' are forced into double and antithetical senses, becoming the pivotal points of an inversion working in terms of an interrogative irony. Certainly it is an irony which is dynamic and quite remote from the static formal ironic patterns which critics of this drama have so often charted. This can be seen even more clearly in the double inversion of masque and 'antic' or antimasque (in, for example, plays like *Antonio's Revenge* and *The Revenger's Tragedy*).

The masque was just one of several symbolic and ritualistic celebrations of royal power; others included royal progresses and their associated entertainments. As Stephen Orgel, Stuart Clark and Louis Montrose (among others) have shown, their capacity to legitimate the power structure was considerable.[22] The masque, a spectacular display of dance, mime and music, came eventually to include its inversion, the so-called antimasque. Preceding the main masque, it was performed by professionals and 'presented a world of disorder or vice, everything that the ideal world of the second, the courtly main masque, was to overcome and supersede' (Orgel, *The Illusion of Power*, p. 40). This was a time in which inversion signified in powerful and complex ways; in part this was because 'Contrariety was . . . a universal principle of intelligibility as well as a statement about how the world was actually constituted' (Clark, 'Inversion, Misrule and the Meaning of Witchcraft', p. 110). Ritualised inversion, especially the image of the world turned upside down, figured prominently in folkrites, carnival, festival and court celebrations: 'By "correspondence" it endowed acts of social disorder with a significance far beyond their immediate character, attributing to them repercussions in every other plane of "government"' (Clark, p. 111). The disorder in question took many forms but dealt especially with the reversal of relationships of authority, sexuality and status generally – for example women over men, father over son, subject over prince. Was such inversion reinforcing of the status quo – licensed misrule acting as the safety valve for social conflict and thus perpetuating the dominant order – or did it endanger it, stimulating rebellion? The answer is a socio-historical one: it could be either depending on occasion and context. That in certain circumstances it undoubtedly could be subversive is shown by among others Peter Burke, Natalie Zemon Davis and David Kunzle.[23]

The court masque was clearly an ideological legitimation of the power structure, as was the preliminary antimasque. Working in terms of the principle of contrariety, virtue (masque proper) is defined, initially, in terms of its opposite (antimasque). As James I put it: 'since the Devill is the very contrarie opposite of God, there can be no better way to know God, than by contrarie' (quoted in Clark, 'Witchcraft and Kingship', p. 175). As masque proper displaced the inversion of antimasque, it was typically the royal figure who was shown to be responsible for accomplishing this, restoring order and equilibrium analogically with God or even more directly as His delegate. In a play like *The Revenger's Tragedy*, however, all this is contradicted because of, and through, a process of double inversion: crucially, antimasque displaces masque rather than vice-versa. To begin with we see how the ideal masque is used as a front for, and is then dislocated by, the sexual brutality of the anti-masque; so, we are told 'Some courtiers in the masque,/Putting on better faces than their own,/Being full of fraud and flattery' rape the Duchess (I. iv. 28–30). Correspondingly and more generally, we see at the play's close how the ideal masque is merely an aesthetic, ritualised execution of antimasque violence. This is Vindice setting up the massacre of the final masque:

> Then, ent'ring first, observing the *true form*,
> Within a strain or two we shall find leisure
> To steal our swords out handsomely,
> And when they think their pleasure sweet and good,
> In midst of all their joys, they shall sigh blood.
>
> (V. ii. 18–22; my italics)

The priority of masque over antimasque is reversed in order finally to collapse the former into the latter, just as in Webster 'lecherous' is collapsed into 'courteous'. Thus the masque is being undermined at a metaphysical level, as a vehicle for providentialism and idealist mimesis, and also at the specifically political level at which it functioned as a ritualised, ideological legitimation of the court. In effect the drama disallows such legitimation: the court is shown as ineradicably corrupt and the aesthetic front which mystified its violent appropriation of power is ruptured from within – 'in midst' – by like violence.[24] Sometimes a kind of poetic justice emerges from the dramatic 'antic' masque, but only as perfunctory closure – that is, a *formal* restoration of providentialist/political orthodoxy, a compliance with its letter after having destroyed its spirit. In such ways does Jacobean tragedy ironically inscribe a subordinate viewpoint within a dominant one. A sub-literal encoding which bypasses the perfunctory surveillance of the censor, it cannot help but be reactivated in performance.

2

Emergence: Marston's *Antonio* Plays (c. 1599–1601) and Shakespeare's *Troilus and Cressida* (c. 1601–2)

Marston's *Antonio* plays show how individuals become alienated from their society. Bereaved, dispossessed, and in peril of their lives, they suffer extreme disorientation and are pushed to the very edge of mental collapse. Self-reintegration can only be achieved through social reintegration, the creation of a sub-culture dedicated to revenge: 'vengeance absolute' (*Antonio's Revenge*, III. ii. 75).

Running through Marston's dramatisation of this process are attitudes to human identity, to revenge and to providence which are radical: thus his protagonists are not defined by some spiritual or quasi-metaphysical essence, nor, even, a resilient human essence; rather, their identities are shown to be precariously dependent upon the social reality which confronts them. Correspondingly, revenge action is not a working out of divine vengeance,[1] but a strategy of survival resorted to by the alienated and dispossessed. Moreover, in that action is a rejection of the providential scheme which divine vengeance conventionally presupposed.

Antonio's Revenge is radical in yet another respect: it eschews the kind of structure which effaces conflict by *formally* resolving it; instead, the play's structure incorporates and intensifies the sense of social and political dislocation which is its subject.

In what follows I propose to substantiate this reading of Marston, primarily with reference to *Antonio's Revenge* (c. 1600–01), and then explore the extent to which *Troilus and Cressida* (c. 1601–02) shares these radical attitudes to identity, revenge and providence, and articulates them through a similar dramatic structure. If my analysis is correct, these two plays, despite their obvious and considerable differences, have thematic concerns and structural characteristics which are not only similar, but seminal for the development of Jacobean tragedy.

Discontinuous Identity (1)

Antonio and Mellida begins with a battle between two Dukes, Piero and Andrugio. Piero wins and Andrugio, together with his son Antonio, is banished. The experience of father and son is one of extreme alienation. They are estranged from family and society, stripped of their former identities, cast out and hunted under sentence of death. Initially they are separated, each believing the other to be dead; Andrugio laments the loss of everything: 'country, house, crown, son' (IV. i. 89).

Through the burlesque of Tamburlaine in the Induction a significant point is being made; Alberto tells Piero to

> . . . frame your exterior shape
> To haughty form of elate majesty
> *As if* you held the palsy-shaking head
> Of reeling chance under your fortune's belt
> In strictest vassalage;
>
> (7–11; my italics)

Tamburlaine's capacity to 'hold the Fates bound fast in iron chains,/And with my hand turn Fortune's wheel about' (Part I, I. ii. 174–5), is seen as exhilarating fiction, evoking legends of 'Hercules/Or burly Atlas' (18–19) but without the capacity to deceive: 'Who cannot be proud, stroke up the hair and strut?' (14). Such is the fictional aspiration of human kind but, for Andrugio and Antonio, the reality is different – they, in the words of the Prologue to *Antonio's Revenge*, are impotently 'Nail'd to the earth with grief . . . /Pierc'd through with anguish' (ll. 22–3). Being nailed to the earth with grief[2] is inextricably bound up with the despairing knowledge of 'what men were, and are,/ . . . what men must be' (ll. 18–19). I shall come back to *Antonio's Revenge* after further consideration of *Antonio and Mellida*, which anticipates the themes of the later play.

Alienation and grief generate a confusion which is so intense that it threatens Antonio's sanity and brings his very identity into question. In a delirious soliloquy he tells himself: 'Antonio's lost;/He cannot find himself, not seize himself' (IV. i. 2–3; cf. IV. i. 102–5, and *Antonio's Revenge*, IV. i. 229). Andrugio's way of responding to all this is to attempt a posture of stoical independence and self-sufficiency:

> . . . There's nothing left
> Unto Andrugio, but Andrugio;
> And that nor mischief, force, distress, nor hell can take.
> Fortune my fortunes, not my mind shall shake
>
> (III. i. 59–62)

In this play stoicism is an attempt to redefine oneself solely from within, to reconstitute one's sense of self by withdrawing from the social reality which has threatened it. As such it is a position precariously attained and incapable of being maintained; attitudes of stoical resistance simply break down. The characters of this play attempt to disengage themselves from hostile circumstance but cannot; they internalise the confusions and contradictions of their world, becoming themselves confused and contradictory. Faced with a dislocated world, individual consciousness itself becomes dislocated.

The serious dramatic and philosophical intention I am attributing to Marston is entirely compatible with his attraction to parody and melodrama. Parody was a complex dramatic process for the Jacobeans, not merely a source of comic effect. By the time of the appearance of these plays stoical endurance had been memorably embodied in such figures as Kyd's Hieronimo and Shakespeare's Titus. A philosophical attitude had become a stage convention. Marston, through parody, undermines the convention and so discredits the attitude. First, there is the self-conscious, sardonic distrust of stage convention as an adequate representation of the experience and the reality which it claims to represent (see especially IV. ii. 69–76 – discussed below); second, there is distrust of the sufficiency of stoicism as a philosophy of mind; *contemptus mundi* and stoic *apathia* are no longer possible responses: individuals may want to be independent of their society but they cannot be: like it or not, they are inextricably 'nailed' to it.

This theme is epitomised in the instability and ambivalence of

Feliche. In Act III we see him scorning Castilio's social vanity from a position of stoical superiority (III. ii. 41ff). Within moments his resolve shatters under the pressure of his own insecurity: 'Confusion seize me . . ./Why should I not be sought to then as well?' Andrugio, under the pressure of different but equally contradictory experiences, undergoes a similar collapse (IV. i. 46–70).

In *Antonio's Revenge* the probing of stoicism, as both attitude and convention, is more searching. In the opening scenes we learn that Andrugio and Feliche have been murdered. It now falls to Pandulpho, Feliche's father, to take up the role of stoic hero. Again, stoicism is in opposition to 'passion'. Pandulpho begins by rejecting the latter, together with its typically hyperbolic mode of expression:

> Would'st have me cry, run raving up and down
> For my son's loss? Would'st have me turn rank mad,
> Or wring my face with mimic action,
> Stamp, curse, weep, rage, and then my bosom strike?
> Away, 'tis apish action, player-like.
>
> (I. ii. 312–16)

Notably, it is the theatrical convention, as well as the experience, which is being repudiated: passion is a kind of dramatic posturing.

Pandulpho's stoic resolve lays claim to a perfect transcendence of the event, a spiritual resolution of suffering which is beyond the event:

> If he [Feliche] is guiltless, why should tears be spent?
> Thrice blessed soul that dieth innocent.
> . . .
> The gripe of chance is weak to wring a tear
> From him that knows what fortitude should bear.
>
> (I. ii. 317–18; 321–2)

When we next encounter Pandulpho his stoicism is even stronger. Piero attempts to corrupt him but cannot and so, in fury, banishes him instead;

> Piero   Tread not in court! All that thou hast I seize.
>   [aside] His quiet's firmer than I can disease.

> *Pandulpho*   Loose fortune's rags are lost; my own's my own.
>   'Tis true, Piero; thy vex'd heart shall see
>   Thou hast but tripp'd my slave, not conquer'd me.
>   (II. i. 166–72)

'Slave' according to Hunter is 'the merely physical and temporal aspects of Pandulpho'; so, the basis of his stoicism is transcendence of the temporal, and its corollary, a duality of mind and body: 'The earth's my body's, and the heaven's my soul's/Most native place of birth' (II. i. 158–9). Thereafter Pandulpho disappears until Act IV, scene ii, where he again preaches fortitude to Antonio. In short, his command of self in the face of the 'grief' and 'anguish' which the Prologue described, appears total.

Suddenly however the resolve shatters; his philosophy of noble transcendence is rejected outright:

> *Pandulpho*   Man will break out, despite philosophy.
>   Why, all this while I ha' but play'd a part,
>   Like to some boy that acts a tragedy,
>   Speaks burly words and raves out passion;
>   But when he thinks upon his infant weakness,
>   He droops his eye. I spake more than a god,
>   Yet am less than a man.
>   (IV. ii. 69–76)

What is being rejected here is the Christian-stoic view of man as capable of defining himself from within, independently of the world in which he lives and which acts upon him. Try as he might, Pandulpho was unable to find the spiritual essence which would sustain him in the face of grief and, ultimately, enable him to transcend it altogether. He acknowledges the soul to be earthbound after all: 'I am the miserablest *soul* that *breathes*' (IV. ii. 76; my italics). Earlier Pandulpho had repudiated passion as 'mimic action', favouring instead the authentic state of stoic resolve. Now stoicism itself is similarly rejected as a kind of dramatic posturing.

Antonio's attitude to suffering is very different; he wants to confront rather than withdraw (stoically) from it, to be revenged on the world rather than passively endure it:

> Confusion to all comfort! I defy it.
> Comfort's a parasite, a flatt'ring Jack,

And melts resolv'd despair.

(I. ii. 284–6)

At II. ii. 47ff he reads from, only to reject, Seneca's *De Providentia* (VI. 6). It is, he says, a philosophy inadequate to the reality of his position. Antonio has known all along that there is no inner self into which one can withdraw; disorientation penetrates the whole self simply because 'grief's invisible/And lurks in secret angles of the heart' (II. ii. 71–2). He endures this grief by translating it into action, into an active search for reintegration. And by IV. ii he realises that the only path to that reintegration is through the role of revenger.

The moment when Pandulpho's resolve suddenly breaks is central for understanding attitudes to identity and the psychology of revenge in Jacobean tragedy. Let us reconsider what has led to this moment: *Antonio's Revenge* first of all dramatises the way that dislocation in the world generates dislocation in consciousness. 'Grief' and all that it stands for in terms of estrangement, alienation, and disorientation threatens not just the individual's capacity to survive the world, *but his very identity within it.* Pandulpho's stoic strategy proved unsuccessful as a way of coping with this because it posited a non-existent autonomous realm of being. And so he too turns to revenge: it enables him to regain his identity, to resist disintegration through a purposeful – albeit violent – re-engagement with the society which has displaced him. Antonio speaks for Pandulpho and a generation of revengers when he translates his misery into revenge; he is, he says, 'The wrack of splitted fortune. the very ooze,/The quicksand that devours all misery'. But, he adds,

> For all this, I dare live, and I will live,
> Only to numb some others' cursed blood
> With the dead palsy of like misery.

(IV. ii. 15–20)

Suddenly we understand his attitude of 'resolv'd despair' (I. ii. 286):

> We must be stiff and steady in *resolve.*

(IV. ii. 109; my italics)

> *Resolved hearts* . . . Steel your thoughts, sharp your
> *resolve,* embolden your spirit . . .
> (V. ii. 79–81; my italics)

In *Antonio and Mellida* reintegration, of self, and of self with
society, is achieved artificially through the play's tragicomic denouement; the main characters confer familial identity upon each other
(V. ii. 225–9) and after being further consolidated by 'wedlock'
(l. 255), their harmony is complete: 'Now there remains no discord
that can sound/Harsh accents to the ear of our accord' (ll. 251–2).
By contrast, in *Antonio's Revenge*, reintegration is achieved through
a resolve which derives from a vengeful commitment which is itself
conditional upon brutalisation: 'pity, piety, remorse,/Be alien to our
thoughts' (V. iii. 89–90). Antonio and the others shake off the
'dead palsy' (IV. ii. 20) which has afflicted them, creating a new
intimacy among themselves, an intimacy which becomes the basis
of a ritualistically confirmed counter-culture:

> Lets thus our hands, our hearts, our arms involve.
> *They wreathe their arms.*
> (IV. ii. 110)

Antonio [To Pandulpho]: Give me thy hand, and thine, most noble heart;
Thus will we live and, but thus, never part.
> *Exeunt twin'd together*
> (V. ii. 88–9)

*

Central to the theatre of Bertolt Brecht is a rejection of the notion
that human nature is unalterable and eternally fixed. Brecht associates this concept of man with what he calls bourgeois or
'Aristotelian' theatre; it erroneously assumes 'that people are what
they are, and will remain so whatever it costs society or themselves:
"indestructibly human"' (*Brecht on Theatre*, p. 235). It further
assumed that the eternally human, precisely because it is eternal,
can be understood independently of man's environment (pp.
96–7). In challenging these assumptions Brecht is, of course, following the fundamental Marxist proposition that human consciousness is determined by social being (p. 250) rather than the
converse. Brecht has said of Baal, the nihilistic, anti-social 'hero' of

the play of that name: 'he is anti-social [*asozial*] but in an anti-social society' (*Gesammelte Werke*, 17.947). *Antonio's Revenge* likewise shows how identity, not just survival, is dependent upon social being, how alienation dislocates consciousness, how individuals reachieve identity by purposefully re-engaging with society – albeit at the cost of brutalisation.

Providence and Natural Law (1)

For Pandulpho, the impossibility of stoic resolve is inseparable from his rejection of the stoic's conception of providence and natural law:

> . . . all the strings of nature's symphony
> Are crack'd and jar . . .
> . . . there's no music in the breast of man . . .
>
> (IV. ii. 92–4)

G. D. Aggeler observes that in the speech from which these lines are taken, 'Pandulpho is rejecting a belief that underlies all of stoic moral doctrine, the belief in the rationality of Nature. According to the stoics, God imparted a rational design to the decrees of Fate which govern Nature.' Pandulpho has realised the falseness of the stoic doctrine that man 'need only adhere to the dictates of right reason and he will be in harmony with a divinely and beneficently ordered scheme' ('Stoicism and Revenge in Marston', p. 511). It is the absence of such a scheme which encourages relativism in morality:

> Most things that morally adhere to souls
> Wholly exist in drunk opinion,
> Whose reeling censure, if I value not,
> It values nought.
>
> (IV. i. 31–4)

Suffering is not explained with reference to a wider moral order because none is available; man is 'confounded in a maze of mischief,/ Stagger'd, stark fell'd with bruising stroke of chance' (IV. i. 56–7).

There are, however, several references to heaven as a providential force. The first important example occurs in Antonio's description of the 'prodigies' he has seen. Viewing these, he says:

I bow'd my naked knee and pierc'd the star
With an outfacing eye, pronouncing thus:
Deus imperat astris.

(I. ii. 121–4)

'God rules the stars': but does He? In the Christian tradition the stars were the instruments of Fortune while Fortune itself was under God's control. Antonio here reassures himself with an orthodoxy in which he later loses faith. Mellida similarly reassures herself of God's providential control: 'Heaven permits not taintless blood be spilt' (IV. i. 151). The death of the innocent Julio, already witnessed, gives the lie to this piety, and Mellida's own death is to follow. In fact, by the time she dies, we are more inclined to see Fortune as a force independent of, not subordinate to, divine order. Everywhere Fortune is evoked to explain catastrophe and suffering; nowhere does anything occur that could be seen as the intervention of a beneficent deity. Antonio envisages 'His epitaph thus: *Ne plus ultra* [nothing beyond]' (II. ii. 133). Further, both Piero and Strotzo ideologically exploit, for purposes of tyranny, the Christian idea of a deity administering retributive justice:

Strotzo   Supreme Efficient,
            Why Cleav'st thou not my breast with thunderbolts
            Of wing'd revenge?
Piero   Why, art not great of thanks
            To gracious heaven for the just revenge
            Upon the author of thy obloquies?

(IV. i. 159–161; 214–16)

In the final sadistic revenge sequence, retributive providence and secular revenge are forcibly conjoined:

Andrugio   Now down looks providence
            T'attend the last act of my son's revenge.

(V. i. 10–11)

This and other references like it (cf. V. ii. 30, V. iii. 67–8, and especially V. iii. 108–9) constitute perhaps the most problematic aspect of the play. Obviously there is no conceivable way that Christian teaching could condone such revenge. It is true that providence was thought to operate through evil agents, that God would use the sinful to destroy the sinful. Yet here Antonio and his accomplices not only survive, but are held in high esteem socially for what they have done.

We have to acknowledge that the fervid commitment to 'vengeance absolute' involves an ethic totally at odds with the religious absolute; *Antonio's Revenge* forces them into an open disjunction, stressing the fact that the one contravenes the other in a deadly serious challenge to conventional providentialist dogma as it related to revenge. Providence has been discovered to be inoperative in a dislocated world where men struggle for secular power. Antonio and his accomplices overcome their alienation by uniting as the bereaved and dispossessed and creating a sub-culture dedicated to violent revenge. As revengers, far from being the instruments of divine providence, they subversively arrogate its retributive function:

Ghost of Andrugio	I taste the joys of heaven, Viewing my son triumph in his black blood.
Antonio	Thus the hand of heaven chokes The throat of murder. This for my father's blood!

(V. iii. 67–8; 108–9)

In thematic and theatrical terms the whole scene involves a process of ritual inversion: the marriage ceremony becomes a sadistic execution, the religious absolute is violated by 'vengeance absolute', the masque by a kind of antic- or antimasque, the decorum of the dance ('The Measure', V. iii. 49 S.D.) by the ritual torture of Piero: '*They offer to run all at* Piero, *and on a sudden stop*' (V. iii. 105 S.D.).

The entire scene adds up to a subversion of providentialist orthodoxy. As William R. Elton has demonstrated in an important study, the Elizabethan–Jacobean period witnessed 'the skeptical disintegration of providential belief' (*King Lear and the Gods*, p. 335). This scene instances that disintegration, together with the dramatic structure appropriate for its expression. To understand that structure we need to see it in an historical context. The formal coherence of the morality play reflected the coherence of the metaphysical doctrine which was its principal subject. Disorder and suffering are finally rendered meaningful through faith in, and experience of, a providential order. As Everyman puts it: God is a 'glorious fountain that all uncleanness doth clarify' (*Everyman*, 1. 545). The best morality plays are anything but flatly didactic; they confront, experientially, some of the deepest religious paradoxes. Nevertheless, they are paradoxes which are articulated through, and contained by, the same formal pattern: human kind exists in the shadow of original sin; we fall, suffer, and eventually repent; there is usually a relapse, incurring despair, before a secure recovery to redemption.

In Jacobean tragedy, the rejection of metaphysical harmony provokes the rejection of aesthetic harmony and the emergence of a new dialectic structure. Coherence comes to reside in the sharpness of definition given *to* metaphysical and social dislocation, not in an aesthetic, religious or didactic resolution *of* it. Thus the alternative to such resolution is not necessarily 'irresolution' in the sense of intending, yet failing to dispose of contradictions. On the contrary, it may be that contradictory accounts of experience are forced into 'misalignment', the tension which this generates being a way of getting us to confront the problematic and contradictory nature of society itself.

So it is that in the final scene of *Antonio's Revenge* Marston subverts the dramatic conventions which embody a providentialist perspective. In particular, the forced conjunction of the contradictory absolutes – secular and divine revenge – generates an internal strain which only stresses their actual disjunction.

In this period the two themes which I have been exploring – the rejection of Christian-stoic accounts of identity and the subversion of providentialist orthodoxy – were inextricably linked: the sense that reality can no longer be adequately explained in terms of an in-forming absolute goes hand in hand with the realisation that subjectivity is not constituted by a fixed, unchanging essence. Thus, for Montaigne,

> . . . *there is no constant existence, neither of our being nor of the objects* [of experience]. And we, and our judgement, and all mortall things else do uncessantly rowle, turne and passe away.

Moreover,

We have no communication with being; for every humane nature is ever in the middle between being borne and dying; giving nothing of itselfe but an obscure apparence and shadow, and an uncertaine and weake opinion. And if perhaps you fix your thought to take its being; it would be even, as if one should go about to grasp the water: for, how much the more he shal close and presse that, which by its owne nature is ever gliding, so much the more he shall loose what he would hold and fasten. (*Essays*, II, 323)

Discontinuous Identity (2)

Shakespeare, like Marston, explores the way in which the disintegrating effects of grief are resisted not through Christian or stoic renunciation of society, but a commitment to revenge – a vengeful re-engagement with the society and those responsible for that grief. As in Marston, it is a society which has fallen into radical disharmony.

Once Troilus has witnessed what he sees as Cressida's betrayal he cannot again be the same person. Shattered idealism finds concentrated expression in disjunction: 'O beauty! Where is thy faith?' (V. ii. 66). Like Antonio he is brought to the edge of mental collapse (V. ii. 137ff) and, again like Antonio, he resists the grief by taking on the role of revenger. Even his explanation for doing so is like Antonio's: 'Hope of revenge shall hide our inward woe' (V. x. 31). Troilus insists on going out to fight the final battle even though Hector tries to dissuade him. Hector thinks Troilus too young to die but Troilus scorns his concern:

> Let's leave the hermit Pity with our mother;
> . . . venom'd vengeance ride upon our swords.
>
> (V. iii. 45 and 47)

To which Hector replies: 'Fie, savage, fie!' Savage indeed, but that is exactly what Troilus has become.

The fate of Troilus is an ironic refutation of Agamemnon's account of 'grief' (I. iii. 2) and its 'bracing' effect on identity. He argues that the Greeks' misfortunes have been

> . . . nought else
> But the protractive trials of great Jove
> To find persistive constancy in men . . .
>
> (I. iii. 19–21)

'Distinction', he adds,

> Puffing at all, winnows the light away,
> And what hath mass or matter by itself
> Lies rich in virtue and unmingled.

(I. iii. 28–30)

To endure misfortune is to reveal one's true self – a pure essence of *virtus* – and, simultaneously, to discover that the universe is significantly ordered.

What happens to Troilus is exactly the opposite: misfortune brutalises him. He must depend for his identity and survival not on a stoic inner virtue but, quite simply, on his society; moreover what his society is, he ultimately becomes: 'savage'. In a sense then Troilus *has* become exactly what Agamemnon's true man, tempered by misfortune, should become: a 'thing of courage' which 'As rous'd with rage, with rage doth sympathise,/And with an accent tun'd in selfsame key' (I. iii. 52–3). This intensifies the irony, especially if we recall that, at the very outset of the play, Troilus – anxious, self-regarding, but in love – could dismiss the warmongers as 'Fools on both sides' (I. i. 89). Now he is one of them, lover turned savage warrior, a thing of courage to whom mercy is 'a vice' (V. iii. 37). Ulysses describes him in action:

> Troilus . . . hath done today
> Mad and fantastic execution,
> Engaging and redeeming of himself
> With such a careless force and forceless care . . .

(V. v. 37–40)

Troilus has acquitted himself as an adult by becoming an 'heroic warrior'. Alternatively we might understand him thus: a thwarted lover rescues himself from his own vulnerability by acting out a savage revenge (cf. *Antonio's Revenge*, V. iii. 89–90). In short, we see in both *Antonio's Revenge* and *Troilus and Cressida* the way that sensitive people brutalise themselves in order to survive in a brutal world. The irony, or rather the tragedy, lies in the fact that, in so doing, they earn the esteem of their society.

Providence and Natural Law (2)

Troilus, in V. ii., is thrust into confrontation with a world which contradicts his, and others', idealisation of it. His description of macrocosmic chaos is more than just a metaphorical declaration of his own disorientation. For Troilus to 'suffer into truth' is not to achieve tragic insight but rather to internalise the sense of contradiction which defines his world:

> Within my soul there doth conduce a fight
> Of this strange nature, that a thing inseparate
> Divides more wider than the sky and earth
> . . .
> The bonds of heaven are slipp'd, dissolv'd and loos'd.
>
> (V. ii. 145–7 and 154)

The scene is the climax of a play which, like *Antonio's Revenge*, not only disposes of the myth of a resilient human essence, but relentlessly undermines the related myth that the universe is providentially governed. This particular speech shows, again, how in this period the two issues were inseparable.

The setting of the play precluded a too explicitly Christianised form of providentialism. Instead Shakespeare uses natural law, the appropriate 'pagan' equivalent of Christian providentialism and, of course, one of its major sources. Briefly, natural law conceives of the universe as 'encoded' in creation with order, value and purpose. Man, in virtue of his rational capacity, synchronises with this teleological design and discovers within it the main principles of his own moral law. Richard Hooker was the most celebrated Elizabethan exponent of such law; he combines with it a version of Christian providentialism which was, arguably, the most persuasive ever.[3]

Troilus and Cressida has two prolonged philosophical debates, one in the Greek camp, primarily on order, the other in the Trojan camp, primarily on value. The main speech in each debate (by Ulysses and Hector respectively) embraces natural law and parallels quite closely passages from Hooker's *Laws*. Ulysses' famous 'degree' speech concentrates on hierarchical order in the universe and in human society: 'degree, priority, and place, . . /in all line of order'

(I. iii. 86 and 88). Without order 'That by a pace goes backward, with a purpose/It hath to climb' (I. iii. 128–9). Hector, in affirming the existence of 'moral laws/Of nature and of nations' (II. ii. 184–5), captures the other essential tenet of natural law: human law derives from the pre-existent laws of nature; human kind discovers rather than makes social law.

Both of these appeals to natural law are contradicted elsewhere within the speeches in which they occur, and, moreover, by the play in virtually every respect. Thus Ulysses claims that order is encoded in nature yet simultaneously concedes that society is disordered and the universe in a state of incipient chaos. Additionally, there is a strong relativist tendency in Ulysses' speech which runs exactly counter to the objectivism of natural law.[4] Hector invokes in some detail the apparatus of natural law only to advocate action which flatly contradicts it (II. ii. 189–93). Further, in place of hierarchical order there exist disintegration and chaos, and instead of intrinsic purpose, 'checks and disasters' which

> Grow in the veins of actions highest rear'd,
> As knots, by the conflux of meeting sap,
> Infects the sound pine, and diverts his grain
> Tortive and errant from his course of growth.
>
> (I. iii. 5–9)

The play is pervaded with imagery of this kind, again suggesting that in Nature itself there is something which runs directly counter to the teleological harmony and integration of natural law. Nature is presented as self-stultifying or paralysed by dislocated energies. The 'Tortive and errant . . . growth' seems self-generated, and thwarted effort the consequence of effort itself:

> He that is proud eats up himself.
>
> (II. iii. 150)

> O madness of discourse,
> That cause sets up with and against itself!
>
> (V. ii. 140–1)

In the ultimate state of chaos envisaged by Ulysses 'Each thing melts/In mere oppugnancy' (I. iii. 110–11); everything is reduced to 'Force' (l. 116) which becomes increasingly self-stultifying and ultimately self-consuming:

> Then everything includes itself in power,
> Power into will, will into appetite;
> And appetite, an universal wolf,
> So doubly seconded with will and power,
> Must make perforce an universal prey,
> And last eat up himself.
>
> (I. iii. 119–24)

Disjunctions of this kind are central to the play's structure and, in this connection, Richard D. Fly has usefully analysed his sense of the play's 'imminent and radical chaos' in terms of its imitative form – that is, the 'disjunction in the plot, discontinuity in the scenario, inconsistency in characterization, dissonance, redundancy [and] lack of emphatic closure and resolution in Act V' ('Suited in Like Conditions', p. 291). Fly implies that chaos and 'universal cataclysm' (p. 291) is the play's final 'vision'. But there is much more happening. To the extent that it posits an underlying, primordial state of dislocation, the language of chaos mystifies social process. To the extent that it interrogates providentialist belief – robbing the absolute of its mystifying function – it foregrounds social process.

Ideology and the Absolute

Lukács has said: 'The absolute is nothing but the fixation of thought, it is the projection into myth of the intellectual failure to understand reality concretely as a historical process' (*History and Class Consciousness*, p. 187). Lukács' perspective was not Shakespeare's but a similar conception of the absolute was available to the Renaissance. More strategically than nihilistically, *Troilus and Cressida* exploits disjunction and 'chaos' to promote critical awareness of both the mystifying language of the absolute and the social reality which it occludes. We are for example compelled by the apparent fact of chaos to think critically about the way characters repeatedly make fatalistic appeals to an extra-human reality or force: natural law, Jove, Chance, Time and so on. Philosophically all of these are very different from each other but experientially they seem interchangeable: in effect they all serve to legitimate fatalistic misrecognition. Consider for example the 'fate' of Troilus and Cressida's love.

It is customary to see this love as destroyed by Time. For Troilus, initially, the cause is nothing less than divine interference:

> Cressid, I love thee in so strain'd a purity,
> That the bless'd gods, as angry with my fancy,
> More bright in zeal than the devotion which
> Cold lips blow to their deities, take thee from me.
>
> (IV. iv. 23–6)

Moments later he blames not the gods but 'Injurious Time' (i. 42). From the point of view of fatalistic misrecognition the one is as effective as the other; both the 'gods' and 'Time' obscure from Troilus as well as Cressida his own passive complicity in the sacrifice of love to political expediency (Cressida is of course being exchanged for Antenor).

Here and throughout the play Time functions as a surrogate universal. It cannot confer universal meaning and value – indeed in one sense it actually erodes them. Yet by doing just that it retains in negative form a crucial attribute of the universal: the certainty which legitimates fatalism:

> *Hector*   . . . The end crowns all,
>   And that old common arbitrator, Time,
>   Will one day end it.
> *Ulysses.*   So to him we leave it.
>
> (IV. v. 224–7)

(Cf. *Henry IV* (Part II), III. ii. 343: 'Let time shape, and there an end.') Such is the rationalisation, by two of its most powerful antagonists, of deadlocked combat. Moments before, we have witnessed a similar exchange in the meeting between Agamemnon and Hector; as they embrace, Agamemnon declares:

> Understand more clear,
> What's past and what's to come is strew'd with husks
> And formless ruin of oblivion;

> But in this extant moment, faith and troth,
> Strain'd purely from all hollow bias-drawing,
> Bids thee, with most divine integrity,
> From heart of very heart, great Hector, welcome.

(IV. v. 164–70)

Conciliation is (literally?) within Agamemnon's grasp. Yet he dissociates 'this extant moment' from the political imperatives of the occasion, construing it instead as almost a transcendent moment out of time. By thus handing over history to Time he divests himself of political will ('hollow bias drawing') and affirms instead his 'divine integrity' – divine because like the moment it is 'strain'd purely'. As used here integrity has no implications for future behaviour but rather denotes a static 'uncorrupted moral state' (*OED*).

With a teleology unique to itself, Time moves all through transience and decay into the formless ruins of oblivion, the reassuring, negative unity of universal formlessness. Time becomes a surrogate universal that confers the hollow structure of certainty on a society which has lost its *raison d'être* in terms of praxis. Time is, in effect, an idealist deformation: not the universal which confirms the integration of meaning, purpose, and identity, but a surrogate which mystifies and occludes the fact of their loss.

From those other instances of this play's tendency to use disjunction to subvert the ideology of war, two must suffice. First there is the contradiction between 'humane' gentleness and martial honour:

> *Aeneas:*   . . . In humane gentleness,
>   Welcome to Troy . . . I swear,
>   No man alive can love in such a sort
>   The thing he means to kill, more excellently.
> *Diomedes:* We sympathise. Jove, let Aeneas live,
>   If to my sword his fate be not the glory.

(IV. i. 22–3; 24–8)

As Paris observes:

> This is the most despiteful'st gentle greeting,
> The noblest hateful love, that e'er I heard of.

(IV. i. 34–5)

Second there is the insistence that all of those things which the martial ideology mystifies as the innate attributes of the outstanding warrior are, in fact, socially conferred and also socially dependent:

> no man is the lord of anything –
> Though in and of him there be much consisting –
> Till he communicate his parts to others;
> Nor doth he of himself know them for aught
> Till he behold them formed in th'applause
> Where th'are extended
>
>   (III. iii. 115–20)

Social Contradiction and Discontinuous Identity

One effect of the notorious discontinuity of 'character' in Jacobean tragedy is to make it virtually impossible to telescope the implications of all this back into the individual, thereby seeing it as ultimately a question of his or her moral culpability. Collectively the inhabitants of the world of *Troilus and Cressida* are responsible for a war and the ideology which legitimates and thereby perpetuates it; individually they are more or less powerless to escape either the war or its ideology. (By 'more or less' we must understand a difference of degree rather than kind, but a very important one nevertheless.) Consider in this respect the case of Cressida.

Her seduction by Diomedes is clever and callous. Alternatively abrupt, pressing and indifferent, it plays on an insecurity endemic to Cressida's *position* as a woman in a brutally male dominated society, and now exacerbated by her social displacement. It is an insecurity which gives rise to a conflict in allegiance:

> *Diomedes*: But will you, then?
> *Cressida*:   In faith, I will, lo; never trust me else.
>
>   (V. ii. 57–8)

Infidelity to Troilus and the society she has left is to be a test of trustworthiness to Diomedes and the society she has been compelled to join. Such is the contradiction which characterises her position now and, soon, her identity – something which Troilus suggests after he has witnessed the seduction: 'This is, and is not, Cressid' (V. ii. 144). In a very real sense Cressida internalises the contradiction of the war itself. She tells Diomedes: 'Ay, come – O Jove! Do come – I shall be plagu'd' (V. ii. 102). It is half submission, half an undirected, imploring plea for help. Refused that help and left *alone* Cressida makes her own fatalistic rationalisation of the submission: 'Ah, poor our sex! This fault in us I find,/The error of our eye directs our mind' (V. ii. 107–8). By concurring with the powerful and dominant myth of female 'frailty', Cressida makes ideological 'sense' of sudden dislocation and dispossession. But *Troilus and Cressida* makes available a counter-perspective: the discontinuity in Cressida's identity stems not from her nature but from her position in the patriarchical order.[5] We might remember in this connection that the object of Troilus's provocative assertion of relativism – 'What's aught but as 'tis valued? (II. ii. 52) – is Helen, who also has a mythical identity; it is a complex male construct to legitimate the war:

> a theme of honour and renown,
> A spur to valiant and magnanimous deeds,
> Whose present courage may beat down our foes.
>
> (II ii. 199–201)

The identification of Helen changes of course depending on the position of those identifying her and their reasons for so doing.

The conflicting estimates of Cressida's actual worth indicate what is so frequently the case: the position of the subordinate becomes contradictory when there occurs a power struggle in the dominant. Identity is a function of position, and position of power; to be the object of power is also to be in part its effect. This is why even before her displacement Cressida conceives herself not only as subordinate to maleness but also obscurely derivative of it (she is speaking to Troilus):

> I wish'd myself a man,
> Or that we women had men's privilege
> Of speaking first . . .
> I have a kind of self resides with you;
> But an unkind self, that it self will leave
> To be another's fool.
>
> (III. ii. 124–6; 144–6)

Cressida, like Webster's protagonists, can her fate foresee but not prevent.

Renaissance Man versus Decentred Malcontent

Central to the development of essentialist humanism is a view of tragedy which sees it almost exclusively in terms of man's defeated potential. But it is a kind of defeat which actually confirms the potential. Perhaps this is the significance of 'tragic waste': the forces destructive of life (fate, fortune, the gods or whatever) paradoxically pressure it into its finest expression in the events which lead to, and especially those which immediately precede, the protagonist's death. In one sense what is being identified is a potential somehow passively realised in its very defeat. We see, for example, protagonists learning wisdom through suffering, willing to know and endure their fate even as it destroys them. It may be that the individual, in virtue of a 'tragic flaw', is partly responsible for his or her suffering. Even so, the extent of that suffering is usually disproportionate to the weakness (hubris, passion, ambition or whatever); to this extent the individual is more sinned against than sinning, and his or her potential is finally reaffirmed in a capacity to suffer with more than human fortitude: 'There is a grace on mortals who so nobly die.' Additionally the protagonist's potential may be realised in a sacrificial sense, death leading to regeneration of the community and, perhaps, of the universe.

None of this is the case with the early seventeenth-century tragedy considered here: Antonio, Pandulpho and Troilus are 'heroes' who lack that essentialist self-sufficiency (Christian or stoic) which is the source of the individual's tragic potential in the foregoing view of tragedy (the discrepancy between myth and actuality which identifies Hector, Ulysses and Achilles indicates that they too lack traditional heroic potential). Antonio, Pandulpho and Troilus internalise rather than transcend the violence of their society, being incapable of surviving its alienating effects except by re-engaging with it – the first two as kinds of terrorist-revengers, the third as a warrior revenger. By contrast, the customary death of the tragic hero can seem mystifying; a greatness which has been established and then questioned is suddenly reaffirmed by being put *beyond* question. It is sometimes offered as the profound paradox of tragedy: in defeat and death 'man' finds his apotheosis. Alternatively, we might see it thus: through mystifying closure tragic death works to evade tragic insight, by cancelling the question 'with such knowledge, what can he done?'

In *Antonio's Revenge* and *Troilus and Cressida* we find the prototypes of the contradictory Jacobean anti-hero: malcontented – often because bereaved or dispossessed – satirical, and vengeful; at once agent and victim of social corruption, condemning yet simultaneously contaminated by it; made up of inconsistencies and contradictions which, because they cannot be understood in terms of individuality alone, constantly pressure attention outwards to the social conditions of existence. The Jacobean malcontent can in turn be seen as a prototype of the modern decentred subject, the bearer of a subjectivity which is not the antithesis of social process but its focus, in particular the focus of political, social, and ideological contradiction.

I have argued that the attack on Christian providentialism in Jacobean tragedy is inseparable from this effect of decentring 'man'. Taken together, attack and effect comprise nothing less than a subversion of Christian humanism.

PART II

STRUCTURE, MIMESIS, PROVIDENCE

3

Structure: From Resolution to Dislocation

In his analysis of Anglo-American literary criticism John Fekete has identified what he sees as its fundamental preoccupation, namely:

> A questioning of all forms of objectivity in relation to a *telos* of harmonic integration . . . The central problematic of the tradition is structured by questions of unity and equilibrium, of order and stability. From the beginning, but increasing systematically, the tradition embraces the 'whole' and structures a totality without struggle and historical movement. (*The Critical Twilight*, p. 195)

In this chapter I propose to look first at this tradition's[1] mediation of Jacobean tragedy, second at an alternative, almost entirely ignored yet far more productive critical perspective deriving from Brecht. I propose Brecht as the crucial link between Jacobean drama and the contemporary materialist criticism – first, because he was closely involved with adapting that drama (especially plays by Marlowe, Shakespeare and Webster), acknowledging in the process that it was a formative influence on his own work;[2] second, because Brecht anticipated most of the important issues in materialistic critical theory.

Bradley[3]

No theory of tragedy has been more influential for interpreting the drama of the early seventeenth century than A. C. Bradley's. Rejection of his speculative character analysis in Shakespeare has tended to obscure the extent to which Bradley's metaphysic of tragedy has remained dominant.

Bradley denied that the ultimate power in the tragic universe could be adequately described in terms of Christian providentialism (*Shakespearean Tragedy*, pp. 26, 278–9, 325). Nevertheless he insists that such a power does exist, and, in effect, he recuperates the fundamental metaphysical tenets of providentialism in a theory which blends mystical intuition with an etiolated version of the Hegelian dialectic. So, for Bradley, tragedy gestures constantly towards – even though it can never fully reveal – an ultimate order of things, an order monistic and mystical, beyond the realm of language, rooted in paradox and accessible only as 'a presentiment, formless but haunting and even profound' (p. 38). But to the extent that the ultimate force of the tragic universe is on the side of good and antagonistic to evil, it can still be described as moral (p. 33). Tragedy is a movement through massive cosmic eruption – 'the self division and intestinal warfare of the ethical substance, not so much the war of good with evil as the war of good with good' (*Oxford Lectures*, p. 71) – to a final Hegelian reconciliation; tragic catastrophe is 'the violent self-restitution of the divided spiritual unity' (p. 91). Thus even in the bleakest of tragedies, *King Lear*, we are left with neither depression nor despair but 'a sense of law and beauty . . . a consciousness of greatness in pain, and of solemnity in the mystery we cannot fathom' (*Shakespearean Tragedy*, p. 279).[4] This sense of tragedy as 'piteous, fearful and mysterious' (p. 25) is something Bradley comes back to time and again (e.g. pp. 23, 30, 38 and 325).

In Bradley the conceptual apparatus of continental metaphysics is largely dispensed with and the metaphysical truth reconstituted experientially (or pseudo-experientially). Likewise, crucially, with the subsequent critical tradition; as a recent critic of Shakespeare puts it (though making no mention here of Bradley):

> In Macbeth . . . the sanctions of divine law become the laws of human consciousness, and the vengeance of God becomes the purgative action of the diseased social organism. [Moreover] the sense of moral order, far from being stunted by this pruning away of the transcendental leafage, merely strikes deeper roots into the soil of consciousness, and grows more compelling as it is less definable. (Sanders, *The Dramatist and the Received Idea*, p. 109)

'Less definable': compare this, and also Bradley's 'mystery that we cannot fathom', with the assurance of Hegel:

> The true course of dramatic development consists in the annulment of contradictions. (*Hegel on Tragedy*, p. 71)

> Over and above mere fear and tragic sympathy we have therefore the feeling of *reconciliation*, which tragedy affords in virtue of its vision of eternal justice. (p. 51)

> Eternal justice is operative . . . under a mode whereby it restores the ethical substance and unity in and along with the downfall of the individuality which disturbs its repose. (p. 49)

From those more recent theorists and critics of tragedy who could be cited in support of the contention that Bradley has been, and remains, a powerful influence, three may suffice.

'Tragedy' says Richard B. Sewall speaks 'of an order that transcends time, space and matter . . . some order behind the immediate disorder'. Like Bradley he is at pains to stress that this is 'nothing so pat as The Moral Order, the "armies of unalterable law", and it is nothing so sure as the orthodox Christian God'. Like Bradley, again, he sees it as much more mystical and mysterious than any of these, involving 'faith in a cosmic good; [a] vision, however fleeting, of a world in which all questions could be answered' (Michel and Sewall, *Tragedy*, pp. 121–3; cf. *Shakespearean Tragedy*, p. 324). G. K. Hunter has offered a providential account of Elizabethan tragedy which also shows a specific resemblance to Bradley's. Elucidating Fulke Greville's famous account of the difference between ancient and contemporary tragedy (see below, chapter 7) Hunter adds that, in the latter, the massacre of innocents 'is part of a larger catastrophic movement which is eventually moral: the universe in casting out the particular evil casts out the good' (*Dramatic Identities and Cultural Tradition*, p. 183; cf. Bradley's view that the moral order, in making its tragic heroes 'suffer and waste themselves', actually 'suffers and wastes itself; . . . to save its life and regain peace from this intestinal struggle, it casts them out', *Shakespearean Tragedy*, p. 37).

In *Elements of Tragedy* Dorothea Krook, ignoring all historical contexts and differences, posits four 'fundamental, universal ele-

ments of tragedy' (p. 8): first an act of shame or horror which violates the moral order, second expiatory suffering, third knowledge
of the necessity of that suffering, fourth an affirmation of the
dignity of the human spirit, and, in the greatest tragedy, affirmation of a transcendent moral order (pp. 8–9, 17). Linking these
four elements is a principle of teleological coherence:

> The final 'affirmation' of tragedy springs from our reconciliation to,
> or acceptance of, the necessity of the suffering rendered intelligible
> by the knowledge: by illuminating the necessity of the suffering the
> knowledge reconciles us to it; by being reconciled to ('accepting') the
> suffering as necessary, we reaffirm the supremacy of the universal
> moral order; and by the act of recognition of and submission to the
> universal moral order . . . we express and affirm the dignity of man.
> (p. 17)

The underlying structure of Krook's tragedy is undoubtedly
Christian but equally important is the humanist centring of 'man':
the tragic hero who suffers into truth 'is all mankind' and represents 'all humanity in embodying some fundamental persistent
aspect of man's nature' (p. 36); the universal qualities of the hero
are courage and nobility (p. 41).

Archer and Eliot

William Archer's *The Old Drama and the New* appeared in 1923,
T. S. Eliot's 'Four Elizabethan Dramatists' in 1924. Archer argued,
contentiously, that Elizabethan drama was seriously vitiated by its
dependence upon unrealistic conventions. Eliot boldly asserted the
contrary: 'The weakness of the Elizabethan drama is not its defect
of realism, but its attempt at realism; not its conventions, but its
lack of conventions' (*Selected Essays*, p. 112). This makes the drama
an 'impure art' – that is, one which tries to combine 'complete
realism' with 'unrealistic conventions' (pp. 114, 112).

For Archer dramatic form simply reflected, unproblematically,
the real world – hence his advocacy of a 'pure and consistent form
of imitation' (p. 134). For Eliot also purity of form was an objective of art but one to be achieved through *abstraction* from life
rather than direct representation of it – hence his insistence on the

importance of conventions and his rejection of realism. It is, says Eliot, 'essential that a work of art should be self-consistent, that an artist should consciously or unconsciously draw a circle beyond which he does not trespass: on the one hand actual life is always the material, and on the other hand an abstraction from actual life is a necessary condition to the creation of the work of art' (*Selected Essays*, p. 111).

Archer wanted 'realism', Eliot convention. And they wanted different things precisely because they held different conceptions of, first, *reality itself*, second and consequently, what the relationship of art to reality should be. Archer's scathing criticism of the Elizabethans' 'semi-barbarous drama' and his own faith in 'realism' was based on a 'rationalist's' conception of the world and a faith in the correspondence of appearance and reality; for him drama had to imitate 'the visible and audible surfaces of life', to be 'sober and accurate' and in accord with 'common sense' (*The Old Drama and the New*, p. 20). Further, as Jonas Barish has remarked, for Archer 'everything surprising, contradictory, bewildering in human nature . . . [was] ruled out of court as unnatural' ('The New Theatre and the Old', p. 4). Eliot saw the world totally differently. In fact, in the very year that Archer's book appeared Eliot had spoken of 'the immense panorama of futility and anarchy which is contemporary history' ('*Ulysses*, Order and Myth', p. 681).

The principal theme of 'Four Elizabethan Dramatists' is that inner consistency is a major criterion of aesthetic achievement; its underlying assumption – one which sheds light on that theme – is that reality is chaotic. Consequently, the aesthetic consistency in question could only be achieved through a careful filtering of reality, followed by adjustment of the selected elements in relation to each other through the use of non-realistic conventions.[5] Occasionally the Jacobean dramatists fulfilled this requirement. Thus Eliot says of *The Revenger's Tragedy* (somewhat oddly), 'the whole action . . . has its own self-subsistent reality' (*Selected Essays*, p. 185); and in *The Sacred Wood*: 'The worlds created by artists like Jonson are like systems of non-Euclidean geometry' (pp. 116–17; interestingly this sentence was omitted from this essay as it appeared later in *Selected Essays*).

To an important extent then art from this perspective becomes formalist – an internally coherent alternative to, rather than a direct representation of, reality; the chaos of the real, the contradictions in experience, are to be excluded rather than, as in Bradley, confronted and transcended in accord with a more ultimate reality. In his essay on Shakespeare and Seneca, Eliot makes a strong distinction between poetry on the one hand and thought, philosophy and intellect on the other. He goes so far as to doubt whether the philosophy of Machiavelli, Montaigne and Seneca could even be said to have influenced Elizabethan writers but, even if it is to be allowed that it did, the influence was not important; so, in Donne for example, he finds 'only a vast jumble of incoherent erudition on which he drew *for purely poetic effects*' (*Selected Essays*, p. 139; my italics). This suggests an even more uncompromising formalism. But Eliot cannot abandon the idea that poetry refers beyond itself and significantly so; thus, although 'In truth neither Shakespeare nor Dante did any real thinking' nevertheless 'the *essential* is that each expresses, in perfect language, some permanent human impulse . . . something *universal* and personal' (*Selected Essays*, pp. 136–7; my italics). By the time of *The Four Quartets* metaphysical and aesthetic significance are re-aligned: 'Only by the form, the pattern/Can words or music reach/The stillness.' Chaos is no longer excluded through unrealistic conventions but transcended through mystical insight into an ultimate reality and articulated now in terms of its appropriate form.

The positions represented by Bradley and Eliot remained central in twentieth-century criticism of Jacobean tragedy; time and again we find the *telos* of harmonic integration as a dominant critical ideal, sometimes in uncompromisingly formalist terms (Eliot) but more usually as an aesthetic reflection of the eternally true, the unchanging human condition (Bradley, later Eliot). In either alternative, history plays no effective part, being either aesthetically/formally excluded or metaphysically transcended. Of course for others in the dominant tradition history *was* deemed important and very much so, but it was still a history filtered through the same ideological imperatives of order. As J. W. Lever has shown in an excellent survey of twentieth-century Shakespearean scholarship, it was this playwright's 'politics' that received most scholarly attention during the years which culminated in the Second World War. His alleged conformity to received ideas was constantly proclaimed, ideas which expressed confident belief in order, degree, constituted authority, obedience to rulers and a corresponding contempt for the populace, and so on. In particular, E. M. W. Tillyard extracted from these ideas '*a symmetrical design* whose natural or metaphysical aspects served mainly to justify the social political *status quo*' ('Shakespeare and the Ideas of His Time', p. 85; my italics).

Coherence and Discontinuity

In recent years critics have continued to ascribe to Jacobean drama an ultimate ethical and/or metaphysical coherence revealed in and through dramatic structure. If that has not been possible, the drama has been judged deficient. Again, numerous studies could be cited; I choose one which seems especially worthy of attention, Arthur C. Kirsch's *Jacobean Dramatic Perspectives*. According to Kirsch this drama declines when it is 'no longer sustained by metaphysical reverberations, when Providence disappears *as a principle of structure as well as belief*' (p. 129; my italics). John Webster has been the most controversial of all Jacobean dramatists in this respect. On the one hand he has been yoked by violence to the supposed moral orthodoxies of his age – being seen by D. C. Gunby for example as an orthodox Christian offering 'a confident assertion of the power of God to counter and destroy evil' ('*The Duchess of Malfi*: A Theological Approach', p. 204) – or, at the other extreme, seen as a decadent nihilist trapped in his own obsession with chaos. Ian Jack and Wilber Sanders are among those who have advanced the second view, but it gets its most cautious and persuasive formulation from Kirsch: 'Aside from the broad assumption that life is hell, there is nothing resembling a coherent moral attitude in [*The White Devil*] and more important, nothing which enables us to integrate or organise its discontinuities of action and character' (*Jacobean Dramatic Perspectives*, p. 104).

More formalist critical perspectives have rescued the drama from such charges by reidentifying its coherence in terms of theme and image. Richard Levin, in his analysis of post-war criticism of English Renaissance drama, identifies as the most influential movement of all what he calls 'thematic criticism', that which finds in the plays underlying homogeneity, deep structures and organic unity, all of which serve as the formal articulation of a predictable content: profound and universal truths about 'man'. One such study which he cites declares that Jonson's *Volpone* 'is not simply a satire of avarice in Jacobean England. It is not a play of topical interest; it is a play for everybody concerned with the eternal verities' (quoted, intentionally unascribed, on p. 30 of Levin, *New Readings*). Hereward T. Price in an important article, 'The Function of Imagery in Webster', makes less exalted claims but implies that the eternal verities are at least implicit in Webster's plays to the extent that their formal coherence amounts to a profound unity which transcends the chaos of their subject matter. Price sees the basic conflict in both *The White Devil* and *The Duchess* as one between 'outward appearance and inner substance' in a universe 'so convulsed and uncertain that no appearance can represent reality'. So form itself becomes the reality; it does so in terms of 'double construction, an outer and an inner . . . figure in action and figure in language', all of which serves to bind the scenes of the plays 'into a whole of the highest possible unity'. Thus through form the chaos of content is transformed by 'an irony so varied, so subtle, and so profound' (G. K. and S. K. Hunter, *John Webster*, pp. 178–80, 202).

Conceived thus, in terms of a final profound coherence, irony becomes something very different from what is actually encountered in these plays: that is, irony as the startling dramatic moment with its own (momentary) subversive thrust. More generally, the very appeal to this notion of structural coherence has in practice neutralised the destabilising effect of contradictory dramatic *process*, subordinating it to notions of totality, effacing it in the closure of formalist (and often, by implication, universalist) truth. Of course Jacobean tragedy does often effect some kind of closure, but it is usually a perfunctory rather than a profound reassertion of order (providential and political). We may feel that such closure was a kind of condition for subversive thought to be foregrounded at all. But we should recognise too that such a condition cannot control what it permits: closure could never retrospectively guarantee ideological erasure of what, for a while, existed prior to and so independently of it.

Meanwhile the point of view typified by William Archer has recently been revived by Christopher Ricks. His argument is much more sophisticated than Archer's and is, moreover, an important corrective to the exalted claims made by the thematic, imagist and formalist critics. For Ricks 'most Elizabethan and Jacobean drama is crude stuff'; he concurs with Bernard Shaw's attack on its 'factitiousness . . . the way in which it is all merely made up – crudely and unconvincingly'. Especially objectionable are its contrived plots, improbable events and inconsistent characterisation. The absence of naturalistic character and behaviour in a play like *The Revenger's Tragedy* makes it a severely limited achievement. Not surprisingly then, Ricks, though critical of Archer, finds that he 'attacked Elizabethan and Jacobean drama very intelligently' and he agrees with Archer's contention that 'Dramatists who could produce effects with such total disregard of nature, probability and common-sense, worked in a soft medium' (*English Drama to 1710*, pp. 338, 306, 330; Archer, p. 46).

One problem with the Archer/Ricks perspective is that it takes 'nature, probability and common-sense' as more or less given. This, as we shall see, is what the Brechtian alternative refuses to do, recognising that these things are too often the ideological property of the dominant discourse. Thus we might, *pace* Archer and Ricks, advise an audience comprised of subordinate groups: be realistic, demand the improbable. Archer's assumption, and to a lesser extent Ricks', is that dramatic realism must involve a straightforward reflection or *simulation* of reality. In fact, realism *constructs* representations of the real and it does this by, among other things, '*reference to independently acquired knowledge of that to which they refer*' (Lovell, *Pictures of Reality*, p. 91). The constructed representation and independently acquired knowledge go together; typically the first invokes the second, via convention.

In illustration of this we might consider the dumb-shows – one of the most improbable and artificial of conventions – in Webster's *The White Devil* (at the beginning of II. ii). John Russell Brown notes in his Revels edition of the play that the dumb-show was originally an allegorical representation of events but came to be used as a convenient means of compressing dramatic action (p. 56). That Webster's dumb-shows are made to serve the second of these functions is obvious enough, but it is their function as a modified form of the first that is especially interesting. First there is the bizarre aspect of the executions: 'Enter suspiciously, Julio and another . . . they put on spectacles of glass, which cover their eyes and noses, and then burn perfumes afore the picture, and wash the lips of the picture; that done, quenching the fire, and putting off their spectacles they depart laughing' (II. ii. 24 S.D.). The result here is not just effective theatre; that final touch, 'they depart laughing' – gratuitous and indeed incongruous from the point of view of plot compression – makes for a lingering sense of the unnaturalness and *deliberate* inhumanity of court intrigue, an effect heightened by the subsequent pathos of Isabella's death in Giovanni's presence. This sudden alteration and deliberate contrast of mood (from brutality to pathos) – an alteration related to the *single* action – catches in brief another aspect of Webster's world: while events themselves have a predictable sequence of cause and effect, the power struggle, sexual and political, makes for a court lacking in emotional coherence, unity of purpose or predictability – in a word, discontinuous.

The second show elaborates the distinctive kind of treachery already encountered in the first – a treachery inextricably a part of courtly adroitness ('– now turn another way,/And view Camillo's far more politic fate, –' II. ii. 34–5). 'Enter Flamineo, Marcello, Camillo . . . they drink healths and dance; a vaulting-horse is brought into the room; Marcello and two more *whisper'd* out of the room, while Flamineo and Camillo strip themselves into their shirts, as to vault; *compliment* who shall begin; as Camillo is about to vault Flamineo pitches him upon his neck . . . etc.' (my italics). These shows do not just compress action, they also epitomise what the play develops – a kind of callous brutality operating behind the guise of court sophistication – the deferential gesture which becomes, suddenly, the murderous thrust (cf. Flamineo's 'I have brought your weapon back' [Flamineo runs Marcello through], V.

ii. 15). I described Webster's use of the dumb-show as a modification of the first function mentioned by Brown because it has little of the schematic, abstract significance of allegory; rather these shows briefly ritualise the sensibility which animates Webster's world.

In the critical perspectives so far considered, there is an unwillingness or inability to see the 'discontinuities' which Kirsch criticises as anything other than a failure of the dramatist to apprehend and register first, the *telos* of harmonic integration – aesthetic, religious, Elizabethan or whatever; second, the subjective embodiment of that integration – the unitary, integrated, plausible 'character'.[6] Alternatively the discontinuities are claimed to be apparent only and Webster is retrieved for a perspective which sees universal and orthodox 'truth' conveyed in and through formal coherence.[7] One of the main aims of this book is to argue that these discontinuities serve a social and political realism; to see how this might be we need to outline a completely different critical perspective deriving from Brecht. Terry Eagleton has put the central issue very well, and what he here asserts of Brecht is exactly true also of the discontinuities in Jacobean drama (as Brecht himself recognised): 'For Brecht it is not quite that art can "give us the real" only by a ceaseless activity of dislocating and demystifying; it is rather that this *is*, precisely, its yielding of the real . . . "Rationality" for Brecht is thus indissociable from scepticism, experiment, refusal and subversion' (*Walter Benjamin*, p. 85).

Brecht: A Different Reality

Brecht completely rejected the *telos* of harmonic integration as the objective of theatre, and he discovered that in this respect Elizabethan drama concurred with his own work. In some respects, as he recognised, Elizabethan drama anticipated epic theatre.

Brecht attacked the contemporary theatre, which he called (somewhat misleadingly) bourgeois or Aristotelian. This was in fact just the kind of theatre which Archer championed over and above the 'semi-barbaric' plays of the Elizabethans. It presents itself as a predetermined totality thus disguising the fact that it is in fact fabricated (ideologically structured) to appear as such; in the face of its inevitability the audience becomes enthralled rather than critically engaged.

Brecht's so-called 'epic' alternative is a theatre which encourages the reverse; as Walter Benjamin has put it, '"it can happen this way, but it can also happen quite a different way" – that is the fundamental attitude of one who writes for epic theatre' (*Understanding Brecht*, p. 8). Contradiction is incorporated in the very structure of the epic play rather than simply being ignored or, alternatively, acknowledged but ultimately transcended. Actors *show* rather than *become* the characters they play; different genres are juxtaposed, sometimes jarringly so. One effect of this is that epic theatre 'incessantly derives a lively and productive consciousness from the fact that it is theatre' (*Understanding Brecht*, p. 4). Another effect is what Brecht called estrangement (*Verfremdungseffekt*) whereby the 'obvious' is made in a certain sense incomprehensible but only in order that it be made the easier to comprehend – that is, it is properly understood, perhaps for the first time. To defamiliarise the 'obvious' – Archer's 'nature, probability and common sense' – is a crucial step towards ideological demystification. Its effect is to 'historicise, that is, consider people and incidents as historically conditioned and transitory. The spectator will no longer see the characters on the stage as unalterable, uninfluenceable, helplessly delivered over to their fate'. Estrangement makes use of dialectical materialism which, says Brecht, 'treats social situations as processes, and traces out all their inconsistencies. It regards nothing as existing except in so far as it changes, in other words is in disharmony with itself' (*Brecht on Theatre*, pp. 144, 193). In the words of Benjamin again: 'Epic theatre does not reproduce conditions; rather, it discloses, it uncovers them' (*Understanding Brecht*, p. 100).

Brecht believed strongly in realism but not in the kind advocated by William Archer and found throughout the contemporary, naturalistic theatre (the so-called stage of the missing fourth wall). This theatre, because of its obsession with verisimilitude, actually misrepresented the real. So, whereas for Archer realism meant the representation of 'the visible and audible surfaces of life', for Brecht these surfaces, far from being reality, were an ideological misrecognition of it.[8] Brecht's conception of realism made a radical distinction between appearance and reality with full recognition of the part played by ideology in the former: 'Realistic means: discovering the causal complexes of society/unmasking the prevailing view of things as the view of those who are in power' (Bloch, *Aesthetics and Politics*, p. 82). In short he defines realism in terms of its object (and objective) rather than of any specific set of conventions. Moreover, 'Literary forms have to be checked against reality, not against aesthetics – even realist aesthetics' (*Brecht on Theatre*, p. 114).

Because Archer identified reality with the natural, the probable and the commonsensical, he argued that its dramatic corollary – that which would adequately represent the real – was a 'pure and logical art form' (*The Old Drama and the New*, p. 5). For Brecht reality – i.e. society – is full of conflict, contradiction and ideological misrepresentation and the art form he advocates is therefore diametrically opposed to Archer's:

> The bourgeois theatre's performances always aim at smoothing over contradictions, at creating false harmony, at idealization. Conditions are reported as if they could not be otherwise; . . . If there is any development it is always steady, never by jerks; the developments always take place within a definite framework which cannot be broken through.
>
> None of this is like reality, so a realistic theatre must give it up.
>
> (*Brecht on Theatre*, p. 277)

Brecht's perspective is also incompatible with Ricks' qualified revival of Archer. Ricks is guarded in making explicit his own first-order critical assumptions, and he also allows qualifications which actually disqualify the thrust of his argument. Thus by conceding that 'to ask that a play be true is not the same as asking that it be naturalistic, realistic, photographic' (p. 307), and further that 'we should not have a rigid idea of what constitutes improbability and inconsistency' (p. 316), Ricks allows in principle what he denies in practice. So, for example, of Bosola's accidental killing of Antonio in *The Duchess of Malfi*, and his exclamation

Antonio!
The man 1 would have sav'd 'bove mine own life!

> We are merely the stars' tennis-balls, struck and banded
> Which way please them
>
>   (V. iv. 51–4)

Ricks says: 'about the whole episode there hangs the unexalted suspicion that the characters (and the audience) are not the stars' tennis-balls but Webster's – struck and banded which way please him' (p. 323). In a sense one wants to say (as does Benjamin of epic theatre): yes, that is precisely the point.

Alternatively it would he possible to reply that the episode is not intrinsically implausible: the play makes it clear that it is night and that Antonio and Bosola are in darkness (the servant exits at line 42 to fetch a lanthorn) – and so on. In this connection John Russell Brown and Lois Potter[9] have suggested that Webster may have been exploiting the partially darkened stage made possible by the enclosed Blackfriars theatre. Historical inquiry of this kind is indeed relevant but not in order to prove that Webster was really – or trying to be – a naturalist. Indeed, from a Brechtian perspective, what is most relevant is the incongruity between Bosola's measured meditation and the sudden disruption of the moment – one *sharpened* by the actual or implied transition from darkness to light (the servant returns with the lanthorn – V. iv. 48). One effect of that incongruity is to check the expected climax; in fact, the episode is a kind of anti-climax: both revenge and poetic justice are anticipated but suddenly denied through the disclosure that it is Antonio not Ferdinand who lies dying. Checked expectation, not enthrallment or empathy, is the result and we are thereby provoked to dwell critically on, for example, the fate/chance disjunction which M. C. Bradbrook has shown to run throughout the play ('Fate and Chance in *The Duchess of Malfi*').

The artifice of the scene does not have to be minimised; on the contrary it is central – as Bosola's reply to Malateste's question about how Antonio was killed makes clear: 'I know not how:/Such a mistake as I have often seen/*In a play*' (V. v. 93–5; my italics). This drawing attention to the play as play (widespread of course in Jacobean drama) is a kind of estrangement effect, an invitation to engage critically with an issue rather than accept a transparent truth; in Raymond Williams' characterisation of the process, a 'falsely involving, uncritical reception' is checked and replaced with 'an involved, critical inspection' (*The Long Revolution*, p. 385). Further, thus alerted, literate members of an audience might pick up the allusion in the scene to Sidney, and possibly Calvin, just two of the several relevant writers who had already used the stars/tennis ball conceit, itself a commonplace (see Dent, *John Webster's Borrowings*). As Alan Sinfield has shown, the important point here is what Webster *declines* to take from his source material, namely the explicit reassurance that what appears arbitrary is in fact divinely ordained[10] (*Literature in Protestant England*, pp. 121–2). My point is not that this is a brilliantly successful passage, or even that it especially illuminates Webster's dramatic technique; it is only that Ricks invokes criteria of plausibility which the play specifically refuses – and it does so precisely to invite a more critical involvement with the issues it dramatises.

What particularly interested Brecht about Elizabethan drama was its structure:

> Take the element of conflict in Elizabethan plays, complex, shifting, largely impersonal, never soluble, and then see what has been made of it today, whether in contemporary plays or in contemporary renderings of the Elizabethans. Compare the part played by empathy then and now. What a contradictory, complicated and intermittent operation it was in Shakespeare's theatre! (*Brecht on Theatre*, p. 161)

In the disconnectedness of Shakespeare's plays 'one recognises the disconnectedness of human fate' (*Schriften*, I, 104–6). It is only quite recently that Brecht's actual indebtedness to the Elizabethans has begun to be explored. W. E. Yuill tells us that Brecht, from his study of the Elizabethan stage, deduced a style of performance akin to his own ideal, namely, 'a stage with minimal technical resources, incapable of creating illusion or mesmeric "atmosphere", depending for its effects upon word and gesture'. He found here a mode of theatrical production which he hoped to resurrect, 'a model for the revolutionary style to which he aspired' (*The Art of Vandalism*, p. 8).[11]

The very elements of Jacobean drama which fascinated Brecht other critics have ignored, explained away or made the focus of their critical condemnation; Brecht's claim that bourgeois theatre aims at 'smoothing over contradictions, at creating false harmony, at idealization' surely applies equally to them.

Recent Marxist critics have attended even more closely than did Brecht to the way that literature becomes internally dissonant because of its relationship to social process, actual historical struggle and ideological contradiction. Brecht clearly thought of the Elizabethans as making some sort of intentional critique of their own historical conjuncture, as he himself did in relation to his own. Pierre Macherey however sees literature as foregrounding ideological contradiction as it were in spite of itself. Ideology 'produces an effect of coherence' but is in reality 'essentially contradictory, riddled with all sorts of conflicts'. Literary texts have inscribed within them this fundamental opposition between attempted coherence and actual incoherence and so 'express the contradictions of the social reality in which they are produced'. Consequently Macherey proposes a type of analysis which reads 'the ideological contradictions within the devices produced to conceal them' (*Red Letters*, no. 5, p. 5). Intentionality of the kind accepted by Brecht need play no part in this process; as Macherey puts it elsewhere: 'the author is the first reader of his own work' (*A Theory of Literary Production*, p. 48).

Terry Eagleton however, in pursuing this mode of analysis, has recourse to the illuminating analogy of the production of a play, one which suggests (to me) that the preoccupation with authorial intention as absent or present, relevant or not, might be misguided:[12] 'just as the dramatic production's relation to its text reveals the text's internal relations to its 'world' under the form of its own *constitution* of them, so the literary text's relation to ideology so constitutes that ideology as to reveal something of its relations to history' (*Criticism and Ideology*, p. 69). The production cannot transcend its text but it may nevertheless interrogate it with a critical rigour (p. 69); likewise the literary text in relation to ideology: 'Textual dissonances . . . are the effect of the work's *production* of ideology. The text *puts* the ideology into contradiction, discloses the limits and absences which mark its relation to history, and in doing so puts itself into question, producing a lack and disorder within itself' (p. 95).

*

Bradley and Eliot can he seen to have represented and perpetuated two dominant positions on the question of the relation of art to reality. According to one position aesthetic form was seen to create an ideal unity, a fictive alternative to the chaotic real; according to the other it was seen to represent or invoke an order of truth beyond the flux and chaos of history and be the more 'real' for so doing. In Renaissance literary theory we find positions which correspond interestingly to these two. We also find an emergent conception of mimesis (I call it 'realist')[13] which bears comparison with the dialectical conception of form just outlined in relation to Brecht.

4

Renaissance Literary Theory: Two Concepts of Mimesis

In the Renaissance a revival of mimetic realism[1] in art coincided with new-found anxieties over the very nature of reality itself. Those anxieties stemmed in part from what Richard H. Popkin regards as the intellectual crisis generated by the Reformation. It was then of course that tradition as the infallible criterion of religious truth was challenged. In its place the reformers substituted the word of God in scripture and the self-evident criterion of subjective conviction (conscience). This, says Popkin, 'raised a most fundamental question: how does one justify the basis of one's knowledge? This problem was to unleash a sceptical crisis not only in theology but also, shortly thereafter, in the sciences and in all other areas of human knowledge' (*The History of Scepticism from Erasmus to Spinoza*, p. 16, see also pp. 52–3).

For those who thought with Montaigne that 'the senses are the beginning and the end of humane knowledge' (*Essays*, II, 307), faith, even as subjective conviction, itself became problematic. Even so confident a theologian as Hooker confirms this. He distinguished between 'certainty of evidence' and 'certainty of adherence'. So far as the first was concerned he allows a great deal to empiricist epistemology: 'That which we see by the light of grace, though it indeed be more certain; yet it is not to us so evidently certain, as that which sense or the light of nature will not suffer a man to doubt of . . . I conclude therefore that we have less certainty of evidence concerning things believed, than concerning sensible or naturally perceived.' Faith is consigned to 'certainty of adherence', but even here there is an anxiety which Kierkegaard would have recognised; for the Christian, says Hooker, even when the evidence of the truth is so small that he 'grieveth . . . to feel his weakness in

70

assenting thereto', there is nevertheless within him, 'a sure adherence unto that which he doth but faintly and fearfully believe' ('Of the Certainty and Perpetuity of Faith in the Elect', pp. 470–1).

These issues, as they relate to the drama, can be focussed in, though not reduced to, one particular tension: on the one hand didacticism, inherited as dramatic conventions from the morality tradition, demanded that the universe be seen to be divinely controlled; that justice and order be eventually affirmed, conflict resolved, and the individual re-established within, or expelled from, the providential design (idealist mimesis). On the other hand, drama was rapidly progressing as a form with empirical, historical and contemporary emphases – all of which were in potential conflict with this didacticism (realist mimesis). An important way of understanding this tension is to approach it through the literary theory of the period.

Poetry versus History

In the sixteenth century the attack on literature, especially drama, gained new force with the growth of puritanism. During what Spingarn has termed the third stage of English criticism – 'the period of philosophical and apologetic criticism' – literature was most persistently defended against the new wave of hostility (*A History of Literary Criticism in the Renaissance*, p. 256). To the charge that literature, as fiction, involves falsity the apologists responded by stressing (under the influence of Aristotle) its mimetic function; the further charge that such literature inevitably inclined towards obscenity and blasphemy was met by advancing its didactic purpose. In some instances this didactic justification was explicitly ideological:

> playes are writ with this ayme, and carryed with this methode, to teach their subjects obedience to their king, to show the people the untimely ends of such as have moved tumults, commotions, and insurrections, to present them with the flourishing estate of such as live in obedience, exhorting them to allegeance, dehorting them from all trayterous and fellonious stratagems. (Heywood, *An Apology for Actors*, p. 53)

But it was also an integral part of a complex theological and ethical world view and as such was embedded in the literary consciousness of the sixteenth century, particularly the Morality drama.

Central to literary didacticism has been the notion of poetic justice. We find the idea in the literary theory of both Sidney and Bacon.[2] But before examining their work I propose to move forward in time and see what happened to poetic justice during the period when it was most vigorously expounded. The idea refers, of course, to the rewarding of the virtuous and the punishing of the vicious, usually in a proportional and appropriate way. Moreover, almost always this just distribution of deserts is portrayed as evidence of providential concern. Stated thus crudely the theory seems to merit the scorn that it has often attracted. Thomas Rymer, who coined the expression and advocated, though he did not invent, the idea, has been particularly open to attack. But the idea is not, necessarily, either crudely didactic or naïve. For the Elizabethans, and Rymer, the idea was protected from this charge because it was actually a part of a sophisticated (though problematic) distinction between poetry and history – a distinction which also goes back to Aristotle. Sophocles and Euripides, says Rymer, found in history:

> the same *end* happen to the *righteous* and to the *unjust, vertue* often *opprest*, and *wickedness* on the Throne: they saw these particular *yesterday-truths* were imperfect and unproper to illustrate the *universal* and *eternal truths* by them intended. Finding also that this *unequal* distribution of rewards and punishments did perplex the *wisest*, and by the *Atheist* was made a scandal to the *Divine Providence*. They concluded, that a *Poet* must of necessity see *justice* exactly administered, if he intended to please. (*The Critical Works*, p. 22)

History, then, contradicts poetic justice and even provides evidence for questioning providence. There is no pretence that in life itself justice is seen to be done; poetic justice is administered by the artist as a result of a rather uneasy alliance between aesthetic and didactic interests: in tragedy, says Rymer, 'Something must stick by observing that constant order, that harmony and beauty of Providence, that necessary relation and chain, whereby the causes and the effects, the vertues and rewards, the vices and their punishments are proportion'd and link'd together' (p. 75). Here, however, the precept is showing signs of strain since Rymer's idea of 'harmony and beauty' is poised ambiguously between being a sub-

stitute for reality on the one hand, and a revelation of a more ultimate reality on the other. Moreover, Rymer's aesthetic delight in
the 'harmony and beauty of Providence' is at odds with his reference elsewhere to 'God Almighty, whose holy will and purposes are
not to be *comprehended* . . . ' (p. 22).

Samuel Johnson, in preferring Tate's *King Lear* (in which the
ending is altered and Cordelia rewarded) makes the same alignment between poetic justice and aesthetic pleasure: 'A play in
which the wicked prosper and the virtuous miscarry may doubtless
be good, because it is a just representation of the common events
of human life. But since all reasonable beings naturally love justice,
I cannot easily be persuaded that the observation of justice makes a
play worse' (*Selected Writings*, pp. 294–5). Again, the crucial question poses itself: is this 'justice' – which, it is conceded, does not
actually exist – simply a pleasing illusion, a fictive construct, or a
relevation of a more ultimate (providential) order? Significantly,
another advocate of poetic justice, John Dennis, interpreted the
lack of it in Shakespeare's plays in this way: 'the Good and the Bad
. . . perishing promiscuously in the best of Shakespear's Tragedies,
there can be either none or very weak Instruction in them: For
such promiscuous Events call the Government of Providence into
Question, and by Scepticks and Libertines are resolv'd into
Chance'.[3] Exactly so; realist mimesis represents an actuality which
obviously differs from the providential order. Now it is not this difference *per se* which disturbs Dennis – it is, after all, a difference
presupposed in the very distinction between mundane and divine –
but, rather, its *dramatic* representation; drama foregrounds, perhaps
more acutely than any other literary genre, the problematic relations between the two realms. Addison criticised Rymer's defence
of poetic justice because he found the notion 'contrary to the experience of life . . . nature and reason' (*The Spectator*, no. 40, 16 April
1711). A century earlier theatre audiences had found just the same.

The Fictive and the Real

Sidney, like Rymer, and also following Aristotle, advocated poetry
in preference to history. Discussing their relative merits in terms of
what they depicted (respectively, the ideal and the actual) Sidney

said: 'if the question be for your own use and learning, whether it be better to have it set down as it should be, or as it was, then certainly is more doctrinable the feigned Cyrus of Xenophon than the true Cyrus in Justin' (*Apology*, pp. 109–10). Sidney repeatedly stressed this point; the poet, with his 'feigned example' (p. 110) can instruct, whereas the historian 'being captivated to the truth of a foolish world, is many times a terror from well-doing, and encouragement to unbridled wickedness' (p. 111). Moreover, poetry instructs pleasurably, even though this pleasure is achieved through radical deception: 'those things which in themselves are horrible, as cruel battles, unnatural monsters, are made in poetical imitation delightful' (p. 114). For Sidney poetic justice is the instructive principle of poetry generally: 'Poetry . . . not content with earthly plagues, deviseth new punishments in hell for tyrants' (p. 112). And, indeed, of drama specifically: 'if evil men come to the stage, they ever go out (as the tragedy writer answered to one that misliked the show of such persons) so manacled as they little animate folks to follow them' (p. 111). The emphasis is strongly prescriptive; 'right poets' he says, 'imitate to teach and delight, and to imitate borrow nothing of what is, hath been, or shall be; but range, only reined with learned discretion, into the divine consideration of what may be and *should* be' (p. 102). But if this didacticism is achieved by completely disdaining 'what is, hath been, or shall be' what, finally, is the ontological status of that which is imitated? Sidney implies that it is wholly fictive. The poet ranges 'only within the zodiac of his own wit'; he 'nothing affirms and therefore never lieth' (pp. 100, 123). Apparently then the poet is not imitating a pre-existent, eternal ideal, but one which he himself creates.[4]

Elsewhere, however, Sidney seems to realise the implications of such a theory and affirms the contrary. Of the different kinds of mimesis he says: 'The chief, both in antiquity and excellency, were they that did imitate the inconceivable excellencies of God' (p. 101). Also, and with Aristotelian and Platonic emphasis, he speaks of poetry's 'universal consideration', its 'perfect pattern', and 'the *idea* or fore-conceit of the work' (pp. 101, 109, 110).[5]

The ambiguity remains unresolved in the *Apology*. Critics,

inclining one way or another in their commentary on the work, have offered incompatible interpretations. Thus Geoffrey Shepherd, a recent editor of the *Apology*, sees Sidney's ideal as metaphysical:

> [Sidney's] religious faith and his poetic theory rest on the belief that intelligent design, not chance, is inherent in nature itself. It is from this position that Sidney urges that poetry can provide what history cannot guarantee, a grasp of the universal design and order. (*Apology*, Introduction, p. 53)[6]

Daiches, on the other hand, concludes that it is fictive: for Sidney, says Daiches,

> *imagination does not give us insight into reality, but an alternative to reality* . . . He almost proceeds to develop a theory of 'ideal imitation', the notion that the poet imitates not the mere appearances of actuality but the hidden reality behind them, but stops short of this to maintain the more naïve theory that the poet creates a better world than the one we actually live in. (*Critical Approaches to Literature*, p. 58)

But why stress this ambiguity? It is of the first importance in that it concerns the ontological status of what poetry represents and, therefore, its didactic function. In the context of Christian theology, morality depends ultimately on a metaphysical sanction for its prescriptive force; if it is accepted that what is being apprehended (and imitated) is a metaphysical ideal with real ontological status, then the prescriptive force of poetry is considerable; conversely, if the object of imitation is ideal in a fictive sense only, it cannot thus prescribe.[7]

Now, Francis Bacon in his account of poetry in *The Advancement of Learning*[8] argues that the ideal world represented by poetry *is* entirely fictive. He thereby completely undermines its didactic function. Bacon divides human learning into three groups: History, Poesy and Philosophy. Each stems from a corresponding faculty of understanding – respectively, Memory, Imagination and Reason. The difference between History and Poesy is defined unambiguously: 'History is properly concerned with individuals, which are circumscribed by place and time . . . *I consider history and experience to be the same thing* . . .' (*De Augmentis Scientiarum*,

p. 426; my italics). Poesy is 'nothing else but Feigned History' (*Advancement*, p. 87); Memory and History are concerned with empirical reality; Poesy and Imagination are confined to the world of fiction. Poesy 'commonly exceeds the measure of nature, joining at pleasure things which in nature would never have come together, and introducing things which in nature would never have come to pass' (*De Augmentis*, p. 426).

Bacon goes on to describe the interrelationship between poesy, poetic justice and providence:

> The use of this Feigned History [i.e. poetry] hath been to give some shadow of satisfaction to the mind of man in those points wherein the nature of things doth deny it; the world being in proportion inferior to the soul; by reason whereof there is agreeable to the spirit of man a more ample greatness, a more exact goodness . . . than can be found in the nature of things . . . because *true history* propoundeth the successes and issues of actions not so agreeable to the merits of virtue and vice, therefore poesy feigns them more just in retribution, and more according to revealed providence. (*Advancement*, p. 88; my italics)

In *De Augmentis* this suggestion that poetry is agreeable illusion is even stronger: 'Poesy seems to bestow upon human nature those things which history denies to it; and to satisfy the mind with the shadows of things when the substance cannot he obtained' (p. 440). Consequently the fictive and ideal elements of poetry are inferior by comparison with those branches of knowledge which engage, albeit painfully, with empirical reality:

> So as it *appeareth* that poesy serveth and conferreth to magnanimity, morality, and to delectation. And therefore it was ever thought to have some participation of divineness, because it doth raise and erect the mind, by submitting the shews of things to the desires of the mind; whereas reason *doth buckle and bow the mind unto the nature of things.* (*Advancement*, p. 88; my italics)

Note how reason, and by implication its corresponding category of learning, philosophy, are now aligned with history and memory on the side of reality.[9] By organising categories of knowledge in this way Bacon retains the Aristotelian categories of poetry and history, but effectively reverses their priority.

Sidney concurs with Aristotle's judgement that poetry 'is more philosophical and more studiously serious than history' (Sidney, *Apology*, p. 109). Bacon asserts exactly the contrary, and the reversal results from the different ontological status accorded to the ideal world of poetry. Bacon's priorities are clear; moving from poetry to the other branches of knowledge he declares: 'It is not good to stay too long in the theatre. Let us now pass on to the judicial place or palace of the mind, which we are to approach and view with more reverence and attention' (*Advancement*, p. 89). Bacon gives poetry an idealist function only to undercut idealism itself. Moreover, a brief re-examination of the foregoing quotations will indicate the extent to which providentialism generally, and poetic justice specifically, are steered into the fictive world of poetry and imagination (see especially p. 76 above). In this connection Bacon makes a fascinating remark on the contemporary theatre:

> Dramatic Poesy, which has the theatre for its world, would be of excellent use if well directed. For the stage is capable of no small influence both of discipline and corruption. Now of corruptions in this kind we have enough; but the discipline in our times has been plainly neglected. And though in modem states play-acting is esteemed but as a toy, except when it is too satirical and biting; yet among the ancients it was used as a means of educating men's minds to virtue. (*De Augmentis*, p. 440)

One might add that the neglect of this 'discipline' on the contemporary stage, the reluctance to use the theatre as a means of 'educating men's minds to virtue' was in part due to a distrust of poetic justice and providentialism similar to Bacon's own! Much of the didactic drama of the sixteenth century conformed to Bacon's view of what the theatre should do.[10] Clearly, however, contemporary drama, with its 'corruptions' and capacity to be 'too satirical and biting' was not conforming to this pattern. Significantly, satire was one of the manifestations of a new dramatic realism, both in tragedy and comedy. Given his own assertion that history and experience are identical (see p. 75 above), and his remarkable classification of drama as 'History made visible' (*De Augmentis*, p. 439), Bacon should have realised that the theatre could not easily be incorporated in his aesthetic. Drama in this period was fulfilling increasingly the function of History rather than Poesy: 'History made visible'.

Fulke Greville makes this point. Like Bacon, he classified knowledge within the categories of the ideal and the actual. In *A Treatise of Human Learning*[11] he asserts that the function of the 'arts' in general, and poetry in particular, is the truthful portrayal of reality. Moreover, analysing the relationship between word and object, Greville strongly implies that this reality is empirical. He rejects intellectual speculation which fails to produce concrete results (stanza 28). He attacks arts like philosophy which are 'Farre more delightfull than they fruitfull be' (stanza 29). Those who engage in linguistic sophistry he calls '*Word-sellers*' and 'Verbalists' (stanzas 30, 31) adding, in one of many conclusions to the same effect:

> *What then are all these humane Arts, and lights,*
> *But Seas of errors? In whose depths who sound,*
> *Of truth finde onely shadowes, and no ground.*

> (stanza 34)

Greville prefers the usefully active life to the idly contemplative, and argues for general truths, gathered from experience and nature and applied to present circumstances. He distrusts language and rejects

> . . . termes, distinctions, axioms, lawes,
> Such as depend either in whole, or part,
> Vpon this stained sense of words, or sawes:
> Onely admitting precepts of such kinde,
> As without words may be conceiu'd in minde.

> (stanza 106)

'*Grammar*', '*Logike*', 'the *Schooles*', '*Rhetorike*' – all come under scathing attack. For Greville linguistic structures constantly carry the danger of obscuring reality or, worse, actually becoming a substitute reality. He condemns such fabrications as 'the painted skinne/Of many words' (stanza 107). He wants language to refer to empirical reality, and therefore he advocates uses of language which

> . . . most properly express the thought;
> For as of pictures, which should manifest

The life, we say not that is fineliest wrought,
Which fairest simply showes, but faire and like.

(stanza 109)[12]

The essential point is made in stanza 112:

> *if the matter be in Nature vile,*
> *How can it be made pretious by a stile?*

So far Greville's theory is wholly in accordance with his preference, expressed in the *Life of Sir Philip Sidney*, for 'images of life' in literature rather than 'images of wit' (p. 224).[13] Greville sees his own images of life appealing 'to those only, that are weather-beaten in the Sea of the World' (p. 224). Such images engage with the reality of experience and the imperfection of the world whereas 'images of wit' do not. These latter images he associates with 'witty fictions; in which the affections, or imagination, may perchance find exercise, and entertainment, but the memory and judgement no enriching at all' (p. 223).

If Greville is here echoing Bacon's classification of the faculties and their corresponding categories of knowledge, there is an implied preference for history as the subject of literature. Actually, it is contemporary society as well as 'life' and history in the wider sense which Greville saw his own drama as representing. He destroyed one of his tragedies because he believed it politically dangerous; it could, he said, have been construed as 'personating . . . vices in the present Governors, and government' (p. 156). Moreover, the 'true Stage' for his plays, says Greville, is not the theatre but the reader's own life and times – 'even the state he lives in . . . the vices of former Ages being so like to these of this Age, as it will be easie to find out some affinity' (p. 225). Thus Greville expresses a strong preference for a form of realist mimesis, both in the *Life* and the early sections of *Human Learning*. Yet, when giving a specific account of poetry later on in *Human Learning* he suddenly switches tack, investing the art with an idealist function. It has, he says, the potential for showing a disordered fallen nature 'how to fashion/Her selfe againe' by reference to the ideal – the '*Ideas*' of 'Goodnesse, or God'. Further, poetry '. . . like a Maker,

her creations raise/On lines of truth' and 'Teacheth us order under
pleasures name' (*Human Learning*, stanza 114). Here Greville
embraces a Platonic conception of the artistic function at odds
with the earlier renunciation:

> *These Arts, moulds, workes can but expresse the sinne,*
> *Whence by mans follie, his fall did beginne.*

> (stanza 47)

H. N. Maclean has argued that Greville discounted the fictive
element in poetic creation to the extent of considering himself one
of the 'meaner sort of Painters' disparaged by Sidney in the *Apology*.
These are painters who represent what they actually see rather than
its idealisation.[14] But despite embracing realist mimesis, Greville
retains the didactic function of art even though his 'images of life'
reveal a world so ineradicably corrupt that little moral instruction
of a positive kind can be extracted from it. It is an instance of the
conflict between the absolute and the relative which characterises
his work and, according to a recent account, his life (Ronald
Rebholz, *Life*). Underlying the conflict is uncertainty about the
final relationship of secular and divine. The desired relationship is
for the empirical reality to reveal the absolute order, yet this is what
the Calvinist will usually deny; the secular realm is corrupt and his
transcendent God can only be known through faith and scriptural
authority. Furthermore, if the Calvinist accepts the doctrine of the
decay of nature (as did Greville), then, through 'declination', the
disjunction between the mundane and the divine increases with
time. As the possibility of experiencing divine order through
secular experiences decreases, it becomes increasingly necessary to
affirm its existence through faith.

The distinction in stanza 18 of *Human Learning* between 'apprehension' and 'comprehension' reflects the dilemma (perhaps, too,
its tortuous, obscure syntax is a way of registering the paradoxical
strain which the dilemma involves):

> Besides, these faculties of apprehension;
> Admit they were, as in the soules creation,
> All perfect here, (which blessed large dimension
> As none denies, so but by imagination

> Onely, none knowes) yet in that comprehension,
> Euen through those instruments whereby she works,
> Debility, misprision, imperfection lurkes.

The 'faculties of apprehension' are wit, will and understanding. 'Comprehension' is the successful exercise of those faculties with regard to true knowledge. Essentially it is a distinction which points to a gap between awareness and understanding:

> . . . our capacity;
> How much more sharpe, the more it apprehends,
> Still to distract, the lesse truth comprehends.

> (*Human Learning*, stanza 20)

'Apprehension' becomes the acute, anxious awareness of the 'comprehension' which is desired but denied.

To recapitulate: Sidney equivocates on what, as Tatarkiewicz reminds us, was one of the central problems of Renaissance aesthetics: 'What is the object, the material cause of poetry: reality or fiction?' (*History of Aesthetics*, III, 167). Sidney retains the didactic function of literature but begins to undermine the providential sanction which, in the late sixteenth century, it presupposed and depended upon. Once it is denied that the source of the didactic scheme is a reality both ultimate and more real than the phenomenal world, the scheme itself withers in the face of a world which contradicts it. And, of course, this is what Bacon, by implication, does deny. He answers the question 'reality or fiction?' by opting firmly for the latter. As such his illusionist account of poetry has little application for the contemporary theatre. Yet he also argues that the ideal order which literature has traditionally portrayed, together with the vehicle of that portrayal, poetic justice, are fictions. In this respect Bacon concurs with some contemporary dramatists: intentionally or otherwise both he and they subvert the didactic function of art together with the metaphysical categories which it presupposed. Further, and notwithstanding all the enormous differences between them, the dramatists would have identified with Bacon's conception of what knowledge should be: the world was 'not to be narrowed till it will go into the understanding' but, on the contrary, the understanding must be 'expanded and opened till it can take in the image of the world, as it is in fact' (*Works*, p. 404).

Thus, the ambiguity found in Sidney's *Apology* can be seen as preparing the way for Bacon's subversion of idealist mimesis. Bacon, in turn, leads writers like Greville to a profound distrust of illusion as an aesthetic objective; Greville felt that if literature is to be prevented from becoming mere escapism it must confront reality without any 'formalist' misrepresentation: '*if the matter be in Nature vile,/How can it be made pretious by a stile?*' But he cannot press the theory to its conclusion since the portrayal of this vile matter threatens both the metaphysical absolute and the didactic scheme (nowhere is this more true than in his own play, *Mustapha*). Aristotle and Sidney affirm the superiority of poetry to history; Bacon reverses this priority while for Greville the very distinction between poetry and history collapses into an outright contradiction between absolute and relative, ideal and actual.[15] Metaphysical categories become susceptible to experiential disconfirmation and especially so in the contemporary theatre. As David Bevington has shown: 'the diversity of aim between realistic expression of factual occurrence and the traditional rendering of a moral pattern inevitably produced an irresolution in the English popular theatre' (*From Mankind to Marlowe*, p. 261).

I have argued here that this irresolution is not merely a technical issue, or the lapse in dramatic propriety reprimanded by Eliot as 'faults of inconsistency, faults of incoherency, faults of taste . . . faults of carelessness' (Eliot, *Selected Essays*, p. 111). Rather it is nothing less than a manifestation of the struggle in that period between residual, dominant and emergent conceptions of the real. And the literary theory of that period gives this struggle a particular focus, especially the debates over poetic versus actual justice, 'poesy' versus 'history', the fictive representation versus the actual representation – in short, idealist mimesis versus realist mimesis. Thus, additionally, I have tried to show that the received view that Renaissance literary theory has little relevance to Renaissance literary practice is misleading; certainly it has little direct critical application, but it does have considerable relevance.

5

The Disintegration of Providentialist Belief

Chapter 2 showed how *Antonio's Revenge* and *Troilus and Cressida* subvert providentialist ideology and its corollary, natural law. Here I want to explore further the ideological dimension of providentialist belief in the period and also some of the forces making for what W. R. Elton describes as its sceptical disintegration. Since what follows is concerned almost entirely with these forces – which, in relation to providentialism, were intentionally and unintentionally subversive – it should be stressed at the outset that the very fact of their existence presupposed providentialism as a dominant discourse. Further, even when successfully challenged, ideologies rarely dissolve quietly away; rather, they go through various stages of reaction, displacement, and transformation.

Atheism and Religious Scepticism

In churches, attendance at which was compulsory on Sundays, the congregation would hear many homilies commanding obedience to authority at all levels and threatening dire punishments from God for those who transgressed. In certain respects society at this time became more authoritarian than it had been hitherto (Stone, *The Crisis of the Aristocracy*, pp. 27–36). Doubtless the homilies were an important ideological underpinning of this development. Consider the *Sermon of Obedience* or *An Exhortation concerning good Ordre and Obedience to Rulers and Magistrates*, much admired by E. M. W. Tillyard. It is worth quoting at some length because of the way it constructs the social order in ideological terms: it is an order represented as immutable not only because it derives from God (though this is primary) but also because it is coextensive with the natural order:

83

> Almightie God hath created and appoyncted all thynges, in heaven,
> yearth, and waters, in a moste excellent and perfect ordre. In heaven
> he hath appoynted distincte Orders and states of Archangelles and
> Angelles. In the yearth he hath assigned Kynges, princes, with other
> gouernors under them, all in good and necessarie ordre . . . The
> Sonne, Moone, Starres . . . do kepe their ordre . . . All the partes of the
> whole yere, as Winter, Somer Monethes, Nightes and Dais, continue
> in their ordre . . . Every degree of people, in their vocacion, callyng,
> and office, hath appointed to them their duetie and ordre. Some are in
> high degree, some in lowe, some Kynges and Princes, some inferiors
> and subjectes. (Tillyard, *Shakespeare's History Plays*, p. 19)

Homilies like this one did not correspond to what people could
not help but believe; they were, in part, a dominant reaction to
emergent social forces. So, for example, contrary to the insistence
in this homily on fixed hierarchy, this was a period when social
mobility was more extensive than at any other time before the
nineteenth and twentieth centuries (Stone, *The Crisis*, p. 36).
Further, against its precise theological compartmentalisation of the
universe we might cite Stone's contention that the Elizabethan
period was 'the age of greatest religious indifference before the
twentieth century' (Review, *EHR*, p. 328).

Evidence of actual atheism among intellectuals like Marlowe,
Raleigh, Thomas Harriot and others has been well documented,
albeit in terms of reaction to it rather than first-hand testimonies.[1]
But since the punishments meted out even for religious unorthodoxy
could be death by torture the lack of such testimonies is not surprising. Nashe in *Christ's Tears Over Jerusalem* avows that 'there is no
Sect now in *England* so scattered as Atheisme', and as for Renaissance
sceptics, William R. Elton summarises as follows the criteria which
marked them out: they denied the immortality of the soul; held
God's providence to be faulty; held that man was not different from
the beasts; denied creation *ex nihilo*; attributed to nature what was
said to belong to God (*King Lear and the Gods*, pp. 50, 54).

For Elton atheism is just one aspect of a more general development in the latter half of the sixteenth century whereby it came to
be felt 'first, that providence, if it existed, had little or no relation
to the particular affairs of individual men; and, second, that it
operated in ways bafflingly inscrutable and hidden to human

reason' (p. 9). He explores these attitudes in relation to the Epicurean revival, and to the influence of Montaigne, Calvin, Bacon and others.

Keith Thomas shows that atheistical thoughts troubled even the most devout. He records too a number of fascinating instances of scepticism among the lower orders, including the denial of the soul's immortality, and of the existence of heaven and hell. Behaviour in church seems to have been not dissimilar to that in the theatres: 'Members of the congregation jostled for pews, nudged their neighbours, hawked and spat, knitted, made coarse remarks, told jokes, fell asleep and even let off guns' (*Religion and the Decline of Magic*, pp. 199, 191). In 1598 a Cambridge man was charged with indecent behaviour in church, his offence being 'most loathsome farting, striking, and scoffing speeches'. And according to the same record, although this greatly offended 'the good', not everyone was displeased; indeed, it was to 'the great rejoicing of the bad' (Thomas, p. 192). The inculcation of religion was, concludes Thomas, a difficult business.

Selimus (1594), significantly described by the Prologue as 'a most lamentable historie/Which this last age acknowledgeth for true', contains a fascinating discourse on atheism and one which takes up the debate on the ideological dimension of religion. Selimus advances the familiar idea that the world once enjoyed peace and equality. But ownership generated conflict and the need for authority. In order better to ensure obedience ('quiet awe', l. 332) 'The names of Gods, religion, heauen, and hell' were invented (l. 329). But for Selimus these things are 'meere fictions'. Even familial bonding is part of the same 'policie' to 'strike/Into our minde a certaine kind of loue . . . To keepe the quiet of societie' (ll. 333, 345, 343–6). Selimus then advances a parodic inversion of the dominant order. Accordingly, religion is a disgrace to man (l. 251) while amoral desire, even that involving patricide, fratricide and other forms of brutality, is couched in terms of humanist aspiration:

> We, whose minde in heauenly thoughts is clad,
> Whose bodie doth a glorious spirit beare . . .
> Why should we seeke to make that soule a slaue,
> To which dame Nature so large freedome gaue?

> (ll. 349–53)

And as for the after-life: 'Parricides, when death hath giuen them rest/Shall haue as good a part as the rest' since 'In deaths voyd kingdome raignes eternall night' (ll. 359–60, 362).

Selimus is a good instance of how even a relatively unsophisticated play could problematise religion by probing its status as ideology. Its title character, though 'evil', is successful, intriguing, witty and, in the closing stages of the action, glorified. But this is not at all problematic compared with the fact that this is a play which, by presenting as it does the terror and violence wreaked by Selimus, might well have persuaded an audience that religion *was* indispensable for maintaining the social order while at the same time casting serious doubt as to its veracity. After all, nothing in the play effectively contradicts Selimus' argument that religion is a mystification of the social order, and 'meere fictions' cannot continue to work effectively in that respect when successfully exposed.

Even though we cannot say finally how widespread it was, atheism in this period certainly constituted a coherent discourse. Nevertheless (to anticipate the later part of this chapter) it should be said that, just as subversive as the atheistical sub-text of some Jacobean tragedies, is the way that others sceptically activate contradictions within Christianity. This was a dramatic strategy made possible in part by the wider historical process described by Alan Sinfield: 'The political and social conditions of the sixteenth century facilitated an institutional split in Christendom, and the consequence was a polarisation and hardening of doctrine. Issues which at other times were accommodated by logical evasions and evocative phraseology were teased out and stated in uncompromising terms, and the problems which ultimately confront all traditional Christianity come sharply into focus' (*Literature in Protestant England*, p. 8). The scepticism encouraged by this constitutes in part the interrogative aspect of Jacobean tragedy even when that tragedy does not advance the atheistical conclusions of *Selimus*. Lastly, the various sceptical perspectives current in this period should be borne in mind not just as the prerogative of the individual playwright but also as possible audience positions,[2] different from each other yet similar in being distrustfully distanced from establishment ideology.

Providentialism and History

Establishment providentialism, as the homily on obedience shows, aimed to provide a metaphysical ratification of the existing social order. God encoded the natural and social world with a system of regulative (and self-regulating) law. The existing order, give or take a few aberrations, is the legitimate one. To depart from it is to transgress God's law. Regulative encoding was the teleological premise on which rested many of the different appeals to providence. But it was reinforced in this period by the idea of specific intervention (particular or special providence), usually, though not always, involving a punitive action by God or one of His agents. This was the form of providentialism favoured by protestantism, implying as it did constant and active surveillance. Its occurrence in the Elizabethan drama has been interpreted by some critics as proof that these playwrights adhered to a fundamentally orthodox Christianity.

Divine intervention could be invoked to explain virtually anything that happened but it was most often used to show that 'misfortune' was in fact divine punishment. The theatrical world was subjected to much providentialist analysis; instances of the plague were interpreted as God's vengeance for people's attendance at plays rather than church; likewise with the collapse of an auditorium in 1583;[3] while Thomas Beard in his *Theatre of God's Judgement* (1597) claimed that Christopher Marlowe's violent death – he was stabbed in a tavern fight – was 'a manifest sign of God's judgement' on this blasphemous dramatist (chapter xxv). Judging by the extent to which it was invoked, the idea of a retributive providence held great sway. But it was by no means an unquestioned orthodoxy. Montaigne was just one who dissented from such ideas: 'If the frost nips the vines in my village, my priest concludes that the wrath of God is hanging over the human race.' Others, adds Montaigne, interpret the civil wars in similar fashion 'without thinking that many worse things have been seen, and that times are good in ten thousand other parts of the world' (I, 56). Those in the middle classes who were upwardly mobile and gaining positions of power – and there were many of them – could be expected to be sceptical of providentialist legitimations of the existing order (though they might also substitute similar legitimations of their own position). At the lower end of the social scale many were suffering terribly from the gathering crisis which, in socio-economic terms, characterised the period 1580 to 1630 (Wrightson, *English Society*, p. 142). Hardship caused by long-term changes like population expansion, inflation and declining real wages, was exacerbated by catastrophic harvest failures. The explanation of misfortune favoured by those who actually suffered it was not divine punishment but the rival doctrine of bad luck (Thomas, *Religion and the Decline of Magic*, p. 131). So there were those right across the social scale for whom, in principle, a sceptical view of retributive providence would make good sense. I explore this in relation to *The Revenger's Tragedy* later in this section; here I want to illustrate it briefly with reference to a play which might seem the least amenable to such analysis, namely Tourneur's *The Atheist's Tragedy*.

Ostensibly this play is a piece of unmitigated propaganda for a retributive providentialism. Its main protagonist, D'Amville, is a monstrous atheist who finally gets his comeuppance (from God). Yet throughout it is a play unsettled by a mocking intelligence which constantly threatens to transgress its own providentialist brief. In Act III the imprisoned Charlemont ponders the injustice of his position:

> I grant thee, heaven, thy goodness doth command
> Our punishments, but yet no further than
> The measure of our sins. How should they else
> Be just? Or how should that good purpose of
> Thy justice take effect by bounding men
> Within the confines of humanity
> When our afflictions do exceed our crimes?
> Then they do rather teach the barb'rous world
> Examples that extend her cruelties
> Beyond their own dimensions, and instruct
> Our actions to be more, more, barbarous
>
> (III. iii. 1–11)

The stirrings of rebellion which this questioning brings about are quickly stilled and in any case shown to be premature. Eventually the justice which Charlemont wants is effected, albeit in an episode which hilariously parodies the by then rather tired dramatic convention whereby divine punishment is not only done but seen to be done; D'Amville, about to execute the innocents, Charlemont and Castabella, has an 'accident' or, in the words of the stage direction, '*As he raises up the axe strikes out his own brains*' (V. ii. 235). The Executioner dispels any doubt: 'In lifting up the axe I think h'as knocked his brains out' (V. ii. 236). It is a scene which relegates providentialism to the same fictive category as poetic justice (which is what Bacon also does with it: *Works*, p. 88, quoted above, p. 76). As he dies, D'Amville confirms 'a power above' which, in striking him down, 'knew the judgement I deserved/And gave it'. But it is left to the judge to push the poetic reach of providential justice to its fictive limit:

> The power of that eternal providence
> Which overthrew his projects in their pride
> Hath made your griefs th'instruments to raise
> Your blessings
>
> (V. ii. 264–7)

Thus contained by the aesthetic neatness of comedic closure, the tragic-didactic status of providentialism is rendered suspect; as an answer to Charlemont's questioning this is, quite consciously, no answer at all but an ironic use of 'Feigned History [i.e. poetry] to give some shadow of satisfaction to the mind of man in those points wherein the nature of things doth deny it' (Bacon, above, p. 76).

Providentialism also constituted an ideological underpinning for ideas of absolute monarchy and divine right. Here of course the doctrine existed in a more complex and sophisticated form. James I uses it in defending the claims of royal power against the challenges of Puritan and Papist,[4] for example, and it is in this domain that we encounter providentialism in the form of the notorious 'Tudor myth' – a teleological interpretation of history as the revelation and consolidation of God's design for England with the Tudor rulers being His agents and heirs on earth. Not so long ago it was accepted by many critics (and generations of their students) that the Tudor myth was the fundamental structuring principle of Shakespeare's English history plays. According to E. M. W. Tillyard (in a book which went through nine impressions in the first thirty years of its publication): 'Behind the disorder of history

Shakespeare assumed some kind of order or degree on earth having its counterpart in heaven.' In this he was at one with his 'educated contemporaries'. And as for the 'orthodox doctrines of rebellion and of the monarchy', doctrines underpinned by the Tudor myth, these 'were shared by every section of the community' (*Shakespeare's History Plays*, pp. 21, 64).

This notion of what both Shakespeare and the Elizabethans fundamentally believed has now been discredited, most recently and conclusively by those who, like H. A. Kelly, have looked at the actual political uses of the myth (*Divine Providence in the England of Shakespeare's Histories*). By so looking we find that there was not one but several, rival providentialist accounts of history, Lancastrian, anti-Lancastrian and Yorkist. Depending on which was advanced the monarch was seen either as agent or transgressor of God's plan. In the light of this we see not just that most of Shakespeare's history plays fail to substantiate this (non-existent) unitary myth, but also that some of them have precisely the opposite effect of revealing how myth is exploited ideologically.[5] We can also find confirmation of this in Bacon's contention that a man is likely to be unimpeded by the envy of others in his own pursuit of power if he attributes his successes 'rather to divine Providence and felicity, than to his own virtue or policy' (*Essays*, p. 160).

Organic Providence

In explicit opposition to the view of Shakespeare as the advocate of 'a timid and unoriginal Christianity' (Sanders, *The Dramatist and the Received Idea*, p. 361), there has emerged the view of him as an immanent providentialist, believing not in the crude idea of retributive intervention from above, but the more sophisticated (and older) idea of natural law. Thus Sanders finds in certain of Shakespeare's plays what he calls 'natural providence', that 'which has emerged out of the natural, an enactment of universal moral law, not a mere proclamation of it; . . . it grows out of the soil of human life, rather than descending supernaturally from above' (p. 104).[6]

Sanders identifies Shakespeare with the so-called Christian humanists of the period (e.g. Huarte and Hooker) who believed in 'the order and disposition which God placed amongst naturall things' (Huarte, quoted from Sanders, p. 114). Natural providence informs the vision of the mature Shakespeare and involves an act of faith in the morality of the universe, says Sanders, adding with commendable directness: 'One is prompted to ask whether some such faith in the essential morality of the universe is not a necessary faith for the dramatist' (p. 119). Here again is the *telos* of harmonic integration and in a typically 'English' version: by construing it as immanent, the cumbersome apparatuses of dogma and metaphysics are dispensed with (see above, chapter 3).

Natural law and ideas associated with it have served to recuperate Shakespeare as a providentialist and, at the same time, to denigrate some of his contemporaries as playwrights of lesser 'vision' fatally seduced by the disintegrative tendencies of their age. D. L. Frost for example finds that whereas both Webster and Ford are oppressed by 'a hopeless complication and ambiguity of moral issues' Shakespeare by contrast 'seems unbewildered' because of an adherence to 'a "natural" moral order, a self-righting world' (*The School of Shakespeare*, p. 119). Nothing of course could be less true of a play like *King Lear* where the concept of nature is interrogated and its multiple meanings, often contradictory, laid open. Commenting on nature in *Lear* Raymond Williams declares: 'What in the history of thought may be seen as a confusion or an overlapping is often the precise moment of the dramatic impulse, since it is because the meaning and the experiences are uncertain and complex that the dramatic mode is more powerful . . . All at once nature is innocent, is unprovided, is sure, is unsure, is fruitful, is destructive, is a pure force and is tainted and cursed' (*Problems in Materialism and Culture*, p. 72).

Lear is only one of several texts which confirm that the concept of natural law was nowhere near as stable and coherent as advocates of organic providence would have us believe; Donne, for example, declares in *Biathanatos* (p. 36) that 'this terme the law of Nature, is so variously and unconstantly deliver'd, as I confesse I read it a hundred times before I understood it once, or can conclude it to signifie that which the author should at that time meane'.[7] And as for Shakespeare's contemporaries, far from being inadequate to the task of affirming natural law, some of them actually saw it for what it might be, namely an ideological legitimation of the dominant social order. For them (as Macherey argues in relation to other kinds of literature) 'chaos and chance are never excuses for confusion, but the token of the irruption of the real' (*A Theory of Literary Production*, p. 39). And theirs are plays whose interrogation of providentialism is sometimes the stronger for being internal rather than external; that is, rather than offering a simple atheistic repudiation of providentialist belief, they play upon the contradictions and the stress-points within it. In effect they inscribe a subversive discourse within the dominant one.

From Mutability to Cosmic Decay

Milton's *Comus* declares a faith in natural law – or at least a self-regulating world, one in which evil is programmed to self-destruct. Such a vision is a delight to the providentialist. But just as interesting as the assertion of faith in this order is the inference to be drawn if history and experience prove otherwise:

> Virtue may be assailed, but never hurt,
> Surprised by unjust force, but not enthralled;
> . . . evil on itself shall back recoil,
> And mix no more with goodness, when at last,
> Gathered like scum, and settled to itself,
> It shall be in eternal restless change
> Self-fed and self-consumed. If this fail,
> The pillared firmament is rottenness,
> And earth's base built on stubble
>
> (589–99)

'if this fail': one implication to be drawn from the controversy over cosmic decay, to which I now want to turn, is an underlying and pervasive fear of just such a failure. But first a general point.

Although chaos is the opposite of order and therefore the opposite of traditional metaphysical mainstays of order (the Platonic

Form for example, or Christian providentialism) it nevertheless often gets construed – especially in literary criticism – as a kind of inverted metaphysical category; its very ubiquity is made to imply a transhistorical irreducible state of disorder, essentially the same behind its different manifestations and to be explained *a priori* – in terms of human nature, say, or the events of pre-history. But just as the critique of the positive universal can disclose the historical conditions which it occludes or seeks to transcend, so with its negative counterpart. To explore any period's conception of chaos is to discover not the primordial state of things, but fears and anxieties very specific to that period. To put it another way, that order and chaos comprise a binary opposition is obvious enough; to take up this relation historically is to render the obvious both interesting and revealing.

In the early seventeenth century the preoccupation with chaos, even when expressed in metaphoric, abstract or theological terms, was undoubtedly rooted in a fear of social change and social disorder (the two things often being equated); because of a 'crushing burden of belief in the need for social stability, all change had to be interpreted as the maintenance of tradition' (Stone, *The Crisis*, p. 22). But some change could only be seen as the disintegration of tradition, and so too of order. And to dwell on that disintegration, particularly at the level of belief, seemed to hold out the possibility of chaos come again. There was nothing intrinsically progressive about the Jacobean obsession with chaos; in some respects just the reverse was true. As we have already seen, the inculcation of belief could seem doubly important in a state which lacked more overtly coercive means of control. Thus Bacon could write to some judges in 1617: 'There will be a perpetual defection, except you keep men in by preaching, as well as law doth by punishing' (*Works*, XIII, p. 213). One thing preaching would dwell on in order to 'keep men in' would be the horror of chaos. Thus the Jacobean obsession with disintegration may reveal, directly or indirectly, some of the real forces making for social instability and change (just as does Bacon's anxiety over defection); further, time and again what is involved is a disintegration of ideological formations which reveals the phenomenon of secular power relaitions. To this extent it was an obsession which could be used subversively as well as conservatively.

*

That the Elizabethan/Jacobean preoccupation with the supposed decay of nature and the universe was a major cause of melancholy and pessimism in the literature of this period has been persuasively argued by, among others, George Williamson and Victor Harris.[8] Often however, crucial differences between ideas of decay and those of mutability have been overlooked. Such differences are important since, in its most extreme form, decay theory came to threaten the religious context out of which it grew and it is at this point that Jacobean tragedy makes subversive use of the idea.

If we tend to forget the Elizabethan capacity to have the sensory imagination triggered by a commonplace abstraction, we are suddenly reminded of it when confronted by the range of meanings encoded in a word like 'dust':

> Leave me O Love, which reachest but to dust.
>
> > (Sidney, *Certain Sonnets*)

> O that thou shouldst give dust a tongue
> > To crie to thee,
> And then not heare it crying!
>
> > (Herbert, 'Deniall')

> Dust hath closed Helen's eye.
>
> > (Nashe, 'Adieu, Farewell Earth's Bliss')

Each poem implies a contradiction intrinsic to mortality: for Sidney it is that to live life at its most intense is only to hasten its ruin ('Love . . . which *reachest* but to dust'); for Herbert it is that we are created dependent only to be abandoned; for Nashe it is that the dust which closes Helen's eye signifies a mutability at once an agent of external destruction and of inner dissolution. Yet each contradiction is only apparent; each, in the context of its respective poem, is resolved into a paradox of faith. However, the different degrees of certitude which accompany these resolutions are revealing.

Sidney's resolution is the most familiar and the most confident: 'Then farewell world, thy uttermost I see,/Eternal Love maintain thy life in me.' Herbert's resolution has the initially rebellious voice finally acquiescing in humility and a request for grace. His poem ends with a rhyming couplet, omitted from all previous stanzas: 'thy favours granting my request,/They and my minde may chime,/And mend my rhyme'. Nashe's lyric is the least confident by far. Its form and cadences indicate that mutability and death are here the subject of elegiac lament. But the poet is also contemplating them from a state of sickness, and the second stanza startles us with the substitution of 'plague' for the anticipated commonplace (Time): 'All things, to end are made,/The plague full swift goes bye.'

Mutability as a literary convention with familiar and recurring signifiers could, then, be easily contained within a providential scheme. But when, as with the Nashe lyric, it was presented as plague and disease this was less clearly the case. That much can be seen from the way the final stanza presses suffering against formal closure:

> Mount we unto the sky.
> I am sick, I must dye:
> Lord have mercy on us.

The second line interposes a stark reality which at once checks the transcendent aspiration of the first line and makes the last into more of a questioning plea than faith-full acquiescence.

Perhaps the least disturbing conception of mutability in this period was that which saw it as an aspect of a natural order both cyclical and regenerative: 'Times go by turns and chances change by course,/From foul to fair, from better happ to worse' (Southwell, *Times Go By Turns*). From this position it is only a short step to Spenser's idea of mutability informed by eternity: 'Yet is eterne in mutability' (*Faerie Queene*, III. 6. 47).

Mutability as a manifestation of Fortune rather than eternity was far more problematic. Simply put, there had been three main conceptions of Fortune: a goddess independent of God, one who shares power with him, and one who is completely subservient to him. One of the developments charted by Willard Farnham in *The Medieval Heritage of Elizabethan Tragedy* was the Christian substitution of divine determinism for pagan fatalism, the third of these conceptions for the first.[9] But the transition was not easily accomplished; Fortune could never quite be divested of its pagan fatalism. Thus we find Puttenham for example arguing that the drama shows 'the mutability of Fortune and the just punishment of God in revenge of a vicious and evil life' (*Elizabethan Critical Essays*, II, 35). Suggested here is that tension which Jacobean tragedy frequently exploits.

The pagan conception of Fortune was not as simple as is sometimes imagined. L. G. Salingar points out that the concept has never expressed 'a single unitary idea, but always a state of mental tension' (*Shakespeare and the Tradition of Comedy*, pp. 131–2). So on the one hand Fortune is the personification of earthly instability and as such the obverse of order, on the other hand, 'by a striking contradiction of thought, one at least of Fortune's principal emblems, the wheel, suggests the exact opposite of caprice and unpredictability' (p. 132).

Conceptions of mutability which pointed toward the decay of nature were the most disturbing of all. Belief in the decay of nature and the universe is an old one. Lucretius in *De Rerum Natura* saw the imperfections of the universe as evidence of its decline. The idea is taken up later in Augustinian theology and from the mid-sixteenth century onwards becomes increasingly prevalent, intensified by among other things protestant theology and the so-called new philosophy. As it existed in the early seventeeth century cosmic decay needs to be distinguished from mutability in at least two crucial respects.

First, in its most extreme form, it draws on a model of an absolute, irreversible decline which precludes the reassuring idea of 'eterne in mutability':

> as all things vnder the Sunne haue one time of strength, and another weakenesse, a youth and beautie, and then age and deformitie: so Time it selfe (vnder the deathfull shade of whose winges all things decay and wither) hath wasted and worne out that liuely vertue of Nature in Man, and Beasts, and Plants; yea the Heauens themselues being of a pure and cleansed matter shall waxe old as a garment. (Raleigh, *History of the World*, p. 144)

Cosmic decay thus tended to make for an absolute distinction between eternity and mutability:

Heaven waxeth old, and all the *Spheares* above
Shall one day faint, and their swift motion stay;
And *Time* it selfe in *Time* shall cease to move;
Onely the Soule survives, and lives for aye.

(John Davies, *Nosce Teipsum*, ll. 1593–6)

Second, whereas mutability, Fortune, and time all tended to be expressed as forces or agents external to and acting upon that which they erode – a tendency reinforced in literature by the conventions of abstraction and personification: 'And Time that gave doth now his gift confound' – decay, by contrast, tends to denote an inner process, an agency of self-destruction which is self-generated and self-stultifying.[10] '*Life*,' says Montaigne, '*is a materiall and corporall motion, an action imperfect and disordered by its own essence*' (*Essays*, III, 237). Cosmic decay typically represented individual, society, and nature in terms of four related but separately identifiable states: paralysed dislocation, self-stultifying conflict, disintegrating form and ineradicable corruption and disease. All four states occur in Donne's *First Anniversary*, probably the most famous literary exposition of decay.

Paralysed dislocation here finds expression in terms of both mankind and the world:

Then, as mankind, so is the world's whole frame
Quite out of joint, almost created lame:
For, before God has made up all the rest,
Corruption entered . . .

(191–4)

Here, additionally, there is the intriguing suggestion that God was in less than complete control of the creation.

Lines like those borrowed from the *First Anniversary* by Webster for the *Duchess of Malfi* express as clearly as any the state of self-stultification:

We seem ambitious, God's whole work to undoe;
Of nothing he made us, and we strive too,
To bring ourselves to nothing back

(155–7; cf. *Duchess*, III. v. 79–80)

Referring to the belief that coitus shortens life, Donne insists too on the stultifying basis of sexuality: 'We kill ourselves, to propagate our kind' (109–10). The idea recalls Spenser: 'For thy decay thou seekest by thy desire' (*Mutability Cantos*, VII. 59).

As regards disintegrating form, this world, says Donne, is 'crumbled out again to his atomies,/'Tis all in pieces, all coherence gone'; moreover, 'what form so'er we see,/Is discord, and rude incongruity' (213; 323–4).

Lastly, images of ineradicable disease penetrating to and from the core of life pervade the poem: 'Sick world, yea dead, yea putrified . . . Corrupt and mortal in thy purest part . . .' (56, 62); not only is the world 'rotten at the heart' (242) but we have to endure the fact that there are 'Corruptions in our brains, or in our hearts,/ Poisoning the fountains, whence our actions spring' (330–1).

It is difficult today to comprehend the extent to which life at that time was subject to illness and disease and why for example they constitute not just the occasion for, but the informing, obsessive, theme of a work like Donne's *Devotions*. Not only was the mortality rate high, but even those who survived were liable to experience considerable pain and sickness during a life of comparatively brief expectation. Epidemics accounted for a large proportion of deaths; as is only too well known, the bubonic plague wiped out thousands of people in each of its outbreaks. In his fifth meditation Donne remarks that 'A long sicknesse will weary friends at last, but a pestilentiall sicknes averts them from the beginning' (p. 23). This makes the sick bed worse than the grave for 'thogh in both I be equally alone, in my bed I *know* it, and *feele* it' (p. 26). The tenth meditation describes the sheer insecurity and precariousness of health, and the fear of sudden illness and death: whereas the world had foreknowledge of the flood 'the *fever* shall break out in an instant, and consume all' (p. 51).

If ever there was needed a providentialist rationalisation of misfortune it was in relation to the plague. But by the same token nowhere were the shortcomings of that rationalisation more apparent (see Thomas, *Religion and the Decline of Magic*, pp. 99–102, 125–6, 129–30). In 1603, the same year that Holland's translation of Plutarch's *Morals* appeared, some 30,000 people in London alone – one sixth of its inhabitants – died from the plague. In Plutarch could be found an alternative to (for example) the puritan explanation of the plague as God's punishment for tolerating catholics, the theatres, drunkenness etc. (Thomas, pp. 99–100): 'there is no other cause of good and evill accidents of this life, but either fortune or els the will of man' (*Morals*, 1603, p. 538). And in Holland's translation of Pliny's *History* (1601) could be found the assertion that the doctrine of providence 'is a toy and vanity worthy to be laughed at' (p. 27).

Of course the devout might insist that decay was part of the divine plan, at least to the extent that original sin, from which decay stems, was part of that plan. Man has ruined himself and God in His wisdom not only permits the process to continue but actually wills it. Thus in a passage which links two characteristics of decay, ineradicable disease and self-stultification, Donne tells us that life is 'poisoned in the fountain, perished at the core, withered in the root, in the fall of Adam' (*LXXX Sermons*, no. 13). Additionally or alternatively, the Christian might argue that what this world lacks the other one possesses, it being man's duty to renounce the first in favour of the second. This is Donne's answer in *The Second Anniversary*:

> Only in heaven joy's strength is never spent,
> And accidental things are permanent.
> Joy of a soul's arrival ne'er decays.
>
> (487–9)

But for others neither answer seemed adequate to the task of reconciling providentialism with the belief in decay. It is hardly surprising that Donne in *The First Anniversary* suggests that 'ruin' (l. 99) and 'Corruption' (l. 194) frustrated 'Even God's purpose' (l. 101) and, consequently, that both man and the world were 'almost *created* lame' (l. 192; my italics). Given a belief in decay the inference that the human race and the world have been either miscreated or abandoned was an easy one to draw, especially since decay, as we shall see, contradicts the idea of an immanent God.

Goodman and Elemental Chaos

Godfrey Goodman was the most noted advocate of the decay thesis. His *The Fall of Man, or the Corruption of Nature* appeared in

1616. In it he argued that the material world was subject to progressive and irreversible deterioration. There were two interrelated processes whereby this occurred, privation and the conflict of opposites.

Deriving from Aristotle, Goodman's idea of privation is rather obscure but it refers generally to the idea of unrealised potential: 'a privation is, when a thing is capable to be, and ought to be, but is not' (p. 390). But what really makes for the world's disintegrative tendency is the opposition and 'contrarietie of elementarie qualities . . . ever active and opposing each other' (p. 32). The conflict exists in everything comprised of the four elements, from microcosm through to macrocosm, within individuals and between species. Even the universe is subject to it. God retards but does not halt the process.

Goodman insisted that his argument was compatible with Christian providentialism. Occasionally he pauses in his elaboration of the world's appalling dislocation to reassure the reader of this. At one stage he actually reassures God himself. 'Sure I am, that thou hast done and permitted all things for the best: I do not here intend to dishonour thee, to disparage the great work of thy creation.' On the contrary: 'in relating these miseries, thy goodness may better appear' (p. 65). Unfortunately for Goodman it did not so appear; the disjunction between divine perfection and secular chaos was too great. Even Goodman comes close to saying that God botched the creation: He 'created not the elements thus rebellious, but leaving them to themselves, then began the insurrection' (p. 18).

It is not surprising then that those like George Hakewill – Goodman's main opponent in the contemporary debate – opposed the belief in decay because it 'makes men murmure and repine against God under the name of Fortune and Destinie' (Preface, *Apologie*).[11] Another (later) opponent of decay argued that by it 'the majesty of God is dishonoured, the commendable indeavours of Man are hindered'.[12] Decay theory was controversial in another respect too. Bizarre as it may now seem, it was then thought to have clear political as well as doctrinal implications. Goodman claimed that a belief in decay was the best way to keep the masses in acquiescent awe; to offer them hope of a better future was to run the risk of exciting a 'mutinee' or an 'innovation' (this latter word then being a common word of abuse). Conversely, Hakewill argued that 'there is not so much feare of Innovation from the country *boares* . . . by meanes of my opinion, as of laziness and murmuring in them by meanes of yours, if they be once persuaded that nothing can bee improved by industry but all things by a fatall necessity grow worse and worse' (*Apologie*, pp. 20, 22; quoted p. 52 of Harris, *All Coherence Gone*). Hakewill, on this and other issues, speaks to the future; those following him take up the ideas of uniformity in change and nature's encoded order (the 'constancy of nature'), aligning them now with an optimistic protestantism, itself on the side of the new science, the 'moderns' against the 'ancients'.[13]

By glancing forward we can see this as just one dimension of the radical protestantism which fed into the English revolution. More generally, and most importantly perhaps, it was a protestantism which challenged the idea that providence entailed passive obedience to divine and secular authority, advocating instead oppositional activity on God's behalf. This is what Hill has called a 'transitional' conception of providence, one moving away from passive obedience towards activity for the relief of man's estate (*God's Englishman*, p. 237). It was also one which rendered providentialism's status as political strategy even clearer than before, and so contributed eventually to it being dispensed with altogether. Thus Cromwell for example, speaking in the Commons of the proposed challenge to the king, was reported as follows by Clement Walker: 'if any man moved this upon design, he [Cromwell] should think him the greatest traitor in the world; but since providence and necessity had cast them upon it, he should pray God to bless their counsels, though he were not provided on the sudden to give them counsel' (quoted from Hill, p. 233).

Goodman was at the furthest possible remove not only from the forward-looking Hakewill but also from contemporaries like Richard Hooker. Thus whereas Goodman finds in the essence of things only ineradicable decay, destruction through perpetual elemental strife, Hooker in total contrast finds a divinely sanctioned essence: 'God hath his influence *into the very essence of all things*, without which influence . . . their utter annihilation could not choose but follow . . . all things which God hath made are in that respect the offspring of God, they are *in him* as effects in their highest cause, he likewise actually *is in them*' (*Laws*, II, 226–7; Hooker's emphasis).

Hooker concurs with Goodman in thinking that the world would he annihilated but for God's providence but differs in thinking that annihilation is prevented by what he calls '*the first law eternal*', a law made by God and which even He 'hath eternally purposed to keep'. This law precedes, and informs, the other kinds of law which encode a regulative order in the universe, in particular the law of nature and the law of reason (*Laws*, I, 153–5, 158). In short, decay theory threatens what was perhaps the most powerful tenet of providentialism (and the one upon which 'natural providence' of the kind advanced by Sanders and other critics is premised), the idea of purpose and order teleologically encoded both in the universe generally and in the identity of things in particular. Instead it posits a universe where future, purpose, and identity disintegrate in perpetual strife.

In the *Devotions* Donne dwells imaginatively on the wholesale annihilation which decay, working at and from the centre of things, implies for a geocentric and hierarchical universe. Not even the heavens escape: 'The *Heavens* containe the *Earth*, the *Earth, Cities, Cities*, Men. And all these are Concentrique; the common *centre* to them all, is *decay, ruine . . . Annihilation*' (p. 51).

Cosmic decay rested on an unstable conjunction of residual and emergent. Based on the one hand on a deeply pessimistic, Christian sense of the implications of original sin, it at the same time drew impetus from the writings of such as Copernicus, Kepler and Galileo, indicating that the earth was not at the centre of the universe and, moreover, that the heavens as well as the earth were subject to mutability. Again it is Donne who testifies to the way that the new philosophy could, if necessary, reinforce the old teaching: 'I need not call in new Philosophy, that denies a settled-nesse, an acquiescence in the very body of the Earth to move in that place, where we thought the Sunne had moved; I need not that helpe, that the Earth it selfe is in Motion, to prove this, That nothing upon Earth is permanent' (Sermon LXXX).

The renewed sense of universal decay seems to have been in part a reaction formation to crisis and doubt from within Christianity itself. Ironically that crisis could only be exacerbated by the fact that advocates of decay drew for support on an emergent 'philosophy' which in the long term would displace not just belief in decay – it ceased to be an issue by about the middle of the seventeenth century – but the specific Christian world view from which it derived.

Providence and Protestantism

It might be objected that while the decay thesis runs counter to the providentialism of Christian humanists like Hooker, this was not so in relation to the severer protestant theology; what might be a heresy for any theology which postulated an immanent god is compatible with one whose god is punitive, transcendent and incomprehensible. Protestantism was, however, more complicated than this suggests. To begin with, Calvin did not subscribe to the idea of increasing decay (though Luther did). Moreover, as might be expected, Calvin states repeatedly that God is in complete control of the universe; not the slightest thing occurs without His willing it; He makes 'manifest his perfections in the whole structure of the universe' such that 'no man . . . is incapacitated for discerning such proofs of [God's] creative wisdom' (*Institutes*, I. v. 1, 2). This is Calvin as propagandist for God's goodness and power. When he contemplates human depravity the story is very different. As Walzer remarks in his discussion of natural law theory, 'the only aspect of the organic image that appealed to Puritan preachers was the idea of disease' (*The Revolution of the Saints: A Study in the Origins of Radical Politics*, p. 176). Calvin, in language which strongly evokes the decay thesis, describes the human body as not just the receptacle but the nurse of disease carrying with it its own destruction; human life is 'interwoven with death' (I. xvii. 10). Adam not only corrupted the race but 'perverted the whole order of nature in heaven and earth [and] deteriorated his race by his revolt'; moreover 'through man's fault a curse has extended above and below, over all the regions of the world' (II. i. 5). The entire human race, 'corrupted by an inherent viciousness', brings 'an innate corruption from the very womb'; 'the impurity of parents is transmitted to their children, so that all, without exception, are originally depraved' (II. 1. 6). Nor does nature escape; Calvin talks of its 'overthrow and destruction' and tells us decisively that 'its ruin is complete' (II. iii. 2). In short, although in the Fall 'the image of God was not utterly effaced and destroyed' in Adam, nevertheless, it was 'so corrupted that *anything which remains* is fearful deformity . . . a ruin, confused, mutilated, and tainted with impurity' (I. xv. 4).

It is not only in relation to the corruption of human kind that Calvin seems to contradict his earlier assertion of the visibility of providence; he also tells us that although 'the order, method, end, and necessity of events' are controlled by God 'to us, however, they *are* fortuitous . . . such being the form under which they present themselves to us'. And this is so because they are in fact 'hidden in the counsel of God'. The manifest contradiction is, as always in Calvin, diverted by appeal to faith: 'what seems to us contingence, faith will recognise as the secret impulse of God' (I. xvi. 9). Elsewhere Calvin acknowledges the full extent of the adversity which these 'fortuitous' (i.e. divinely ordained) events involve; among 'the accidents' to which life is liable he lists, with not a little relish, disease, pestilence, war, sterility, penury and death, adding: 'these are the events which make men curse their life, detest the day of their birth, execrate the light of heaven, even censure God, and (as they are eloquent in blasphemy) charge him with cruelty and injustice' (III. vii. 10). Calvin contends that people reason in this way because they are ignorant of his explanation as to why things are thus. Equally it may well have been because they found his explanation and others like it woefully inadequate. Granted that, it is not difficult to see how Calvin's own graphic portrayal of adversity, his insistence on the incomprehensibility of providence and the extent of people's and nature's inherent corruption, actually fuelled despair, nihilism and, even, the 'censure [of] God'. Significantly, Calvin was himself aware of the danger of attending too much 'to the natural ills of man, and thereby seem to ascribe them to the Author of nature; impiety . . . not hesitating, when accused, to plead against God, and throw the blame of its guilt upon Him' (I. xv. 1).

Protestantism thus intensified religious paradox. In a sense this was intentional: for Calvin faith was generated on the axis of paradox and from within experienced contradiction.[14] The problem of divine order versus secular chaos is only one of several notorious instances of this: God is good, yet evil only occurs because he actively wills it; God offers salvation to his people through Christ yet predestines many to damnation; God is merciful yet the reprobate is given no chance, and so on.[15] In retrospect we might feel that Calvin's fatal mistake was to charge too much to faith. The paradoxical leap of faith which protestantism finally and crucially demanded proved impossible for many; what in Calvin's eyes demonstrated the necessity for and unavoidability of faith, in theirs seemed to contradict its very possibility.[16] Michael Walzer is surely correct in arguing that Calvin 'sought a cure for anxiety not in reconciliation but in obedience' and that, in the service of this aim, his is a theology which is strategically ambiguous and which posits alienation in order to encourage discipline (*The Revolution of the Saints*, pp. 28, 30). But its effect could be, and was, otherwise: the anxious might dwell disobediently upon the very alienation and ambiguity which was supposed to make them acquiesce. Luther had put the point at issue with dangerous clarity: 'God governs the external affairs of the world in such a way that, if you regard and follow the judgement of human reason, you are forced to say, either that there is no God, or that God is unjust, *as the poet said*: "I am often tempted to think there are no gods"' (*On the Bondage of the Will*, p. 315; my italics; Plutarch, in 'Of Superstition' [*Morals*, trans. 1603], makes much the same point).

The English Calvinist William Perkins tells us that an evil conscience, Hell and Death 'are good, because they are ordained of God, for the execution of his justice, howsoever in themselves and to us they be evill' (*The Whole Treatise of Cases of Conscience*, I. 1. 2). Notice that Perkins too intensifies rather than suppresses the paradox: these things in themselves and to us *are* evil, not just apparently so. Again, it is not surprising that Milton's Adam (for example) comes close to accusing God of being a rather powerful sadist (*Paradise Lost*, 10, 743ff). Dramatists like Marlowe exploit these contradictions for explicitly subversive effect, those like Greville became ensnared in them – the effect of which is hardly less subversive when, as in *Mustapha*, it leads to just that censure of God which Calvin warns against.

Ralph Cudworth was one of those who later criticised the determinism of Calvinism, calling it a 'Theologick Fate' whereby 'God's will is not regulated by his essential and immutable Goodness and Justice [but] meer arbitrary will omnipotent'. According to Cudworth this was a theology which had actually encouraged rather than checked the disintegration of moral life. Dominic Baker-Smith cites this passage from Cudworth in support of his contention that the effect of Calvinism could be one of alienation ('Religion and John Webster', p. 212).

One instance of this, intriguing in its association of cosmic decay with the arbitrariness of God's will, occurs in Nashe's *Summer's Last Will and Testament*. The character Ver, by conjoining 'Theologic Fate' with the idea of cosmic decay, comes up with an argument in favour of reckless hedonism. He begins as follows: 'This world is transitory; it was made of nothing, and it must to nothing. Wherefore, if we will do the will of our high Creator, whose will it is that it pass to nothing, we must help to consume it to nothing' (Nashe, p. 155). Here surely is a protest against 'mere arbitrary will omnipotent'; behind Ver's blasphemous wit is a damning indictment of divine sadism: 'Gold is more vile than men. Men die in thousands, and then thousands, yea, many times in hundred thousands, in one battle. If then the best husband be so liberal of his best handiwork, to what end should we . . . doubt to spend at a banquet as many pounds as He spends men at a battle?' (p. 155). It constitutes another instance of subversion from within: the spirit of a theology is sabotaged not in spite but because of adherence to its letter; paradox is intensified into contradiction; an authoritarian discourse is indicted through ironic allegiance. This curious mixture of despair, transgression and hedonism figures centrally in *Dr Faustus* (see chapter 6).

Providence, Decay and the Drama

Some Jacobean tragedies seem to dis-cover the contradictions and shortcomings of providentialist theory even when they have set out to validate it or at least assume its validity. Other tragedies interrogate providentialism more directly. They attack, in particular, the idea of a particular, retributive, providence by (for example) undermining the dramatic conventions which embody it. They also challenge the basic premise of providentialism as it grows out of, and draws upon, natural law: the idea of a teleologically encoded law governing the nature, identity and interrelationships of all things and, ultimately, the very *telos* of the universe itself. One way they do this is with ideas and attitudes associated with cosmic decay which, as I have suggested, was the site of anxiety, conflict and uncertainty *within* Christianity. One reason why few 'Christian' plays have been as difficult for Christianity to contain as *Dr Faustus* is that this one takes contradiction to the heart of the creation; hell, declares Mephistopheles, is 'Within the bowels of these elements,/Where we are tortur'd (v. 120–1).

As we saw in chapter 2, the very structure of *Troilus and Cressida*, often considered to be the most radically disordered of Shakespeare's plays, seems to be based on a principle of self-stultification. Andrugio in *Antonio and Mellida* gives the lie to teleology:

> Philosophy maintains that Nature's wise
> And forms no useless or unperfect thing . . .
> Go to, go to, thou liest Philosophy!
> Nature forms things unperfect, useless, vain.
>
> (III. i. 27–8; 34–5)

The earth, says Andrugio, 'this monstrous animal/That eats her children' is blind and deaf.

In other plays too there occurs the strategic moment when the disintegration of providentialism is underpinned by images of cosmic decay. Experientially it is expressed as self-stultification and self-destruction: 'I love what most I loath and cannot live/Unless I compass that which holds my death' (*Bussy D'Ambois*, II. ii. 170–1; cf. IV. i. 29 and V. iii. 67–8); 'all delight doth itself soon'st devour', 'There's nothing of so infinite vexation/As man's own thoughts', 'we confound/ Knowledge with knowledge' (*The White Devil*, I. ii. 193–4; V. vi. 202–3, 256–7); in *Sejanus* Tiberius refers to 'that chaos bred in things' (II. ii. 313; cf. I. i. 86–8 and III. ii. 689–92), while Shakespeare's Antony resolves to kill himself when 'all labour/Mars what it does; yea, very force entangles/Itself with strength' (IV. xiv. 47–9; cf. II. vi. 123–4, III. xiii. 114–15, IV. vi. 10–11).

A brilliant image of Webster's shows the sudden switch (a kind of 'epistemological break') which the familiar 'dust' metaphor undergoes in the context of decay stultification rather than the dissolution of mutability:

> Whether we fall by ambition, blood, or lust,
> Like diamonds we are cut with our own dust.
>
> (*Duchess of Malfi*, V. v. 71–2)

In some plays (e.g. *Sejanus*, *King Lear* and *Antony and Cleopatra*) the experience of stultification goes along with explicit reference to the contemporary philosophy of cosmic decay. In *Mustapha* and *The Revenger's Tragedy* decay imagery figures in important but different ways. In the former it works to contradict from within the idealist mimesis of its formal vision. In the latter – to anticipate the analysis below in somewhat schematic terms – we find a residual ideology (decay) used to subvert a dominant one (providentialism), and this from the perspective of an emergent scepticism.

In the plays analysed in Part III the principle of contradiction remains paramount but, crucially, its imagery is less that of cosmic stultification and more that of social dislocation.

6

Dr Faustus (c. 1589–92): Subversion Through Transgression

One problem in particular has exercised critics of *Dr Faustus*: its structure, inherited from the morality form, apparently negates what the play experientially affirms – the heroic aspiration of 'Renaissance man'. Behind this discrepancy some have discerned a tension between, on the one hand, the moral and theological imperatives of a severe Christian orthodoxy and, on the other, an affirmation of Faustus as 'the epitome of Renaissance aspiration . . . all the divine discontent, the unwearied and unsatisfied striving after knowledge that marked the age in which Marlowe wrote' (Roma Gill, ed., *Dr Faustus*, p. xix).

Critical opinion has tended to see the tension resolved one way or another – that is, to read the play as ultimately vindicating either Faustus or the morality structure. But such resolution is what *Dr Faustus* as interrogative text[1] resists. It seems always to represent paradox – religious and tragic – as insecurely and provocatively ambiguous or, worse, as openly contradictory. Not surprisingly Max Bluestone, after surveying some eighty recent studies of *Dr Faustus*, as well as the play itself, remains unconvinced of their more or less equally divided attempts to find in it an orthodox or heterodox principle of resolution. On the contrary: 'conflict and contradiction inhere everywhere in the world of this play' ('*Libido Speculandi*: Doctrine and Dramaturgy in Contemporary Interpretations of Marlowe's *Dr Faustus*', p. 55). If this is correct then we might see it as an integral aspect of what *Dr Faustus* is best understood as: not an affirmation of Divine Law, or conversely of Renaissance Man, but an exploration of subversion through transgression.

Limit and Transgression

Raymond Williams has observed how, in Victorian literature, individuals encounter limits of crucially different kinds. In *Felix Holt* there is the discovery of limits which, in the terms of the novel, are enabling: they vindicate a conservative identification of what it is to be human. In complete contrast *Jude the Obscure* shows its protagonist destroyed in the process – and ultimately because – of encountering limits. This is offered not as punishment for hubris but as 'profoundly subversive of the limiting structure' ('Forms of English Fiction in 1848', p. 287). *Dr Faustus,* I want to argue, falls into this second category: a discovery of limits which ostensibly forecloses subversive questioning in fact provokes it.[2]

What Erasmus had said many years before against Luther indicates the parameters of *Dr Faustus'* limiting structure:

> Suppose for a moment that it were true in a certain sense, as Augustine says somewhere, that 'God works in us good and evil, and rewards his own good works in us, and punishes his evil works in us' . . . Who will be able to bring himself to love God with all his heart when He created hell seething with eternal torments in order to punish His own misdeeds in His victims as though He took delight in human torments? (*Renaissance Views of Man,* ed. S. Davies, p. 92)

But Faustus is not *identified* independently of this limiting structure and any attempt to interpret the play as Renaissance man breaking out of medieval chains always founders on this point: Faustus is constituted by the very limiting structure which he transgresses and his transgression is both despite and because of that fact.

Faustus is situated at the centre of a violently divided universe. To the extent that conflict and contradiction are represented as actually of its essence, it appears to be Manichean; thus Faustus asks 'where is the place that men call hell?', and Mephostophilis replies 'Within the bowels of these elements', adding:

> when all the world dissolves
> And every creature shall be purify'd,
> All places shall be hell that is not heaven.
>
> (v. 117, 120, 125–7)

If Greg is correct, and 'purified' means 'no longer mixed, but of one essence, either wholly good or wholly evil' (*Marlowe's Dr Faustus*, Parallel Texts, p. 330), then the division suggested is indeed Manichean.[3] But more important than the question of precise origins is the fact that not only heaven and hell but God and Lucifer, the Good Angel and the Bad Angel, are polar opposites whose axes pass through and constitute human consciousness. Somewhat similarly, for Mephostophilis hell is not a place but a state of consciousness:

> Hell hath no limits, nor is circumscrib'd
> In one self place, but where we are is hell,
> And where hell is, there must we ever be.

(v. 122–4)

From Faustus' point of view – one never free-ranging but always coterminous with his position – God and Lucifer seem equally responsible in his final destruction, two supreme agents of power deeply antagonistic to each other[4] yet temporarily co-operating in his demise. Faustus is indeed their subject, the site of their power struggle. For his part God is possessed of tyrannical power – 'heavy wrath' (i. 71 and xix. 153), while at the beginning of scene xix Lucifer, Beelzebub and Mephostophilis enter syndicate-like 'To view the *subjects* of our monarchy'. Earlier Faustus had asked why Lucifer wanted his soul; it will, replies Mephostophilis, 'Enlarge his kingdom' (v. 40). In Faustus' final soliloquy both God and Lucifer are spatially located as the opposites which, *between them*, destroy him:

> O, I'll leap up to my God! Who pulls me down?
>
> see where God
> Stretcheth out his arm and bends his ireful brows
>
> My God, my God! Look not so fierce on me!
>
> Ugly hell, gape not! Come not, Lucifer.

(ll. 145, 150–1, 187, 189)

Before this the representatives of God and Lucifer have bombarded Faustus with conflicting accounts of his identity, position and destiny. Again, the question of whether in principle Faustus can repent, what is the point of no return, is less important than the fact that he is located on the axes of contradictions which cripple and finally destroy him.

By contrast, when, in Marlowe's earlier play, Tamburlaine speaks of the 'four elements/Warring within our breasts for regiment' he is speaking of a dynamic conflict conducive to the will to power – one which 'Doth teach us all to have aspiring minds' (1. II. vii. 18–20) – not the stultifying contradiction which constitutes Faustus and his universe. On this point alone *Tamburlaine* presents a fascinating contrast with *Dr Faustus*. With his indomitable will to power and warrior prowess, Tamburlaine really does approximate to the self-determining hero bent on transcendent autonomy – a kind of fantasy on Pico's theme of aspiring man. But like all fantasies this one excites as much by what it excludes as what it exaggerates. Indeed exclusion may be the basis not just of Tamburlaine as fantasy projection but *Tamburlaine* as transgressive text: it liberates from its Christian and ethical framework the humanist conception of man as essentially free, dynamic and aspiring; more contentiously, this conception of man is not only liberated from a Christian framework but re-established in open defiance of it. But however interpreted, the objective of Tamburlaine's aspiration is very different from Pico's; the secular power in which Tamburlaine revels is part of what Pico wants to transcend in the name of a more ultimate and legitimate power. Tamburlaine defies origin, Pico aspires to it:

> A certain sacred striving should seize the soul so that, not content with the indifferent and middling, we may pant after the highest and so (for we can if we want to) force our way up to it with all our might. Let us despise the terrestrial, be unafraid of the heavenly, and then, neglecting the things of the world, fly towards that court beyond the world nearest to God the Most High. (*On the Dignity of Man*, pp. 69–70)

With *Dr Faustus* almost the reverse is true: transgression is born not of a liberating sense of freedom to deny or retrieve origin, nor from an excess of life breaking repressive bounds. It is rather a transgression rooted in an *impasse* of despair.

Even before he abjures God, Faustus expresses a sense of being isolated and trapped; an insecurity verging on despair pre-exists a damnation which, by a perverse act of free will, he 'chooses'. Arrogant he certainly is, but it is wrong to see Faustus at the outset as secure in the knowledge that existing forms of knowledge are inadequate. Rather, his search for a more complete knowledge is itself a search for security. For Faustus, 'born, of parents base of stock', and now both socially and geographically displaced (Prologue, ll. 11, 13–19), no teleological integration of identity, self-consciousness and purpose obtains. In the opening scene he attempts to convince himself of the worth of several professions – divinity, medicine, law, and then divinity again – only to reject each in turn; in this he is almost schizoid:

> Having commenc'd, be a divine in show,
> Yet level at the end of every art,
> And live and die in Aristotle's works.
> Sweet Analytics, 'tis thou hast ravish'd me!
>
> When all is done, divinity is best.
>
> Philosophy is odious and obscure,
> Both law and physic are for petty wits,
> Divinity is basest of the three,
> Unpleasant, harsh, contemptible, and vile.
>
> (i. 3–6, 37, 105–8)

As he shakes free of spurious orthodoxy and the role of the conventional scholar, Faustus' insecurity intensifies. A determination to be 'resolved' of all ambiguities, to be 'resolute' and show fortitude (i. 32; iii. 14; v. 6; vi. 32, 64) is only a recurring struggle to escape agonised irresolution.

This initial desperation and insecurity, just as much as a subsequent fear of impending damnation, suggests why his search for knowledge so easily lapses into hedonistic recklessness and fatuous, self-forgetful 'delight' (i. 52; v. 82; vi. 170; viii. 59–60). Wagner cannot comprehend this psychology of despair.

> I think my master means to die shortly:
> He has made his will and given me his wealth
>
> I wonder what he means. If death were nigh,
> He would not banquet and carouse and swill
> Amongst the students.
>
> (xviii. 1–2, 5–7)

Faustus knew from the outset what he would eventually incur. He willingly 'surrenders up . . . his soul' for twenty-four years of 'voluptuousness' in the knowledge that 'eternal death' will be the result (iii. 90–4). At the end of the first scene he exits declaring 'This night I'll conjure though I die therefor.' Later he reflects: 'long ere this I should have done the deed [i.e. suicide]/Had not sweet pleasure conquer'd deep despair' (vi. 24–5). This is a despairing hedonism rooted in the fatalism of his opening soliloquy: 'If we say that we have no sin, we deceive ourselves, and there's no truth in us. Why, then, belike we must sin, and so consequently die' (i. 41–4). Half-serious, half-facetious, Faustus registers a sense of human kind as miscreated.

Tamburlaine's will to power leads to liberation through transgression. Faustus' pact with the devil, because an act of transgression without hope of liberation, is at once rebellious, masochistic and despairing. The protestant God – 'an arbitrary and wilful, omnipotent and universal tyrant' (Walzer, p. 151) – demanded of each subject that s/he submit personally and without mediation. The modes of power formerly incorporated in mediating institutions and practices now devolve on Him and, to some extent and unintentionally, on His subject: abject before God, the subject takes on a new importance in virtue of just this direct relation.[5] Further, although God is remote and inscrutable he is also intimately conceived: 'The principal worship of God hath two parts. One is to yield subjection to him, the other to draw near to him and to cleave unto him' (Perkins, *An Instruction Touching Religious or Divine Worship*, p. 313). Such perhaps are the conditions for masochistic transgression: intimacy becomes the means of a defiance of power, the new-found importance of the subject the impetus of that defiance, the abjectness of the subject its self-sacrificial nature. (We may even see here the origins of sub-cultural transgression: the identity conferred upon the deviant by the dominant culture enables resistance as well as oppression.)

Foucault has written: 'limit and transgression depend on each other for whatever density of being they possess: a limit could not exist if it were absolutely uncrossable and, reciprocally, transgression would be pointless if it merely crossed a limit composed of illusions and shadows' (*Language, Counter-Memory, Practice*, p. 34). It is a phenomenon if which the anti-essentialist writers of the Renaissance were aware: 'Superiority and inferiority, maistry and subjection, are joyntly tied unto a naturall kinde of envy and contestation; they must perpetually enter-spoile one another' (Montaigne, *Essays*, III, 153).

In the morality plays sin tended to involve blindness to the rightness of God's law, while repentance and redemption involved a renewed apprehension of it. In *Dr Faustus* however sin is not the error of fallen judgement but a conscious and deliberate transgression of limit. It is a limit which, among other things, renders God remote and inscrutable yet subjects the individual to constant surveillance and correction; which holds the individual subject terrifyingly responsible for the fallen human condition while disallowing him or her any subjective power of redemption. Out of such conditions is born a mode of transgression identifiably protestant in origin: despairing yet defiant, masochistic yet wilful. Faustus is abject yet his is an abjectness which is strangely inseparable from arrogance, which reproaches the authority which demands it, which is not so much subdued as incited by that same authority:

> *Faustus:* I gave . . . my soul for my cunning.
> *All:* God forbid!
> *Faustus:* God forbade it indeed; but Faustus hath done it.
>
> (xix. 61–4)

Mephostophilis well understands transgressive desire; it is why he does not deceive Faustus about the reality of hell. It suggests too why he conceives of hell in the way he does; although his sense of it as a state of being and consciousness can be seen as a powerful recuperation of hell at a time when its material existence as a *place* of future punishment was being questioned, it is also an arrogant appropriation of hell, an incorporating of it into the consciousness of the subject.

A ritual pact advances a desire which cancels fear long enough to pass the point of no return:

> Lo, Mephostophilis, for love of thee
> Faustus hath cut his arm, and with his proper blood
> Assures his soul to be great Lucifer's,

Chief lord and regent of perpetual night.
View here this blood that trickles from mine arm,
And let it be propitious for my wish.

(v. 54–8)

But his blood congeals, preventing him from signing the pact. Mephostophilis exits to fetch 'fire to dissolve it'. It is a simple yet brilliant moment of dramatic suspense, one which invites us to dwell on the full extent of the violation about to be enacted. Faustus finally signs but only after the most daring blasphemy of all: 'Now will I make an end immediately/ . . . *Consummatum est*: this bill is ended' (v. 72–4). In transgressing utterly and desperately God's law, he appropriates Christianity's supreme image of masochistic sacrifice:[6] Christ dying on the cross – and his dying words (cf. John xix. 30). Faustus is not liberating himself, he is ending himself: 'it is finished'. Stephen Greenblatt is surely right to find in Marlowe's work 'a subversive identification with the alien, one which 'flaunts society's cherished orthodoxies, embraces what the culture finds loathsome or frightening' (*Renaissance Self-Fashioning*, pp. 203, 220). But what is also worth remarking about this particular moment is the way that a subversive identification with the alien is achieved and heightened through travesty of one such cherished orthodoxy.

Power and the Unitary Soul

For Augustine the conflict which man experiences is not (as the Manichean heresy insisted) between two contrary souls or two contrary substances – rather, one soul fluctuates between contrary wills. On some occasions *Dr Faustus* clearly assumes the Augustinian conception of the soul; on others – those expressive of or consonant with the Manichean implications of universal conflict – it presents Faustus as divided and, indeed, constituted by that division. The distinction which Augustine makes between the will as opposed to the soul as the site of conflict and division may now seem to be semantic merely; in fact it was and remains of the utmost importance. For one thing, as *Dr Faustus* makes clear, the unitary soul – unitary in the sense of being essentially indivisible and eternal – is the absolute precondition for the exercise of divine power:

> O, no end is limited to damned souls.
> Why wert thou not a creature wanting soul?
> Or why is this immortal that thou hast?
> Ah, Pythagoras' *metempsychosis*, were that true,
> This soul should fly from me and I be chang'd
> Unto some brutish beast: all beasts are happy,
> For when they die
> Their souls are soon dissolv'd in elements;
> But mine must live still to be plagu'd in hell.
>
> (xix. 171–9)

Further, the unitary soul – unitary now in the sense of being essentially incorruptible – figures even in those manifestations of Christianity which depict the human condition in the most pessimistic of terms and human freedom as thereby intensely problematic. In a passage quoted below, the English Calvinist William Perkins indicates why, even for a theology as severe as his, this had to be so: if sin were a corruption of man's 'substance' then not only could he not be immortal (and thereby subjected to the eternal torment which Faustus incurs), but Christ could not have taken on his nature (see p. 168).

Once sin or evil is allowed to penetrate to the core of God's subject (as opposed to being, say, an inextricable part of that subject's fallen *condition*) the most fundamental contradiction in Christian theology is reactivated: evil is of the essence of God's creation. This is of course only a more extreme instance of another familiar problem: how is evil possible in a world created by an omnipotent God? To put the blame on Adam only begs the further question: Why did God make Adam potentially evil? (Compare Nashe's impudent gloss: 'Adam never fell till God made fools' [*The Unfortunate Traveller*, p. 269]).

Calvin, however, comes close to allowing what Perkins and Augustine felt it necessary to deny: evil and conflict do penetrate to the core of God's subject. For Calvin the soul is an essence, immortal and created by God. But to suggest that it partakes of God's essence is a 'monstrous' blasphemy: 'if the soul of man is a portion transmitted from the essence of God, the divine nature must not only be liable to passion and change, but also to ignorance, evil desires, infirmity, and all kinds of vice' (*Institutes*, I. xv.

5). Given the implication that these imperfections actually constitute the soul, it is not surprising that 'everyone feels that the soul
itself is a receptacle for all kinds of pollution'. Elsewhere we are told
that the soul, 'teeming with . . . seeds of vice . . . is altogether
devoid of good' (I. xv; ii, iii). Here is yet another stress point in
protestantism and one which plays like *Dr Faustus* (and *Mustapha*)
exploit: if human beings perpetuate disorder it is because they have
been created disordered.

The final chorus of the play tells us that Dr Faustus involved
himself with 'unlawful things' and thereby practised 'more than
heavenly power permits' (ll. 6, 8). It is a transgression which has
revealed the limiting structure of Faustus' universe for what it is,
namely, 'heavenly *power*'. Faustus has to be destroyed since in a
very real sense the credibility of that heavenly power depends upon
it. And yet the punitive intervention which validates divine power
also compromises it: far from justice, law and authority being what
legitimates power, it appears, by the end of the play, to be the other
way around: power establishes the limits of all those things.

It might be objected that the distinction between justice and
power is a modern one and, in Elizabethan England, even if enter-
tained, would be easily absorbed in one or another of the paradoxes
which constituted the Christian faith. And yet: if there is one thing
that can be said with certainty about this period it is that God in
the form of 'mere arbitrary will omnipotent' could not 'keep men
in awe'. We can infer as much from many texts, one of which was
Lawne's *Abridgement* of Calvin's *Institutes*, translated in 1587 –
around the time of the writing of *Dr Faustus*. The book presents
and tries to answer, in dialogue form, objections to Calvin's theology. On the question of predestination the 'Objector' contends
that 'to adjudge to destruction whom he will, is more agreeable to
the lust of a tyrant, than to the lawful sentence of a judge'. The
'Reply' to this is as arbitrary and tyrannical as the God which the
Objector envisages as unsatisfactory: 'It is a point of bold wickedness even so much as to inquire the causes of God's will' (p. 222;
quoted from Sinfield, p. 171). It is an exchange which addresses
directly the question of whether a tyrannical God is or is not
grounds for discontent. Even more important perhaps is its unin-
tentional foregrounding of the fact that, as embodiment of naked

power alone, God could so easily be collapsed into those tyrants who, we are repeatedly told by writers in this period, exploited Him as ideological mystification of their own power (see above, chapter 1). Not surprisingly, the concept of 'heavenly power' interrogated in *Dr Faustus* was soon to lose credibility, and it did so in part precisely because of such interrogation.

Dr Faustus is important for subsequent tragedy for these reasons and at least one other: in transgressing and demystifying the limiting structure of his world without there ever existing the possibility of his escaping it, Faustus can be seen as an important precursor of the malcontented protagonist of Jacobean tragedy. Only for the latter, the limiting structure comes to be primarily a socio-political one.

Lastly, if it is correct that censorship resulted in *Dr Faustus* being one of the last plays of its kind – it being forbidden thereafter to interrogate religious issues so directly – we might expect the transgressive impulse in the later plays to take on different forms. This is in fact exactly what we do find; and one such form involves a strategy already referred to – the inscribing of a subversive discourse within an orthodox one, a vindication of the letter of an orthodoxy while subverting its spirit.

7

Mustapha (c. 1594–6): Ruined Aesthetic, Ruined Theology

The very structure of *Mustapha*,[1] like the idealist mimesis which informs it, constitutes a reaction formation to doubt, anxiety and emergent scepticism. As such the play provokes more disquiet than it allays: Greville's interrogative text undermines its own providentialist brief, reconstituting, even as it struggles to foreclose, the disjunction between idealist and realist mimesis and, relatedly, the contradictions within protestant theology. It is a brilliant, fascinating and still underrated text.

Tragedy, Theology and Cosmic Decay

Greville's writing is marked by a pessimism which stems in part from his belief that the post-lapsarian world is prey to cosmic decay or, in his word, 'declination'. It is a process of disintegration which intensifies with time and thereby also widens the gulf between God and man, divine and secular, spiritual and material, absolute and relative. In *Mustapha* we, like the Eternity of its third chorus, 'see the finite still itself confound' (l. 120; cf. III. ii. 32–3, V. iii. 49). In the past scholars have typically represented Greville as moving beyond this pessimism. Ellis-Fermor speaks of Greville's 'almost mystical rejection of the seen in favour of the unseen' (*Jacobean Drama*, p. 197), and Geoffrey Bullough of Greville's 'religious faith which transcends the earth's chaos' (*Works*, I, 23). These are views of the dramatist as one who moved from a world-weary apprehension of the secular to a clear-eyed apprehension of the eternal.

Greville's recent biographer, Ronald A. Rebholz, is far more responsive to the complexity and tension in the man's thought.

Analysing the Treatises, Rebholz discerns 'a movement away from the hope for redeeming the world towards a despairing contempt for its institutions, and a corresponding diminution of the area in which man contributes towards his union with God' (*The Life of Fulke Greville*, p. 312). The circumstances of Greville's life doubtless contributed to the conflict in his thought. The dilemma of being a radical protestant,[2] the hallmark of which was an insistence that religion should determine state policy, could only intensify the contradiction between religion and *realpolitik* which, as we shall see in relation to Jonson's *Sejanus*, increasingly characterised the politics of this period.

The 'images of life' which, according to Greville's own testimony, were the basis of his plays, are an inextricable blend of protestant pessimism and the mimetic realism to which, as we have seen, he was strongly committed (see above, chapter 4). Both, but especially the latter, eventually force faith into a reaction formation characterised by an extreme disjunction between grace and experience, divine and temporal. It is the logical conclusion of a certain kind of protestantism, one already breaking up and giving way to its more progressive and revolutionary forms. *Mustapha* is a text which enacts that breakdown.

Because of his adherence to mimetic realism Greville explicitly distinguishes his own tragedies from those of his contemporaries who aimed 'to point out Gods revenging aspects upon every particular sin, to the despaire, or confusion of mortality'. Such is the drama of providential intervention. By contrast his own work is concerned 'to trace out the high waies of ambitious Governours, and to shew in the practice, that the more audacity, advantage and good successe such Soveraignties have, the more they hasten to their owne desolation and ruine' (*Life of Sidney*, chapter 18). Greville here invokes the zenith – nadir contrast of fortune's wheel, the proverbial belief that the higher one climbs the harder one falls, but also suggests a concept of secular power in-formed by the contradiction of cosmic decay: 'successe' generates its own 'ruine' (cf. II. iii. 1–6). But in certain important respects *Mustapha* is closer to the Senecan tragedy which Greville actually distinguished it from. The purpose of Senecan ('the Ancient') tragedy was, he says, 'to exemplifie the disastrous miseries of mans life, where Order, Lawes, Doctrine, and Authority are unable to protect Innocency from the exorbitant wickednesse of power, and so out of that melancholike Vision, stir horrour, or murmer against Divine Providence' (chapter 18). This is an extraordinary description which in every respect could stand as an epigraph for much Jacobean tragedy generally and, specifically, Greville's *Mustapha*. By delineating 'the high waies of ambitious Governours . . . in the practice' Greville commits himself to a mimetic realism whereby 'the disastrous miseries of mans life' *are* exemplified, where 'Order etc.' *are* shown unable to protect 'Innocency' and where, moreover, from this 'melancholike Vision' there *does* emerge a challenge to 'Divine Providence'.

Greville saw the world in terms of an extreme disjunction between divine and temporal:

> Mixe not in functions God, and earth together;
> The wisdome of the world, and his, are two;
> One latitude can well agree to neither.
>
> (*Treatise of Religion*, st. 98)

Neither human kind nor its institutions can bridge the divide, the Church being the major instance of institutional failure in this respect (*Caelica*, cix; *Religion*, st. 17); all that can bridge it is that arbitrary gift of grace which generates faith: 'all rests in the hart' (*Religion*, st. 95). Elsewhere Greville allows rather more to human capacity; this is where his construct of the 'shaddowes' comes in. This is a theory which allows that although the discrepancy between divine and secular is appalling (and getting worse), we do at least have the opportunity to try and live according to the closest approximation to the divine order: 'Yet in the world those *Orders* prosper best/Which from the *word*, in seeming varie least' (*Human Learning*, st. 87). At best this achieves only a partial alleviation of human kind's 'confounded' condition; it can only retard, never stop, the process of declination (*Human Learning*, st. 63). The construct of the shadows is, then, a compromise solution. When Greville is affirming the complete disjunction of secular and divine he uses the shadow metaphor in a pejorative sense (e.g. *Religion,*

st. 17); when he is more optimistic, in a positive sense. The ambiguity signifies his shifting position between metaphysical absolutism and pragmatic relativism. In fact the construct itself can be
seen as Greville's attempt to theorise the relativism and pragmatism
which his own political involvement presupposed. So, for example,
he approves of 'shaddowed' tyranny on the pragmatic grounds that
it is a lesser evil than the tyranny which is not even a shadow of the
ideal order. But what begins as a compromise so easily becomes a
contradiction – the perpetuation of evil in the pursuit of partial
good (cf. Rebholz, pp. 150–1, 306–7). Such is the dilemma which
Mustapha confronts.

Mustapha: Tragedy as Dislocation

In *Mustapha* there is no unequivocal damnation for the evil protagonists, no wholesale repentance, no recourse to poetic justice.
Greville's extensively revised version of the play ends with the
Chorus Sacerdotum following on directly from the *Chorus
Tartarorum*, both of which sabotage the metaphysical scheme
which the play formally struggles to ratify: in effect, the play
disconfirms its own attempt at formal and ideological coherence.

Greville's characterisation, like his images of life generally, grows
from a fusing of mimetic realism and protestant pessimism. At one
level his protagonists are destroyed by a life of murderous competition whose focus is the court – both general symbol and specific
instance of a social conflict which is stultifying rather than
dynamic. Laid across this perspective is a more formal scheme of
identity, one which situates the play's main protagonists between
the opposing poles of secular and divine, the corrupt and the virtuous. Mustapha, one of the 'pure souls' (V. iv. 100), is possessed of
a totally divine orientation. By contrast Rossa is bent on secular
power at any cost. Situated between them is Soliman for whom
consciousness is synonymous with uncertainty, conflict and contradiction. Encircling him are advisers, also victims of the conflicting
pulls of the two poles:

> . . . flesh and blood, the means 'twixt heaven and hell,
> Unto extremes extremely racked be
>
> (II. iii. 179–80)

> . . . the self-accusing war
> Where knowledge is the endless hell of thought.
>
> (IV. iv. 60–1)

As in *Dr Faustus*, the consciousness of such protagonists is situated on the axes of contradictions which simultaneously constitute and cripple them.

If stultification and disequilibrium intrinsically characterise both society and human consciousness, it is equilibrium – ethical, theological and aesthetic – which formally structures the play and two of its character symbols, Mustapha and Carmena. Both embody Christian-stoic endurance; by obeying the moral imperatives of the other world the individual becomes self-sacrificial in this:

> Mustapha, with thoughts resolvèd, and united,
> Bids them [i.e. his executioners] fulfil their charge and looks no further.
> . . . in haste to be an angel,
> With heavenly smiles and quiet words foreshows
> The joy and peace of those souls where he goes.
>
> (V. ii. 75–6; 81–3)

Mustapha's death is not an event of redemption: far from bringing the two worlds closer together, it only confirms their disjunction. The divine remains separate and self-sufficient whereas the secular is abandoned as inherently stultifying and meriting nothing but a beautifully articulated attitude of *contemptus mundi*:

> . . . life is but the throne of woe,
> Which sickness, pain, desire, and fear inherit,
> Ever most worth to men of weakest spirit:
> Shall we, to languish in this brittle jail,
> Seek, by ill deeds, to shun ill destiny?
> And so, for toys, lose immortality?
>
> (IV. iv. 133–8)

At this level the play's metaphysical orientation – a fusion of Christianity and stoicism – has rigour and consistency. It is, however, interrogated by the consciousness of those dislocated in relation to it;[3] human consciousness as dramatic focus disconfirms dramatic resolution.

The most obvious contrast is between Mustapha's certainty – 'thoughts resolved and united' – and Soliman's tormented 'self-division':

> Horror I apprehend, danger, despair:
> All these lie hidden in this word 'Conspire'.

(IV. iii. 42–3)

Governor and governed are involved in a vicious circle: tyranny encourages sedition which in turn reinforces tyranny. Soliman is pulled in conflicting directions, now believing his son to be a traitor, now believing him innocent. Carmena and Achmat argue for Mustapha's innocence, Rossa for his guilt. Soliman's insecurity leads him to an extreme relativism:

> In what strange balance are man's humours peised?
> Since each light change within us, or without,
> Turns fear to hope, and hope again to doubt.
> If thus it work in Man, much more in thrones,
> Whose tender heights feel all thin airs that move,
> And work that change below they use above.
> For on the axis of our humours turn
> Church-rites, and Laws; subjects' desire, and wit,
> All which, in all men, come and go with it.

(I. ii. 18–26)

Act II finishes with Soliman unable to decide between the counsels of Rossa and Carmena. He tells them:

> . . . she and you a strife within me move,
> And rest I will with counsel from above.

(II. iii. 230–1)

We next encounter him in Act IV scene i where he has a vision of an angel holding a mirror. He cannot decide whether it is an illusion or an objective revelation:

> Visions are these, or bodies which appeared?
> Raised from within, or from above descending?

The mirror reflects the absolute moral imperative, the structural principle of the play itself:

> *Safety, right and a crown,*
> *Thrones must neglect that will adore God's light.*

Soliman is incapable of placing faith in the vision:

> This glass, true mirror of the infinite,
> Shows all; yet can I nothing comprehend.

Everything the vision might stand for is made inaccessible by his inability to believe in or, as he puts it, 'feel' a superior power:

> This empire, nay the world, seems shadows there,
> Which mysteries dissolve me into fear.
> I that without feel no superior power,
> And feel within but what I will conceive,
> Distract, know neither what to take nor leave.

The effect of the vision is then an even more intense confusion:

> In my affections man, in knowledge more,
> Protected nowhere, far more disunited,
> Still king of men, but of myself no more.

He has begun by seeking divine reassurance and ends

> . . . with prayer thus confused,
> Nor judge, nor rest, nor yield, nor reign I can,
> No God, no devil, no constant king, nor man.
> The earth draws one way and the sky another.

Other characters in the play attempt to reconcile adherence to an ethical absolute with political involvement in a corrupt world. They too experience extreme dilemmas. Achmat, adviser to Soliman, is first faced with the impossible choice of either betraying his king or tacitly condoning the murder of Mustapha. After the murder he has to decide whether to save Soliman, thus preserving in power one who is totally unfit to rule, or allow anarchy to reign in the state. Heli, a priest, and another of Soliman's advisers, finds himself in a similar position. The stichomythic exchange between him and Mustapha, striking in a play dominated by extended monologues, effectively underpins the clash of relativist and absolutist perspectives. Heli is attempting to persuade Mustapha to save himself by fleeing. It would have been easy to discredit Heli's pragmatism but in fact it is invested with ethical as well as political intelligence (especially at IV. iv. 153–69).

Inter-act choruses explore similar conflicts. The reflections of the Bashas or Cadis (first chorus) move to and fro between the particular theme of political allegiance and the seemingly inseparable theme of futile endeavour in a corrupt world. Both are expressed in terms of inherent stultification:

> We silly bashas help power to confound,
> With our own strength exhausting our own ground.
>
> (ll. 77–8; cf. 11–12, 83–4, 190, 219–22)

'Disproportioned humours' lead to a 'confused estate' (ll. 150, 153); moreover the sickness is deeply rooted and that which should cure is itself corrupted by the disease (ll. 155–8).

The third chorus, a debate between Time and Eternity, embodies two mutually antagonistic perspectives. Time offers a vision of creation where mutability is desirable and human kind, if it knew it, would actually be miserable with eternal life. But Eternity sees Time as complicit with a world subject to decay:

> . . . since time took her fall
> Mankind sees ill increase, no good at all.
>
> (ll. 83–4)

Eternity, in some absolute sense, represents that 'good' which is absent yet we learn little of what constitutes it; Eternity stresses only the division between itself and earthly perfection: 'Goodness of no mixed course can be the mother' (l. 130).

The fourth chorus, that of the *Converts to Mahomedanism*, proves the subjective limits of human awareness; our 'once happy states' can now barely be glimpsed (ll. 5–8). Increasingly human kind can comprehend only 'deprivings' (l. 6). The Absolute comes inevitably to be defined negatively, as a determining absence. And this is why its ontological and epistemological status becomes intensely problematic and why finally we get the outburst of scepticism in the *Chorus Tartarorum* and the *Chorus Sacerdotum*. This same chorus (the fourth) contains another vivid image of dislocation as cosmic decay; it describes the stultification caused by the political antagonism of Church and Crown:

> They strive, turn and descend, feel error's destiny,
>
> Thus, in disorder's chain, while each link wresteth other,
> Incestuous error to her own is made both child and mother.
>
> (II. 53, 55–6)

The *Chorus Tartarorum* is an outburst of cynicism, the *Chorus Sacerdotum* of sceptical, interrogative despair. The ostensible purpose of the first is to reject superstition:

> Vast superstition! Glorious style of weakness!
> Sprung from the deep disquiet of man's passion,
> To desolation and despair of nature.
>
> (ll. 1–3)

But it becomes progressively clearer that religion itself is being brought into question. Indeed, in the 1609 Quarto 'Religion' is actually substituted for 'superstition'. Thus line 1 reads: 'Religion, thou vain and glorious style of weakness' and line 10: 'Mankind! trust not this dream, religion.' Moreover, a copy of the 1633 Folio in the Bibliothèque Nationale has a manuscript annotation alongside line 1 which reads: 'In the original it is Blind Religion, thou glorious etc. But this seemed too atheistical to be licensed at the press.'[4] In the later text distrustful references to God (l. 7), Heaven (l. 30), and Faith (l. 27) clearly retain the sense of this earlier version. Against a repressive religion which aids tyranny, encourages 'Cruelty for God's sake' and ties the 'senses to . . . senseless glories' the chorus advocates nature.

By contrast the *Chorus Sacerdotum* attacks nature but now it is identified with the very source of creation itself – the 'majesty of power':

> Oh wearisome condition of humanity!
> Born under one law, to another bound:
> Vainly begot, and yet forbidden vanity,
> Created sick, commanded to be sound:
> What meaneth nature by these diverse laws?
> Passion and reason self-division cause:
> Is it the mark or majesty of power
> To make offences that it may forgive?

Essentially then, human kind is miscreated. Perhaps 'Created sick, commanded to be sound' refers only to birth in the post-lapsarian world where all have inherited original sin? But Greville does not make this distinction, and, in that the subjects of the passage are generic 'Humanity' and the laws of existence, and also the ultimate power controlling both of these, 'created' must be understood to refer to *the* Creation. As such it is a passage which contrasts strikingly with the beginning of the fourth Chorus where responsibility for dislocation is precisely located in the Fall: 'Angels fell first from God, man was the next that fell:/Both being made by Him for Heaven, have for themselves made hell' (ll. 1–2). And there is an even more explicit contrast with the Chorus of good Spirits in *Alaham* where Man is described as 'A crazed soul, unfixed;/Made good, yet fallen, not to extremes, but to a mean betwixt' (ll. 21–2).

The experience of self-division was of course familiar to the Christian tradition. What makes Greville interesting in this respect is the way he relieves human kind and even the Fall of responsibility for this. In *A Treatise of Wars* a similar idea occurs. Everything, says Greville, yet again, eventually becomes prey to declination:

> *Mortality is Changes proper stage:*
> *States haue degrees, as humane bodies haue,*
> *Springs, Summer, Autumne, Winter and the graue.*

Moreover the responsibility is God's:

> though God do preserue thus for a time,
> This *Equilibrium,* wherein Nature goes,

> Yet he both by the cure, and the disease,
> Proues, *Dissolution, all at length must sease.*

Again it is not, ultimately, the Fall that causes violence and injustice to be the condition of the world, but God's intent:

> if it had beene Gods intent
> To giue Man here eternally possession,
> Earth had beene free from all misgouernment,
> *Warre,* Malice, could not then haue had progression,

Man (as at first) had bin mans nursing brother,
And not, as since, *One Wolfe unto another.*

(st. 42, 44, 45)

This section of the Treatise shows Greville moving from a conservative decay of nature argument, based on the analogy of natural
senescence and the nature cycle,[5] to a vision of cosmic decay based
on the principle of self-stultification initiated by God (cf. stanza
48). What begins as a vision of the world informed by the natural
principles of mutability and transience, ends as a vision of men
being '*One Wolfe unto another*', characterised also by 'Antipathy of
Minde'. Moreover, 'as Man vnto Man, so State to State/Inspired is,
with the venime of this hate' (st. 46).

Calvin had explicitly rejected the Thomistic view that the Fall
was a matter of divine permission. On the contrary, it was the
result of positive divine ordination: 'The first man fell because the
Lord deemed it meet that he should: why he deemed it meet, we
know not' (*Institutes*, III. xxxiii. 8). Paradoxically yet effectively,
Calvinism revitalised faith precisely through an emphasis on doubt
and anxiety; in *Mustapha*, repeatedly, paradox collapses into the
disjunctions and contradictions which, eventually, will undermine
faith itself: 'Born under one law, to another bound:/Vainly begot,
and yet forbidden vanity' [etc.]. John Hick reminds us that
Calvinist theodicy, like most other theodicies, finally asserts 'God's
ultimate responsibility for the existence of evil' (*Evil and the God of
Love*, p. 264; see also chapter VI passim, and pp. 69, 197, 234–7).
Mustapha is a rebellious cry against that fact: 'Created sick, commanded to be sound'; this is the play's major emphasis and one
developed with a bitter insistence at the furthest possible remove
from the aesthetic and theological harmony characteristic of idealist mimesis (cf. IV. i. 38: 'The earth draws one way and the sky
another' and IV. iv. 39: 'God's law . . . wills impossibility'). It
brings to the fore the most provocative tenets of Calvinism: evil is
so extensive it seems to promise the annihilation of human kind;
God is ultimately *responsible* for this – and yet we cannot hold Him
culpable. Greville was wrestling with a contradiction which was to
prove irresolvable – at least in his terms. At the end of the seventeeth century Pierre Bayle was to press home the implications for

any theology which allowed God's responsibility for evil, and he does so in terms which seem most appropriate for the *Chorus Sacerdotum*. Such theologies, according to Bayle, incorporated into God the principle of evil itself, and so moved from Christian monotheism to Manichean dualism. Further, according to Bayle: 'all religion is here at stake . . . as soon as one dared to teach that God is the author of sin, one would necessarily lead men to atheism'.[6] This indicates why (in Rebholz' words) the *Chorus Sacerdotum* 'delivers the most penetrating attack on the conventional Christian concept of the good God before *King Lear* and the plays of Webster'. And, more generally, why 'As a mode of inquiry, the choruses undermine the coherence of viewpoint essential to *exemplum*, just as the shift to a political focus in the last act [of *Mustapha*] confuses the play's thematic concern and destroys its dramatic unity' (*The Life of Fulke Greville*, p. 107).

Mustapha moves, then, towards a state of radical dislocation. Its aesthetic/theological frame, precarious from the first, finally fractures. The consequences are extreme since 'as in circles, who breaks any part/That perfect form doth utterly confound' (*Chorus Secundus*, ll. 91–2). Suggested in this image is the potentially unstable nature of the essentialist counterpart of the Absolute as conceived in this play. Its very perfection attests to its vulnerability and powerlessness; it is conceived not as the basis of worldly intervention but as an ideal unity. Like the circle, its survival is conditional upon it being detached, perfectly self-referring – in fact, like Mustapha. Eager to die in a state of spiritual equipoise – 'with thoughts resolvèd, and united' (V. ii. 75) – Mustapha is 'That perfect form', a reaction formation whose survival as such is paradoxically conditional upon extinction. But the play's *a priori*, formal counterpart of Mustapha cannot be so removed but rather disintegrates under interrogation from the text it cannot contain. And yet chaos is not its final 'vision'; it is, rather, the condition and ground of its realism: from within a ruined theology, a ruined aesthetic, we discern the phenomenon of power.

Astonishingly, the word 'power' and its derivatives recur rnore than 110 times in *Mustapha*; power is hypostatised as a surrogate absolute, invested with the determining authority of providence itself:

> So is frail mankind . . .
> Formèd, transformèd, and made instruments
> In many shapes, to serve power's many bents.
>
> (*Chorus Primus*, ll. 11–14)

More specifically, power is inseparable from a social structure ante-
rior to individual subjects – and even kings – and into which they
are inscribed:

> The saint we worship is authority,
> Which lives in kings, and cannot with them die.
>
> (IV. iv. 17–18)

> Power hath great scope; she walks not in the ways
> Of private truth.
>
> (I. ii. 5–6; cf. I. ii. 237–8, II. iii. 178, *Chorus Secondus*, ll. 97–8)

All this can only occur because ideology – that 'art by which man
seems, but is not free' (*Chorus Secundus*, l. 115) – makes the people
acquiescent to power:

> . . . power can neither see, work, or devise,
> Without the people's hands, hearts, wit, and eyes:
> So that were man not by himself oppressed
> Kings would not, tyrants could not make him beast.
>
> (*Chorus Secandus*, ll. 207–10)

It is a process of mystification in which priests play an important
part:[7]

> We priests, even with the mystery of words,
> First bind ourselves, and with ourselves the rest
> To servitude.
>
> (IV. iv. 41–3)

In Rossa power and desire – 'This unbound, raging, infinite
thought-fire' (V. iv. 26) – seem to unite; for a while she becomes
the powerfully unified subject riding roughshod over those crippled
by their respective experiences of dislocation. Integrated and apparently autonomous, she figures as the anarchic, evil counterpart of
Mustapha. But only temporarily: as events both defeat and punish
Rossa she enters a state of dislocation even more extreme than that
of the others. Because she has at once 'transgressed/The laws of

nature and . . . of state' (IV. iii. 5–6), Rossa cannot herself re-establish, or be re-established within, the order she has violated.

In virtue of that transgression the advice which Greville gives to the unfortunate addressee of his *Letter to an Honourable Lady*, namely, 'That obedience is just, the customes of Nations and lawes of Nature will assure you' (p. 279), cannot apply to Rossa. She has refused such obedience, identifying both the customs of nations and the laws of nature as complex forms of legitimation of state power and as providing opportunities for abusing that power. In the *Letter* Greville is reassuring on this question of abuse in a way which *Mustapha* cannot be: 'those excesses which arise out of Authority, are they not . . . rods of trials which we inferiors must kisse, and that God onely may burne, which made them . . . ?' (p. 279).

It is not that the play's theology is simply repudiated or even that it finally becomes redundant; rather it foregrounds, and is eventually subverted by, that which it was supposed to explain: 'images of life', of the 'wearisome condition of humanity' in a sixteenth-century political context.[8] In this respect Greville's play, otherwise so different from the world of Elizabethan and Jacobean stage plays, is typical: it articulates a radical critique not in spite of its problematic structure but precisely because of it.

8

Sejanus (1603): History and *Realpolitik*

Sejanus, like *Mustapha*, seeks to represent the mechanisms of state power and in so doing confronts without resolving the disjunctions between idealist and realist mimesis, religion and policy, providentialism and *realpolitik*.

History, Fate, Providence

The concluding paragraph of 'The Argument' gives to history, politics and ethics an explicitly providential perspective; essentially, political opposition is represented as 'unnatural' (l. 42) to the extent that it deviates from a divine prescription which happens to ratify the status quo. Even evil princes are part of the design and therefore not to be challenged.

> This [i.e. the fall of Sejanus] do we advance as a mark of terror to all traitors, and treasons; to show how just the heavens are in pouring and thundering down a weighty vengeance on their unnatural intents, even to the worst princes: much more to those, for guard of whose piety and virtue, the angels are in continual watch, and God himself miraculously working.

The fact that *Sejanus* was thought seditious when first acted and Jonson summoned to the Privy Council (and possibly imprisoned) might explain why this passage was included in the first (1605) Quarto edition of the play, two years after it was first acted, although left out of the 1616 folio, when presumably it was thought safe to do so. Whether or not The Argument's providentialist gloss was dictated by expediency the fact remains that most of Act V involves a crude attempt to interpret history according to this same providentialist justice.

For plays like *Sejanus* shifts in contemporary historiography are of paramount importance. Machiavelli, Guicciardini, and Raleigh (among others) present history in terms which qualify, problematise and even contradict providentialist explanations. It is their conception of history which realist mimesis draws upon.[1]

Jonson insisted on the importance for art of historical truth and, more specifically, of experience: 'Experience, Observation, Sense, Induction, are the fower Tryers of Arts. It is ridiculous to teach any thing for undoubted Truth that Sense, and Experience, can confute' (Preface to *The English Grammar, Works,* VIII, 465). So detailed are the historical sources which Jonson provided for *Sejanus* that it has been described as a work of 'historical realism', one disclosing as much about Jonson's present as about the past and thereby remaining 'one of the most devastating accounts the drama has given us of dictatorship in action' (Jonas Barish, ed., *Sejanus,* pp. 15, 19).

Historical writing of this kind came specially under the ban of the authorities and its writers ran serious risks; as we saw, Greville felt obliged to destroy one of his plays for fear of reprisals from the state, Shakespeare's *Richard II* was almost certainly exploited for seditious purposes, and, sure enough, *Sejanus* got Jonson in trouble with the Privy Council. Raleigh in the Preface to his *History of the World* expressed the danger in no uncertain terms: 'who-so-euer, in writing a moderne Historie, shall follow truth too neare the heeles, it may happily strike out his teeth'.[2]

In the earlier acts of *Sejanus* history is presented as radically contingent; political power, not providence is the fundamental determinant:

Tiberius:	When the master-prince
	Of all the world, Sejanus, saith, he fears;
	Is it not fatal?
Sejanus:	Yes, to those are feared.
Tiberius:	And not to him?
Sejanus:	Not, if he wisely turn
	That part of fate he holdeth, first on them.
Tiberius:	That nature, blood, and laws of kind forbid.
Sejanus:	Do policy, and state forbid it?
Tiberius:	No.
Sejanus:	The rest of poor respects, then, let go by:
	State is enough to make th'act just, them guilty.

(II. 165–73)

Thus speak the two most powerful men in Rome. Especially interesting is the way that Sejanus conceives of 'fate' as almost synonymous with 'power'; more generally, both Sejanus' amoral self-assertiveness and the extent of its deviation from the moral norm – 'the rest of poor respects' – are sharply focussed in the semantic changes which 'fate' undergoes. Tiberius' use of 'fatal' suggests awareness of an extra-human agency to whose influence even the prince is potentially subject; for Sejanus the prince subjects fate. Fate is similarly conceived as personal power when at the end of Act I Sejanus, after having refused to fight with Drusus (who has just struck him), remarks in soliloquy:

> He that, with such wrong moved, can bear it through
> With patience, and an even mind, knows how
> To turn it back. Wrath, covered, carries fate.

> (I. 576–8)

Two things are happening here: first, stoic 'patience' is being appropriated for *realpolitik*, second – and relatedly – 'fate' is made almost synonymous with purpose (cf. Tiberius' remark to Sejanus: 'Dearest head,/To thy most fortunate design I yield' (III. 502)). Sejanus' attitude to fate contrasts strikingly with the fatalism of the virtuous and powerless people in this play; for them 'fate' either signifies the way events transpire (always beyond their control) or the more or less vaguely conceived extra-human agency responsible for that outcome.

These semantic shifts are a primary manifestation of the underlying tension in *Sejanus* between a pagan-secularist discourse and a Christian one, each interrogating the other. In the earlier scenes it is the former which dominates; even Silius and Arruntius offer a kind of choric commentary which tacitly acknowledges the primacy of state power:

> *Arruntius:*   O desperate state
> Of grovelling honour! Seest thou this, O sun,
> And do we see thee after? Me thinks, day
> Should lose his light, when men do lose their shames,
> And, for the empty circumstance of life,
> Betray their cause of living.

Silius:	Nothing so.
	Sejanus can repair, if Jove should ruin.
	He is now the court-god . . .
	He will do more than all the house of heav'n
	Can, for a thousand hecatombs. 'Tis he
	Makes us our day, or night.

(I. 196–207)

Stressed too is the fact that ethical determinants have no external or objective existence; once again power is the sole criterion:

Sejanus:	Sir, you can lose no honour,
	By trusting ought to me. The coarsest act
	Done to my service, I can so requite,
	As all the world shall style it honourable.

(I. 326–9)

Similarly, according to Macro, 'A prince's power makes all his actions virtue' (III. 717). The same relativist challenge lies behind the most subversive statement of Sejanus' *realpolitik*: ''tis place,/Not blood, discerns the noble, and the base' (V. 11–12). Nobility, on this estimation, derives not from innate *virtus* but one's place within the power structure. This is the last of Sejanus' several repudiations of hierarchy, and it is made just before providentialist retribution sets in: we see, or are meant to see, Sejanus' *realpolitik* as nothing more than hubristic strutting. In a kind of supernatural melodrama Sejanus' statue belches black smoke and there leaps from it a 'monstrous serpent' (V. 37); his servants slip over and break their necks while ravens croak.

Sejanus remains sceptical:

> What excellent fools
> Religion makes of men! Believes Terentius
> (If these were dangers, as I shame to think them)
> The gods could change the certain course of fate?

(V. 69–72)

If the answer is 'yes' – and at one level it is clearly meant to be – then fate is firmly relocated within a providential scheme and no longer the open-ended concept undergoing shifting definition in a power struggle which, dramatically disclosed, threatens to subvert that scheme.

Sejanus thus foregrounds a contradiction between the providentialist ratification of power and the demystifying strategies of survival and gain resorted to by those actually holding power; further, it substantiates Felix Raab's identification of such a conflict in Jacobean England: at the beginning of the seventeenth century the same men involved in ruthless struggles for power would also be those who, 'in a different context, would defend the power of kings and/or popes in terms of Scripture, the patristic texts and scholastic philosophy . . . That there was a basic contradiction between this conceptual framework and the world of affairs in which many of its exponents were involved is obvious' (*The English Face of Machiavelli*, pp. 24–5). In *Sejanus* this is nowhere more apparent than in the disparity between the paragraph from 'The Argument' with which I began, and the sentence which immediately precedes it: 'at last, when Sejanus least looketh, and is most secure (with pretext of doing him an unwonted honour in the Senate) he [Tiberius] trains him from his guards, and with a long and doubtful letter, in one day, hath him suspected, accused, condemned, and torn in pieces, by the rage of the people'.

Of course there were those in the period who openly advocated both policy and a belief in providential design. Thus as early as 1548 we find William, Lord Paget of Beaudesert arguing that only 'arte, pollycie and practise must helpe (for these be the meanes in myne opynion) that God will nowe vse for our helpe' (*Camden Miscellany*, vol. XXV, ed. Beer and Jack, p. 24). This illustrates the way ideology may suppress contradictions but only by incorporating them within itself; if the element of suppression enables the process of ideological legitimation, that of incorporation offers the possibility of it being challenged: it renders the ideology potentially unstable – vulnerable, for instance, to the sceptical interrogation to which it was being subjected in the Jacobean theatre.

9

The Revenger's Tragedy (c. 1606): Providence, Parody and Black Camp

Many critics have felt that if *The Revenger's Tragedy*[1] cannot be shown to he fundamentally orthodox then it cannot help but be hopelessly decadent. If, for example, it can be shown to affirm morality-play didacticism and its corresponding metaphysical categories (and hence idealist mimesis), an otherwise very disturbing play is rendered respectable. Moreover, the embarrassing accusation of a critic like Archer – that the play is 'the product either of sheer barbarism, or of some pitiable psychopathic perversion' – can be countered with the alternative view that it is a 'late morality' where 'the moral scheme is everything'.[2]

Numerous critics have tried to substantiate the morality interpretation by pointing to (i) the orthodox moral perspective which is, allegedly, implicit in characters' responses to heaven, hell, sin and damnation, and (ii) the extensive use of ironic peripeteias which allegedly destroy evil according to a principle of poetic justice. I want to challenge in turn each of these arguments.[3]

Providence and Parody

In Vindice's rhetorical invocations to heaven there is a distinctive sense of mockery:

> Why does not heaven turn black, or with a frown
> Undo the world? – why does not earth start up,
> And strike the sins that tread upon't?

(II. i. 254–6)

The implied parody of the providential viewpoint, the *caricature* of the vengeful god, becomes stronger as the play progresses:

> *Vindice:*   O, thou almighty patience! 'Tis my wonder
> That such a fellow, impudent and wicked,
> Should not be cloven as he stood, or with
> A secret wind burst open.
> Is there no thunder left, or is't kept up
> In stock for heavier vengeance? [*Thunder sounds*] There it goes!
>   (IV. ii. 194–9)

Here the traditional invocation to heaven becomes a kind of public stage-prompt ('Is there no thunder left . . . ?') and God's wrath an undisguised excuse for ostentatious effect. In performance such lines beg for a facetious Vindice, half turned towards the audience and deliberately directing its attention to the crudity of the stage convention involved.[4] In effect, the conception of a heavenly, retributive justice is being reduced to a parody of stage effects. In the following pun on 'claps' heaven is brought down to the level of a passive audience applauding the melodrama: 'When thunder claps, heaven likes the tragedy' (V. iii. 47). Vindice becomes the agent of the parody and is invested with a theatrical sense resembling the dramatist's own: 'Mark, thunder! Dost know thy *cue*, thou big-voic'd cryer?/Duke's groans are thunder's *watchwords*' (V. iii. 42–3; my italics; cf. Vindice's earlier line: 'When the bad bleeds, then is the tragedy good' – III. v. 205).

It gives an intriguing flexibility to Vindice's role, with the actor momentarily stepping through the part and taking on – without abandoning the part – a playwright's identity. This identity shift is instrumental to the parody: at precisely the moments when, if the providential references are to convince, the dramatic illusion needs to be strongest, Vindice (as 'playwright') shatters it. He does so by prompting for thunder from the stage, by representing thunder as a participant in a melodrama waiting for its 'cue', and by re-casting the traditionally 'frowning' heaven as a spectator clapping the action. The convention linking 'heaven', 'thunder' and 'tragedy' is, together with its related stage effects, rendered facile; providentialism is obliquely but conclusively discredited.[5] The letters of providentialist orthodoxy and, perhaps, of censorship, are respected but in performance their spirit is subverted through a form of parody akin to 'the privy mark of irony' described in the

Dedication to Beaumont's *The Knight of the Burning Pestle.*

Peter Lisca, in seeing the references to thunder and heaven as eliminating any doubt as to the play's 'sincere moral framework' (Lisca, p. 250), seems to miss an irony in tone and delivery which, in performance, would actually contradict the kind of moral conclusions he draws. Discussions of the extent to which a play is indebted to older dramatic forms are often marred in this way by an inadequate discrimination between the dramatic use of a convention and wholesale acceptance of the world view that goes (or went) with it. Obviously, the distinction becomes more than usually crucial when, as is the case here, the convention is being subjected to parody.

This play also exposes the hypocritical moral appeals which characters make to the providential order. An audience will, for example, simply bear the sermonising rhetoric of the Duchess's attack on illegitimacy:

> O what a grief 'tis, that a man should live
> But once i' th' world, and then to live a bastard,
> The curse o' the womb, the thief of nature,
> Begot against the seventh commandment,
> Half-dammn'd in the conception, by the justice
> Of that unbribed everlasting law.

(I. ii. 159–64)

The hollowness of this rhetoric is, of course, compounded by the sheer hypocrisy of its delivery: the Duchess is seen speaking not from the pulpit, but in the act of seducing her stepson and inciting him to murder his own father.

Still in Act I there is a moral posturing more revealing even than that of the Duchess. Antonio, celebrating publicly his wife's 'virtue' (she has committed suicide after being raped), is seen to value it even more than her life. 'Chastity' and 'honour' emerge in fact as the ideological imposition and self-representation of the male ego in a male dominated world. What compels us to consider the episode thus is not the simple facts themselves but the fact of their caricature; thrown into exaggerated relief, 'honour' and 'chastity' are turned inside out and held up for inspection. As with the interrogative representation of providence, parody here invites distrust,

ironic distance and refusal. Thus, discovering his wife's dead body
to 'certain lords' Antonio exclaims:

> be sad witnesses
> Of a fair, comely building newly fall'n . . .
> Piero: That virtuous lady!
> Antonio: Precedent for wives!
>
> (I. iv. 1–7)

A language of artificial grandeur reeking of affected grief tells us
that what is being celebrated is not her innate virtue but her dutiful
suicide, her obedience to male-imposed terms of sexual honour:

> Antonio: I joy
> In this one happiness above the rest . . .
> That, being an old man, I'd a wife so chaste.
>
> (I. iv. 74–7)

Chastity in this court involves a life-denying insularity dictated by
male vanity, not disinterested virtue. Again, it involves a hypocrisy
masked by an appeal to the providential order: 'Virginity is paradise, lock'd up./You cannot come by yourselves without fee,/And
'twas *decreed* that man should keep the key' (II. i. 157–9). Male
relations of power and possession are sanctioned in terms of female
virtue and providential design, while the death of Antonio's wife,
though presented as the cause of ensuing conflict, is in fact the
excuse for its continuation. In effect she is the instrument of a
power struggle quite independent of her.

   Peripeteias allegedly constitute the structural evidence for the
providential interpretation of the play. Lisca for example has argued
that its moral attitude 'proceeds from a Christian point of view (the
Puritan)' and that the peripeteias indicate 'the intestinal division of
evil itself, a division which while seeming to lead to multiplication
ironically ends in cross cancellation' (pp. 242, 245). Often the
assumption behind this approach is that peripeteia possessed an
inherently providential meaning. This was not the case with
Aristotle's definition of it and nor, at this time, with its use in the
Italian *novelle* and the plays influenced by them.[6] In *The Revenger's
Tragedy* the ironic reversal is manifestly bound up with Vindice's

(and the theatre's) sense of artistry and 'jest' (V. i. 64) and what Nicholas Brooke characterises as a humour 'in marvellously bad taste' (*Horrid Laughter in Jacobean Tragedy*, p. 14). In particular the art of revenge is seen to aim at a vicious blend of the appropriate and the unexpected. Vindice's advice to Lussurioso on how to kill the Duchess and Spurio (whom they expect to find in bed together) is an extreme case in point: 'Take 'em finely, finely now . . . Softly, my lord, and you may take 'em twisted . . . O 'twill be glorious/To kill 'em doubled, when they're heap'd. Be soft,/My Lord' (II. ii. 169; II. iii. 4). Here both peripeteia and poetic justice are construed in terms of a villainous aesthetic delight. It is a mode of appropriation which makes for a kind of double subversion: the play not only refuses two principles of moralistic drama, it presses them ignominiously into the service *of* play. Likewise with its own formal closure: 'Just is the law above!' cries Antonio with orthodox solemnity in relation to the series of murders in the final scene; ''twas somewhat witty carried, though we say it' replies Vindice coyly, referring to one of the same. In that reply, as elsewhere, the play's mocking intelligence and acute sense of parody – the kind that 'hits/Past the apprehension of indifferent wits' (V. i. 134) – converge in a 'witty' subversion of Antonio's crude, providential rationalisation.

Desire and Death

Inseparable from this play's subversion of some of the conventions of idealist mimesis is an alternative representation of the relations which bind sexuality, power and death. It centres on the frenetic activity of an introverted society encompassed by shadows and ulti-mately darkness – the 'heedless fury' and 'Wildfire at midnight' which Hippolito describes (II. ii. 172). The Court, 'this luxurious circle', is a closed world where energy feeds back on itself perpetu-ating the 'unnatural' act in unnatural surroundings: the location of the Duke's death is an 'unsunned lodge', 'Wherein 'tis night at noon'. Decay and impermanence stress the futility of each person's obsessive struggle for power. Yet there is no anticipation of other-worldly compensation, Junior's cynical rejection of the relevance of heaven to his impending death (III. iv. 70–4) being typical. The play's view of mortality is reminiscent of Schopenhauer; I quote briefly from his *Parerga and Paralipomena* simply to emphasise that it is not necessarily a view which entails a conception of man as inherently sinful or governed by divine law. The experience Schopenhauer describes is a contingent one with secular boundaries:

> The vanity of existence is revealed in the whole form existence assumes . . . in the fleeting present as the sole form in which actuality exists, in the contingency and relativity of all things . . . in continual desire without satisfaction; in the continual frustration of striving of which life consists . . . Thus its form is essentially unceasing *motion* without any possibility of that repose which we continually strive after . . . existence is typified by unrest. . . . Yet what a difference there is between our beginning and our end! We begin in the madness of carnal desire and the transport of voluptuousness, we end in the dissolution of all our parts and the musty stench of corpses.[7]

One is reminded too of the more restrained, yet somehow almost as pessimistic, account of London by Tourneur (or whoever that 'C.T.' was)[8] at the opening of 'Laugh and Lie Downe: Or, the Worldes Folly':

> Now in this Towne were many sundrie sorts of people of all ages; as Old, and young, and middle age: men, women and children: which did eate, and drinke, and make a noyse, and die . . . they were Creatures that serued the time, followed Shaddowes, fitted humours, hoped of Fortune, and found, what? I cannot tell you.[9]

In *The Revenger's Tragedy* this sense of court life as futile striving is intensified by the dramatist's insistence that here there is no alternative: activity occupying the immediate dramatic focus – 'this present minute' – is made, through graphic 'off-stage' description, to appear as just a bolder representation of that which pervades the rest of life:

> My lord, after long search, wary inquiries,
> And politic siftings, I made choice of yon fellow,
> Whom I guess rare for many deep employments;
> This our age swims within him . . .
> He is so near kin to this present minute.
>
>   (I. iii. 21–6)

Moreover, characters move into the line of vision already 'charged' with a common motivating energy – sexual, aggressive or otherwise – which varies in intensity only depending on whether it is the dramatic foreground or background that they occupy. It is, consequently, a world whose sense ends with its activity – a world, that is, whose senselessness becomes instantly apparent when activity culminates in death. Vindice highlights this through a detached awareness which Tourneur exploits to full effect as part of a structural interplay between movement and stasis.

Movement illustrates repeatedly the forces that impel, but simultaneously constrain and destroy people; the most extreme is the sexual – the 'riot' of the blood (I. i. 11). 'I am past my depth in lust,/And I must swim or drown' says Lussurioso (I. iii. 88–9), testifying to the destructive yet compulsive force of desire. Social forces are powerfully realised as either grinding poverty or thwarted ambition – both of which render the individual vulnerable to court exploitation. Thus we see Hippolito being sent from court –

> To seek some strange-digested fellow forth,
> Of ill-contented nature, either disgrac'd
> In former times, or by new grooms displac'd –
>
> (I. i. 76–8)

while for Lussurioso 'slaves are but nails, to drive out one another'. For his second slave he demands one who,

> being of black condition, suitable
> To want and ill content, hope of preferment
> Will grind him to an edge.
>
> (IV. i. 69–71)

Both Machiavellian intrigue and lust are depicted as inherent aspects of the frenetic movement and become inextricably linked with it in imagination:

> *Vindice:*   my brain
> Shall swell with strange invention; I will move it
> Till I expire with speaking, and drop down
> Without a word to save me; but I'll work –
> *Lussurioso:* We thank thee, and will raise thee.
>
> (I. iii. 119–23)

The point is stressed throughout with the recurrence of that word 'swell' in imagery of tumescence: 'drunken adultery/I feel it swell me' (I. ii. 190–1); 'I would embrace thee for a near employment,/ And thou shouldst swell in money' (I. iii. 76–7); 'Thy veins are swell'd with lust, this shall unfill 'em' (II. ii. 94); see also I. ii. 113 and IV. i. 63.

Movement involves an incessant drive for self-fulfilment through domination of others.[10] It is also represented as a process of inevitable disintegration; dissolution and death seem not in opposition to life's most frantic expression but inherent within it: 'O, she was able to ha' made a usurer's son/*Melt* all his patrimony in a kiss' (I. i. 26–7; my italics); 'I have seen patrimonies washed a-pieces, fruit fields turned into bastards, and, in a world of acres, not so much dust due to the heir 'twas left to, as would well gravel a petition' (I. ii. 50–3). The assertion of life energy does not stand in simple contrast to the process of disintegration but rather seems to feed – to become – the very process itself.[11]

Vindice's silk-worm image makes for the same kind of emphasis at a point immediately prior to the height of the dramatic action (the bizarre murder of the Duke with a skull, poisoned and disguised as a 'country lady'): 'Does the silk worm expend her yellow labours/For thee? for thee does she undo herself?'[12] (III. v. 72–3). Dissolution, the sense of helpless movement and lack of purpose are all concentrated in this image. The sense of uncontrollable movement towards dissolution also recalls Vindice's earlier lines where drunkenness releases barely conscious desire: 'Some father dreads not (gone to bed in wine)/To slide from the mother, and cling the daughter-in-law' (I. iii. 58–9). Here, in lines whose meaning is reinforced by the stress falling on 'slide' and 'cling', the involuntary action of a human being is reduced (casually yet startlingly) to the reflex action typical of an insentient being. In all these ways the futility and destructiveness of social life seem to have their source in some deeper condition of existence; at the very heart of life itself there moves a principle of self-stultification.

Contrary to this use of movement, the stasis with which it contrasts involves a form of detachment, the medium of insight and a limited foresight. Whereas to be caught up in the temporal process is to be blindly preoccupied with the present 'minute' (a recurring expression – see especially I. ii. 168; I. iii. 26; I. iv. 39; III. v. 75), the brief moments of inaction allow for a full realisation of just how self-stultifying is this world's expenditure of energy, of just how poor is the benefit of the 'bewitching minute'. It is reflected, initially, in the way Vindice's opening commentary is delivered from a point of detached awareness – a detachment represented spatially with him withdrawn into the shadowed region of the stage and directing attention at the procession. And at III. v. 50ff, just before the (by now) anticipated climax, his own contemplative state directs attention to the lifelessness of the skull, a wholly static but tangible representation of death and a striking visual contrast to the frenetic activity of life in this court. Insight of this kind is limited to Vindice; by others it is actually evaded. Thus whereas Vindice realises that 'man's happiest when he forgets himself' (IV. iv. 84) but cannot in fact forget himself for very long, Ambitioso checks his realisation that 'there is nothing sure in mortality, but mortality' with a resolve to action: 'Come, throw off clouds now, brother, think of vengeance,/And deeper settled hate' (III. vi. 89–90; 92–3).

There is one view of the characters in this play which sees them as morality type abstractions – 'simply monstrous embodiments of Lust, Pride and Greed' (Salingar, '*The Revenger's Tragedy* and the Morality Tradition', p. 404). But their subhumanity indicates more: displaying considerable desire, some intelligence but little self-awareness, they fit this play's depiction of life lived obsessively and destructively within the dislocated social 'minute'. Moreover such awareness as does exist is turned inward, brought to bear on immediate desire, but always in a way that fails to discover a unified, autonomous self. Instead their soliloquies indicate the forces which in-form and dislocate them. The Duchess, for example, is first seen as a voice of 'natural' mercy pleading for her 'youngest, dearest son' (I. ii. 103). But in her first soliloquy, while presumably retaining this affection, she becomes the ruthless schemer intent on having her husband killed by his bastard son and herself having an illicit – in the terms of the play, 'incestuous' (I. ii. 175) – sexual relationship with the latter. Moments later, the bastard, Spurio, accedes to both proposals only to then repudiate the Duchess just as she repudiated her Duke: 'Stepmother, I consent to thy desires,/I love thy mischief well, but I hate thee' (I.

ii. 193–4). Thus Spurio casts himself as the avenger, making the appropriate alliance, but in so doing makes a distinction in commitment that stalls all possibility of empathy. In the same soliloquy, brilliant, imaginative compression of mood and image suggests a dissolving of Spurio's present consciousness into the very circumstances of his conception: '. . . some stirring dish/Was my first father . . . / . . . drunken adultery/I feel it swell me' (ll. 181–2; 190–1). 'Impudent wine and lust' now infuse his veins such that 'Adultery is my nature' (l. 179), while alliteration and stressed single-syllable words give a rhythmic insistence blending into the 'withdrawing hour' to insinuate exactly the concealed activity in which he was 'stol'n softly':

> In such a whisp'ring and withdrawing hour,
> When base male-bawds kept sentinel at stair-head,
> Was I stol'n softly.
>
> (I. ii. 187–9)

Imagery of sexuality becomes this play's most powerful signifier of a society deriving initial impetus from, yet finally stultified by, the contradictions within it. Thus the old Duke is sexually 'parch'd and juiceless' – one with 'scarce blood enough to live upon' (I. i. 9, 10) – yet his very impotence is paradoxically though not untypically the source of a sterile and destructive life force.

Given a world of dislocated energy as its dramatic subject, what kind of formal unity is such a play likely to possess? The answer is suggested in Vindice. Disguise, intelligence and the capacity to see the futility of others' endeavour, give him a kind of freedom. Yet it is at best partial and probably illusory, being, in effect, a knowledge of the fate of the society to which he is inescapably confined. It is as such that, at the play's close, he surrenders his life with comparative indifference, a surrender recalling his earlier expression of estrangement: 'My life's unnatural to me, e'en compelled/As if I lived now when I should be dead' (I. i. 120–1). Unemployed and with his family in poverty he articulates the tensions and contradictions of his world, becoming the focal point for those dimensions of the play which, though inextricably linked, will not – indeed, cannot – be finally resolved into a single coherent 'vision'. Even when he is most apparently an agent – as for example in the famous fifth scene of Act III – he is really a victim and he knows it; hence his sharply alternating moods: detached, exhilarated, despairing, sadistic. Vindice as malcontented satirist is corrupted by the society he condemns because inescapably a part of that society; to put it another way, he condemns it because he is corrupted – inevitably corrupted by it. In this respect satirist figures like Vindice and Flamineo (*The White Devil*) share much in common with other malcontented rebels like, for example, Antonio (*Antonio's Revenge*), Bussy d'Ambois, and Edmund (*King Lear*): estrangement from society, whether because of poverty, dispossession, unemployment, injustice or thwarted ambition, provokes in them an aggressive reaction; heroic or criminal it adds up to the same thing: a desperate bid for reintegration. In its vindictiveness this bid becomes the contradictory attempt to destroy that which they are within and which they cannot survive without. The experience of estrangement reveals on the one hand the futility and worthlessness of the existing social order, on the other the estranged subject's dependence upon it; most extremely, to be reintegrated is to embrace destruction. Yet the alternative – estrangement itself pushed to an extreme – leads to poverty, mental collapse or suicide.

In *The Revenger's Tragedy* a vital irony and a deep pessimism exist in disjunction; if they are held together dramatically they are not in any sense aesthetically integrated, either in tone or character. And if there is an attitude yoking them by violence together it is not that of the unified sensibility once thought to characterise the period, but rather that of a subversive black camp. It is sophisticated and self-conscious, at once mannered and chameleon; it celebrates the artificial and the delinquent; it delights in a play full of innuendo, perversity and subversion; by mimicking and misappropriating their glibness it exposes the hypocrisy and deception of the pious; through parody it declares itself radically sceptical of ideological policing though not independent of the social reality which such scepticism simultaneously discloses. Vindice, living that reality in terms of social displacement and exploitation, lives also the extreme instability of his society and is led thereby to meditate on mutability and death. Even the meditation takes on a subversive edge because transferred from the study to that place to which Vindice's displacement has led him: the domain of sexuality and power, the 'accursed palace' where his brother finds him 'Still sighing o'er death's vizard' (I. i. 30, 50). Just as displacement compels action so the meditation is, as it were, enacted. Yet no one in the process is allowed the role of heroic despair; in relation to no one is human suffering made to vindicate human existence. To that extent *The Revenger's Tragedy* is beyond – or before – 'tragedy'.

PART III

MAN DECENTRED

10

Subjectivity and Social Process

Jacobean tragedy anticipates, and is therefore usefully explored in relation to, a central tenet of materialist analysis, namely that the essentialist concept of 'man' mystifies and obscures the real historical conditions in which the actual identity of people is rooted.

Marx in his famous sixth thesis asserts: 'Feuerbach resolves the essence of religion into the essence of *man*. But the essence of man is not an abstraction inherent in each particular individual. The real nature of man is the totality of social relations.' And elsewhere: 'It is not the consciousness of men that determines their being, but, on the contrary, their social being that determines their consciousness' (*Selected Writings*, pp. 83, 67). Chapter 16 addresses the wider implications for cultural studies and literary criticism of this materialist, anti-essentialist conception of subjectivity. Here I provide only a preliminary indication of its importance for developing a critical perspective which both recovers an historical understanding of subjectivity in the Jacobean period and its drama, and counters the essentialist misrepresentation of period and drama in modern literary criticism.

Of especial importance for drama is, of course, Brecht's account of decentred subjectivity in his theory of epic theatre. Brecht resolutely refused the traditional representation of human nature as fixed, presenting instead a protagonist embodying the Marxist proposition that human consciousness is determined by social being or, in Benjamin's description, an 'untragic hero' who is 'like an empty stage on which the contradictions of our society are acted out' (*Understanding Brecht*, p. 17).[1] This, I shall argue, is true also of protagonists in Jacobean theatre. Important also is the more recent work of Michel Foucault which analyses both subjectivity and the relations between subject and society in terms of power. Foucault conceives of power not as something possessed by subjects but as that which constitutes them; the individual is both the effect and the object of power:

> The individual is not to be conceived as a sort of elementary nucleus, a primitive atom, a multiple and inert material on which power comes to fasten or against which it happens to strike, and in so doing subdues or crushes individuals . . . The individual, that is, is not the *vis-à-vis* of power; it is, I believe, one of its prime effects. The individual is an effect of power, and at the same time, or precisely to the extent to which it is that effect, it is the element of its articulation. The individual which power has constituted is at the same time its vehicle. (*Power/Knowledge*, p. 98)

This is a perspective which helps us recover something of fundamental importance for the late sixteenth and early seventeenth century when some writers at least were discovering the implication of the fact that 'man' is a binary function of 'God': to demystify the latter is to decentre the former.

It might be thought that to use the writing of Marx, Brecht, Foucault and others to elucidate early seventeenth-century England, far from restoring a correct historical context for its drama, is itself an unhistorical procedure. Certainly the obvious differences between that period and a more recent materialist tradition should not be minimised. Nevertheless the one has its roots in the other. Brecht develops his dramatic theory in relation to the theatre of the earlier period, and there are real similarities between Althusser's theory of ideology and Montaigne's account of custom (see chapters 1 and 3). Additionally Perry Anderson has pointed out that much of Althusser's Marxism was drawn directly from Spinoza (1632–97) and also that Althusser, in developing Marxism with reference to earlier philosophers, was not unique; the philosophical ancestry of Marxism has been taken to include Hegel, Nietzsche, Rousseau, Kant, Hume, Machiavelli and Galileo.[2] For the purposes of the present argument the most significant figures in this list are the last two; Galileo because the decentring of man in Jacobean tragedy was contemporaneous with, and influenced by, the revolution whereby 'man' and 'his' planet were displaced both from the real and the metaphysical centre of the universe; Machiavelli because, as Gramsci has argued, he was a pioneer of the 'philosophy of praxis', the most important formulation of which, says Gramsci, is Marxism. Especially relevant to the present subject is Gramsci's claim – in a section of the *Prison Notebooks* entitled in its original version 'Marx and Machiavelli' – that the most original contribution of the philosophy of praxis is its anti-essentialism, that is, its 'demonstration that there is no abstract "human nature", fixed and immutable (a concept which certainly derives from religious and transcendentalist thought) but that human nature is the totality of historically determined social relations' (p. 133). Machiavelli's philosophy of praxis, adds Gramsci, 'bases itself entirely on the concrete action of man, who, impelled by historical necessity, works and transforms reality' (pp. 248–9).

Just as important as this question of antecedents is the argument which follows, namely that the incorrect procedure is that which insists on reading the early seventeenth century through the grid of an essentialist humanism[3] which in historical fact post-dates it and in effect only really emerges with the Enlightenment; in other words, what makes a materialist analysis of subjectivity in that period seem inappropriate is itself a thoroughly anachronistic perspective. In fact, during that period the essentialist conception of man was in a vulnerable state of transition, being, roughly speaking, between its Christian/metaphysical formulations and the later secular/Enlightenment mutations of these (the latter being the object of Marx's attack). The paradigm of Christian essentialism presented the soul as metaphysically derivative and to this extent simply disallowed the idea of the autonomous, unified self-generating subject postulated by essentialist humanism. Obviously, with the decline of Christian essentialism there did not instantly emerge the humanist ideology of individual man. On the contrary, in the England of the early seventeenth century that decline led to a decentring of man and a corresponding emphasis on the extent to which subjectivity was to be socially identified. That such identification was possible is not surprising given that, prior to the Renaissance, 'what mattered was . . . not the individual but society, the corpus of all individuals' (Walter Ullmann, *The Individual and Society in the Middle Ages*, p. 48). In fact, in the early seventeenth century 'individual' was often used in the non-essentialist sense of 'eccentric', and Raymond Williams has found that it was not perhaps until 1690 that the essentialist sense of the word emerges, and even then it was as an adjective and not a noun: 'our idea of any individual Man' (Locke, *Human Understanding*, III, vi). At any rate, the idea of 'the individual as a substantial entity' emerges only in the latter part of the seventeenth century and in the eighteenth century (*Keywords*, p. 135). Of course there is not a simple persistence of the medieval conception of identity as hierarchical location any more than there is a sudden appearance of the autonomous subject. But the former does remain as an important residual conception of identity as subjective dependence – only now of course dependence itself as a category of social relations is being contested.[4]

Jacobean tragedy challenged Christian essentialism, and indeed its stoic and humanist derivatives – just as Marxist materialism challenged the (by then) deeply rooted Enlightenment mutations of it. Idealist literary criticism has been unwilling to recognise either challenge, preferring instead to interpret that tragedy in terms of, first, the metaphysical essentialism which it was in fact subjecting to sceptical interrogation, and second, an essentialist humanism which, as I have already indicated and argue more fully in chapter 16, only really emerges in the Enlightenment, and then undergoes important transformations through romanticism and modernism which further distance it from the early seventeenth century. The result has been a criticism which insists on finding in Jacobean tragedy its own humanist deformation of transcendent subjectivity.

Tragedy, Humanism and the Transcendent Subject

In one sense the humanist theory of tragedy repudiates the religious desire to be folded within the absolute; moreover, in such tragedy the absolute is typically construed not redemptively but as a force permanently hostile to man's deepest needs. Nevertheless, tragic death restores transcendent unity to the subject and to man, not despite but because of the fact that now it ceases to be conditional upon a redemptive identification with the absolute. Man gathers that unity into himself; his essential nature is pressured into its full being. Individual extinction leads to the apotheosis of man, who now becomes his own universal. Further – and this too is a consequence of this view being a displaced theology – suffering and loss are mystified, rendered inevitable and unalterable and, as such, become the precondition for instantiation of the universal. John Tinsley has recently (1982) characterised very clearly this tragic sense of life; it always contains, he says, 'a vision of man remaining incomparably superior to all those circumstances which seem only to underline his ultimate insignificance and transitoriness . . . it expresses a solicitude for, and a stoic pride in, man who is the victim of so much pain, and a resentment against the fortuitous character of human calamity and against any God, who, if he exists, must be held to permit this'; further, it replaces ideas of creation and providence with some kind of fatalism ('Tragedy and Christian Beliefs', pp. 101–2). For Tinsley, a bishop, such a view as it stands is of course unacceptable to the Christian faith. But, situated as it is 'equally removed from both faith and despair' (p. 100), it is redeemable.

Bishop Tinsley is quite right: the tragic sense of life as articulated in idealist culture *is* redeemable for Christian faith, and the parameters of his discussion – faith and despair, the tragic and the comic, atonement and redemption, Christian irony, fatalism and reconciliation – indicate why this is so: both perspectives, the tragic and the Christian, remain within the same idealist problematic, one which can be best characterised in terms of what it excludes, namely the single most important concept in materialist analysis: praxis. It is a concept which severs the connection between individuality and man, between subjectivity and the human condition. Consequently it rejects the 'tragic' belief in a human essence which, by its own nature as well as its relation to the universal order of things, must inevitably suffer. On the contrary, as Raymond Williams says of Brecht: 'We have to see not only that suffering is avoidable, but that it is not avoided, And not only that suffering breaks us but that it need not break us' (*Modem Tragedy*, pp. 202–3).

The Jacobean Displacement of the Subject

In the early seventeenth century older ideas of the universe and of society as functioning on a metaphysical principle of hierarchy and interdependence were being displaced, as was the related idea of identity as metaphysically derivative. Donne's famous complaint in the *First Anniversary* that all coherence has gone is perhaps most interesting not as an evocation of impending anarchy but as an indication that individual identity had hitherto depended ultimately on the 'coherence' of a geocentric cosmology and a corresponding ideology of *centred* structure:

> New philosophy calls all in doubt,
> The element of fire is quite put out;
> The sun is lost, and th' earth . . .
> 'Tis all in pieces, all coherence gone;
> All just supply, and all relation:
> Prince, subject, father, son, are things forgot.
>
> (ll. 205–7; 213–15)

Relational identity has, suggests Donne in the passage which follows, given way to anarchic egotism. But the latter is not at all the humanist idea of a quasi-spiritual subject at once essentially autonomous and partaking of a universal human nature. Such notions will come later. In the interim we have a period deeply receptive to the implications of the decentred subject. The egotism of which Donne complains was a part of the individualism associated with the new social and geographical mobility, one which encouraged a view of identity as less a matter of performing a certain function within a fixed order (as in medieval society) than of 'initiating certain kinds of activity, choosing particular directions'; thus 'what I am' (what I do) becomes by extension 'what I want to be' – again, a non-essentialist form of individualism (Raymond Williams, *The Long Revolution*, p. 92).

It may be right to see in western philosophy at this time what

Hiram Haydn has called 'the ultimate desertion of the universal for the particular' (*The Counter-Renaissance*, p. 143); indeed, the sceptical disintegration of providentialism is one aspect of this change. But we should not underestimate just how difficult it was, then and subsequently, to make the particular signify independently of the universal. Nowhere was this more so than with regard to human subjectivity (it is no accident that two of the most radical sceptics of universal truth, Montaigne and Hume, also problematise and decentre the subject). Perhaps the most fundamental error of idealist criticism is to assume that with the ultimate deconstruction of metaphysics (God), the particular (Individual) was foregrounded in all its intrinsic uniqueness. There are several reasons why this was not so. For one thing metaphysics was recuperated in ways which proved it to be, as it were, profoundly resilient – principally in idealist culture itself where 'individual' comes to presuppose its own universal. Moreover, because the particular had for so long been constructed as a binary function of the universal, any independent foregrounding of it had to be problematic, arguably impossible: because of this binary relationship the particular is not simply foregrounded by the destabilising of the universal, but is itself destabilised.

Michel Foucault, examining the history of the decentring of man, remarks that 'Nietzsche *rediscovered* the point at which man and god belong to one another, at which the death of the second is synonymous with the disappearance of the first' (*The Order of Things*, p. 342; my italics). Who Foucault has in mind as previously or first discovering this binary relation between God and man is not clear, but certainly writers in the Renaissance were aware of it. Calvin opens the *Institutes* with in insistence that 'knowledge of God and of ourselves . . . are connected by many ties'. In the first place, to consider oneself is inescapably to consider God because 'our very being is nothing else than subsistence in God alone'. Conversely, 'it is evident that man never attains to a true self-knowledge until he has previously contemplated the face of God' (I. i. 1–2). The disturbing implications which can be drawn from this are made later by Calvin: 'As Adam's spiritual life would have consisted in remaining united and bound to his Maker, so estrangement from Him was the death of his soul' (*Institutes*, II.

i. 5). Montaigne makes the same point in more dramatic terms: 'God had made man like unto a shadowe, of which who shall judge, when the light being gone, it shall vanish away? *Man is a thing of nothing*' (*Essays*, II, 199).

To see how the dramatists went further we might set against the traditional idea of, say, Hooker – that 'God hath his influence into the very essence of all things, without which influence of Deity supporting them their utter annihilation could not choose but follow' (*Laws*, II, 226) – Chapman's contention that 'purblind Chance/ . . . pipes through empty men, and makes them dance' (*Bussy D'Ambois*, V. iii. 47–8). Chapman's parallel between '*empty men*' and 'purblind chance' (purblind = totally blind) is the *precise inversion* of Hooker's positive, binary dependence of man upon God, man in-formed by God. (Similarly, in Marston's *Antonio's Revenge*, Pandulpho declares that disharmony in 'the breast of man' is the inevitable corollary of disharmony in nature – IV. ii. 90–5).

It is worth glancing forward at this point if only to register the fact that as later writers develop the implication of the first great decentring of man (the heliocentric theory of the universe) it is by no means always an occasion for anguish. Henry Power says in *Experimental Philosophy* (1664): 'as for the Earth being the Centre of the World, 'tis now an opinion so generally exploded that I need not trouble you nor my self with it' (pp. 164, 190). John Spencer in *A Discourse Concerning Prodigies* (1663–5) indicates how cheerfully some at least were prepared to accept the consequences of this decentring. It is, says Spencer, only our 'fond valuation of our selves' which leads us to seek a relationship between man and the universe. Spencer mocks both this anthropocentrism and its teleological corollary; for him geocentrism and egocentrism seem inextricably related: 'we first conceit Man the *great measure* of things . . . next that he is the *great End* of things . . . Hence we easily fancy no New Star or Comet shines from Heaven but we are extremely concerned in the occasion . . .' (pp. 279–81; cited in Harris, pp. 165, 168).

The rest of this section outlines first, the essentialist view of man which derives from sixteenth-century Christianity and its stoic and humanist derivatives, and which is drawn upon in the modern Christian and humanist interpretations of Elizabethan and Jacobean tragedy; second, the tensions within the essentialist view; third, the alternative tradition drawn upon by those dramatists who interrogated the essentialist view and, in contradistinction to it, decentred man; lastly, the way that this decentring of man is the basis of an increasingly penetrating social and political realism in a sequence of plays ranging from Chapman's *Bussy D'Ambois*, through Shakespeare's *Lear* and *Coriolanus* and culminating with Webster's *The White Devil*. Progressively in these plays the mechanisms of state,[5] of ideology and of power are disclosed. Power especially is foregrounded but not (as in the work of some recent theorists) hypostatised as a universal in its own right. It is, rather, identified in complex manifestations and relations – also in terms which contest its equally complex ideological misrepresentations.

The Essentialist Tradition: Christianity, Stoicism and Renaissance Humanism

Christianity allots to man a spiritual essence, albeit one derived from and dependent upon God and, further, rendered problematic by the Fall. Generally speaking the soul as construed by Christianity retains an essential identity, especially if conceived as fundamentally indivisible. In the Renaissance and Reformation not only Christians but also stoics and humanists explored and consolidated this idea of man's spiritual identity. Two significant sources were Augustine and Aquinas.

Augustine (354–430) insisted on the perfection of God and, by contrast, the depravity of man. God himself is omnipotent, omniscient and omnipresent. Man is sinful, his flesh weak, his will perverted and his reason ineffectual. The relationship between fallen man and an omnipotent God proved notoriously problematic in Augustine's account. For example: God willed that Adam should sin yet Adam had free will nevertheless, says Augustine. The question of how this is possible is, he confesses, 'Of such obscurity that I can neither bring it home to the intelligence of other people, or understand it myself' (*On the Soul and its Origin*, IV. 16; quoted from Baker, *The Image of Man*, p. 174).

Aquinas' (1225–74) view of man is more optimistic. He affirms man's potential, especially his rational potential: a man's mind is 'the very essence of the soul' (*Selected Writings*, p. 177). Man's *raison d'être* as a rational creature is knowledge of God, which he obtains by experience of the world about him, a world governed by natural law, itself grounded in God's eternal law. Thus whereas Augustine's universe is governed by God's absolute but inscrutable will, Aquinas' universe manifests God's intelligible design. And man's exalted nature is inseparable from that design. Subsequent Christian estimates of man – whether in the severer tradition of Augustine or the more optimistic tradition of Aquinas – remain, as one would expect, ultimately essentialist.

The Renaissance development of classical humanism tended to reinforce the Thomistic view.[6] Thus for Peter de La Primaudaye, man is 'a creature made of God after his own image, just, good and right by nature' (*The French Academy*, 1618, p. 5). The emphasis falls increasingly on man's quasi-divine attributes – his unique powers of reasoning, the immortality of his soul, his rule over the rest of creation. Sir John Davies asserts:

> thy whole image thou in man hast writ;
> There cannot be a creature more divine,
> Except like thee it should be infinit.
>
> (*Nosce Teipsum*, ll. 266–8)

Davies concentrates almost exclusively on man's exalted nature. His position is that of a Christian humanist: man exists at the centre of a theocentric universe; he is rational by nature – indeed, his desire for knowledge 'from the *Essence* of the *Soule* doth spring' (l. 1308); moreover certain kinds of knowledge are innate. Additionally the universe is magnificently inter-connected and human law 'doth her Roote from God and Nature take' (l. 790). Davies accepts the theory of evil as privation (l. 18) and that man has free will (ll. 854ff). For Walter Raleigh also man is 'eternally endued with a divine understanding' (*History*, p. 126).

Humanists like Ficino and Pico, under the influence of neo-platonism, advocate man's spiritual self-sufficiency and even come close to suggesting an *independent* spiritual identity for man:

'With his super celestial mind he transcends heaven . . . man who
provides generally for all things both living and lifeless, is a *kind*
of God' (Ficino, *Platonic Theology*, p. 234). In the same work
Ficino asserts that man possesses almost the same genius as the
author of the heavens, and could also make the heavens had he
the materials.

In the revival of stoicism there is a similar emphasis. Seneca had
said:

> in a man praise is due only to what is his very own . . . Praise in him
> what can neither be given nor snatched away . . . You ask what that
> is? It is his spirit, and the perfection of his reason in that spirit. For
> man is a rational animal. Man's ideal state is realised when he has
> fulfilled the purpose for which he was born. And what is it that
> reason demands of him? Something very easy – that he live in accor-
> dance with his own nature. (*Letters*, pp. 88–9)

Neo-stoics like Lipsius, Du Vair and Joseph Hall endeavoured to
show that such philosophy was compatible with Christianity. How
successful they were is debatable but they could find in Seneca
something approximating to Christian providence. In fact in the
very same letter from which the above extract is taken, Seneca
insists that the soul 'is impelled by a force that comes from heaven.
A thing of that soul's height cannot stand without the prop of a deity'
(p. 87; my italics). Man withdraws into his essential self not to be
independent of the universal order but better to apprehend it. Here
then is the same binary dependence of essence upon universal as
that found in Christianity. And it suggests why, in a play like
Marston's *Antonio's Revenge*, stoic essentialism is rejected: initially
embraced as a substitute for the disintegrated universal, it is abandoned because found to be dependent upon that universal; the
latter is indeed its 'prop', as Seneca says.

Internal Tensions

Even within the Christian tradition, man's spiritual identity was
often felt to be more problematic than the foregoing suggests. In
general terms essentialism might at least be qualified by both the
Augustinian and the Thomistic theologies, the first because of its

emphasis on man's helpless depravity, the second because of its tendency to subsume man into the cosmic system. Additionally there was the problem of man's *divided* nature. Neoplatonic dualism leads even Ficino to acknowledge that 'because we are all separated from God on earth, none of us is a true man; each one of us is divided from his own Idea and nature' (*Commentary on Plato's Symposium*, 1574 edition, chapter 19). Thomas Browne described man as 'that amphibious piece between a corporeal and spiritual essence' who has to live 'in divided and distinguished worlds' (*Religio Medici*, p. 53).

As I indicated earlier, the paradoxes of religious thought are not effaced but rather formally contained by the structure of the morality play; the possibility of paradox intensifying into contradiction is formally foreclosed but paradox itself nevertheless remains central. This is especially so in the representation of man's divided nature.

In *Mankind* (c. 1470) the conflict between soul and body is overcome in a progression from 'diverse transmutation' to '*vitam eternam*', life everlasting (ll. 916 and 920). On his first appearance Mankind, the protagonist, testifies to his state of self-division:

> My name is Mankind. I have my composition
> Of a body and of a soul, of condition contrary.
> Betwixt the twain is a great division:
> He that should be subject, now he hath the victory.
> This to me is a lamentable story:
> To see my flesh, of my soul to have governance.
>
> (ll. 193–8)

This is the view often echoed in the later drama. It should be emphasised however that in *this* play man's 'condition contrary' is under providential control. To quote the above lines out of context conceals the fact that immediately before uttering them Mankind has firmly stated that 'By the providence of God thus we be derivate'.

Throughout the moralities a similar pattern recurs: because man exists in the shadow of original sin he falls and suffers but eventually repents. There is usually a relapse and the experience of despair before a final recovery to secure redemption. The inevitability of the pattern seems to assume a deterministic relation between the Fall and man's subsequent repetition of the event. Yet there is an equally strong assumption that man possesses a sufficiently uncontaminated will either to avoid his fall, or to choose redemption once he has fallen.

The dramatic force of *The Castle of Perseverance* (1405–25, the second earliest of the extant Medieval moralities) derives from the tension between these two assumptions. There is a close and insistent juxtaposition of the helpless and the responsible sides of man's nature. He is vulnerable because divided against himself.

> I wolde be ryche in gret a-ray,
> And fayn I wolde my sowle save

(ll. 378–9)

Yet he is also responsible:

> God hathe govy[n] Man fre arbitracion
> Whethyr he wyl hymse[lf] save or hys soule [spyll]

(ll. 25–6)

Mankind's vulnerability is represented in vivid and immediate terms at his first entry. He is flanked by the Good and Bad Angels and these are his first words:

> This nyth I was of my modyr born.
> Fro my modyr I walke, I wende,
> Full feynt and febyl I fare you beforn.
> I am nakyd . . .
> I was born this nyth in blody ble . . .
> A, Lord God in trinite,
> Whow Mankende is Unthende!

(ll. 276–87)

In this condition he is forced to choose between the two Angels. Predictably he is deceived by the Bad Angel and falls into sin. After he has repented but fallen again (to Covetousness) the Good Angel wants to imprison him for protection. But Meekness insists that Mankind must be left to reject sin for himself. This time he is claimed by Death before he has time to repent and so is apparently damned. (We see Soul being taken to Hell on the back of the Bad Angel.) Nevertheless, Mankind's last words were a cry for mercy

and there follows a trial before that mercy is finally granted to him
by God. Willard Farnham, referring to this merciful denouement,
argues that so long as dramatist and audience 'conceive that a universal law of justice, under which man lives and engages himself
with his destiny, is dominated by the force of mercy their recognition of tragedy must necessarily be small' (*Medieval Heritage*, p.
193). Yet there is in this play, as I have tried to indicate, an especially acute awareness of the conflicting demands of man's nature:
he is vulnerable and divided to the extent that he cannot live up to
the responsibility demanded of him. In one, intriguing, sequence
(ll. 3008ff) we see Mankind's Soul, although apparently without
power to control the body, nevertheless taking responsibility for the
latter's sin. Mankind has died. His Soul crawls from beneath the
bed and reproaches the body:

> Thi sely sowle schal ben akale;
> I beye thi dedys wyth rewly rowte
>
> (ll. 3038–9)

but then turns to the Good Angel and accepts responsibility for
the body's sin by assuming an identity with it (especially at
ll. 3069–70).

To dislocate or abandon morality form – the formal guarantee of
resolution – was always potentially to activate such tensions, especially this experience of dislocated subjectivity. Its most extreme
images in later literature include that of the rack, already encountered in Greville's *Mustapha*: 'flesh and blood, the means 'twixt
heaven and hell,/Unto extremes extremely racked be'. Herbert in
'The Temper' pleads with God 'O rack me not to such a vast
extent' and asks too why He 'dost stretch/A crumme of dust from
heav'n to hell?' In this instance faith leads to reintegration: 'Thy
power and love, my love and trust/Make one place ev'ry where'
(not so with Lear of course, who dies on the rack of this tough
world – V. iii. 316).

An even more important source of tension was the protestant
revival of Augustinianism. Calvin, repudiating the Renaissance
exaltation of man, claimed that

the mind of man is so entirely alienated from the righteousness of God that he cannot conceive, desire or design anything but what is wicked, distorted, foul, impure and iniquitous; that his heart is so thoroughly envenomed by sin that it can breath out nothing but corruption and rottenness.

(*Institutes*, II, 5, 19).

In the hands of Marston, the Calvinist insistence on man's abject state, rather than intimidating him into an attitude of self-abnegation before God, becomes evidence for questioning whether any relationship with God could, or ever did, exist:

> Sure I nere thinke these axioms to be true,
> That soules of men, from that great soule ensue,
> And of his essence doe participate,
> As't were by pypes, when so degenerate,
> So adverse is our natures motion,
> To his immaculate condition:
> That such foule filth, from such faire puritie,
> Such sensuall acts from such a Deitie,
> Can nere proceed. But if that dreame were so,
> Then sure the slime that from our soules doe flow,
> Have stopt those pypes by which it was convai'd
> And now no humane creatures, once disrai'd
> Of that fayre jem.
> Beasts *sence*, plants *growth*, like being as a stone,
> But out alas, our *Cognisance* is, gone.

('A Cynicke Satyre', ll. 188–202)

The 'Deitie' in question is stoic and the passage as a whole is arguing against a specifically Senecan view (lines 189–90 refer to Seneca's *Epistles*, CXX, 14). Thus Marston uses a protestant estimate of man to deny the stoic belief in man's rational essence but, in suggesting also that man is so degenerate that he has *no* relation to God, he simultaneously violates the central premise of Calvinism (or at least jars its most sensitive nerve). And the upshot of it all is an emphatic denial that man's nature is coextensive with a spiritual essence.

Such counter-tendencies to the Renaissance optimism about man's nature figure in Jacobean tragedy's decentring of the subject. But if that process were merely confined to the tensions within Christianity – catholic or protestant – it might not extend beyond the pessimism familiar from medieval traditions of *contemptus mundi*, *de casibus* tragedy, the *memento mori* and so on (see Farnham, chapter 11). The severity of Calvin was more disturbing than any of those, yet even this was an attitude to man which kept him obsessively central even as it castigated him. As one unsympathetic critic has put it, the Calvinist's demand for man's self-abasement before God can be shown to originate in 'an arrogant pride . . . and religious subjectivism' (P. Murtz, *The Place of Hooker in the History of Thought*, p. 37). In this respect Calvinism can be seen as a variant – rather than a denial – of the same essentialism which lies behind the humanist exaltation of man, at least to the extent that it wants to define, once and for all, his essential nature. Nevertheless, by making that nature so depraved, Calvinism creates a destabilising tendency all of its own (one of many in fact): a creature so corrupt would seem finally to be so removed from God that even the relationship of dependence is called in question. For the English Calvinist William Perkins it seemed imperative to prevent this by positing a kind of super-essence which remains incorruptible even by original sin: 'Sin is not a corruption of man's substance, but only of faculties. Otherwise neither could men's soul be immortal, nor Christ take upon him man's nature' (*A Golden Chain*, p. 192). In the plays discussed below there is no such essence; man is decentred to reveal the social forces that both make and destroy him. In part this is because both the problem of man's divided nature and the Calvinist belittling of him were put to subversive use by being loosened or transferred from original theological contexts where they were 'tied down' by the doctrine of providence. Once again then, it is not necessary to see the radicalism of the drama as constituting an absolute break with dominant cultural forms; rather, it emerges, at least initially, from potential contradictions *within* those forms. But by being (for example) intensified and/or transposed, these same contradictions become challenges *to* those forms.

More important even than the foregoing is the way that Jacobean tragedy drew on estimates of human nature which were largely outside, or even in opposition to, these dominant forms and their internal strains. Those estimates included some of the more radical implications of the humanists like Pico, together with the more explicit radicalism of More, Machiavelli, Montaigne, Bacon and Hobbes (who, although he is writing shortly after the drama, is anticipated by it).[7] It is to these that I now turn.

Anti-Essentialism in Political Theory and Renaissance Scepticism

Ficino's notion of man's divinity involved not a fixed nature but, rather, a process of deification. Pico takes this even further, and in the celebrated *Oration On the Dignity of Man* he represents the Creator as telling Adam that he has deliberately been made without a fixed identity – 'neither of heaven, nor of earth, neither mortal nor immortal' (*The Renaissance Philosophy of Man*, ed. Cassirer, p. 225). Instead he has been created with abundant freedom to 'obtain for thyself the limits of thy identity' (p. 225). Ernst Cassirer finds here 'a specifically modern pathos of thought' stemming from the fact that 'the dignity of man cannot reside in his being, i.e., in the place allotted man once and for all in the cosmic order' (*The Individual and the Cosmos in Renaissance Philosophy*, p. 84). In fact, continues Cassirer, there is a reversal of the traditional relationship between *being* and *acting*: 'It is not being that prescribes once and for all the lasting direction which the mode of action will take; rather, the original direction of action determines and places being' (a prefiguring in this view, then, of the existentialist philosophy whereby existence precedes essence). One can imagine how Pico's account of man, and for that matter Pomponazzi's argument that the doctrine of the soul's immortality runs counter to reason, could, for a later generation, contribute to the sense of man's spiritual identity as problematic. On the question of immortality, it is interesting that Sir John Davies asserts confidently that man's immortality is the precondition for belief in God. It is, he says, an absolutely universal rule:

> None that acknowledge God or providence,
> Their *Soules* eternitie did ever doubt;
> For all religion takes her roots from hence,
> Which no poore naked nation lives without.
>
> (*Nosce Teipsum*, ll. 1837–40)

La Primaudaye is even more explicit on the implications for providence of disbelief in the soul's immortality: 'the religion of God, his
providence, and the immortalitie of our soule are . . . fast lincked
and joyned together . . . if our soules be not immortall, there is
neither punishment nor reward, either for vertue or vice . . . Which
if it were so, then shoulde God have no care of men: and if he have
no care of them howe shall hee be their God and Creator . . . ?'
(*The French Academy*, 1596, pp. 553–4). One would expect that
the undermining of providence would make spiritual identity
problematic; what is interesting is that in this case the reverse was
also thought to be true: to repudiate man's immortality is to challenge providence. In this respect, then, God is a binary function of
man as well as man of God.

One clearly radical tendency in humanism is to be found in
Thomas More's recognition of the extent to which social institutions form human nature. This is what J. H. Hexter, in his
analysis of the radicalism of *Utopia*, calls More's 'environmen-
talism' (*The Complete Works of St Thomas More*, vol. IV, p. cxviii).
What *Utopia* omits is the idea of a fixed human nature, depraved
or otherwise, of which society is an inevitable and unalterable
reflection. On the contrary, More believed many if not all evils to
be generated by social institutions; for him, according to Hexter:
'It is the social environment of Europe, its laws and customs, that
leads Christian men to prey on Christian men in a society based
not on community but on the thinly masked oppression of the
poor by the rich' (p. cxxi). It is surely this awareness which lies
behind More's radicalism, especially his contempt for the
European warrior class, his repudiation of hierarchy and his corresponding advocacy of communist equality, and his demystification
of law (see above, p. 16).

Machiavelli and Hobbes demystify man and society in at least
three important respects. Two of these are well known: politics is
separated from morality and both are in turn separated from divine
prescription. The third involves the rejection of essentialism; these
two philosophers dispense not only with the idealised human
essence, but the depraved one as well.

Although he never speaks of the soul, there are places in *The*

Discourses where Machiavelli appears to posit an unchanging human nature. For example: 'in constituting and legislating for a commonwealth it must needs be taken for granted that all men are wicked' (pp. 111–12). But such statements are more pragmatic assumptions than essentialist definitions which seek to delimit *a priori* the nature of man. In fact, what becomes increasingly apparent is that Machiavelli is concerned not with man's intrinsic nature, but with people in history and society. He remarks, for example, that in coming to power a leader will often realise that he was mistaken in thinking particular individuals responsible for social disorder; rather it is larger political and social forces (p. 228). Such a perspective leads Machiavelli to account for man's acquisitiveness not in terms of his nature, but of the individual's relative position in society (pp. 117–18, and below, chapter 14).

Francis Bacon refers to and agrees with Machiavelli on the issue of human nature. It is, says Bacon in a passage already cited in an earlier context and worth repeating here, custom and education rather than nature which are the crucial determinants of human behaviour: 'His [i.e. Machiavelli's] rule holdeth still, that nature, nor the engagement of words, are not so forcible as custom.' Men behave, he adds (with a strikingly deterministic simile), 'as if they were dead images and engines moved only by the wheels of custom' (*Essays*, p. 119).

Hobbes' view of man is thoroughly anti-essentialist. It is rooted in an uncompromising materialism:[8] 'The world, (I mean not the earth only . . . but the *universe*, that is, the whole mass of things that are), is corporal, that is to say, body . . . that which is not body, is not part of the universe: and because the universe is all, that which is no part of it, is *nothing*; and consequently, *nowhere*' (*Leviathan*, chapter 46). Hobbes uses this materialism as the basis for a scathing attack on the doctrine of '*separated essences*, built upon the vain philosophy of Aristotle' (chapter 46). In that attack the concept of the soul is jettisoned – not just the idea of its immortality but its existence in any form separate from the body (earlier in *Leviathan* we find Hobbes dismissing the concept of 'incorporeal substance' as 'contradictory and inconsistent', chapter 4; see also chapter 44). Nevertheless Hobbes still finds it necessary to speak of a given human nature – but now we are confronted not with essence but with the much more malleable notion of instinct or passion: 'I put for a general inclination of all mankind, a perpetual and restless desire of power after power, that ceaseth only in death.' This makes the condition of man 'a condition of war of everyone against everyone' and leads to Hobbes' notorious 'state of nature' in which the life of man is 'solitary, poor, nasty, brutish and short' (chapter 13). Although Hobbes' state of nature allegedly refers to a pre-social condition, it has been shown by C. B. Macpherson to presuppose man *in a particular kind of society*. So, for example, Hobbes says that two principal causes of conflict between men in the state of nature are competition and the desire for glory – both of which presuppose social interaction and socially sanctioned goals. The society presupposed is, says Macpherson, a possessive market society – that is, one in which labour is alienable and 'invasion' is institutionalised in the market situation. In effect Hobbes' state of nature is 'a logical abstraction drawn from the behaviour of men in a civilised society', his 'natural man' only a 'civilised man with the restraint of law removed' (*The Political Theory of Possessive Individualism*, pp. 26, 29). If there is a confusion in Hobbes at this point it is a revealing one. Hobbes retains elements of a 'dominant' conception of man in the context of a radical 'emergent' alternative: the (dominant) notion of an unchanging human nature – one given *a priori* – conflicts with an (emergent) concern to see the individual within, and constituted by, society.

Hobbes is often taken to be an advocate of individualism. This is misleading. His philosophy is individualistic to the extent that it takes as its starting point hypothetically dissociated individuals; it is anti-individualistic to the extent that it denies those individuals any effective autonomy – metaphysical or pre-social. As Otto Gierke long ago remarked, Hobbes 'made the individual omnipotent with the object of forcing him to destroy himself instantly' (*Natural Law and the Theory of Society*, I, 61). It is because of his relativism and anti-essentialism that Hobbes unequivocally denies that man is intrinsically evil: 'The desires, and other passions of man, are in themselves no sin. No more are the actions, that proceed from those passions . . .' (chapter 13; see also *De Cive* in *Man and Citizen*, p. 100). Moreover, because he gets rid of essences Hobbes can be reasonably optimistic about man's capacity to exchange the state of nature for social harmony. It is partly man's passions, and partly his reason which accomplish this (p. 102; cf. p. 271). And in *De Cive* we are told unequivocally that 'man is made fit for society not by nature but by education' (*Man and Citizen*, p. 110).[9]

Between Machiavelli and Hobbes comes Montaigne – profoundly different from either of them, yet also contributing to a mode of thought whereby man and society are demystified. Thus, when he tells us that 'the laws of conscience [i.e. morality], which we say to proceed from nature', in fact 'proceed from custome' (*Essays*, I, 114), he is reminding us that laws which were hitherto thought of as innate and absolute are in fact relative values which have been internalised (see above, pp. 9–19). Yet there is a fundamental contradiction in Montaigne. In one respect his essays are a quest for his essential substantial autonomous self: 'I write not my gests [i.e. actions] but my selfe and my essence' (II, 60). But he is prevented from ever finding that self because his own radical scepticism deconstructs the ideological framework on which it depended. Once again we see how the unitary subject is a binary function of the universal. Perhaps no other writer in the period does more to decentre man. He does this not simply by refusing ideology but by inadvertently revealing its profound pull even as he challenges it. On the one hand he confidently declares that there are at least 'inclinations' and 'passions' which are given: 'Natural inclinations are by institution helped and strengthened, but they neither change nor exceed.' And this can lead to a rather smug conservatism: '*Those which in my time, have attempted to correct the passions of the world by new opinions, reforme the vices of apparence; those of essence they leave untouched if they encrease them not*' (III, 29–30). Yet elsewhere in the *Essays* he experiences himself in entirely contrary terms: 'I have nothing to say entirely, simply, and with soliditie of my selfe without confusion, disorder, blending, mingling . . .' (II, 12); moreover: 'the more I frequent and know myselfe . . . the less I understand myselfe' (III, 282); indeed, 'whosoever shall heedfully survey and consider himselfe, shall finde

. . . volubility and discordance to *be in himself* (II, 12; my italics).
Intriguingly, in the act of searching for his essential self we find
Montaigne reversing the priority of essence over action in the quotation just given: 'I describe not the essence, but the passage' (III,
23). That it is a passage alarmingly affected by context is indicated
by Montaigne's repeated stress on the formative power of circumstance and the material conditions of existence: 'we . . . change as
that beast that takes the colour of the place wherein it is laid . . . all
is but changing, motion and inconstancy . . . We goe not but we
are carried: as things that flote, now gliding gently, now hulling
violently, according as the water is, either stormy or calme' (II,
8–9). Even more explicitly: 'He whom you saw yesterday so boldly
venturous, wonder not if you see him a dastardly meacocke
tomorrow . . . circumstances have setled the same in him: therefore
it is no marvell if by other contrary circumstances he became a
craven and change coppy' (II, 11). Finally the quest for an essential, autonomous self is virtually abandoned by Montaigne and
man is seen by his 'nature' to be in perpetual and restless motion,
lacking an essence and finding himself if at all only by embracing
otherness: 'Oh man . . . there's not one so shallow, so empty, and so
needy as thou art who embracest the whole world' (III, 253). In
short, man is put on a par with the rest of nature, being, says
Montaigne, 'without any prerogative or *essentiall pre-excellencie*' (II,
151; my italics).[10]

In their different ways the foregoing writers decentre the subject
and so provide the bases for a materialist understanding of the
interrelations between the social, the political and the subjective.
Whether or not Gramsci's claim that Machiavelli was the most
important precursor of Marx is conceded, it is surely correct that
the thought of this period was potentially, and in certain respects
actually, revolutionary. All of the plays analysed in the rest of this
section draw upon that thought.

Renaissance Individualism?

It might be objected, the foregoing notwithstanding, that we can
still speak of something called Renaissance individualism – a phenomenon based on the emergence in that period of secular essen-

tialism, itself coterminous with the demise of metaphysical essentialism. Individualism has become a notoriously problematic term, used indiscriminately to cover a wide range of concepts and theories. The confusion surrounding its use is especially prevalent in relation to the Renaissance, one reason being that far-reaching material and ideological changes in Elizabethan and Jacobean England – in particular the breakup of hierarchical social structures with a corresponding increase in social mobility – have been erroneously interpreted in terms of Enlightenment and Romantic conceptions of individuality.[11] Thus the attempt to clarify the term is not just an exercise in conceptual tidiness but a programme for identifying some crucial ideological parameters, especially with regard to the cultural appropriation of the Renaissance in our own time. Jacob Burckhardt's Romantic construction of that period is a famous case in point. On his view the Renaissance discerned and brought to light 'the full, whole nature of man' and gave 'the highest development to individuality'; in short, man in this period became 'a spiritual *individual*, and recognised himself as such' (*The Civilisation of the Renaissance in Italy*, pp. 81, 284). Leaving aside the question of the relevance of this account for Italy, it can be said with confidence that it is entirely inappropriate for Elizabethan and Jacobean England. Yet we find even Christopher Hill assuming somewhat uncritically the Romantic view whereby 'the boundless individualism of Marlowe's heroes, or of Macbeth, their unlimited desires and ambitions for power beyond power, set them in conflict with the standards of existing society' (*The Century of Revolution 1603–1714*, p. 80).

Although Hill does not do so, literary critics often take such an assessment as justification for an essentialist view of dramatic characters, one which seeks ultimately to identify them independently of an informing socio-historical context; as Burckhardt put it: 'in the face of all objective facts, of laws and restraints of whatever kind', the Renaissance individual retains the feeling of his own sovereignty' (p. 279).

But what of the growing *complexity* of character in the Elizabethan theatre; does not that at least partially substantiate Burckhardt's view? In fact, the development in that drama of character representation – especially via the soliloquy – is evidence less of Renaissance individualism than of an emergent realism of the kind described in chapter 3. Moreover, if the argument in the rest of this book is at all correct then it is a realism which problematises subjectivity rather than foregrounding man as a spiritual or psychological unity. Hence, in part, that absence of character 'consistency' for which Jacobean tragedy has often been criticised. Another aspect of that growing complexity in characterisation was of course the realisation that identity itself is a fiction or construct. Theatrical disguise and play were not merely a representation of this, but in part the very means of its discovery: 'Nay, if you cannot bear two subtle fronts under one hood, idiot go by, go by, off this world's stage' (*Antonio and Mellida*, Induction, ll. 75–6). Ben Jonson knew well how 'play' could reveal the illusion of the essential self, and, conversely, how 'habit' could become 'another nature': 'our whole life is like a Play: Wherein every man forgetfull of himselfe, is in travaile with expression of another. Nay, wee so insist in imitating others, as wee cannot (where it is necessary) returne to our selves . . . [we] make the habit of another nature, as it is never forgotten' (*Discoveries*, p. 44).

A late play, *The Witch of Edmonton*, is remarkable for the way it depicts how habit, socially coerced, becomes another – or rather 'anti' – nature. The witch (Mother Sawyer) complains:

> Some call me Witch;
> And being ignorant of myself, they go
> About to teach me how to be one: urging,
> That my bad tongue (by their bad usage made so)
> Forespeaks their Castle, doth bewitch their Corn,
> Themselves, their Servants, and their Babes at nurse.
> This they enforce upon me: and in part
> Make me to credit it.
>
> (II. i. 8–15)

This is no simple case of mistaken identity; Mother Sawyer 'really' seems to become a witch. But this emphasis upon identity as socially coerced offers the opportunity for an interrogation of the demonising mentality and, not surprisingly, the injustice and hypocrisy it masks:

Mother Sawyer:	A Witch? who is not?
	Hold not that universal Name in scorne then.
	What are your painted things in Princes Courts?
	Upon whose Eye-lids Lust sits blowing fires
	To burn Men's Souls in sensual hot desires ...
Justice:	But these work not as you do.
Mother Sawyer:	No, but far worse:
	These, by Inchantments, can whole Lordships change
	To Trunks of rich Attire: turn Ploughs and Teams
	To *Flanders* Mares and Coaches ...
Justice:	Yes, yes, but the Law
	Casts not an eye on these.

(IV. i. 101–17)

Even the amoral 'individualist' of the drama possesses not a fixed identity but a chameleon one; 'subtle, false, and treacherous' (*Richard III*, I. i. 37: cf. *Sejanus*, III. 978). *Selimus* (1594) indicates how the power appropriated by such individuals actually creates their autonomous-seeming *virtus*. So, for example, at the height of his success the atheistical and chameleon Selimus is suddenly transformed into the superlative warrior. Significantly it is his enemy, Tonembey, who attests to this: 'A matchless knight is warlike Selinus ... this heroicke Emperour' (ll. 2467 and 2474). Anticipated here is a central theme of the plays discussed below: *Virtus* is an effect and vehicle of power, not the independent virtue antecedent to, and generative of it. *Selimus* also depicts the process whereby power has disintegrative as well as formative effects on identity – especially of those being displaced by it. Anticipating his own murder (by his son) the Emperor Biazet declares: 'Thus is our minde in sundry pieces torne/By care, by feare, suspition and distrust' (ll. 475–6). Likewise with Richard III at that point when power is slipping from him; an attempt to reassert autonomy collapses into paradoxical self-division:

What do I fear? Myself? There's none else by.
Richard loves Richard; that is, I am I.
Is there a murderer here? No – yes, I am.
Then fly. What, from myself? Great reason why –
Lest I revenge. What, myself upon myself!
Alack, I love myself. Wherefore? For any good
That I myself have done unto myself?
O no! Alas, I rather hate myself

For hateful deeds committed by myself!
I am a villain; yet I lie, I am not.

(V. iii. 182–91)

A related effect of anti-essentialism is the dissociation of social
rank from innate superiority. Middleton's *The Changeling* contains
a powerful instance of this. Beatrice hires De Flores to murder her
betrothed. De Flores obliges and then demands sexual recompense,
threatening to reveal Beatrice's part in the murder. She, appalled,
tries desperately to buy him off but every offer is refused. Finally
she invokes her innate superiority: 'Think but upon the distance
that creation/Set 'twixt thy blood and mine, and keep thee there'.
De Flores' reply is devastating:

> Look but into your conscience, read me there,
> 'Tis a true book, you'll find me there your equal.
> Push! Fly not to your birth, but settle you
> In what the act has made you, y'are no more now;
> You must forget your parentage to me:
> You are the deed's creature; by that name
> You lost your first condition, and I challenge you,
> As peace and innocency has turn'd you out,
> And made you one with me.

(III. iv. 132–40)

There is here an ironic, disjunctive displacement of the fall into
social terms, the 'first condition' which Beatrice has fallen from being
that of the ruling elite. If the biblical Fall uses the two human conditions (pre-lapsarian and fallen) to mythicise history and society, the
reverse is true of Beatrice's social fall: an act of transgression and its
consequences actually disclose 'blood' and 'birth' to be myths in the
service of historical and social forms of power, divested of which
Beatrice becomes no more than what 'the act' has made her.

Paul Delany, in his recent study of British seventeenth-century
autobiography, concludes that the 'semi-mystical theory that a
powerful obscure and widely-diffused impulse labelled "Renaissance individualism" came into being at this time has to be discounted' (*British Autobiography in the Seventeenth Century*, p. 168).
Delany also observes that in medieval thought conflicting mental
states are personified in the *psychomachia*: good and bad angels

fight for man's soul but the essence of his personality remains intact. Conversely, the new man of the Renaissance 'succumbs to a more or less destructive schizophrenia in the same circumstances: his core of self-hood splits and his very identity becomes doubtful'[12] (pp. 11–12; such, as I have already indicated, is the condition of protagonists in *Antonio's Revenge* and *Troilus* – see chapter 2). For Delany, Hamlet is the obvious instance of this and he would presumably concur with Robert Ellrodt's astute remark that 'Hamlet's brooding introspection does not achieve, but defeats, self-knowledge' ('Self-Consciousness in Montaigne and Shakespeare', p. 47). The struggle for self-knowledge might legitimately be said to have its roots in protestantism and Renaissance humanism, but just how different its modern form is from them can hardly be overestimated. In fact, in respect of both it seems more useful to talk not of the individualism of this period but its self-consciousness, especially its sense of the self as flexible, problematic, elusive, dislocated – and, of course, contradictory: simultaneously arrogant and masochistic, victim and agent, object and effect of power.[13]

One of the most celebrated humanist accounts of man, Pico's *Oration*, was, as we have seen, anti-essentialist in its emphasis. Juan Vives in his *Fable about Man* (1518) and Castiglione in *The Book of the Courtier* (1528, trans. 1561) and, above all, Machiavelli in *The Prince* (1513) take up and develop in different ways the idea of the protean self artificially constructed and capable of extraordinary diversity. On this view the individual becomes 'a being of astonishing flexibility because he lacks a fixed nature or a commitment to anything' (Greenblatt, *Sir Walter Ralegh*, p. 40). Not only manuals of court behaviour but handbooks of rhetoric emphasised culture as theatre, as dissimulation and feigning, advising on the construction of an artificial identity in the service of power (Greenblatt, *Renaissance Self-Fashioning*, pp. 162–3). Machiavelli's Prince is no longer the agent of God or the supreme representative of man teleologically and eternally located in the divine scheme, but an agent whose identity is dictated by the necessities of political intervention and the pressures of the contingent historical moment.

So far as protestantism is concerned we need only look at, say, Donne's *Holy Sonnets* to see how, at that time, the obsessive intro-

spection which it incited situated the individual in anything but a
'boundless' condition or, indeed, any kind of essentialist autonomy:
'Despair behind and death before' (1). Registered here is an experience of dislocation which overrides even the relocating potential of
the sonnet form, an experience of identity as intensely problematic:
'Oh to vex me contraries meet in one' (19); 'Not one hour I can
myself sustain' (1; the placing of the pronoun maybe attempting to
cheat the fact?). Arrogant yet abject, the subject of almost every
meditation wrestles with the experienced paradoxes and contradictions of protestant subjectivity (cf. Herbert's 'The Cross': 'These
contrarieties crush me: these crosse actions/Doe winde a rope
about, and cut my heart').

As John Carey has said of Donne more generally: 'Among the
transient and contradictory surges of consciousness, he could
isolate no firm personality'; for Donne even spiritual qualities were
condemned to flux (*John Donne: Life, Mind and Art*, pp. 170,
188). Not surprisingly Donne's corrosive scepticism embraces both
the universal – '*Man*, who is the noblest part of the *Earth*, melts so
away, as if he were a *statue*, not of *Earth*, but of Snowe' (*Devotions*,
p. 11) – and its subjective instantiations – 'ourselves' says Donne in
'Negative Love' are 'what we know not'. Donne was preoccupied
not just with the fragmentation of self and the decentring of man
but also with the inherent instability of matter and the world's
never absent potential to collapse back into nothingness (see Carey,
chapter 6). Emerging from this obsession with instability and
change is a sense of the complex interrelations between power, violence, and desire, as they traverse and constitute subjectivity. Thus
the fourteenth Holy Sonnet, 'Batter my heart, three personed God'
finds the speaker in a relationship with sado-masochistic power
(and desire) very different from, say, the exploitative rake of 'Love's
Usury' who determines to 'mistake by the way/The maid, and tell
the Lady of that delay'. Even those famous expressions of love
which rhetorically strive to transcend the world of power (e.g. 'The
Canonisation', 'The Sun Rising') have internalised its structures.
So, even at the moment of ecstatically declared independence of
power relations, they remain ineradicably there, actively (ironically?) informing the love which has supposedly left them behind:

> She'is all states, and all princes, I,
>   Nothing else is.
> Princes do but play us; compared to this,
> All honour's mimic, all wealth alchemy.

'The Sun Rising'

Lastly, Marston is just one of many other writers in the period who declare the protean nature of man; he registers, especially in his verse satires, the extreme instability of the satiric persona while at the same time negating the humanist affirmation of man's transcendent potential (see A. D. Cousins, 'The Protean Nature of Man in Marston's Verse Satires'; also Alvin Kernan: 'instability, incoherence, wildness, uncertainty, contradiction, these are the very essentials of the satyr character' – *The Cankered Muse*, p. 116).

In one of the most important recent (1980) studies of Renaissance literature, Stephen Greenblatt declares that his intention was to explore what he saw as 'the very hallmark of the Renaissance' namely, 'the role of human autonomy in the construction of identity'. Yet as the work progressed he discovered just the opposite: 'In all my texts and documents there were, so far as I could tell, no moments of pure, unfettered subjectivity; indeed, the human subject itself began to seem remarkably unfree, the ideological product of the relations of power in a particular society' (*Renaissance Self-Fashioning*, p. 256). It is a discovery which leaves him anxious, because to abandon the illusion that we make our identity is 'to abandon the craving for freedom'; moreover, 'to let go of one's stubborn hold upon self-hood, even self-hood conceived as a fiction, is to die' (p. 257). But perhaps the reverse is true, by abandoning the fiction we may embrace freedom in and through the '*affirmation* [which] *determines the noncentre otherwise than as loss of the centre*' (Jacques Derrida, *Writing and Difference*, p. 292; his italics). It is a related subject to which I return in the final chapter.

11

Bussy D'Ambois (c. 1604): A Hero at Court

Bussy D'Ambois (c. 1604) occupies an interesting position in the radical drama of the period. Like the earlier plays it interrogates providence and decentres the tragic subject but now the emphasis is shifted; before, the emphasis had tended to fall on the first of these projects, now and henceforth the reverse tends to be the case.

Shadows and Substance

The very first line of *Bussy* repudiates stoic providence in a way even more direct than that found in the *Antonio* plays and *Troilus and Cressida*: 'Fortune, not Reason, rules the state of things.' Bussy is preoccupied with the instability of this 'state' (i.e. the body politic): 'Reward goes backwards, Honour on his head;/Who is not poor, is monstrous' (I. i. 2–3). He repudiates politicians ('statists', l. 10) who, with their 'Authority, wealth, and all the spawn of Fortune' are deluded into thinking they are everything whereas in fact – and in Time – they are nothing: 'Man is a torch borne in the wind; a dream/But of a shadow, summ'd with all his substance' (ll. 18–19). That word 'substance' had a fascinating range of meanings in this period not dissimilar from those it retains today. But it possessed an ambiguity more telling then than now: it could mean 'essential nature' – especially when, as here, it was contrasted with 'shadow' (cf. 'He takes false shadows for true substances', *Titus Andronicus*, III. ii. 80); alternatively, it could mean virtually the opposite – that is, not what man intrinsically is, but what he acquires: 'Authority, wealth and all the spawn of Fortune' (l. 13). There is not here the Christian belief that the ways of the world tempt man from the ways of the spirit; on the contrary, man is seen to construct an identity from shadows because they are in some sense prior. What Montsurry says of princes – that 'form gives all their essence' (II. ii. 123) – is the view of man presented in this play: his essential nature goes missing as does the universe's teleological design; reluctantly yet determinedly Chapman concentrates on the social realities disclosed by their absence.

Given its political dimension, the play's opening stage direction – *Enter* Bussy D'Ambois, *poor* – is hardly less significant than its first line. Bussy's poverty runs quite contrary to the circumstances of his historical source. It is an innovation of Chapman's and serves as the precondition for Bussy's understanding of human identity and of the state. Exclusion and poverty give him – or rather force upon him – a true view of things yet one which is anything but disinterested; that is, they offer to Bussy a vantage point from which he experiences the relative worthlessness of the social order and, simultaneously, his dependence upon it. Monsieur politically exploits such dependence and his view of the exploited is simple: 'None loathes the world so much . . . /But gold and grace will make him surfeit of it' (I. i. 52–3). Tamyra later speaks of 'great statesmen' who 'for their general end/In politic justice make poor men offend' (III. i. 44–5); Monsieur is one such but with the important distinction that justice is not his objective. Bussy accepts Monsieur's offer of preferment but rationalises his choice: 'I am for honest actions, not for great.' He will, he tells himself, 'rise in Court with virtue' (I. i. 124 and 126). It is this rationalised – and compromised – position which characterises Bussy from here on.

Monsieur sends to Bussy, via Maffe, one thousand crowns. Maffe is the state servant who is eminently employable as an instrument of power because shrewd yet gullible: shrewd enough to play the game, gullible enough to internalise its rules. He has been instructed to give Bussy the money but has not been told why. Seeing the impoverished Bussy he asks: 'Is this man indu'd/With any merit worth a thousand crowns?' (I. i. 140–1). By 'merit' he means usefulness – specifically, the capacity to serve his master, Monsieur. Maffe thus invokes a criterion of human worth which is, as it were, second nature to those bound up in the struggle to maintain or achieve power. It is a criterion which Hobbes later

makes the corner stone of his theory of the state: 'The *value*, or
WORTH of a man, is as of all other things, his price; that is to say, so
much as would be given for the use of his power: and therefore is
not absolute; but a thing dependent on the need and judgement of
another' (*Leviathan*, chapter 10). Maffe aspires to understand
'policy' (l. 202) but as he himself admits (ll. 199–200), he does not
have the ears of great men, nor does he understand such men. His
view of the court is both determined and ideologically distorted by
his position within it – a position which, for example, leads him
erroneously to assume a conventional range of potential roles for
Bussy – the poet-pamphleteer, a soldier or joker. Bussy is angered
by this and turns Maffe's criterion of merit back upon Maffe; referring to those parts of the latter's dress which signify his steward-
ship, he demands: 'What qualities have you sir (beside your
chain/And velvet jacket)?' (I. i. 191–2). Thus Bussy taunts Maffe
with being nothing apart from his position as state servant. Such is
his own impending position, and such too is the recurring
emphasis of this play: identity is shown to be constituted not essentially but socially.

Bussy arrives at court dressed in a new suit. His entry follows
immediately after Henry and Montsurry have been criticising the
vanity of dress. In the previous scene Bussy showed himself especially anxious not to have to appear at court 'in a threadbare suit'
(I. i. 106). This anxiety is another aspect of the same awareness
which prompted his interrogation of Maffe. In this society man's
identity, like his worth, is, in the words of Hobbes, 'a thing dependent on the need and judgement of another'; more exactly, this
identity exists in terms of the role ascribed to the individual by
others or, alternatively, a role which he proposes for their ratification. It is precisely the courtiers' refusal to ratify Bussy's new role
which leads to the quarrel in which five die. Bussy, manifestly insecure, is over-assertive. This prompts L'Anou to observe: 'See what a
metamorphosis a brave suit can work' (I. ii. 118). But Barrisor's
taunt is the more vicious for being even closer to the truth: 'This
jealousy of yours sir, confesses some close defect in yourself, that we
never dreamed of' (I. ii. 185–6). Unerringly he provokes in Bussy
insecurity born of dependence. They vow to fight and so the first
act concludes.

Court Power and Native Noblesse

Monsieur and the King eulogise Bussy, or rather they construct for him a conception of himself as innately noble, self-determining and uncompromised. To the extent that he 'lives' this identity he becomes not in fact autonomous but the more exploitable. Monsieur is especially accomplished in achieving this. His initial description of Bussy as incomparably heroic (I. ii. 140–6) is not a spontaneous recognition of him as such but the testing out of a predetermined role for him. Monsieur's hyperbole picks up on something more general: even as a life and death struggle is developing between Bussy and Guise, a self-consciously theatrical court is construing it as performance; for the king the quarrel is a kind of entertainment (l. 147) while L'Anou (later to die in the fight) describes it as 'one of the best jigs that ever was acted' (I. ii. 152). By the close of this scene Bussy has taken on the part devised for him by Monsieur. Later, after Bussy has deserted him, Monsieur gives a very different assessment of his former protégé, one which speaks very much to the conditions in which he found him. Lacking a rational soul, he is, says Monsieur, not 'diffused quite through' with that which would make him all 'of a piece'. As such he is unpredictable and erratic; he is, in effect, the decentred, soulless subject who 'wouldst envy, betray,/Slander, blaspheme, change each hour a religion,/*Do anything*. . .' (III. ii. 349–56; my italics).

Bussy, once raised by Monsieur (the king's brother), is taken up by the one person even more powerful: the king. To the latter Bussy becomes protector and play-thing ('my brave Eagle', IV. i. 108). The king's similarly hyperbolic praise of Bussy is especially revealing at the point where he indulges in role reversal; Bussy is, he says –

> Man in his native noblesse, from whose fall
> All our dissensions rise; that in himself
> (Without the outward patches of our frailty,
> Riches and honour) knows he comprehends
> Worth with the greatest: Kings had never borne
> Such boundless eminence over other men,
> Had all maintain'd the spirit and state of D'Ambois.

> (III. ii. 91–7)

Subscribing to the myth of transcendent virtue in another permits the ruler to mystify the true extent of his own material power. This comes across quite clearly in the scene where Bussy is pardoned by the king. He declines the pardon, insisting that he has committed no offence when events are considered in the light of his essentialist autonomy: 'Who to himself is law, no law doth need' (II. i. 203). The king replies: 'Enjoy what thou entreat'st, we give but ours', which might be glossed: enjoy your illusion of autonomy only in so far as it does not transgress my authority. Indeed, thus encouraged and controlled, Bussy's mythical autonomy will actually enhance that authority. One indication of the extent to which Bussy's *virtus* is shown to be not innate but the effect – and thus the vehicle – of court power is the way he takes on the hyperbolic terms in which Monsieur had set it up:

> What insensate stock
> Or rude inanimate vapour without fashion,
> Durst take into his Epimethean breast
> A box of such plagues as the danger yields,
> Incurr'd in this discovery?
>
> (IV. ii. 9–13)

Even more conclusive (and in the same scene) is the moment when the hyperbole, and indeed *virtus* itself, is shown to dissolve into the policy of which it was only ever the effect; plotting against Monsieur, Bussy declares: 'I'll soothe his plots: and strew my hate with smiles . . . And policy shall be flank'd with policy' (ll. 155, 161).

The play does not merely show noblesse defeated by policy. Were this in fact the case it might be legitimately defined as humanistic tragedy in the sense already outlined in chapter 2: that is, a tragedy of defeated potential in which the defeat only confirms the potential. Rather, the play shows the putative noblesse to be the effect of policy and thus, by noblesse's own essentialist criteria, to suffer erasure.

Bussy dies in a scene which begins with one of the most direct repudiations of teleology, providence and natural law to be found anywhere in Jacobean tragedy:

Nature hath no end
In her great works, responsive to their worths,
That she who makes so many eyes, and souls,
To see and foresee, is stark blind herself:

So nature lays
A mass of stuff together, and by use,
Or by the mere necessity of matter,
Ends such a work, fills it, or leaves it empty
Of strength, or virtue, error or clear truth.

(V. iii. 1–4; 12–16)

Even the play's supernatural dimension works against providence. In fact Act IV, scene ii works as a burlesque of the supernatural similar to that which we have already seen in *The Revenger's Tragedy* (above, pp. 139–43; Chapman's is of course the earlier play). Behemoth and his spirits are shown to be incompetent (l. 60) and at cross purposes (ll. 73–5); finally they exit ('descend') in disarray advising that Bussy have recourse to 'policy' (l. 138). In fact they seem themselves to be instruments of policy: they are controlled by 'Fate' while 'Fate's ministers' are said to be 'The Guise and Monsieur' (V. ii. 61–2; cf. the association of 'Destiny' with 'Great statesmen' at III. i. 43–4). Thus the significance of the supernatural comes back, via a kind of closed circuit, to the secular.

Just as Monsieur rejects the notion that nature is encoded with a teleological design, so Bussy dies repudiating the existence of the soul (once again the disintegration of providentialism is accompanied by this decentring of the tragic subject):

is my body then
But penetrable flesh? And must my mind
Follow my blood? Can my divine part add
No aid to th' earthly in extremity?
Then these divines are but for form, not fact.

(V. iii. 125–9)

Echoing lines from his opening speech he adds:

let my death
Define life nothing but a Courtier's breath.

Nothing is made of nought, of all things made;
Their abstract being a dream but of a shade.

(V. iii. 131–4)

The sense of those last two lines is as follows: 'all things are created from and return to nothing. Therefore the idea of substantial essence is an illusion'.[1]

12

King Lear (c. 1605–6) and Essentialist Humanism

When he is on the heath King Lear is moved to pity. As unaccommodated man he feels what wretches feel. For the humanist the tragic paradox arises here: debasement gives rise to dignity and at the moment when Lear might be expected to be most brutalised he becomes most human. Through kindness and shared vulnerability human kind redeems itself in a universe where the gods are at best callously just, at worst sadistically vindictive.

In recent years the humanist view of Jacobean tragedies like *Lear* has been dominant, having more or less displaced the explicitly Christian alternative. Perhaps the most important distinction between the two is this: the Christian view locates man centrally in a providential universe;[1] the humanist view likewise centralises man but now he is in a condition of tragic dislocation: instead of integrating (ultimately) with a teleological design created and sustained by God, man grows to consciousness in a universe which thwarts his deepest needs. If he is to be redeemed at all he must redeem himself. The humanist also contests the Christian claim that the suffering of Lear and Cordelia is part of a providential and redemptive design. If that suffering is to be justified at all it is because of what it reveals about man's intrinsic nature – his courage and integrity. By heroically enduring a fate he is powerless to alter, by insisting, moreover, upon *knowing* it, man grows in stature even as he is being destroyed. Thus Clifford Leech, an opponent of the Christian view, tells us that tragic protagonists 'have a quality of mind that somehow atones for the nature of the world in which they and we live. They have, in a greater or lesser degree, the power to endure and the power to apprehend' (*Shakespeare's Tragedies*, p. 15). Wilbur Sanders in an influential study argues for an ultimately

optimistic Shakespeare who had no truck with Christian doctrine
or conventional Christian conceptions of the absolute but nevertheless affirmed that 'the principle of health – grace – is not in
heaven, but in nature, and especially in human nature, and it
cannot finally be rooted out'. Ultimately this faith in nature and
human nature involves and entails 'a faith in a universal moral
order which cannot finally be defeated' (*The Dramatist and the
Received Idea*, pp. 336–7).

Here as so often with the humanist view there is a strong residue
of the more explicit Christian metaphysic and language which it
seeks to eschew; comparable with Sanders' use of 'grace' is Leech's
use of 'atone'. Moreover both indicate the humanist preoccupation
with the universal counterpart of essentialist subjectivity – either
ultimately affirmed (Sanders) or recognised as an ultimate tragic
absence (Leech).[2] The humanist reading of *Lear* has been authori-
tatively summarised by G. K. Hunter (he calls it the 'modern' view
of the play):

> [it] is seen as the greatest of tragedies because it not only strips and
> reduces and assaults human dignity, but because it also shows with
> the greatest force and detail the process of restoration by which
> humanity can recover from degradation . . . [Lear's] retreat into the
> isolated darkness of his own mind is also a descent into the seed-bed
> of a new life; for *the individual mind is seen here as the place from
> which a man's most important qualities and relationships draw the
> whole of their potential*. (*Dramatic Identities and Cultural Tradition*,
> pp. 251–2; my italics)

What follows is an exploration of the political dimension of
Lear. It argues that the humanist view of that play is as inappropriate as the Christian alternative which it has generally displaced –
inappropriate not least because it shares the essentialism of the
latter. I do not mean to argue again the case against the Christian
view since, even though it is still sometimes advanced, it has been
effectively discredited by writers as diverse as Barbara Everett,
William R. Elton and Cedric Watts.[3] The principal reason why the
humanist view seems equally misguided, and not dissimilar, is this:
it mystifies suffering and invests man with a quasi-transcendent
identity whereas the play does neither of these things. In fact, the

play repudiates the essentialism which the humanist reading of it presupposes. However, I do not intend to replace the humanist reading with one which rehearses yet again all the critical cliché's about the nihilistic and chaotic 'vision' of Jacobean tragedy. In *Lear*, as in *Troilus*, man is decentred not through misanthropy but in order to make visible social process and its forms of ideological misrecognition.

Redemption and Endurance: Two Sides of Essentialist Humanism

'Pity' is a recurring word in *Lear*. Philip Brockbank, in a recent and sensitive humanist reading of the play, says: 'Lear dies "with pity" (IV. vii. 53) and that access of pity, which in the play attends the dissolution of the senses and of the self, is a condition for the renewal of human life' ('Upon Such Sacrifices', p. 133). Lear, at least when he is on the heath, is indeed moved to pity, but what does it mean to say that such pity is 'a condition for the renewal of human life'? Exactly whose life is renewed? In this connection there is one remark of Lear's which begs our attention; it is made when he first witnesses 'You houseless poverty' (III. iv. 26): 'Oh, I have ta'en/Too little care of this!' Too little: Lear bitterly reproaches himself because hitherto he has been aware of yet ignored the suffering of his deprived subjects. (The distracted use of the abstract – 'You houseless poverty' – subtly suggests that Lear's disregard has been of a general rather than a local poverty.) He has ignored it not through callous indifference but simply *because he has not experienced it.*

King Lear suggests here a simple yet profound truth. Far from endorsing the idea that man can redeem himself in and through an access of pity, we might be moved to recognise that, on the contrary, in a world where pity is the prerequisite for compassionate action, where a king has to share the suffering of his subjects in order to 'care', the majority will remain poor, naked and wretched. The point of course is that princes only see the hovels of wretches during progresses (walkabouts?), in flight or in fairy tale. Even in fiction the wheel of fortune rarely brings them that low. Here, as so often in Jacobean drama, the fictiveness of the genre or scene

intrudes; by acknowledging its status as fiction it abdicates the
authority of idealist mimesis and indicates the better the reality it
signifies; resembling in this Brecht's alienation effect, it stresses artifice not in the service of formalism but of realism. So, far from
transcending in the name of an essential humanity the gulf which
separates the privileged from the deprived, the play insists on it.
And what clinches this is the exchange between Poor Tom (Edgar)
and Gloucester. The latter has just arrived at the hovel; given the
circumstances, his concern over the company kept by the king is
faintly ludicrous but very telling: 'What, hath your Grace no better
company?' (III. iv. 138; cf. Cordelia at IV. vii. 38–9). Tom tells
Gloucester that he is cold. Gloucester, *uncomprehending rather than
callous*, tells him he will keep warm if he goes back into the hovel
(true of course, relatively speaking). That this comes from one of
the 'kindest' people in the play prevents us from dismissing the
remark as individual unkindness: judging is less important than
seeing how unkindness is built into social consciousness. That
Gloucester is unknowingly talking to his son in this exchange
simply underscores the arbitrariness, the woeful inadequacy of
what passes for kindness; it is, relatively, a very precious thing but
as a basis for human kind's self-redemption it is a non-starter.
Insofar as Lear identifies with suffering it is at the point when he is
powerless to do anything about it. This is not accidental: the
society of *Lear* is structured in such a way that to wait for shared
experience to generate justice is to leave it too late. Justice, we
might say, is too important to be trusted to empathy.

Like Lear, Gloucester has to undergo intense suffering before he
can identify with the deprived. When he does so he expresses more
than compassion. He perceives, crucially, the limitation of a society
that depends on empathy alone for its justice. Thus he equates his
earlier self with the 'lust-dieted man . . . *that will not see/Because he
does not feel*' (IV. i. 69–71; my italics). Moreover he is led to a conception of social justice (albeit dubiously administered by the
'Heavens', l. 68) whereby 'distribution should undo excess,/And
each man have enough' (IV. i. 72–3).

By contrast, Lear experiences pity mainly as an inseparable
aspect of his own grief: 'I am mightily abus'd. I should e'en die

with pity/To see another thus' (IV. vii. 3–4). His compassion emerges from grief only to be obliterated by grief. He is angered, horrified, confused and, above all, dislocated. Understandably then he does not empathise with Tom so much as assimilate him to his own derangement. Indeed, Lear hardly communicates with anyone, especially on the heath; most of his utterances are demented mumbling interspersed with brief insight. Moreover, his preoccupation with vengeance ultimately displaces his transitory pity; reverting from the charitable reconcilation of V. iii to vengeance once again, we see him, minutes before his death, boasting of having killed the 'slave' that was hanging Cordelia.

But what of Cordelia herself? She more than anyone else has been seen to embody and symbolise pity. But is it a pity which significantly alters anything? To see her death as *intrinsically* redemptive is simply to mystify both her and death.[4] Pity, like kindness, seems in *Lear* to be precious yet ineffectual. Far from being redemptive it is the authentic but residual expression of a scheme of values all but obliterated by a catastrophic upheaval in the power structure of this society. Moreover the failure of those values is in part due to the fact that they are (or were) an ideological ratification of the very power structure which eventually destroys them.

In *Lear*, as we shall see in the next section, there is a repudiation of stoicism similar to that found in Marston's *Antonio's Revenge*. Yet repeatedly the sceptical treatment, sometimes the outright rejection, of stoicism in these plays is overlooked; often in fact it is used to validate another kind of humanism. For convenience I call the kind outlined so far ethical humanism and this other one existential humanism. The two involve different emphases rather than different ideologies. That of the latter is on essential heroism and existential integrity, that of the former on essential humanity, the universal human condition. Thus, according to Barbara Everett (in another explicitly anti-Christian analysis):

> In the storm scene Lear is at his most powerful and, despite moral considerations, at his noblest; the image of man hopelessly confronting a hostile universe and withstanding it only by his inherent powers of rage, endurance and perpetual questioning, is perhaps the most purely 'tragic' in Shakespeare. ('The New *King Lear*', p. 333)

Significantly, existential humanism forms the basis even of J. W. Lever's *The Tragedy of State*, one of the most astute studies of Jacobean tragedy to date. On the one hand Lever is surely right in insisting that these plays 'are not primarily treatments of characters with a so-called "fatal flaw", whose downfall is brought about by the decree of just if inscrutable powers . . . the fundamental flaw is not in them but in the world they inhabit: in the political state, the social order it upholds, and likewise, by projection, in the cosmic state of shifting arbitrary phenomena called "Fortune"' (p. 10). By the same criteria it is surely wrong to assert (on the same page) that: 'What really matters is the quality of [the heroes'] response to intolerable situations. This is a drama of adversity and stance . . . The rational man who remains master of himself is by the same token the ultimate master of his fate.' In Lever's analysis Seneca is the ultimate influence on a drama (including *King Lear*) which celebrates man's capacity inwardly to transcend oppression (p. 9).

If the Christian mystifies suffering by presenting it as intrinsic to God's redemptive and providential design for man, the humanist does likewise by representing suffering as the mysterious ground for man's *self*-redemption; both in effect mystify suffering by having as their common focus an essentialist conception of what it is to be human: in virtue of his spiritual essence (Christian), essential humanity (ethical humanist), or essential self (existential humanist), man is seen to achieve a paradoxical transcendence: in individual extinction is his apotheosis. Alternatively we might say that in a mystifying closure of the historical real the categories of idealist culture are recuperated. This suggests why both ethical and existential humanism are in fact quasi-religious: both reject the providential and 'dogmatic' elements of Christianity while retaining its fundamental relation between suffering, affirmation and regeneration. Moreover they, like Christianity, tend to fatalise social dislocation; its causes are displaced from the realm of the human; questions about them are raised but only rhetorically, thus confirming man's impotence to alleviate the human condition. This clears the stage for what really matters: man's responsive suffering and what it reveals in the process about his essential nature. Recognisable here is the fate of existentialism when merged with

literary criticism as a surrogate or displaced theology; when, specifically, it was co-opted to the task most symptomatic of that displacement, namely the obsession with defining tragedy. It will be
recalled that for the existentialist existence precedes essence, or so
said Sartre, who later tried to develop this philosophy in the
context of Marxism. In literary criticism the social implications of
existentialism, such as they were, were easily ignored, the emphasis
being instead on a modernist angst and man's thwarted spiritual
potential. This is another sense in which existential humanism is
merely a mutation of Christianity and not at all a radical alternative; although it might reluctantly have to acknowledge that neither
Absolute nor Essence exist, it still relates man to them on a principle of Augustinian privation: man understands his world only
through the grid of their absence.

King Lear: A Materialist Reading

More important than Lear's pity is his 'madness' – less divine furor
than a process of collapse which reminds us just how precarious is
the psychological equilibrium which we call unity, and just how
dependent upon an identity which is social rather than essential.
What makes Lear the person he is – or rather was – is not kingly
essence (divine right), but, among other things, his authority and
his family. On the heath he represents the process whereby man has
been stripped of his stoic and (Christian) humanist conceptions of
self. Consider what Seneca has to say of affliction and philosophy:

> Whether we are caught in the grasp of an inexorable law of fate,
> whether it is God who as lord of the universe has ordered all things,
> or whether the affairs of mankind are tossed and buffeted haphaz-
> ardly by chance, it is philosophy that has the duty of protecting us.
> (*Letters*, p. 64)

Lear, in his affliction, attempts to philosophise with Tom whom he
is convinced is a 'Noble philosopher', a 'good Athenian' (II. iv. 168
and 176). It adds up to nothing more than the incoherent ram-
blings of one half-crazed by just that suffering which philosophy,
according to the stoic, guards against. It is an ironic subversion of

neo-stoic essentialism, one which recalls Bacon's essay 'Of Adversity', where he quotes Seneca: '*It is true greatness to have in one the frailty of a man, and the security of a god*' only to add, dryly: 'This would have done better in poesy, where transcendences are more allowed' (*Essays*, p. 15). As I have already shown (chapter 4), Bacon believed that poesy implies idealist mimesis – that is, an illusionist evasion of those historical and empirical realities which, says Bacon, 'buckle and bow the mind unto the nature of things' (*Advancement*, p. 83). He seems to have remained unaware that Jacobean drama was just as subversive of poesy (in this sense) as he was, not only with regard to providentialism but now its corollary, essentialism. Plays like *Lear* precisely disallow 'transcendences': in this at least they confirm Edmund's contention that 'men/Are as the time is' (V. iii. 31–2). Montaigne made a similar point with admirable terseness: 'I am no philosopher: Evils oppresse me according as they waigh' (*Essays*, III, 189). The Fool tells Lear that he is 'an O without a figure' (I. iv. 192); both here and seconds later he anticipates his master's eventual radical decentredness, the consequence of having separated 'The name, and all th' addition' of a king from his real 'power' (I. i. 129, 135): 'Who is it that can tell me who I am?' cries Lear; 'Lear's shadow' replies the Fool.

After he has seen Lear go mad, Gloucester offers this inversion of stoicism:

> Better I were distract
> So should my thoughts be sever'd from my griefs,
> And woes by wrong imagination lose
> The knowledge of themselves.
>
> (IV. vi. 281–4)

For Lear dispossession and displacement entail not redemptive suffering but a kind of suffering recognition – implicated perhaps with confession, depending on how culpable we take this king to have been with regard to 'the great *image* of authority' which he now briefly demystifies: 'a dog's obey'd in office' (IV. vi. 157; my italics). Lear does acknowledge blame, though deludedly believing the power which made him blameworthy is still his: 'Take that of me, my friend, who have the power/To seal th' accuser's lips' (IV. vi. 169–70). His admission that authority is a function of 'office' and 'power', not intrinsic worth, has its corollary: power itself is in control of 'justice' (l. 166) rather than vice-versa:

> The usurer hangs the cozener.
> Through tatter'd clothes small vices do appear;
> Robes and furr'd gowns hide all. Plate sin with gold
> And the strong lance of justice hurtless breaks;
> Arm it in rags, a pigmy's straw doth pierce it.
>
> (IV. vi. 163–7)

Scenes like this one remind us that *King Lear* is, above all, a play about power, property and inheritance. Referring to Goneril, the distraught Lear cries: 'Ingratitude thou marble-hearted fiend,/More hideous when thou show'st thee in a child/Than the sea-monster' (I. iv. 259–61). Here, as throughout the play, we see the cherished norms of human kindness shown to have no 'natural' sanction at all. A catastrophic redistribution of power and property – and, eventually, a civil war – disclose the awful truth that these two things are somehow prior to the laws of human kindness rather than vice-versa (likewise, as we have just seen, with power in relation to justice). Human values are not antecedent to these material realities but are, on the contrary, in-formed by them.[5]

Even allowing for his conservative tendency to perceive all change as a change for the worse, Gloucester's account of widespread social discord must surely be taken as at least based on fact: 'These late eclipses in the sun and moon portend no good to us . . . Love cools, friendship falls off, brothers divide, in cities, mutinies; in countries, discord; in palaces, treason . . . there's son against father; the King falls from bias of nature: there's father against child' (I. ii. 100–11). ''Tis strange', concludes the troubled Gloucester and exits, leaving Edmund to make things somewhat less so. Significantly, Edmund does not deny the extent of the discord, only Gloucester's mystified sense of its cause. In an earlier soliloquy Edmund has already repudiated 'the plague of custom . . . The curiosity of nations' which label him bastard (I. ii. 3–4). Like Montaigne he insists that universal law is merely municipal law (above, p. 16). Here he goes further, repudiating the ideological process whereby the latter is misrecognised as the former; he rejects, that is, a way of thinking which represents the contingent

as the necessary and thereby further represents human identity and
the social order as metaphysically determined (and therefore unalterable): 'When we are sick in fortune, often the surfeits of our
own behaviour, we make guilty of our disasters the sun, the moon,
and stars; as if we were villains on necessity, fools by heavenly com-
pulsion . . . by a divine thrusting on' (I. ii. 122–31). Closely related
to this refusal of the classical ideological effect is the way Edmund
also denaturalises the theatrical effect: 'Pat! He comes like the catastrophe of the old comedy. My cue is villainous melancholy' (I. ii.
128). Yet this revolutionary scepticism is discredited by the purpose
to which it is put. How are we to take this? Are we to assume that
Edmund is simply evil and therefore so is his philosophy? I want to
argue that we need not. To begin with we have to bear in mind a
crucial fact: Edmund's scepticism is made to serve an *existing*
system of values; although he falls prey to it, he does not introduce
his society to its obsession with power, property and inheritance; it
is already the material and ideological basis of that society. As such
it in-forms the consciousness of Lear and Gloucester as much as
Cornwall and Regan; consider Lear first, then Gloucester.

Lear's behaviour in the opening scene presupposes first, his
absolute power, second, the knowledge that his being king
constitutes that power, third, his refusal to tolerate what he
perceives as a contradiction of that power. Therefore what Lear
demands of Cordelia – authentic familial kind-ness – is precluded
by the very terms of the demand; that is, by the extent to which the
occasion as well as his relationship to her is saturated with the
ideological imperatives of power. For her part Cordelia's real
transgression is not unkindness as such, but speaking in a way
which threatens to show too clearly how the laws of human
kindness operate in the service of property, contractual, and power
relations:

> I love your Majesty
> According to my bond . . .

> I
> Return those duties back as are right fit . . .

> Why have my sisters husbands, if they say
> They love you [i.e. Lear] all?
>
> (I. i. 91–2; 95–6; 98–9)

Presumably Cordelia does not intend it to be so, but this is the patriarchal order in danger of being shorn of its ideological legitimation – here, specifically, a legitimation taking ceremonial form. (Ironically yet predictably, the 'untender' (l. 105) dimension of that order is displaced on to Cordelia.) Likewise with the whole issue of dowries. Prior to Lear's disowning of Cordelia, the realities of property marriage are more or less transmuted by the language of love and generosity, the ceremony of good government. But in the act of renouncing her, Lear brutally foregrounds the imperatives of power and property relations: 'Here I disclaim all my paternal care,/Propinquity and property of blood' (I. i. 112–13; cf. ll. 196–7). Kenneth Muir glosses 'property' as 'closest blood relation' (ed. *King Lear*, p. 11). Given the context of this scene it must also mean 'ownership' – father owning daughter – with brutal connotations of the master/slave relationship as in the following passage from *King John*: 'I am too high-born to be *propertied*/To be a . . . serving man' (V. ii. 79–81). Even kinship then – indeed *especially* kinship – is in-formed by the ideology of property relations, the contentious issue of primogeniture being, in this play, only its most obvious manifestation. Later we witness Lear's correlation between the quantity of retainers Goneril will allow him and the quality of her love: Regan offers twenty-five retainers, upon which Lear tells Goneril: 'I'll go with thee./Thy fifty yet doth double five-and-twenty,/And thou art twice her love' (II. iv. 257–9).

Gloucester's unconscious acceptance of this underlying ideology is conveyed at several points but nowhere more effectively than in Act II, scene i; even as he is coming to terms with Edgar's supposed treachery he is installing Edmund in his place, offering in *exchange* for Edmund's 'natural' behaviour – property:

> of my land
> Loyal and natural boy, I'll work the means
> To make thee capable.
>
> (II. i. 83–5)

Thus the one thing which the kind Gloucester and the vicious Cornwall have in common is that each offers to reward Edmund's 'loyalty' in exactly the same way (cf. III. v. 16–18). All this would be ludicrous if it were not so painful: as their world disintegrates Lear and Gloucester cling even more tenaciously to the only values they know, which are precisely the values which precipitated the disintegration. Hence even as society is being torn apart by conflict, the ideological structure which has generated that conflict is being reinforced by it.

When Edmund in the forged letter represents Edgar complaining of 'the oppression of aged tyranny' which commands 'not as it hath power, but as it is suffered' (I. ii. 47–8), he exploits the same personal anxiety in Gloucester which Cordelia unintentionally triggers in Lear. Both fathers represent a challenge to their patriarchal authority by offspring as unnatural behaviour, an abdication of familial duty. The trouble is they do this in a society where 'nature' as ideological concept is fast losing its power to police disruptive elements – for example: 'That nature which contemns its origin/Cannot be border'd certain in itself' (IV. ii. 32–3). No longer are origin, identity and action a 'natural' ideological unity, and the disintegration of that unity reveals something of fundamental importance: when, as here (also, e.g., at I. ii. 1–22), nature is represented as socially disruptive, yet elsewhere as the source of social stability (e.g., at II. iv. 176–80), we see an ideological construct beginning to incorporate and thereby render visible the very conflicts and contradictions in the social order which it hitherto effaced. In this respect the play activates a contradiction intrinsic to any 'naturalised' version of the Christian metaphysic; to abandon or blur the distinction between matter and spirit while retaining the basic premises of that metaphysic is to eventually construe evil as at once utterly alien to the human condition (unnatural) yet disturbingly and mysteriously inherent within it (natural) and to be purged accordingly. If deep personal anxiety is thus symptomatic of more general social dislocation it is also what guarantees the general reaction formation to that dislocation: those in power react to crisis by entrenching themselves the deeper within the ideology and social organisation responsible for it.

At strategic points in the play we see how the minor characters have also internalised the dominant ideology. Two instances must suffice. The first occurs in Act II, scene ii, where Kent insults Oswald. He does so almost entirely in terms of the latter's lack of material wealth, his mean estate and consequent dependence upon service. Oswald is, says Kent, a beggarly, three-suited, hundred-pound, filthy, worsted-stocking . . . superserviceable . . . one-trunk-inheriting slave' (II. ii. 15ff; as Muir points out, servants were apparently given three suits a year, while gentlemen wore silk as opposed to worsted stockings). The second example involves the way that for the Gentleman attending Cordelia even pity (or more accurately 'Sorrow') is conceived as a kind of passive female commodity (IV. iii. 16–23).[6]

We can now see the significance of Edmund's scepticism and its eventual relationship to this dominant ideology of property and power. Edmund's sceptical independence is itself constituted by a contradiction: his illegitimate exclusion from society gives him an insight into the ideological basis of that society even as it renders him vulnerable to and dependent upon it. In this respect Edmund resembles the malcontents already encountered in previous chapters: exclusion from society gives rise both to the malcontent's sense of its worthlessness and his awareness that identity itself is dependent upon it. Similarly, Edmund, in liberating himself from the myth of innate inferiority, does not thereby liberate himself from his society's obsession with power, property and inheritance; if anything that obsession becomes the more urgent: 'Legitimate Edgar, I *must* have your land' (I. ii. 16; my italics). He sees through one level of ideological legitimation only to remain the more thoroughly enmeshed with it at a deeper level.

Edmund embodies the process whereby, because of the contradictory conditions of its inception, a revolutionary (emergent) insight is folded back into a dominant ideology. Witnessing his fate we are reminded of how, historically, the misuse of revolutionary insight has tended to be in proportion to its truthfulness, and of how, as this very fact is obscured, the insight becomes entirely identified with (or as) its misappropriation. Machiavellianism, Gramsci has reminded us, is just one case in point (*Selections from Prison Notebooks*, p. 136).

The Refusal of Closure

Lionel Trilling has remarked that 'the captains and kings and lovers and clowns of Shakespeare are alive and complete before they die' (*The Opposing Self*, p. 38). Few remarks could be less true of *King Lear*. The notion of man as tragic victim somehow alive and complete in death is precisely the kind of essentialist mystification which the play refuses. It offers instead a decentring of the tragic subject which in turn becomes the focus of a more general exploration of human consciousness in relation to social being – one which discloses human values to be not antecedent to, but rather in-formed by, material conditions. *Lear* actually refuses, then, that autonomy of value which humanist critics so often insist that it ultimately affirms. Nicholas Brooke, for example, in one of the best close analyses of the play that we have, concludes by declaring: 'all moral structures, whether of natural order or Christian redemption, are invalidated by the naked fact of experience', yet manages in the concluding sentence of the study to resurrect from this unaccommodated 'naked experience' a redemptive autonomy of value, one almost mystically inviolable: 'Large orders collapse; but values remain, and are independent of them' (*Shakespeare: King Lear*, pp. 59–60). But surely in *Lear*, as in most of human history, 'values' are shown to be terrifyingly dependent upon whatever 'large orders' actually exist; in civil war especially – which after all is what *Lear* is about – the two collapse together.

In the closing moments of *Lear* those who have survived the catastrophe actually attempt to recuperate their society in just those terms which the play has subjected to sceptical interrogation. There is invoked, first, a concept of innate nobility in contradistinction to innate evil and, second, its corollary: a metaphysically ordained justice. Thus Edgar's defeat of Edmund is interpreted as a defeat of an evil nature by a noble one. Also nobility is seen to be like truth – it will out: 'Methought thy very gait did prophesy/A royal nobleness' (V. iii. 175–6). Goneril is 'reduced' to her treachery ('read thine own evil', l. 156), while Edmund not only acknowledges defeat but also repents, submitting to Edgar's nobility (ll. 165–6) and acknowledging his own contrary nature (ll. 242–3). Next, Edgar invokes a notion of divine justice which holds out the possibility of rendering their world intelligible once more; speaking to Edmund of Gloucester, he says:

> The gods are just, and of our pleasant vices
> Make instruments to plague us:
> The dark and vicious place where thee he got
> Cost him his eyes.
>
> (V. iii. 170–3)

Thus is responsibility displaced; but perhaps Edgar is meant to wince as he says it since the problem of course is that he is making his society supernaturally intelligible at the cost of rendering the concept of divine justice so punitive and 'poetic' as to be, humanly speaking, almost unintelligible. Nevertheless Albany persists with the same process of recuperation by glossing thus the deaths of Goneril and Regan: 'This judgement of the heavens, that makes us tremble,/Touches us not with pity' (V. iii. 230–1). But when he cries 'The Gods defend her!' – i.e. Cordelia – instead of the process being finally consolidated we witness, even before he has finished speaking, Lear re-entering with Cordelia dead in his arms. Albany has one last desperate bid for recuperation, still within the old punitive/poetic terms:

> All friends shall taste
> The wages of their virtue, and all foes
> The cup of their deservings.
>
> (V. iii. 302–4)

Seconds later Lear dies. The timing of these two deaths must surely be seen as cruelly, precisely, subversive: instead of complying with the demands of formal closure – the convention which would confirm the attempt at recuperation – the play concludes with two events which sabotage the prospect of both closure and recuperation.

13

Antony and Cleopatra (c. 1607): *Virtus* under Erasure

In Jonson's *Sejanus*, Silius, about to take his own life in order to escape the persecution of Tiberius, tells the latter: 'The means that makes your greatness, must not come/In mention of it' (III. 311–12). He is of course exposing a strategy of power familiar to the period: first there occurs an effacement of the material conditions of its possibility, second, a claim for its transcendent origin, one ostensibly legitimating it and putting it beyond question – hence Tiberius' invocation only moments before of 'the Capitol,/ . . . all our Gods . . . the dear Republic,/Our sacred Laws, and just authority' (III. 216–18). In *Sejanus* this is transparent enough. In other plays – I choose for analysis here *Antony and Cleopatra* and *Coriolanus* – the representation of power is more complex in that we are shown how the ideology in question constitutes not only the authority of those in power but their very identity.

Staged in a period in which there occurred the unprecedented decline of the power, military and political, of the titular aristocracy, *Antony* and *Coriolanus*, like *Sejanus* before them, substantiate the contention that ''tis place,/Not blood, discerns the noble, and the base' (*Sejanus*, V. i. 11–12). Historical shifts in power together with the recognition, or at least a more public acknowledgement, of its actual operations, lead to the erasure of older notions of honour and *virtus*. Both plays effect a sceptical interrogation of martial ideology and in doing so foreground the complex social and political relations which hitherto it tended to occlude.

In his study of English drama in the seventeenth century C. L. Barber detects a significant decline in the presence of honour as a martial ideal and he is surely right to interpret this as due to changes in the nature and occupations of the aristocracy during

204

that period. These included the professionalising of warfare and the increasing efficiency of state armies. The effect of such changes was that by the end of the seventeenth century there was considerably less scope for personal military initiative and military glory; honour becomes an informal personal code with an extremely attenuated social dimension (*The Idea of Honour in the English Drama 1591–1700*, pp. 269–79).

More recently, and even more significantly for the present study, Mervyn James has explored in depth the changing conceptions of honour between 1485 and 1642; most striking is his conclusion that there occurred 'a change of emphasis, apparent by the early seventeenth century . . . [involving] . . . the emergence of a "civil" society in which the monopoly both of honour and violence by the state was asserted' (*English Politics and the Concept of Honour 1485–1642*, p. 2).[1]

Such are the changes which activate a contradiction latent in martial ideology and embodied in two of Shakespeare's protagonists, Antony and Coriolanus. From one perspective – becoming but not yet residual – they appear innately superior and essentially autonomous, their power independent of the political context in which it finds expression. In short they possess that *virtus* which enables each, in Coriolanus' words, to 'stand/As if a man were author of himself' (V. iii. 35–6). 'As if': even as these plays reveal the ideological scope of that belief they disclose the alternative emergent perspective, one according to which Antony and Coriolanus are nothing more than their reputation, an ideological effect of powers antecedent to and independent of them. Even as each experiences himself as the origin and embodiment of power, he is revealed in the words of Foucault (above, p. 154) to be its instrument and effect – its instrument because, first and foremost. its effect. Bacon brilliantly focusses this contradiction in his essay on martial glory: 'It was prettily devised of AEsop: *The fly sate upon the axle-tree of the chariot wheel and said, What a dust do I raise!*' (*Essays*, p. 158). Throughout Bacon's essay there is a dryly severe insistence on that fact which martial ideology cannot internally accommodate: 'opinion brings on substance' (p. 158). Such is the condition of Antony and Coriolanus, and increasingly so: as they transgress the power structure which constitutes them both their

political and personal identities – inextricably bound together if
not identical – disintegrate.

Virtus and History

Antony and Cleopatra anticipates the dawn of a new age of imperialist consolidation:

> The time of universal peace is near.
> Prove this a prosp'rous day, the three nook'd world
> Shall bear the olive freely

(IV. vi. 5–7)

Prior to such moments heroic *virtus* may appear to be identical
with the dominant material forces and relations of power. But this
is never actually so: they were only ever coterminous and there is
always the risk that a new historical conjuncture will throw them
into misalignment. This is what happens in *Antony and Cleopatra*;
Antony, originally identified in terms of both *virtus* and these dominant forces and relations, is destroyed by their emerging disjunction.

In an important book Eugene Waith has argued that 'Antony's
reassertion of his heroic self in the latter part of the play is entirely
personal. What he reasserts is individual integrity . . . Heroism
rather than heroic achievement becomes the important thing' (*The
Herculean Hero*, p. 118). On this view Antony privately reconstitutes his 'heroic self' despite or maybe even because of being
defeated by circumstances beyond his control. I want to argue that
the reverse is true: heroism of Antony's kind can never be 'entirely
personal' (as indeed Bacon insisted) nor separated from either
'heroic achievement' or the forces and relations of power which
confer its meaning.

The reader persuaded by the Romantic reading of this play is
likely to insist that I'm missing the point – that what I've proposed
is at best only true of the world in which Antony and Cleopatra
live, a world transcended by their love, a love which 'translineates
man [sic] to divine likeness' (Wilson Knight, *The Imperial Theme*,
p. 217). It is not anti-Romantic moralism which leads me to see
this view as wholly untenable. In fact I want to argue for an inter-

pretation of the play which refuses the usual critical divide whereby it is either 'a tragedy of lyrical inspiration, justifying love by presenting it as triumphant over death, or . . . a remorseless exposure of human frailties, a presentation of spiritual possibilities dissipated through a senseless surrender to passion' (Traversi, *An Approach to Shakespeare,* II, p. 208). Nor do I discount the Romantic reading by wilfully disregarding the play's captivating poetry: it is, indeed, on occasions rapturously expressive of desire. But the language of desire, far from transcending the power relations which structure this society, is wholly in-formed by them.

As a preliminary instance of this, consider the nature of Antony's belated 'desire' for Fulvia, expressed at news of her death and not so dissimilar to his ambivalent desire for Cleopatra (as the sudden shift of attention from the one to the other suggests):

> Thus did I desire it:
> What our contempts doth often hurl from us
> We wish it ours again; the present pleasure,
> By revolution low'ring, does become
> The opposite of itself. She's good, being gone;
> The hand could pluck her back that shov'd her on.
> I must from this enchanting queen break off.
>
> (I. ii. 119–25)

True, the language of the final scenes is very different from this, but there too we are never allowed to forget that the moments of sublimity are conditional upon absence, nostalgic contemplation upon the fact that the other is irrevocably gone. As for present love, it is never any the less conditioned by the imperatives of power than the arranged marriage between Antony and Octavia.

Virtus and *Realpolitik* (1)

In *Antony and Cleopatra* those with power make history yet only in accord with the contingencies of the existing historical moment – in Antony's words: 'the strong necessity of time' (I. iii. 42). If this sounds fatalistic, in context it is quite clear that Antony is not capitulating to 'Time' as such but engaging in *realpolitik,* real power relations. His capacity for policy is in fact considerable; not only, and most obviously, is there the arranged marriage with Octavia, but also those remarks of his which conclude the alliance with Lepidus and Caesar against Pompey:

> [Pompey] hath laid strange courtesies and great
> Of late upon me. I must thank him only,
> Lest my remembrance suffer ill report;
> At heel of that, defy him.
>
> (II. ii. 159–62)

In fact, the suggestion of fatalism in Antony's reference to time is itself strategic, an evasive displacing of responsibility for his impending departure from Cleopatra. As such it is paralleled later by Caesar when he tells the distraught Octavia,

> Be you not troubled with the time, which drives
> O'er your content these strong necessities,
> But let determin'd things to destiny
> Hold unbewail'd their way.
>
> (III. vi. 82–5)

The cause of her distress is divided allegiance between brother and husband (Caesar and Antony) who are now warring with each other. Caesar's response comes especially ill from one scarcely less responsible for her conflict than Antony, her marriage to the latter was after all dictated by his political will: 'The *power* of Caesar, and/His *power* unto Octavia' (II. ii. 147–8; my italics). 'Time' and 'destiny' mystify power by eclipsing its operation and effect, and Caesar knows this; compare the exchange on Pompey's galley – Antony: 'Be a child o' th' time./ Caesar: Possess it, I'll make answer' (II. vii. 98–9). Caesar, in this respect, is reminiscent of Machiavelli's Prince; he is inscrutable and possessed of an identity which becomes less fixed, less identifiable as his power increases. Antony by contrast is defined in terms of omnipotence (the more so, paradoxically, as his power diminishes): the 'man of men' (I. iv. 72), the 'lord of lords' (IV. viii. 16).

In both *Antony and Cleopatra* and *Coriolanus* the sense of *virtus* (virtue) is close to 'valour', as in 'valour is the chiefest virtue' (*Coriolanus*, II. ii. 82), but with the additional and crucial connotations of self-sufficiency and autonomous power, as in 'Trust to thy *single virtue*; for thy soldiers/ . . . have . . ./Took their discharge' (*King Lear*, V. iii. 104–6). The essentialist connotations of 'virtue' are also clearly brought out in a passage from *Troilus and Cressida* already discussed (see above, pp. 40–1): 'what hath mass or matter by itself/Lies rich in virtue and unmingled'. In *Antony and Cleopatra* this idea of self-sufficiency is intensified to such an extent that it suggests a transcendent autonomy; thus Cleopatra calls Antony 'lord of lords!/O *infinite virtue*, com'st thou smiling from/ The world's great snare uncaught?' (IV. viii. 16–18). Coriolanus is similarly described as proud, 'even to the altitude of his virtue' (II. i. 38). Against this is a counter-discourse, one denying that virtue is the source and ethical legitimation of power and suggesting instead that the reverse is true – in the words of Macro in *Sejanus*, 'A prince's power makes all his actions virtue' (III. 717). At the beginning of Act III for example, Silius urges Ventidius further to consolidate his recent successes in war, so winning even greater gratitude from Antony. Ventidius replies that, although 'Caesar and Antony have ever won/more in their officer than person' (III. i. 16–17), an officer of theirs who makes that fact too apparent will lose, not gain favour. It is an exchange which nicely illustrates the way power is a function not of the 'person' (l. 17) but of 'place' (l. 12), and that the criterion for reward is not intrinsic to the 'performance' (l. 27) but, again, relative to one's placing in the power structure (cf. *Sejanus*, III. 302–5: 'all best turns/With doubtful princes, turn deep injuries/In estimation, when they greater rise,/Than can be answered').[2]

Later in the same act Antony challenges Caesar to single combat (III. xiii. 20–8). It is an attempt to dissociate Caesar's power from his individual virtue. Enobarbus, amazed at the stupidity of this, testifies to the reality Antony is trying, increasingly, to deny:

> men's judgements are
> A parcel of their fortunes, and things outward
> Do draw the inward quality after them,
> To suffer all alike.

> (III. xiii. 31–4)

In Enobarbus' eyes, Antony's attempt to affirm a self-sufficient identity confirms *exactly the opposite*. Correspondingly, Caesar scorns Antony's challenge with a simple but devastating repudiation of its essentialist premise: because 'twenty times of better fortune' than Antony, he is, correspondingly, 'twenty men to one' (IV. ii. 3–4).

As effective power slips from Antony he becomes obsessed with reasserting his sense of himself as (in his dying words): 'the greatest prince o' th' world,/The noblest' (IV. xx. 54–5). The contradiction inherent in this is clear; it is indeed as Canidius remarks: 'his whole action grows/Not in the power on't' (III. vii. 68–9). Antony's conception of his omnipotence narrows in proportion to the obsessiveness of his wish to reassert it; eventually it centres on the sexual anxiety – an assertion of sexual prowess – which has characterised his relationship with both Cleopatra and Caesar from the outset. He several times dwells on the youthfulness of Caesar in comparison with his own age (e.g. at III. xiii. 20; IV. xii. 48) and is generally preoccupied with lost youthfulness (e.g. at III. xiii. 192; IV. iv 26; IV. viii. 22). During the battle scenes of Acts III and IV he keeps reminding Cleopatra of his prowess – militaristic and sexual: 'I will appear in blood' (II. xiii. 174); 'There's sap in't yet! The next time I do fight,/I'll make death love me' (III. xiii. 192–3); and:

> leap thou, attire and all,
> Through proof of harness to my heart, and there
> Ride on the pants triumphing.
>
> (IV. viii. 14–16)

All this, including the challenge to single combat with Caesar, becomes an obsessive attempt on the part of an ageing warrior (the 'old ruffian' – IV. i. 4) to reassert his virility, not only to Cleopatra but also to Caesar, his principal male competitor. Correspondingly, his willingness to risk everything by fighting on Caesar's terms (III. vii) has much more to do with reckless overcompensation for his own experienced powerlessness, his fear of impotence, than the largesse of a noble soul. His increasing ambivalence towards Cleopatra further bespeaks that insecurity (e.g. at III. xii and IV. xii). When servants refuse to obey him he remarks 'Authority melts from me' – but insists nevertheless 'I am/Antony yet' (III. xiii.

92–3): even as he is attempting to deny it Antony is acknowledging that identity is crucially dependent upon power. Moments later even he cannot help remarking the difference between 'what I am' and 'what . . . I was' (III. xiii. 142–3).

It is only when the last vestiges of his power are gone that the myth of heroic omnipotence exhausts itself, even for him. In place of his essentialist fixedness, 'the firm Roman', the 'man of steel' he once felt himself to be (I. iv. 43; IV. iv. 35), Antony now experiences himself in extreme dissolution:

> That which is now a horse, even with a thought
> The rack dislimns, and makes it indistinct
> As water is in water . . .
>   Eros, now thy captain is
> Even such a body: here I am Antony,
> Yet cannot hold this visible shape
>
> (IV. iv. 9–14)

Virtus, divorced from the power structure, has left to it only the assertion of a negative, inverted autonomy: 'there is left us/ Ourselves to end ourselves' (IV. xiv. 21–2). And in an image which effectively expresses the contradiction Antony has been living out, energy is felt to feed back on itself: 'Now all labour/Mars what it does; yea, very force entangles/Itself with strength' (IV. xix. 47–9). Appropriately to this, he resolves on suicide only to bungle the attempt. The bathos of this stresses, uncynically, the extent of his demise. In the next scene it is compounded by Cleopatra's refusal to leave the monument to kiss the dying Antony lest she be taken by Caesar. Antony, even as he is trying to transcend defeat by avowing a tragic dignity in death, suffers the indignity of being dragged up the monument.

There is bathos too of course in Caesar's abruptly concluded encomium:

>   Hear me, good friends –
> *Enter an Egyptian*
> But I will tell you at some meeter season.
> The business of this man looks out of him
>
> (V. i. 48–50)

The question of Caesar's sincerity here is beside the point; this is, after all, an encomium, and to mistake it for a spontaneous expression of grief will lead us to miss seeing that even in the few moments he speaks Caesar has laid the foundation for an 'official' history of Antony. First we are reminded that Caesar *is* – albeit regrettably – the victor. He then vindicates himself and so consolidates that victory by confessing to a humanising grief at the death of his 'brother' (though note the carefully placed suggestion of Antony's inferiority: 'the *arm* of mine own body'). Caesar further vindicates himself by fatalising events with the by now familiar appeal to necessity, in this case 'our stars,/Unreconcilable'. Earlier Caesar had told Octavia that 'The ostentation of our love . . . left unshown,/Is often left unlov'd' (III. vi. 52–3). Such is the rationale of his encomium, a strategic expression of 'love' in the service of power. The bathos of these episodes makes for an insistent cancelling of the potentially sublime in favour of the political realities which the sublime struggles to eclipse or transcend. Actually, bathos has accompanied Antony throughout, from the very first speech of the play, the last three lines of which are especially revealing (Philo is speaking of Antony):

> Take but good note, and you shall see in him
> The triple pillar of all the world transform'd
> Into a strumpet's fool. Behold and see.
>
> (I. i. 11–13)

The cadence of 'triple pillar of all the world' arches outward and upward, exactly evoking transcendent aspiration; 'transformed' at the line end promises apotheosis; we get instead the jarringly discrepant 'strumpet's fool'. Cynical, perhaps, but Philo's final terse injunction – 'Behold and see' – has prologue-like authority and foresight.

After Antony's death the myth of autonomous *virtus* is shown as finally obsolescent; disentangled now from the prevailing power structure, it survives as legend. Unwittingly Cleopatra's dream about Antony helps relegate him to this realm of the legendary, especially in its use of imagery which is both Herculean and statuesque: 'His legs bestrid the ocean; his reared arm/Crested the world'[3] (V. ii. 82–3). Cleopatra asks Dolabella if such a man ever existed or might exist; he answers: 'Gentle Madam, no.' Cleopatra vehemently reproaches him only to qualify instantly her own certainty – 'But if there be nor ever were one such' – thereby, in the hesitant syntax, perhaps confirming the doubts which prompted the original question.

His legs bestrid the ocean: in dream, in death, Antony becomes at last larger than life; but in valediction is there not also invoked an image of the commemorative statue, that material embodiment of a discourse which, like Caesar's encomium, skilfully overlays (without ever quite obscuring) obsolescence with respect?

Honour and Policy

If the contradiction which constitutes Antony's identity can be seen as a consequence of a wider conflict between the residual/dominant and the emergent power relations, so too can the strange relationship set up in the play between honour and policy. Pompey's reply to Menas' offer to murder the triumvirs while they are celebrating on board his (Pompey's) galley is a case in point:

> Ah, this thou shouldst have done,
> And not have spoke on't. In me 'tis villainy:
> In thee't had been good service. Thou must know
> 'Tis not my profit that does lead mine honour:
> Mine honour, it. Repent that e'er thy tongue
> Hath so betray'd thine act. Being done unknown,
> I should have found it afterwards well done,
> But must condemn it now.
>
> (II. vii. 73–80)

Here honour is insisted upon yet divorced from ethics and consequences; the same act is 'villainy' or 'service' depending on who performs it; ignorance of intent to murder is sufficient condition for approving the murder after the event.

Elsewhere in the play we see these inconsistencies resolved in favour of policy; now honour pretends to integrity – to be thought to possess it is enough. Once again it is a kind of political strategy which takes us back to Machiavelli's *The Prince*.[4] Antony tells Octavia: 'If I lose mine honour/I lose myself' (III. iv. 22–3).

Octavia has of course been coerced into marriage with Antony to heal the rift (now reopened) between him and Caesar, her brother. So, for Antony to speak to her of honour seems hypocritical at least; when, however, Antony goes further and presents himself as the injured party ready nevertheless to forgo his revenge in order to indulge Octavia's request that she be *allowed* to act as mediator – 'But, as you requested/Yourself shall, go between's' (III. iv. 24–5) – the honour in question is shown to be just another strategy in his continuing exploitation of this woman.

When Thidias is persuading Cleopatra to betray Antony and capitulate to Caesar, honour is now a face-saving strategy for *both* sides; because she 'embraced' Antony through fear, says Caesar, he construes the scar upon her honour as 'constrained blemishes,/Not as deserv'd'. Cleopatra quickly concurs: 'He [Caesar] is a god, and knows/What is most right. Mine honour was not yielded,/But conquer'd merely' (III. xiii. 59–62).

In Enobarbus we see how policy aligns positively with realism and judgement. He, like Philo at the outset of the play, Ventidius in III. i. and the soldier in III. vii. who urges Antony not to fight at sea, occupies a role in relation to power very familiar in Jacobean tragedy: he possesses an astuteness characteristic of those removed from, yet involved with and dependent upon – often for their very lives – the centre of power; his is the voice of policy not in the service of aggrandisement so much as a desire for survival. So, for example, we see in III. vi. Enobarbus attempting to dissuade Cleopatra from participating in the war and Antony from fighting on Caesar's terms. Failing in the attempt, Enobarbus leaves Antony's command but is struck with remorse almost immediately. Since he left without his 'chests and treasure' (IV. v. 8) we are, perhaps, to presume that material gain of this kind was not his motive. Enobarbus, like Antony, comes to embody a contradiction; the speech of his beginning 'Mine honesty and I begin to square' (III. xiii. 41) suggests as much, and it becomes clear that he has left his master in the name of the 'judgement' which the latter has abdicated but which is integral still to his, Enobarbus', identity as a soldier. Yet equally integral to that identity is the loyalty which he has betrayed.

The extent of people's dependence upon the powerful is something the play never allows us to forget. Cleopatra's beating of the messenger in II. v. is only the most obvious reminder; a subtler and perhaps more effective one comes at the end of the play when Cleopatra attempts to conceal half her wealth from Caesar. In the presence of Caesar she commands Seleucus, her 'treasurer', to confirm that she has surrendered all; 'speak the truth, Seleucus' she demands and, unfortunately for her, he does, revealing that she has kept back as much as she has declared. Cleopatra has ordered him 'Upon his *peril*' (V. ii. 142) to speak the truth (i.e. lie) while he, with an eye to Caesar, replies that he would rather seal his lips 'than to my *peril*/Speak that which is not'. Here, truth itself is in the service of survival. Cleopatra, outraged, finds this unforgivable; for servants to shift allegiance is, in her eyes (those of a ruler), 'base' treachery (V. ii. 156). The play however, in that ironic repetition of 'peril' (my italics) invites an alternative perspective: such a shift is merely a strategy of survival necessitated precisely by rulers like her.[5] Yet doubly ironic is the fact that while Seleucus is described as a 'slave, of no more trust/Than love that's hir'd' (V. ii. 153–4) her own deceit is approved by Caesar as the 'wisdom' (V. ii. 149) appropriate to one in her position.

Elsewhere Caesar speaks in passing of the 'much tall youth' (II. vi. 7) that will perish in the event of war; Octavia speaks of the consequence of war between Caesar and Antony being as if 'the world should cleave, and that slain men/Should solder up the cleave' (III. iv. 31–2; cf. III. xiii. 180–1; IV. xii. 41–2; IV. xiv. 17–8). It is a simple yet important truth, one which the essentialist rhetoric is never quite allowed to efface: to kiss away kingdoms is to kiss away also the lives of thousands.

Sexuality and Power

Those around Antony and Cleopatra see their love in terms of power; languages of possession, subjugation and conspicuous wealth abound in descriptions of the couple. More importantly, Antony and Cleopatra actually experience themselves in the same terms. Antony sends Alexas to Cleopatra with the promise that he will 'piece/Her opulent throne with kingdoms. All the East/(Say thou) shall call her mistress' (I. v. 45–7). Later Caesar describes the ceremony whereby that promise was honoured, a ceremony aiming for an unprecedented *public* display both of wealth and power: 'Cleopatra and himself in chairs of gold/Were publicly enthron'd'; Antony gives to Cleopatra the stablishment of Egypt and makes her 'Absolute Queen' of Syria, Cyprus and Lydia. 'This in the public eye?' inquires Maecenas; 'I' th' common showplace' confirms Caesar (III. vi. 4–12). Cleopatra for her part sends twenty separate messengers to Antony. On his return from Egypt Enobarbus confirms the rumour that eight wild boars were served at a breakfast of only twelve people, adding: 'This was but as a fly by an eagle: we had much more monstrous matter of feast, which *worthily deserved noting*' (II. ii. 185; my italics).

Right from the outset we are told that power is internal to the relationship itself: Philo tells us that Antony has been subjugated by Cleopatra (I. i. 1–9) while Enobarbus tells Agrippa that Cleopatra has 'pursed up' (i.e. pocketed, taken possession of) Antony's heart (II. ii. 190). As if in a discussion of political strategy, Cleopatra asks Charmian which tactics she should adopt in order to manipulate Anthony most effectively. Charmian advocates a policy of complete capitulation; Cleopatra replies: 'Thou teachest like a fool – the way to lose him!' (I. iii. 10). Antony enters and Cleopatra tells him: 'I have no power upon you', only then to cast him in the role of treacherous subject: 'O, never was there queen/ So mightily betrayed. Yet at the first/I saw the treasons planted' (I. iii. 23–6). Whatever the precise sense of Cleopatra's famous lines at the end of this scene – 'O my oblivion is a very Antony,/And I am all forgotten' – there is no doubt that they continue the idea of a power struggle: her extinction is coterminous with his triumph.

Attempting to atone for his departure, Antony pledges himself as Cleopatra's 'soldier-servant, making peace or war/As thou affects' (I. iii. 70). This is just one of many exchanges which shows how their sexuality is rooted in a fantasy transfer of power from the public to the private sphere, from the battlefield to the bed. In II. v. Cleopatra recalls with merriment a night of revelry when she subjugated Antony and then engaged in cross-dressing with him, putting 'my tires and mantles on him, whilst/I wore his sword

Phillipan' (II. v. 22–3). Inseparable from the playful reversal of sexual roles is her appropriation of his power, military and sexual, symbolised phallically of course in the sword. Later Antony takes up the sword – power motif in a bitter reproach of Cleopatra for her power over him; here he sees her as his 'conqueror' (III. xi. 66, and compare IV. xiv. 22–3). Another aspect of the power–sexuality conjunction is suggested in the shamelessly phallic imagery which the lovers use: 'Ram thou thy fruitful tidings in mine ears,/That long time have been barren' (II. v. 24–5), although again Cleopatra delights in reversing the roles (as at II. v. 10–15).

Here then is another aspect of the contradiction which defines Antony: his sexuality is informed by the very power relations which he, ambivalently, is prepared to sacrifice for sexual freedom; correspondingly, the heroic *virtus* which he wants to reaffirm in and through Cleopatra is in fact almost entirely a function of the power structure which he, again ambivalently, is prepared to sacrifice for her.

Ecstasy there is in this play but not the kind that constitutes a self-sufficient moment above history; if *Antony and Cleopatra* celebrates anything it is not the love which transcends power but the sexual infatuation which foregrounds it. That infatuation is complex: ecstatic, obsessive, dangerous. Of all the possible kinds of sexual encounter, infatuation is perhaps the most susceptible to power – not just because typically it stems from and intensifies an insecurity which often generates possessiveness and its corollary, betrayal, but because it legitimates a free play of self-destructive desire. In Antony's case it is a desire which attends and compensates for the loss of power, a desire at once ecstatic and masochistic and playing itself out in the wake of history, the dust of the chariot wheel.

14

Coriolanus (c. 1608): The Chariot Wheel and its Dust

Coriolanus, perhaps even more than Antony, is constituted by the contradiction inherent in the martial ideal: though identified in terms of an innate superiority he is in fact the ideological effect of powers antecedent to and independent of him. This becomes manifest in the encomium for Coriolanus, delivered as part of a campaign for his election to the consulship. Its language is uncompromisingly essentialist; Coriolanus is, we are told, in possession of 'valour . . . the chiefest virtue'; in battle he becomes omnipotence personified: '*Alone* he ent'red . . . aidless came off . . . Now all's his', and so on. But this is followed immediately by the loaded remark of the *nameless* First Senator: '*He cannot but with measure fit the honours/Which we devise him*' (II. ii. 80–122; my italics).

For as long as this hero remains in service to the state an ideological effect occurs which construes his reputation as following naturally from his *virtus*. When that reputation is used against the state there emerges a contradiction which reveals both reputation and state to be prior to and in some sense constitutive of *virtus*.

Virtus and Realpolitik (2)

If Coriolanus believes his *virtus* to be prior to and determining of his social involvement, essentially independent of it though capable of being in practice contaminated by it, Volumnia knows otherwise; she conceives of *virtus* not as essence but as political strategy. Nevertheless it is she who has nurtured in Coriolanus his essentialist consciousness. Hitherto it has spurred him to greatness, led him to 'with measure fit' the role in which she and other patricians 'devise him'; when, however, as now, it begins to prove politically

218

counterproductive she tries to modify it. By so doing she generates both in and for Coriolanus the tension which will break him.

When Coriolanus returns from war Volumnia is gratified that he has been wounded. It would be wrong to see this only as a grotesque inversion of normal maternal care; it is also a rational estimate of the political capital of a wounded hero: 'There will be large cicatrices [scars] to show the people, when he shall stand for his place' [i.e. stand for the consulship] (II. i. 139–40). The contrast between the political and the essentialist conceptions of *virtus* is expressed again in a memorable exchange between Coriolanus and his mother in III. ii. Coriolanus has refused to compromise in the question of the consulship and she has reproached him for being so intransigent. He then asks her:

Why did you wish me milder? Would you have me
False to my nature?

(III. ii. 14–15)

Volumnia replies, tellingly: 'I would have had you put your power well on/Before you had worn it out.' What Coriolanus understands as his 'nature' Volumnia understands as 'power', something to be appropriated, 'put . . . well on'. For Coriolanus the world is seen in terms of the absolute and the determining essence; for Volumnia the absolute is displaced by a social network of relative interactions, one in which intervention not essence is determining. Volumnia, in some respects the counterpart of Caesar in *Antony and Cleopatra*, has an understanding of all this so astute it will make her, in the wake of her son's death, the most powerful person in Rome:

This Volumnia
Is worth of consuls, senators, patricians,
A city full

(V. iv. 51–3)

says Menenius, while the First Senator welcomes her home as 'our patroness, the life of Rome!' (V. v. 1).

The metaphor of power as strategy, a role to be appropriated, is taken up subsequently and always in ironic opposition to Coriolanus' essentialism; this is Volumnia, still persuading

Coriolanus to compromise: 'perform a part/Thou hast not done before'. Coriolanus resists, always in the name of 'my noble heart' (III. ii. 108–9; 100), 'mine own truth (III. ii. 121). When he does eventually capitulate to his mother's pressure it constitutes the onset of a conflict which will prove more lethal for Coriolanus than anything encountered on the battlefield: it is a demand for compromise which originates from the very same source as his uncompromisable identity, namely, Volumnia. She herself articulates this (the contradiction she is forcing upon her son) when in the name of 'policy' (III. ii. 42) she tells him, rebukingly, 'You are too absolute' (l. 38), adding immediately, as if aware of the contradiction, 'Though therein you can never be too noble'. As Brockbank says: 'the terse syntax masks the anomalies in Volumnia's position' (ed. *Corialanus*, p. 220).

Coriolanus does not show the defeat of innate nobility by policy, but rather challenges the very idea of innate nobility. So when Coriolanus is exiled from Rome he declares confidently 'There is a world elsewhere' (III. iii. 137). But it is the world being left which he needs, because it is there that his identity is located. With unwitting but telling emphasis he testifies to just that fact: 'I shall be lov'd when I am lack'd' (IV. i. 15). And again, moments later:

> While I remain above the ground you shall
> Hear from me still, and never of me aught
> But what is like me formerly.
>
> (IV. i. 51–3)

And if this is not sufficient, we next see Coriolanus offering his *virtus* to Aufidius with the ultimate aim of *avenging* himself upon Rome. It is ironically significant that when they meet, Aufidius repeatedly fails to recognise Coriolanus even though they have many times fought each other:

> Thou hast beat me out
> Twelve several times, and I have nightly since
> Dreamt of encounters 'twixt thyself and me –
> We have been down together in my sleep,
> Unbuckling helms, fisting each other's throat –
> And wak'd half dead with nothing.
>
> (IV. v. 121–6)

Despite this, Aufidius only recognises Coriolanus when he is told his name. The implication is clear: Aufidius loves not the man but the power he signifies; he puts a face to the name, not vice-versa.

Coriolanus assumes that because it is essentially and exclusively his, he can transfer *virtus* intact, with himself; he *is* his *virtus*. In fact, this is just a further escalation of the same destructive conflict; indeed, the soliloquy which precedes his entry into Antium shows Coriolanus close to *anomie*. This is because, as he tells Aufidius, all that remains of his past is his name (IV. v. 73). The martial kudos he has lost he needs at all costs – hence his present deeply contra-dictory position: 'my love's upon/This enemy town' (IV. iv. 23–4). Hence too the tragic absurdity of that position: 'A goodly city is this Antium. City,/'Tis I that made thy widows' (IV. iv. 1–2). At home the patricians continue to mystify Coriolanus as the colossus who makes history of his own accord:

> He is their God; he leads them like a thing
> Made by some other deity than Nature,
> That shapes men better.
>
> (IV. vi. 91–3)

Yet things with Coriolanus are very much otherwise; now in the service of the Volscians, we find him anxiously having to recon-struct his reputation in relation to them: 'You must report to th' Volscian lords how plainly/I have borne this business' (V. iii. 3–4).

No sooner is that done than the contradiction between present and former selves is made manifest with the arrival of his family to plead with him. We should not sentimentalise Coriolanus' eventual capitulation to his family. After all, the appeals of his wife and son carry little weight compared with that of Volumnia. (In Plutarch he tells her: 'I see myself vanquished by you alone' – Brockbank, ed. *Coriolanus*, p. 263). She finally succeeds by appealing to his 'repu-tation' (V. iii. 144) and his obligation to her: 'there's no man in the world/More bound to's mother' (V. iii. 158–9). The appeal is a moral one, but what Volumnia signifies here is not motherhood so much as socialisation; as she herself says: 'Thou art my warrior;/I holp to frame thee' (V. iii. 62–3). The demands which she now makes of him merely lay bare his contradictory insertion in the prevailing social relations between and within Rome and Antium. He perceives as much when he tells her that she has won a victory for Rome at the expense of his ruin. At last though, in the place of the martial myth of transcendent, autonomous *integration* Coriolanus is forced to experience himself as decentred, identified by conflicting social forces which he cannot contain or, now, survive. Significantly – indeed tragically – it is at that moment that he can offer to mediate for peace. In the final scene however, Aufidius provokes Coriolanus into a return to his essentialist rant – 'Alone I did it' (V. vi. 117) – and before the peace stands a chance of ratification, Coriolanus is killed. The two main political conflicts which open the play – patrician against plebeian, Romans against Volscians – remain.

Essentialism and Class War

Essentialist egotism, far from being merely a subjective delusion, operates in this play as the ideological underpinning of class antagonism. At first sight Coriolanus' immoderate hatred of the plebeians might seem like a spontaneous expression of his patrician self-esteem. But it soon becomes apparent that the hatred is a precondition of the esteem; Coriolanus, as patrician, needs the plebeians, not just in battle and as a class to exploit at home, but as objects of inferiority without which his superiority would be literally meaningless. Yet again, identity is revealed to be a complex function of social relations. Thus Coriolanus' pride in his wounds is inextricably bound up with the fact that he got them in the same battle where he saw the plebeians run from 'th' noise of our own drums' (II. iii: 52–3). This suggests why, when under pressure, the patrician assertion of superiority reveals, in its very hatred of the plebeians, a deep insecurity. Whereas the imagery used by the patricians to celebrate Coriolanus is thoroughly essentialist – images of integration, uniqueness, oneness, aloneness, hardness, and so on – that used to describe the plebeians is just the opposite – disorder, formlessness, multiplicity, instability, disease. They are hydra – like: 'the mutable, rank-scented meiny' (III. 1. 66).

Implicit in this contrast is a patrician fear of being contaminated and overwhelmed. Anti-plebeian invective, even as it belittles, attests to this deep fear, one both collective and individual. Menenius speaks of 'Your multiplying spawn . . . /That's thousand to one good one' (II. ii. 76–7) while Coriolanus has an almost manic fear that his oneness will be obliterated by the many. Only disaster will follow, he says,

> By mingling them with us, the honour'd number;
> Who lack not virtue, no, nor power, but that
> Which they have given to beggars
>
> (III. i. 72–4)

In the same scene Cominius speaks of 'odds against arithmetic' and likens the rage of the plebeians to 'interrupted waters' which 'o'er-bear/What they are used to bear'. The potential power of the plebeians, destructive, anarchic or otherwise, is a reality which the essentialist ideology of the patricians registers even as it struggles to suppress and occlude it; that which mystifies the class war also works to give it a displaced focus.

The plebeians in this play need to be seen in relation to the conditions of their existence – material, political and ideological. Brecht comments astutely on those conditions in a study of the first scene of the play (it is in the form of a dialogue):

> I don't think you realise how hard it is for the oppressed to become united. Their misery unites them – once they recognise who has caused it. 'Our sufferance is a gain to them' [I. i. 22]. But otherwise their misery is liable to cut them off from one another, for they are forced to snatch the wretched crumbs from each other's mouths. Think how reluctantly men decide to revolt! (*Brecht on Theatre*, p. 252)

A remark of the Third Citizen at the beginning of II. iii. suggests exactly this: 'We have power in ourselves to do it [i.e. repudiate Coriolanus], but it is a power that we have no power to do.' The accurate complexity of that remark evokes a contradiction familiar to oppressed majorities: disunity prevents them actualising their potential power, while the cause of that disunity is the very oppression which that power, if actualised, could overcome. It is a remark

which also shows that this play neither sentimentalises the plebeians nor, as is much more usually argued, displays the allegedly
universal Elizabethan hatred of the mob.

Critics have been eager to assume, or confidently assert, that the
Jacobean dramatists could not think beyond such hatred and that
any suggestion to the contrary would be simply anachronistic. It is
not surprising perhaps to find Sir Mungo William MacCallum
telling us that Shakespeare invariably treats crowds of citizens as
'stupid, disunited, fickle' (*Shakespeare's Roman Plays and Their
Background*, p. 470), but even A. P. Rossiter insists that when we
consider Shakespeare's 'fear of the mob and disorder' then 'we must
swallow our democracy' (*Angel with Horns*, p. 243), while a recent
critic speaks in passing of 'the worthless rabble of plebeians'
(Richard S. Ide, *Possessed With Greatness*, p. 169). Actually, the plebeians in *Coriolanus* are presented with both complexity and sympathy because understood in terms of the contradiction which the
Third Citizen articulates. It is, moreover, a contradiction corresponding to the material realities of their relationship with the
patricians. This too is registered by one of the citizens: 'the object
[i.e. the sight] of our misery, is an inventory to particularize their
abundance; our sufferance is a gain to them' (I. i. 21–2). This is an
assertion which would find ample support in Machiavelli's
Discourses, which conclude that it is the 'haves' rather than the
'have nots' who are more disruptive of the Republic since it is the
former who think they 'cannot hold securely what they possess
unless they get more at others' expense'[1] (p. 118). In another
chapter of the *Discourses*, headed *The Masses are more Knowing and
more Constant than is a Prince*, Machiavelli declares

> If therefore, it be a question of a prince subservient to the laws and
> of a populace chained up by the laws, more virtue will he found in
> the populace than in the prince; and if it be a question of either of
> them loosed from control by the law, there will be found fewer
> errors in the populace than in the prince. (p. 256)

Moreover: 'The brutalities of the masses are directed against those
whom they suspect of conspiring against the common good; the
brutalities of a prince against those whom he suspects of conspiring

against his own good' (p. 257). Machiavelli goes so far as to compare the voice of the people with that of God because so 'remarkably accurate in its prognostications' (p. 255).

Antagonism towards the mob, the so-called 'many-headed monster', was indeed expressed time and again in Jacobean England but this fact is evidence not of what all educated people could not help but believe but of a complex, deep, and often conscious class hostility: 'Anonymous libels and seditious utterances testify to the existence among at least some of the common people of a bitter hatred of the rich whom they regarded as exploiters. "Yt wold never be merye till some of the gentlemen were knocked down" was the opinion of one prospective leader of an abortive Oxfordshire rising in 1596' (Wrightson, *English Society 1580–1680*, p. 150). Seen against the background of famine and enclosure riots and at a time when 'the standard of living of the mass of the population was steadily declining whilst the wealth of the rich was visibly increasing' this antagonism emerges as 'a contemptuous attitude [which] thinly concealed the fears of the propertied class' (Christopher Hill, *Change and Continuity*, pp. 186, 188). Greville, speaking in the House of Commons in 1593, drew an analogy between the lower classes and the feet, declaring that if they 'knew their strength as well as we know their oppression, they would not bear as they do' (Hill, p. 187). Masterless men, always the first products of the breakdown of tradition, were especially feared. Relatively powerless because largely unorganised, they nevertheless constituted 'anomalies, potential dissolvents of the society', a group who could be mobilised as the mob and politically exploited as such (Hill, *The World Turned Upside Down*, pp. 40–1; see also Walzer, p. 313). As A. L. Beier has argued, London was experiencing unprecedented social problems in this respect: 'By 1600 slums were mushrooming in the suburbs, and hundreds of young, male vagrants, increasingly recruited from the London area itself, were loitering around the streets' ('Social Problems in Elizabethan London', p. 217). Lacking a regular police force and standing army, the authorities were especially anxious about the part such people might play in any insurrection. Recent historical research has established not just that the period witnessed numerous food and enclosure riots, but that it 'possessed an actual tradition of riot, a pattern of crowd action on the part of the common people' (Wrightson, *English Society 1580–1680*, p. 173). Not surprisingly then, dearth in Jacobean England, as in the society of *Coriolanus*, 'could detonate conflicts which sprang ultimately from the underlying socio-economic changes of the period' (Walter and Wrightson, 'Dearth and the Social Order', p. 25).

All this shows, I believe, that Brecht's reading of the first scene of *Coriolanus* is not anachronistic.[2] Consider what, from that scene alone, he concludes about the play:

> B: That the position of the oppressed classes can
>   be strengthened by the threat of war and
>   weakened by its outbreak.
> R: That lack of a solution can unite the oppressed
>   class and arriving at a solution can divide it . . .
> P: That differences in income can divide the oppressed class.
> R: That soldiers, and war victims even, can
>   romanticise the war they survived and be easy
>   game for new ones.
> W: That the finest speeches cannot wipe away realities,
>   but can hide them for a time.
>
> (*Brecht on Theatre*, p. 264)

These conclusions may sound startlingly modern but in fact the play amply confirms them, and not only in the first scene (to which Brecht regrettably limits this analysis). Consider, for example, the contradiction in the attitude of the people of Corioli towards Coriolanus – in effect a tragic instance of false-consciousness – as described by the Second Conspirator in V. vi.:

>   patient fools,
> Whose children he hath slain, their base throats tear
> With giving him glory.

But when the same people finally take revenge on Coriolanus it does not amount to a shift into 'true' consciousness – first, because in yet another of the tragic ironies which pervade this play, they cry for Coriolanus' death just at that moment when he is prepared to work for peace; second, because in this they are manipulated and subjected to propaganda (organised now by Aufidius).

And yet: the same propaganda which keeps the plebeians partially in awe also (like the anti-plebeian invective) constitutes them as potentially subversive of state power. The point is made by Terentlus in *Sejanus* when he speaks of

> The eager multitude, (who never yet
> Knew why to love, or hate, but only pleased
> T'express their rage of power)
>
> (V. 762–4)

It is in part because they are victims of a mystification which at crucial moments fails that the people embody a volatile, unpredictable 'rage of power', one capable of being turned against one ruler by another. Those who, kept in ignorance, 'follow fortune, and hate men condemned,/Guilty, or not' (*Sejanus*, V. 802–3) are, like Coriolanus, instruments and effects of power and consequently – also like him – unstably so: the ruler always in danger of being undermined by the same people upon whom his power is conditional because of the contradictions internal to the ideology which mediates his relationship to them. Finally then, the plebeians in *Coriolanus* have some justice on their side: 'What authority surfeits on would relieve us' (I. i. 15–16). But *Coriolanus* is concerned less with judging or vindicating the plebeians than *showing* the way that they are characterised by hunger, powerlessness and ignorance.

The patricians are seen in a similarly complex relationship to ideology. At one level they are engaged in a straightforward conspiracy; in III. ii. for example, Volumnia explicitly advocates conspiratorial deception of the plebeians in the interest of her own class. Coriolanus agrees reluctantly but in words which are revealing:

> I'll mountebank their loves,
> Cog their hearts from them, and come home belov'd
>
> (III. ii. 132–3)

Nevertheless the conspiratorial view is completely inadequate for other aspects of this play's treatment of ideology – not least the relationship of antagonistic dependence which ideology partly conceals and which I've already discussed. Further, Menenius sincerely believes in the essentialist mystification of Coriolanus which he as much as anyone helps to perpetuate (e.g. 'His nature is too noble for the world' – III. i. 255). Perhaps too he believes what we might now see as a classic instance of conspiratorial mystification: 'For the dearth,/The gods, not the patricians, make it' (I. i. 70–1). And yet it comes too pat and we are entitled to be sceptical, especially bearing in mind a report from Warwickshire during the dearth of 1608 (probably the year of the play's production) which confirmed that the shortage of corn was caused partly by hoarding – something which was widely recognised anyway – and, further, Laud's Star Chamber judgement of 1632 after trials for hoarding which declared 'this last yeares famin was made by man and not by God' (cited by Walter and Wrightson, 'Dearth and the Social Order', pp. 30–1). Perhaps Menenius neither consciously believes nor is consciously exploiting this idea, rather, he is a patrician having 'instinctive' recourse to a familiar strategy for 'keeping men in awe'. But the argument here does not depend upon speculation of this kind about what stage characters 'really' believe. My point is that Menenius represents a type who can both believe and exploit the strategy in question. Moreover, like Gloucester in *King Lear* (see above, p. 200) he is shown to cling to ideological imperatives even from within the midst of the contradictions and disruption which they entail. Hence his response to Coriolanus' betrayal of Rome. Initially he refuses to believe it, having completely failed to understand the psychology and conditions of the possibility of the martial ethos he has celebrated so tirelessly. When it transpires that Coriolanus really has become Rome's enemy, Menenius simply reaffirms with renewed intensity the old class antagonisms (IV. vi. 96–121; V. iv. 30), a fall-back position which 'explains' the inexplicable by ideologically obliterating it. Even when deeply wounded by Coriolanus' rejection of him – 'grief-shot/With his unkindness' (V. i. 44–5) – he clings to an essentialist mystification of his former master: 'He wants nothing of a god but eternity, and a heaven to throne in' (V. iv. 23–4).

Although *Coriolanus*, of all Shakespeare's tragedies, is the least amenable to the perspective of essentialist humanism, it is frequently read in those terms. After giving an excellent analysis of *Coriolanus* as a 'penetrating and sustained analysis of political processes' Brian Vickers turns to Coriolanus' character. In the situation in which Coriolanus finds himself, says Vickers, 'the individual is right to reject a corrupt society and to affirm the authenticity of his own values' (*Shakespeare: Coriolanus*, pp. 56, 37). In the final chapter, significantly titled 'Success in Failure', we are told that Coriolanus is an idealist, possessing 'spontaneity and immediacy of feeling . . . integrity . . . noble trust and loyalty to others' and that the choice becomes one between the individual and his society: 'I would rather have his [Coriolanus'] integrity and innocence, however easily "put upon" than all the calculation and political skill in Rome or Corioli' (p. 59). As I've tried to show, Coriolanus is not identified in terms of innocence or integrity, least of all in the autonomous ethical sense suggested here. More important still, the very dichotomy of innocent, authentic individual versus corrupt society is false to the play; to accept that dichotomy is idealistically to recuperate the political and social realism of *Coriolanus*; the ethically unified subject of a world elsewhere allows us to transcend the political and social realities foregrounded in and by the dislocated subject in this one.

The more accurate assessment of Coriolanus comes from Aufidius' reflections upon the fortunes of this man: 'So our virtues/Lie in th' interpretation of the time' (IV. vii. 49–50). A radical *political* relativism is advanced here. Significantly Aufidius speaks of 'virtues' (rather than, say, reputation) as being socially constructed rather than intrinsically possessed (cf. 'Rights by rights falter, strengths by strengths do fail' – l. 55).

Such then is the radically contingent nature not just of individual identity but, inseparably, of the present historical conjuncture. But there is not here a simple substitution of one universal for another, of Chance for Providential Design. With the dissolution of the universal and its instantiating essence a new kind of history is disclosed, albeit one both obscure and complex and with boundaries necessarily indeterminate. Nevertheless its focus is unmistakable: state power, social conflict and the struggle between true and false discourses. Hence the fascinating tendency in Aufidius' soliloquy, one characteristic of the play as a whole and indeed of other Jacobean tragedies – the tendency to anchor traditional ideas of transience and mutability in an immediate perception of political and historical vicissitude.[3] Coriolanus' 'O world' soliloquy is another case in point: friends, once inseparable, 'break out/To bitterest enmity' while 'fellest foes . . . grow dear friends' (IV. iv. 17–21). These reflections are of course the prelude to Coriolanus' own switch in allegiance of which Sicinius is to remark, incredulously yet profoundly: 'Is't possible that so short a time can alter the condition of a man?' (V. iv. 10).

15

The White Devil (1612):
Transgression Without Virtue

In *The White Devil* the decentring of the tragic subject is most fully in the service of another preoccupation of Jacobean tragedy: the demystifying of state power and ideology. In no other play is the identity of the individual shown to depend so much on social interaction; even as they speak protagonists are, as it were, off-centre. It is a process of displacement which shifts attention from individuals to their context and above all to a dominating power structure which constructs them as either agents or victims of power, or both.

Religion and State Power

For Flamineo religion is the instrument of state power – a façade of sanctity indispensable to its operation. His satire is cynically reductive yet based on accurate insight:

> there's nothing so holy but money will corrupt and putrify it . . . You are happy in England, my lord; here they sell justice with those weights they press men to death with . . . Religion; O how it is commeddled with policy. The first bloodshed in the world happened about religion. (III. iii. 24–5, 27–8, 37–9)

In the following act Flamineo's assessment is vindicated as we witness 'religion' fronting 'policy'; Monticelso enters *in state* (stage direction) and Francisco whispers to him the news that Brachiano and Vittoria have escaped from the house of convertites; as a result Monticelso makes their excommunication his first act as new Pope:

> We cannot better please the divine power,
> Than to sequester from the holy church
> These cursed persons. Make it therefore known,

231

We do denounce excommunication
Against them both.

(IV. iii. 65–9)

It is an episode which shows how state power is rendered invulnerable by identification with its 'divine' origin – how, in effect, policy gets an ideological sanction. In performance of course we will see that it is an appeal further ratified by the awesome apparatus of investiture – a good instance of the ceremonial keeping of men in awe (see above, pp. 17–18). Finally there is the masterful foresight of the true politician: 'All that are theirs in Rome/We likewise banish'. Thus at the same time as it consolidates faith, religious ritual is shown to consolidate the power of those who rule, the second being secured in and through the first. Brachiano, in describing Duke Francisco, makes a similar point in relation to the 'robes of state':

> all his reverent wit
> Lies in his wardrobe; he's a discreet fellow
> When he's made up in his robes of state

(II. i. 184–6)

The Virtuous and the Vicious

In Act I, scene ii, Cornelia, unseen, witnesses the seduction of Vittoria (her daughter) by Duke Brachiano, with Flamineo (her son) acting as pander. At last she intervenes to reprimand all three. As she preaches honour and virtue to Brachiano we realise that she has an entirely false conception of 'The lives of Princes' (I. ii. 276); she is, in fact, a victim to the myth of courtliness, the myth which disguises the real nature of the court and the elite which dominates it (and her). It is the same myth to which Vittoria refers when she is dying – 'O happy that they never saw the court/Nor ever knew great man but by report' (V. vi. 258–9) – and which surrounds the reputed glory of these great men: 'Glories, like glow-worms, afar off shine bright/But look'd to near have neither heat nor light' (V. i. 40–1).

In both of these so-called *sententiae* there is something quite different from the inappropriate moralising that some critics have detected.[1] In fact, they evince a perceptive awareness that those who are geographically and socially removed from the centre of power are deceived as to its true nature. This is an aspect of the ideological ratification of power which Machiavelli refers to in *The Prince*. If a ruler is consistently virtuous, and behaves accordingly – this will be his ruin, says Machiavelli.[2] On the contrary he must be capable of doing evil while appearing virtuous. The reality is concealed by a carefully constructed myth – Vittoria's 'report' – rendered workable at least in part by the ignorance of those who are ruled. Both *The White Devil* and *The Prince* indicate that this is an ignorance resulting from geographical and social distance:

> To those seeing and hearing him, [the prince] should appear a man of compassion, a man of good faith, a man of integrity, a kind and a religious man. And there is nothing so important as to seem to have this last quality. Men in general judge by their eyes rather than by their hands; because everyone is in a position to watch, few are in a position to come in close touch with you. Everyone sees what you appear to be, few experience what you really are. And those few dare not gainsay the many who are backed by the majesty of state. (*The Prince*, p. 101)

In short, *realpolitik* presupposes for its successful operation complicity by the few, ideological misrecognition by the many.

At this same point in *The White Devil* (Act I, scene ii) we witness yet again irony in the service of subversion: Cornelia preaches to the Duke precisely the myth which ratifies his exploitation of subjects like her. Having internalised her position as one of the exploited she does not exactly make the rod for her own back, but when the master drops it she is the one who 'instinctively' returns it to him. By embracing the Christian ethic of humility and passive virtue Cornelia endures poverty and reproaches her son's conduct with the question: 'what? because we are poor/Shall we be vicious?' (I. ii. 304–5). Flamineo, indirectly in what he says here, more directly in his actual conduct, answers that question affirmatively: in *this* society the only means of alleviating poverty is a self-regarding viciousness. Here, as in the very first scene of the play, we see the lie being given to the Christian/stoic belief in the efficacy of adversity. In that first scene Antonelli tells Lodovico: 'affliction/ Expresseth virtue, fully' (he is referring to the latter's banishment).

Lodovico, in his brutal reply – 'Leave your painted comforts – /I'll make Italian cut-works in their guts/If ever I return' (I. i. 51–3) – indicates the contrary. We draw the same conclusion when Lodovico and Flamineo agree to a malcontented allegiance: 'Let's be unsociably sociable' (III. iii. 74). It is a mock pact, broken almost as soon as it is made, and parodying, even as it proposes, the resignation characteristic of *contemptus mundi*. They agree to withdraw from the court and teach all those like them – the dispossessed and the failed – 'To scorn that world which life of means deprives'. It is a large group, embracing

> the beggary of courtiers,
> The discontent of churchmen, want of soldiers,
> And all the creatures that hang manacled,
> Worse than strappado'd, on the lowest felly
> Of Fortune's wheel
>
> (III. iii. 89–93)

Antonelli suddenly announces that Lodovico's fortunes have reversed: he has been pardoned. Instantly Lodovico spurns Flamineo and within seconds they are at each other's throats.

Whereas Cornelia internalises an oppressive conception of virtue, one which keeps her dutifully subservient, Vittoria and Flamineo reject virtue to become, like Lodovico, vicious. It is the tragic contradiction of this society that for those in it virtue involves false-consciousness while the struggle for true consciousness entails viciousness. The crimes of Flamineo and Vittoria reveal not their essential criminality but the operations of a criminal society. Most importantly, those who are most responsible for its viciousness – the powerful – conceal this fact *by and through* their power:

> Vittoria: If Florence be i'th' court, would he would kill me.
> Gasparo: Fool! Princes give rewards with their own hands
>   But death or punishment by the hands of others.
>
> (V. vi. 184–6)

Exploitation – by the prince of his subjects and by them of each other – is a recurring concern of the play (one articulated at, for example, II. i. 317–19; IV. i. 81–6; IV. ii. 134; V. iii. 60–3). Act IV, scene ii, more than anywhere else in the play, uses antagonistic confrontation to reveal the rootedness of power in exploitation. In that scene both Vittoria and Flamineo rebel against their master, Brachiano. More generally Vittoria rebels against her subordination as a woman, Flamineo against the subordination of one forced into service through dispossession.

Sexual and Social Exploitation

Vittoria lives in a society in which women are subordinate to men. But the men are never quite confident of their domination and require that women acquiesce in the role accorded to them: 'A *quiet* woman' says Flamineo, 'Is a still water under a great bridge./A man may shoot her safely' (IV. ii. 175–7; my italics). The same male insecurity flares into misogyny at the least provocation (Brachiano is here speaking to Vittoria):

> Thou hast led me, like an heathen sacrifice,
> With music, and with fatal yokes of flowers
> To my eternal ruin. Woman to man
> Is either a god or a wolf.
>
> (IV. ii. 86–9)

In her trial scene Vittoria refuses to be 'quiet', provoking Monticelso into a furious diatribe against whores as the bane of man[3] (III. ii. 78–101). Misogyny is further apparent in Flamineo's repeated deprecation of women (e.g. at I. ii. 18–20; IV. ii. 147–8; V. iii. 178–84; V. vi. 151–5; V. i. 91–2) and in the fact that evil, lust and jealousy are given female personification by male characters. Isabella laments, 'O that I were a man, or that I had power . . .' (II. i. 242). To be male *is* to have power – in particular, power over women. Monticelso has the power, as Vittoria points out, to name her 'whore' (III. ii. 146–8). Not only does the language of the dominant actually confer identity on the subordinate, but the latter can only resist this process in terms of the same language; thus Vittoria determines to 'personate masculine virtue' (III. ii. 135). And yet, because of her different position in relation to power Vittoria's appropriation of that language can only go so far; in a sense the same language is not the same at all: 'O woman's poor revenge/Which dwells but in the tongue!' (III. ii. 281–2). Nevertheless, to appropriate masculine virtue was still the most extreme form of female insubordination (in Jacobean England 'assertive women' provoked much controversy; even James I intervened, commanding the clergy to preach against them and threatening more direct action if this failed).[4] The extent of Vittoria's power to defy is captured in her declaration to those trying her: 'I scorn to hold my life/At yours or any *man's* entreaty, sir' (III. ii. 137–8).

Flamineo's dispossession (I. ii. 306–7) has pressed him into service and the search for 'preferment'. In that search he has been disillusioned – first by his university education, second by his attendance at court. Education and service have left him just as poor yet even more dissatisfied: each has given him an insight into what he believes to be the false-consciousness of those like his mother which keeps them poor and 'virtuous' and, at the same time, made him want all the more the preferment he has been denied.

There is a fragile bond of loyalty between brother and sister. Thus Flamineo ruins his standing with Brachiano by reproaching him for calling Vittoria a whore; this leads to a confrontation for which Brachiano never forgives Flamineo (see V. ii. 78). But whatever allegiance Flamineo and Vittoria have through kinship or shared grievance, it is over-ridden – indeed, contradicted – by their respective roles in relation to each other and to Brachiano: she is Brachiano's mistress, he the procurer. Flamineo, challenged by his brother about the role of pander to Vittoria, dissolves kinship into shared ambition: 'I made a kind of path/To her and mine own preferment' (III. i. 35–6). But it is a path hardly wide enough for two to travel: brother prostitutes sister and she reproaches him accordingly; Flamineo, for his part, repeatedly degrades her sexuality so as to evade his own humiliation as pander. Finally their relationship explodes into outright antagonism with each prepared to kill the other (V. vi). It is a relationship which enacts the process whereby the individual emerges from familial bonds into adulthood only to find in the latter forms of social identity which contradict or destroy the former. The mother is the first casualty. Here, as throughout Jacobean tragedy, the bonds of 'nature' and 'kind' collapse under pressure and, because they break – indeed precisely *as* they break – they are shown to be not natural at all, but social.

The ambivalence which Flamineo and Vittoria feel towards Brachiano is born of their compromised relationship to him. He represents what each wants yet hates. It is an ambivalence which is most apparent in the angry confrontation of Act IV, precipitated by Francisco's letter to Vittoria pretending his love for her. This is intercepted by Brachiano who promptly assumes Vittoria's infidelity. He abuses her in terms which recall Monticelso's denunciation: 'Where's this whore?' (IV. ii. 43). This angers Flamineo who threatens to break Brachiano's neck. In response to the latter's incredulous 'Do you know me?' (i.e. 'do you realise who you're talking to?') Flamineo tears away the myth of 'degree' and points to the real basis of hierarchy:

> O my lord! methodically.
> As in this world there are *degrees* of evils:
> So in this world there are *degrees* of devils.
> You're a great Duke; I your poor secretary.
>
> (IV. ii. 56–9; my italics)

We recall this exchange later when Francisco, disguised as a soldier, comments as follows on his anticipated meeting with Brachiano:

> I shall never flatter him: I have studied man too much to do that. What difference is between the Duke and I? No more than between two bricks, all made of one clay: only't may be one is placed on the top of a turret, the other in the bottom of a well, by mere chance. (V. i. 104–8)

The force of this repudiation of a Duke's innate superiority is ironically reinforced by the fact that Francisco is one himself. A similar idea is expressed by Bosola, Flamineo's counterpart in *The Duchess of Malfi*: 'Some would think the souls of princes were brought forth by some more weighty cause, than those of meaner persons; *they are deceived* . . . the same reason that makes a vicar go to law for a tithe-pig and undo his neighbours, makes them spoil a whole province, and batter down goodly cities with the cannon' (II. i. 104–10; my italics).

As Brachiano abuses Vittoria she turns on him with a passionate anger which recalls the confrontation with Monticelso in the trial scene. She attacks Brachiano for his failure to provide:

What do you call this house?
Is this your palace? Did not the judge style it
A house of penitent whores? . . .
Who hath the honour to advance Vittoria
To this incontinent college? Is't not you?
Is't not your high preferment? Go, go brag
How many ladies you have undone, like me.

(IV. ii. 109–15)

Vittoria here reveals what she had hoped to get from Brachiano
('high preferment') and what she despises him for (sexual possession – the power to 'undo'; compare lines 129–30 of this same
scene when Brachiano declares: 'Are not those matchless eyes *mine*
. . . Is not this lip *mine*?'). Vittoria remains recalcitrant even when
the repentant though shameless Brachiano tries to win her around
with his reassurance: 'for you Vittoria,/Think of a duchess' title' (ll.
215–16).

The White Devil does not idealise Vittoria. In some respects it
even alienates our sympathy for her. But if it does not invite sympathy it invites even less judgement – especially the kind which
forecloses the play by relegating problematic figures like Vittoria
and Flamineo to the realm of the morally defective. In understanding Vittoria we need to contrast her with Isabella. Isabella has
always been a problem for critics who have wanted to identify her
as the play's point of moral reference. In their terms she can just
about carry moral piety but fails completely to carry moral stature.
Throughout her interview with Brachiano (II. i.) she evinces a
degree of self-abnegation which is the opposite of Vittoria. In the
space of thirteen separate utterances – some no more than single
lines – she addresses Brachiano nine times as 'my dear lord' or
something similar. Finally, despite his callousness, she decides to
feign responsibility for the rift even though, apparently, the blame
is entirely his. She has a strong desire to be self-sacrificial and to be
remembered as such by Brachiano (II. i. 223–4). Hers is sexual
subordination taken to an extreme: the 'lesser sex' willingly takes
upon itself the guilt of the superior in a ritual of self-sacrifice.[5] The
more callous Brachiano is, the more she reverences him as god-like.
In the first dumb-show – a symbolic enactment of the contradictions and false-consciousness which characterise Isabella's relation-

ship with Brachiano – the self-sacrificial role she has internalised is ritualistically underwritten: 'she kneels down *as to prayers*, then draws the curtains of Brachiano's picture, does three reverences to it, and kisses it thrice'. The ritual element highlights not just her self-sacrifice but the simple fact that she is being brutally murdered by the husband she reverences – in the very act of reverencing him.

The Assertive Woman

From the outset and especially in the middle ages, Christianity had a strong misogynist streak. Woman was the sinful temptress, lustful, vain, and the bane of man. But in the sixteenth century both humanists and reformers were in different ways challenging this estimate of women, especially the basic assumption of their 'natural' inferiority.[6] Recent studies of the Elizabethan feminist controversy amply confirm Louis B. Wright's conclusion in an earlier work that it indicated 'a serious undercurrent of intelligent thinking upon women's status in a new commercial society' (*Middle Class Culture in Elizabethan England*, p. 507). Robert Brustein shows how the satiric denigration of women in Elizabethan drama was an anxious reaction to increasing independence and status on the part of some ('The Monstrous Regiment of Women', pp. 37–8). William Heale, writing in 1609 in defence of women, remarks the ethical double standard which we so often find in the drama: 'The Courtier though he wears his Mistresse favour, yet stickes not to sing his Mistresse shame' (*An Apologie for Women*, quoted in Wright, p. 485).

In fact there seems to have been a significant change in attitudes to women in the drama of the second decade of the seventeenth century. Linda Woodbridge argues that whereas the first decade witnessed unprecedented misogyny in the drama, a startling change followed whereby assertive women came to be positively celebrated. She argues here for a correlation with the actual behaviour of women in Jacobean England, also a recognition by playwrights and companies of the economic importance of female playgoers (*Women and the English Renaissance*, esp. chapter 10).

But actual changes for the better in the position of women at this time were distinctly limited. Rightly, the rather complacent but widely held view that some Renaissance women actually achieved equality with men has been challenged in recent years. Joan Kelly-Gadol argues that in the long term the historical changes of that period which were liberating for men resulted in new forms of oppression for women – in particular a diminishing access to property, political power and education, and a greater regulation of their sexuality ('Did Women Have a Renaissance?').[7]

Certainly in Jacobean drama we find not a triumphant emancipation of women but at best an indication of the extent of their oppression. The form that it takes in Webster's two major plays is important. In particular the figure of Vittoria should be viewed in relation to the image of the disorderly or unruly woman – the 'woman on top' – found extensively in literature, wood cuts, broadsheets, pictorial illustrations and popular festivity. It was an image which, like other forms of ritual inversion, could legitimate rather than subvert the dominant order (see above, pp. 25–8). Yet, as Natalie Zemon Davis has argued, because it was a multivalent image it could also 'widen behavioural options for women within and even outside marriage, and . . . sanction riot and political disobedience for both men and women'. Most generally, that image could become part and parcel of conflict resulting from efforts to change the basic distribution of power in society ('Women on Top: Symbolic Sexual Inversion and Political Disorder in Early Modern Europe', pp. 154–5). This seems to describe Vittoria quite aptly. It suggests too that (*pace* Juliet Dusinberre)[8] dramatists like Webster were interested in the exploitation of women (rather than women's rights) as one aspect – and a crucial one – of a social order which thrived on exploitation. So, in a trial in which Vittoria is charged with, among other things, being a whore, we are reminded that marriage was itself a form of prostitution:

> 'twas my cousin's fate –
> may I name the hour – to marry you;
> He bought you of your father . . .
> He spent there in six months
> Twelve thousand ducats, and to my acquaintance
> Receiv'd in dowry with you not one julio
>
> (III. ii. 234–9)

The Comedy of Errors is another case in point. In that play Shakespeare explores the rationale of female subordination: the sisters Adriana and Luciana disagree about man's domination of woman. 'Why should their liberty than ours be more?' complains Adriana. She complains too that her husband, Antipholus, does not appreciate her servitude: 'when I serve him so, he takes it ill' (II. i. 10 and 12). Luciana replies that Adriana's husband is 'bridle of your will', and that among all animals the female species 'Are their males' subjects, and at their controls'. Moreover,

> Man, more divine, the master of all these,
> Lord of the wide world and wild watr'y seas,
> Indu'd with intellectual sense and souls,
> Of more pre-eminence than fish and fowls,
> Are masters to their females, and their lords.

> (II. i. 20–4)

Adriana is questioning this explanation when Dromio the servant appears complaining that Antipholus (his master) has been mistreating him too. Adriana, impatient, falls to doing the same and Dromio exits, still complaining: 'You spurn me hence, and he will spurn me hither;/If I last in this service, you must case me in leather.' So: Adriana is abused by her 'master', while she in turn abuses her slave who is in his turn abused by both master and mistress. The episode is a 'comic' yet penetrating critique of authority and service. Two further points are worth noting about it. First, there is the familiar ideological appeal to natural law – the law encoded in nature according to God's providential design: 'heaven's eye' (l. 16). Second, we here witness the issue of men's domination of women being put alongside men's domination of men. Thus Adriana, later in the same scene, complains that her husband prefers the company of 'minions' to hers. She adds:

> Do their gay vestments his affections bait?
> That's not my fault; he's master of my state.
> What ruins are in me that can be found
> By him not ruin'd?

> (II. i. 94–7)

These are powerful lines and their force is increased rather than diminished by the fact that we have just seen how one such minion is as much at the mercy of Adriana and Antipholus as she is of Antipholus.

The Dispossessed Intellectual

The circumstances which Flamineo struggles against were just as familiar in the first decade of the seventeenth century. He bears some resemblance to the so-called 'alienated intellectuals of early Stuart England' investigated in an article of that name by Mark E. Curtis.[9] It was frustration rather than exploitation which characterised these men; leaving university they encountered a society unable to use their talents or fulfil their sense of duty, self-esteem and honour. This 'generated impatience with the old corruption and helped create the body of men who could be among its most formidable opponents' (p. 314). Flamineo is concerned not with duty but survival and gain. His situation is more desperate: he suffers from frustration *and* exploitation and insofar as they can be distinguished the former makes him susceptible to the latter. As Lussurioso remarks in *The Revenger's Tragedy*, 'discontent and want/Is the best clay to mould a villain' (IV. i. 47–8).

Flamineo's education, which on his own confession (I. ii. 320–4) contributed to his discontent, is as important as Hamlet's though for different reasons. Hobbes, discussing the causes of the civil war, laid some of the blame at the door of the universities: 'The core of rebellion, as you have . . . read of other rebellions, are the universities' (*The English Works of Thomas Hobbes*, VI, 237). And in the year before the appearance of *The White Devil* Bacon had written:

> There [are] more scholars bred than the State can prefer and employ, and . . . it must needs fall out that many persons will be bred unfit for other vocations, and unprofitable for that in which they were bred up, which fill the realm full of indigent, idle and wanton people, who are but materia rerum novarum. (Cited from L. C. Knights, *Drama and Society in the Age of Jonson*, pp. 324–5)

In one of his *Essays* Bacon considers 'Seditions and Troubles' in the state. 'The matter of seditions' says Bacon 'is of two kinds –

much poverty and much discontentment.' And among their causes and motives he lists 'general oppression' and 'factions grown desperate'. One of the remedies open to the state is to ensure it does not arise that 'more are bred scholars than preferments can take off'. Bacon also advocates 'great use of ambitious men in being screens to princes in matters of danger and envy . . . [and] in pulling down the greatness of any subject that overtops' (*Essays*, pp. 44–5; 113). This is exactly how Francisco uses Lodovico and Brachiano uses Flamineo. Moreover, it correlates quite precisely with Gasparo's remark to the effect that 'Princes give rewards with their own hands,/But death or punishment by the hands of others' (quoted in context on p. 234 above). Bacon then advises on how such men, once used, may be 'bridled':

> There is less danger of them if they be of mean birth than if they be noble; and if they be rather harsh of nature, than gracious and popular; and if they be new raised, than grown cunning and fortified in their greatness. (*Essays*, pp. 113–14)

All such characteristics would tend to isolate such men *from each other* as well as from others unlike them. And this is crucial: potential opponents of the prince must not be allowed to unite since 'whatsoever, in offending people, joineth and knitteth them *in a common cause*' is likely to result in sedition and must therefore be avoided at all cost (*Essays*, p. 45; my italics).

In comparing the theatrical malcontent with his historical counterpart in Jacobean society we are concerned with resemblance rather than exact comparisons – not least because, as we saw in chapter 3, that drama gains its realism as much by theatrical exaggeration of essential characteristics as by non-exaggerated representation of surface properties. Thus, just as Flamineo throws the plight of the dispossessed and exploited into exaggerated relief, so too do the two murderers whom Macbeth hires to kill Banquo and Fleance. These murderers are truly *desperate*:

Second Murderer: I am one, my liege,
Whom the vile blows and buffets of the world
Have so incens'd that I am reckless what
I do to spite the world.

First Murderer: And I another
                          So weary with disasters, tugg'd with fortune,
                          That I would set my life on any chance,
                          To mend it or be rid on't.
                                                        (III. i. 107–113)

As hirelings these men are lethal: misfortune has made them very
vicious; they are 'reckless' in the sense of having nothing to lose and
therefore being beyond the reach of an appeal to self-preservation.
Authority has always had most to fear from those who not only
have nothing to gain from it, but also nothing left to lose to it. Of
course, each murderer had his life. But life without means comes to
mean nothing: 'I would set my life *on any chance,/*To mend it or be
rid on't'. The kind of poverty provoking such desperation is graphi-
cally portrayed by Robert Burton. Especially relevant is his insistence on the way that extreme poverty is so completely destructive
of social standing that no aspect of one's identity, no independently
identifiable aspect of oneself, remains untouched; the individual so
afflicted is wholly recast in a new role: '*if once poor, we are metamor-
phosed in an instant*, base slaves, villains, and vile drudges; for to be
poor is to be a knave, a fool, a wretch, a wicked, an odious fellow, a
common eye-sore, *say poor and say all*' (*Anatomy of Melancholy*, I.
350; my italics). Burton is insistent on this point: 'He must turn
rogue and villain . . . poverty alone makes men thieves, rebels, murderers, traitors, assassinates' (I. 354).

In *All's Well that Ends Well* Parolles asserts: 'Simply the thing I
am/Shall make me live . . . There's place and means for everyman
alive' (IV. iii. 310–11 and 316). For malcontents like Flamineo and
Macbeth's murderers the reverse is true: the position they 'live'
makes them what they are, and they kill each other for 'place and
means'.

Living Contradictions

In death Flamineo and Vittoria remain defiant. Many have interpreted this as tragic affirmation – of self[10] if not of life or the moral
order (but sometimes of all three). Yet brother and sister die with
the same dislocated identities. Vittoria claims to be 'too true a
woman' to show fear (l. 220) but as Flamineo observes (ironically

recalling Vittoria's own words at III. ii. 135), she is a woman who has appropriated 'masculine virtue' (1. 242). For his part Flamineo sustains defiance only by isolating himself in the moment – removed from the past, the future, almost from consciousness itself; asked what he is thinking he replies:

> Nothing; of nothing: leave thy idle questions –
> I am I'th'way to study a long silence,
> To prate were idle – I remember nothing.
> There's nothing of so infinite vexation
> As man's own thoughts.
>
> (V. vi. 219–23)

Moments later he declares:

> I do not look
> Who went before, nor who shall follow me;
> No, at myself I will begin and end.
>
> (V. vi. 223–5)

Flamineo dies with a gesture of futile defiance half-acknowledged as such in his being at once aggressively defiant and masochistically demanding: 'Search my wound deeper: tent it with the steel/That made it' (ll. 235–6). This is not the self-affirmation, the essentialist self-sufficiency of stoicism, but the stubborn defiance born of a willed insensibility which recalls his earlier: 'We endure the strokes like anvils or hard steel,/Till pain itself make us no pain to feel' (III. iii. 1–2). His last words –

> farewell glorious villains, –
> This busy trade of life appears most vain,
> Since rest breeds rest, where all seek pain by pain –
>
> (V. vi. 269–71)

surely allude to Bacon's essay *Of Great Place* (especially if we take 'glorious villains' to mean villains in search of glory):

> It is a strange desire, to seek power and lose liberty; or to seek power over others, and to lose power over a man's self. The rising unto place is laborious, and by pains men come to greater pains; and it is sometimes base, and by indignities men come to dignities. The standing is slippery; and the regress as either a downfall, or at least an eclipse, which is melancholy thing. *Cum non sis qui fueris, non esse*

cur velis vivere [When you are no longer the man you have been there is no reason why you should wish to live]. (*Essays*, p. 31)

It is in the death scene that we see fully the play's sense of how individuals can actually be constituted by the destructive social forces working upon them. We have already seen how Cornelia and Isabella internalised roles of subservience with the consequence that they revere that which exploits and destroys them. Conversely Vittoria and Flamineo refuse subservience even as they serve and, in so doing, are destroyed as much by their rebellion as that which they rebel against. Perhaps the most powerful contradiction lies in this simple fact: their stubborn, mindless self-affirmation at the point of death is made with the same life-energy which, up to that point, has been life-destructive. So, though directly opposed in many respects, these two pairs (Cornelia, Isabella; Flamineo, Vittoria) resemble each other in being constituted and ultimately destroyed by what Brecht called 'a great living contradiction'. He uses the description in relation to his own play, *Mother Courage and her Children*, with which, for the purposes of this discussion, I must assume acquaintance. The passage is worth quoting at length; it is appropriate not only for *The White Devil* but as a kind of anti-conclusion to this section:

> The trader mother became a great living contradiction, and it was this that defaced and deformed her, to the point of making her unrecognisable . . . After the maiming of her daughter, she damned the war with a sincerity just as deep as that with which she praised it in the scene immediately following. Thus she gives expression to opposites in all their abruptness and irreconcilability. The rebellion of her daughter against her . . . stunned her completely and taught her nothing. The tragedy of Mother Courage and of her life . . . consisted in the fact that here a terrible contradiction existed which destroyed a human being, a contradiction which could be resolved, but only by society itself and in long, terrible struggles . . . It is not the business of the playwright to endow Mother Courage with final insight . . . his concern is, to make the spectator see.[11]

SUBJECTIVITY: IDEALISM VERSUS MATERIALISM

16

Beyond Essentialist Humanism

Anti-humanism and its declared objective – the decentring of man – is probably the most controversial aspect of Marxist, structuralist and post-structuralist theory. An adequate account of the controversy and the issues it raises – essentialism, humanism, materialism, the subject/society relationship and more – would need a book in its own right and it is perhaps reckless to embark upon such a discussion in the space of a concluding chapter. I do so for three reasons at least.

First, it is a perspective important for the book as a whole since I have argued for the emergence in the Renaissance of a conception of subjectivity legitimately identified in terms of a materialist perspective rather than one of essentialist humanism. Second, for better or worse no issue is more central to English studies as it has been historically constituted than this question of subjectivity. Third, to reject the view that literature and criticism meet on some transhistorical plateau of value and meaning, leads inevitably to a discussion of the differences between incompatible critical perspectives; in this instance we are probably concerned with the most incompatible of all, namely the materialist as opposed to the idealist. But since what follows may seem far removed from the literary criticism familiar in English studies generally and of the Renaissance in particular, perhaps I should acknowledge that in a sense it is, and that its relevance lies in just this fact: the materialist conception of subjectivity (like historical materialism generally) aims not only to challenge all those forms of literary criticism premised on the residual categories of essentialist humanism and idealist culture but, even more importantly, invites a positive and explicit engagement with the historical, social and political realities of which both literature and criticism are inextricably a part.

Origins of the Transcendent Subject

Anti-humanism, like materialist criticism more generally, challenges the idea that 'man' possesses some given, unalterable essence which is what makes 'him' human, which is the source and *essential* determinant of 'his' culture and its priority over conditions of existence.

As I have already argued, it is the Enlightenment rather than the Renaissance which marks the emergence of essentialist humanism as we now know it; at that time concern shifts from the metaphysically derivative soul to what Robert Paul Wolff has termed 'individual centres of consciousness' (*The Poverty of Liberalism*, p. 142) which are said to be self-determining, free and rational by nature. Those forms of individualism (e.g. 'abstract individualism')[1] premised on essentialism tend, obviously, to distinguish the individual from society and give absolute priority to the former. In effect the individual is understood in terms of a pre-social essence, nature, or identity and on that basis s/he is invested with a quasi-spiritual autonomy. The individual becomes the origin and focus of meaning – an individuated essence which precedes and – in idealist philosophy – transcends history and society.

Reflecting here its religious antecedents, idealist philosophy marks off the domain of the spiritual as superior to, and the ultimate counter-image of, actual, historical, social, existence. It is not only that (as Nietzsche contended) the entire counterfeit of transcendence and of the hereafter has grown up on the basis of an impoverished life, but that transcendence comes to constitute an ideological mystification of the conditions of impoverishment from which it grew: impoverishment shifts from being its cause to its necessary condition, that required to pressure one's true (spiritual) identity into its true transcendent realisation. As Robbe-Grillet puts it, in the humanist tragic sense of life 'interiority always leads to transcendence . . . the pseudo-necessity of tragedy to a metaphysical beyond'; but at the same time it 'closes the door to any realist future' since the corollary of that beyond is a static, paralysed present ('Nature, Humanism and Tragedy', pp. 81, 84). The truth that people do not live by bread alone may then be appropriated ideologically to become the 'truth' that spiritual nourishment is an adequate substitute for bread and possibly even preferable to it (Marcuse, *Negations*, pp. 109–22). But most importantly, the *'revolutionary force of the ideal, which in its very unreality keeps alive the best desires of men amidst a bad reality'* (*Negations*, p. 102; my italics) is lost, displaced by ideals of renunciation and acquiescence. Rebellious desire is either abdicated entirely or tamed in service to the cultural reification of 'man', the human condition, the human spirit and so on.

Marcuse, writing in 1936, was trying to explain the transition from liberalism to authoritarianism which Europe was witnessing. We may be unable to accept some of Marcuse's conclusions but the task he set himself then seems as urgent as ever. In one thing he was surely right: the essentialism of western philosophy, especially that of the idealist tradition, could be used to sanction that process whereby 'the soul was able to become a useful factor in the technique of mass domination when, in the epoch of authoritarian states, all available forces had to be mobilised against a real transformation of social existence' (*Negations*, p. 114). The attacks upon idealist culture by Brecht, Walter Benjamin and Theodore Adorno were made from similiar positions.[2] In their very different ways these three writers engage with the materialist conception of subjectivity, one which, in so far as it retains the concept of essence, construes it not as that which is eternally fixed but as social potential materialising within limiting historical conditions. Conditions will themselves change – in part under the pressure of actualised potential – thus enabling new potentialities to unfold.

Arguably, to accept with Marx that Feuerbach was wrong 'to resolve the essence of religion into the essence of *man*', since 'the real nature of man is the totality of social relations' (*Selected Writings*, p. 83), should be to dispense altogether with 'essence', 'nature' and 'man' as concepts implicated irredeemably in the metaphysic of determining origin. Such at least is the implication of cultural materialism and that most famous of its formulations by Marx: 'The mode of production of material life conditions the social, political and intellectual life process in general' (*Selected Works*, p. 182). Consequently it is social being that determines consciousness, not the reverse[3] (see above, chapter 10).

In recent years the critique of essentialism has become even more searching partly in an attempt to explain its extraordinary recuperative power. Thus for Althusser humanism is characterised by two complementary and indissociable postulates: '(i) that there is a universal essence of man; (ii) that this essence is the attribute of "*each single individual*" who is its real subject' (*For Marx*, p. 228; the italicised phrase is a direct reference to Marx's sixth thesis on Feuerbach). Humanism gives rise to the concept of 'man' which, says Althusser, must be abolished: 'It is impossible to *know* anything about men except on the absolute precondition that the philosophical (theoretical) myth of man is reduced to ashes' (p. 229). Against humanism Althusser contends that 'The human subject is decentred, constituted by a structure which has no "centre" either, except in the imaginary misrecognition of the "ego", that is to say in the ideological formations where it finds recognition' (*Lenin and Philosophy*, p. 201).

Before continuing, two general points are worth remarking. First, Althusser is here drawing on psychoanalytic theory whereas I shall not. What follows involves cultural materialist, Marxist and post-structuralist analysis of a different kind.[4] Second, the controversy surrounding not just Althusser but the anti-humanism of Marxism, structuralism and post-structuralism generally has in part been due to a confusion of terms, and it has a long history. Thus Colin Wilson could declare in the fifties that he was an anti-humanist, yet his existentialist idealism is completely alien to the respective positions of, say, Althusser and Foucault. Indeed, according to those positions Wilson's own philosophy would be ineradicably humanist in virtue of its reliance on transcendent subjectivity (best exemplified in Wilson's article 'Beyond the Outsider', pp. 38–40). Wilson acknowledges quite explicitly that his is an idealism struggling to get back to its religious roots: 'Religion *must* be the answer' (p. 46; cf. pp. 37 and 40). And his definition of humanism includes, among other things, 'the values of the mass', 'scientific materialism' and 'progress' (pp. 36, 37, 41) – all of which materialist anti-humanism might endorse, though not uncritically. Anti-humanism would also utterly dissociate itself from Wilson's absurd contention that humanism (thus defined) has engendered 'nothing but mass-boredom and frustration, and periodic outbreaks of war' (p. 41). Wilson is not an anti-humanist in either Althusser's or Foucault's sense; he is, rather, anti-humanitarian and anti-democratic and in this resembles his precursors – T. E. Hulme, Eliot and others (see below, pp. 261–7). Probably it is pointless to try and rescue the term anti-humanism, especially since the important issues can better be focussed by addressing a more fundamental division – of which the humanist/anti-humanist controversy is only a manifestation – namely, that between idealist and materialist conceptions of subjectivity.

Derrida has insisted that metaphysics is so deeply rooted in our discourses that there is no getting beyond it (*Positions*, p. 21); perhaps in this he is too fatalistic. Nevertheless his assertion is strikingly apt for the history of the essentialist humanism which has pervaded English studies and carried within it a residual metaphysic, one which makes for the ideological effacement of socio-cultural difference and historical context. It thereby denies or at least seeks to minimise the importance of material conditions of human existence for the forms which that existence takes. I cannot provide here a detailed history of essentialist humanism in all its post-Enlightenment complexity, but propose instead to indicate, through some important textual landmarks, its centrality for the development of English studies, especially in so far as it informs the critical perspectives argued against in previous chapters.

Essence and Universal: Enlightenment Transitions

Put very schematically, western metaphysics has typically had recourse to three indissociable categories: the universal (or absolute), essence, and teleology. If universals and essences designate, respectively, what ultimately and essentially exists, then teleology designates metaphysical destiny – for the universe as a whole and its essences in particular.

In Descartes we can see a crucial stage in the history of meta-physics, one whereby essence takes on a new importance in the schema: the metaphysically derivative soul gives way to the autonomous, individuated essence, the self-affirming conscious-ness. (But just as the individuated essence typically presupposed its counterpart and origin, the universal form, so the subject of essen-tialist humanism comes to presuppose a universal human nature/condition.) For Descartes the self was a pure, non-physical substance whose 'whole essence or nature . . . is to think'; he also equated mind, soul, understanding and reason (*Works*, I, 101 and 152). Therefore he clearly retained an *a priori* and thoroughly metaphysical account of consciousness, one which was in impor-tant respects challenged, in others assimilated, by empiricists like Locke. But by elucidating in terms of empiricist epistemology a conception of the person which, however modified, contained an irreducibly metaphysical component, these empiricists were embarking upon a philosophical programme inherently problem-atic.

The trouble with Locke's definition of a person is that it still makes it a contingent rather than a necessary truth that people are of human form: 'It being the same consciousness that makes a man be himself to himself, personal identity depends on that only' (*Essay Concerning Human Understanding*, II. 27. 10). But if Locke is here still working with Cartesian assumptions, his empiricist epistemology nevertheless leads him to the radical supposition that the mind is 'as we say, white Paper, void of all Characters, without any *ideas*'. He then asks 'how comes it to be furnished? . . . Whence has it all the *materials* of Reason and Knowledge? To this I answer, in one word, From *experience*. In that, all our Knowledge is founded' (II. i. 2). Elsewhere Locke asserts that of all men 'nine parts of ten are what they are, good or evil, useful or not, by their education' (*Some Thoughts Concerning Education*, p. 114).

Hume for his part conducts a devastating critique of essen-tialism, getting rid of *substance* (an age-old metaphysical category which in this context was the supposed basis of the self) and arguing instead that 'mankind . . . are nothing but a bundle or col-lection of different perceptions which succeed each other with an inconceivable rapidity and are in perpetual flux and movement'.

There is not, he adds, 'any single power of the soul which remains unalterably the same', and regarding 'the mind . . . there is properly no *simplicity* in it at one time nor *identity* in different' (*Treatise*, I. iv. 6). And yet, contrary to what the foregoing might lead us to expect, Hume gives one of the most explicit statements of what Robert Solomon calls the 'transcendental pretence':[5] 'human nature remains still the same in its principles and operations . . . Mankind are so much the same, in all times and places, that history informs us of nothing new or strange in this particular. Its chief use is only to discover the constant and universal principles of human nature by showing men in all varieties of circumstances and situations' (*Enquiry*, section VIII, part 1). In effect, and crucially, 'man' as a universal remains, notwithstanding a radical transition from being given *a priori* to being given contingently, in 'nature'.[6]

There is yet another inconsistency, more important than any so far noted: Hume's 'universal principles of human nature' are not, even in his terms, universal after all, for he suspects 'negroes . . . to be *naturally* inferior to whites. There never was a civilised nation of any other complexion than white.' And the reason? 'Nature . . . made an original distinction betwixt these breeds [i.e. black and white]. Not to mention our colonies, there are NEGROE slaves dispersed all over EUROPE of which none ever discovered any symptom of ingenuity' (*Essays, Moral Political and Literary*, I, 252).

In the period between Locke and Hume we witness the emergence of a conception of man which rejected explicitly metaphysical categories only to re-import mutations of them in the guise of 'nature'. *Pace* Hume, 'history informs us' that nature has been as powerful a metaphysical entity as any, God included.

In contrast to the emerging British empiricism, the tradition of philosophical idealism recast essentialism in an explicitly metaphysical form. Immanuel Kant said of Rousseau that he was 'the first to discover beneath the varying forms human nature assumes, the deeply concealed essence of man' (Solomon, p. 54). Rousseau's essence was, of course, an innate goodness or potentiality existing in contradistinction to the corruption of society. But Kant legitimated essentialism in the context of transcendental idealism, a revolutionary philosophy which posited the phenomenal world as determined by the structure of the human mind itself, by the formal categories of consciousness: 'Hitherto it has been assumed that all our knowledge must conform to objects' says Kant, only then to present the truth as precisely the reverse of this: 'objects must conform to our knowledge' (*Critique of Pure Reason*, p. 22). Man as a rational being is part of the noumenal world possessed of an autonomous will serving its own law; he is an end in himself just as objects in the noumenal world are things in themselves. The enormous differences between the two philosophical traditions represented by Hume and Kant respectively could hardly be exaggerated yet on two things at least they agree: first (like Descartes) they begin with the individual taken in abstraction from any socio-political context; second, Kant concurs with Hume on the (human) condition of blacks: 'Mr Hume challenges anyone to cite a simple example in which a negro has shown talents . . . So fundamental is the difference between these two races of men [black and white] and it appears to be as great in regard to mental capacities as in colour' (*Observations on the Feeling of the Beautiful and Sublime*, pp. 110–11; quoted in Richard Popkin, *The High Road to Pyrrhonism*, pp. 259–60). This second point on which Hume and Kant agree is in part consequence of the first; the abstraction in abstract individualism (i.e. its metaphysics) is the means whereby the historically specific has been universalised as the naturally given.

Discrimination and Subjectivity

The example of racism is included here not as a gratuitous slur but rather as a reminder that the issues involved have not been, and still are not, limited to the realm of contemplative philosophy. As Popkin points out, the Enlightenment was the watershed of modern racial theories (*The High Road to Pyrrhonism*, especially chapters 4 and 14). Essentialist theories of human nature, though not intrinsically racist, have contributed powerfully to the ideological conditions which made racism possible. Similarly, when an ideological legitimation of slavery proved necessary (because of growing opposition to it) such theories helped provide that too. (See Montagu, *Man's Most Dangerous Myth*, pp. 21ff.)

The following is an instance of essentialist legitimation from our own century:

> History has shown, and daily shows anew, that man can be trained
> to be nothing that he is not genuinely, and from the beginning, in
> the depths of his being; against this law, neither precept, warning,
> punishment nor any other environmental influence avails. Realism
> in the study of man does not lie in attributing evil tendencies to
> him, but in recognising that all that man can do emerges in the last
> resort from himself, from his innate qualities.

Here essence and teleology are explicitly affirmed while 'history'
becomes the surrogate absolute. If we are used to finding this
kind of utterance in our own cultural history it comes as something of a shock to realise that these were the words of Alfred
Bäumler, a leading Nazi 'philosopher' writing on race.[7] In part
(that is, taking into account the historical context) they substantiate the claim of Marcuse that since Descartes essentialism has
'followed a course leading from autonomy to heteronomy, from
the proclamations of the free, rational individual to his surrender
to the powers of the authoritarian state' (*Negations*, pp. 44–5).[8]
This in turn underscores the importance of Derrida's contention
that the critique of ethnocentrism, together with the emergence
of ethnology and the corresponding decentring of European
culture, are 'historically contemporaneous with destruction of the
history of metaphysics' (*Writing and Difference*, p. 282).
Metaphysics can be finally displaced only when the twin concepts
of centred structure and determining origin are abandoned (pp.
278–9).

Derrida writes also of the importance of passing beyond 'Man
and humanism, the name of man being the name of that being
who, throughout the history of metaphysics or of ontotheology –
in other words throughout his entire history – has dreamed of
full presence, the reassuring foundation, the origin and the end of
play' (*Writing and Difference*, p. 292). If this echoes Levi-Strauss'
pronouncement that 'the ultimate goal of the human sciences' is
'not to constitute, but to dissolve man' (*The Savage Mind*, p.
247), or Foucault's equally notorious 'man is an invention of
recent date', one likely soon to 'be erased, like a face drawn in
sand at the edge of the sea' (*The Order of Things*, p. 387) – pro-
nouncements upon which some in the humanist tradition have
become fixated in horror – then it is worth interjecting that the

anti-humanism of Foucault's variety at least does not involve the elimination of individuality, only of 'man'. In fact, it is those discourses centred around 'man' and human nature which, historically, have regulated and repressed *actual* diversity and *actual* human difference. To speak of the uniqueness of an individual may mean either that s/he is contingently unlike anyone else actually known or that s/he approximates more closely to a normative paradigm, spiritual or natural, than anyone else who has ever, or will, or can, exist. The materialist view of the subject would at least render the former possible by rejecting the premises of the latter; in that sense, far from eliminating individuality, it realises it (interestingly, Lawrence's conception of individuality seems to be closer to the latter – see below, pp. 264–7).

In a sense Barthes is right to attack the petit-bourgeois for being 'unable to imagine the Other . . . because the Other is a scandal which threatens his essence' (*Mythologies*, p. 151), but we should remember that the experience of this kind of threat has by no means been limited to the petit-bourgeois, and the forms of discrimination which it has invited have operated in terms of several basic categories of identity, including race, sexuality and class.

The crucial point is surely this: essentialism, rooted as it is in the concept of centred structure and determining origin, constitutes a residual metaphysic within secularist thought which, though it has not entailed has certainly made possible the classic ideological effect: a specific cultural identity is universalised or naturalised; more specifically, in reaction to social change this residual metaphysic is activated in defence of one cultural formation, one conception of what it is to be truly human, to the corresponding exclusion of others.[9]

Formative Literary Influences: Pope to Eliot

Although in both the empiricist and the idealist traditions of philosophy universal and essence are never ultimately dissociated, the emphasis falls differently; sometimes it will be on the universal – man's, but also each individual's, underlying nature; sometimes it will be on the individuated essence – that which instantiates or incorporates the universal. We find both positions in English literary criticism – not surprisingly since both the empiricist and the idealist traditions feed into it and, in different ways, underpin one of its central tenets: great literature penetrates beyond the historically and culturally specific to a realm of universal truth whose counterpart is an essentially unchanging human condition.

Pope, in The Design of his *Essay on Man* declares that 'The Science of Human Nature is, like all other sciences, reduced to a *few clear points*' (his italics); appropriate to this he offers 'a general Map of MAN', one concerned with '*fountains*' rather than 'rivers'. Universal man not only constitutes people as one, over and above the inequalities which apparently divide them, but renders those inequalities quite *inessential*:

> Condition, circumstance is not the thing;
> Bliss is the same in subject or in king,

> Heav'n breathes thro' ev'ry member of the whole
> One common blessing, as one common soul.

> (Epistle IV)

Having cited this passage, it has to be conceded that the ideological use of essentialism though no less powerful in recent times, is rarely so blatant! Samuel Johnson, following Hume, found 'such a Uniformity in the Life of Man . . . that there is scarce any Possibility of Good or Ill, but is common to Human Kind' (*Rambler*, 60). And Shakespeare, says Johnson, depicts human nature in its universal forms, appropriately disregarding the 'Particular manners' of any one of its diverse cultural manifestations; his characters 'are the genuine progeny of common humanity, such as the world will always supply and observation will always find'; they exemplify 'those general passions and principles by which all minds are agitated and the whole system of life is continued in motion'. And all this is so because the poet correctly 'overlooks the casual distinction of country and condition, as a painter, satisfied with the figure, neglects the drapery' (*Preface to Shakespeare*, in *Selected Writings*, pp. 264-7).

Kantian metaphysics, together with that of Fichte and Schelling, finds its way into Romantic criticism through

Coleridge who, searching for 'a truth self-grounded, unconditional and known by its own light' finds it in 'the SUM or I AM, which I shall hereafter indiscriminately express by the words spirit, self, and self-consciousness' (*Biographia Literaria*, pp. 150–1; the conflation of spirit, self and self-consciousness is of course exactly what is at issue). Coleridge's celebrated account of the Primary Imagination (derived from Schelling) is a classic statement of essentialism, but note how it manages to harness the absolute and the teleological as well: 'The primary imagination I hold to be the living power and prime agent of all human perception, and as a repetition in the finite mind of the eternal act of creation in the infinite I AM' (p. 167). Elsewhere, and drawing now on a 'native' tradition, Coleridge speaks of Shakespeare's ability to concentrate upon 'our common nature', an ability which makes him 'the pioneer of true philosophy'. A play like *Lear* is, says Coleridge, representative of 'men in all countries and of all times'; we find in it that 'which in all ages has been, and ever will be, close and native to the heart of man' (*Essays and Lectures on Shakespeare*, pp. 56–7, 126); note how in these two extracts the plural 'men' and the singular 'man' signify one and the same, also how 'heart of man' carries inconspicuously the sense of man as both universal and individuated essence.[10]

Bradley, like Coleridge, is seminal in the development of modern literary criticism and, like him, was significantly influenced by the German idealist tradition. His indebtedness was to Hegel,[11] for whom the imperative 'know thyself' concerned not the individual as such but knowledge of 'man's genuine reality – of what is essentially and ultimately true and real – of mind as the true and essential being' (*Philosophy of Mind*, p. 1). The mind or spirit in question is of course the Hegelian Absolute Spirit, the complexities of which it is unnecessary to enter into here since Bradley's indebtedness to Hegel is tentative, highly qualified and full of a 'painful mystery' all its own (*Shakespearean Tragedy*, p. 38). What is important is that Bradley tends to concentrate upon the Hegelian theme of reconciliation rather than that of dialectical process. Moreover he tends to conceive of absolute spirit not in historical but subjective terms (as a function of 'character'). So, in Shakespearean tragedy, a 'conflict of forces in the hero's soul' becomes the focus for the self-division of an ultimately spiritual power (*Shakespearean Tragedy*, p. 18; *Oxford Lectures*, p. 86). This conflict leads to apotheosis in death: 'In any Shakespearean tragedy we watch some elect spirit colliding, partly through its error and defect, with a superhuman power which bears it down; and yet we feel that this spirit, even in the error and defect, rises by greatness into ideal union with the power that overwhelms it' (*Oxford Lectures*, p. 292; see also chapter 3 above). The importance of this double emphasis in Bradley – reconciliation rather than dialectical process, 'character' rather than history – could hardly be overestimated: those aspects of Hegelian philosophy which he declined, and those which he took up, are crucial for the development of the materialist and the idealist traditions respectively.

Even from this brief summary it is, I hope, apparent that the metaphysical underpinning of Coleridge's and Bradley's criticism operates differently in each case yet also contributes to an important similarity: each sees the individual – creative spirit (Coleridge) or tragic spirit (Bradley) – as a transcendent subject constituted either by an essence in its own right or in an essentialist relationship to the absolute.

Believing their society to be in decline or dangerously off course, many literary critics in the English tradition have seen as even more imperative than usual their task of re-affirming the universal values associated with man's essential nature. Seminal for this school has been Matthew Arnold's affirmation of Culture. Once again absolute and essence are conflated to become the teleological motor of man: 'Religion says: *The Kingdom of God is within you*; and culture, in like manner, places human perfection in an *internal* condition, in the growth and predominance of our humanity proper' (*Culture and Anarchy*, p. 8). Arnold speaks often of this given 'human nature' which it is the function of culture to bring into full flower 'by means of its spiritual standard of perfection' (p. 13). In Arnold's writing we see how important was essentialist humanism in reconstituting criticism as a surrogate theology. Eventually though, Arnold's optimistic humanism would be displaced by a more explicit theology, and one avowedly tragic in its implications.

T. E. Hulme rejected humanism in favour of the so-called 'truths' of dogmatic religion – in particular the dogma of Original Sin. Belief in that dogma goes hand in hand with a naked essentialism, albeit Christian rather than humanist: 'I do not imagine that men themselves will change in any way . . . exactly the same type existed in the Middle Ages as now.' And elsewhere: 'Man is an extraordinarily fixed and limited animal *whose nature is absolutely constant*' (*Speculations*, pp. 58, 116; my italics).

Hulme also insisted on the gulf between the absolute and the relative; to recognise this was to understand 'the religious attitude . . . the tragic significance of life . . . the futility of existence' (pp. 33–4). In this, as in his essentialism, Hulme is representative of much subsequent criticism – especially of tragedy. Hulme explicitly embraces an ideology of absolute and essence, but also a kind of inverted teleology: history and the human present are now understood to be ordered not immanently or naturally, but through the grid of a determining absence. At best, the worst effects of this absence can be curtailed through discipline, order and tradition. Similarly Eliot, writing in the context of his own critique of humanism, asserts: 'It is to the immense credit of Hulme that he found out for himself that there is an *absolute* to which Man can *never* attain' (*Selected Essays*, p. 490; Eliot's italics). Recognition of this gulf constitutes the essence of man: 'Man is man because he can recognise supernatural realities' (p. 485).

Existentialism

To structure the world and define man in terms of a determining absence involves a teleological inversion characteristic not just of the Hulme–Eliot tradition of criticism but also, as we saw in chapter 12, of an influential version of existentialism in which the emphasis is shifted back to the romanticism which Hulme and Eliot deplored. Existentialism in this guise also becomes especially susceptible to a materialist critique; thus Henri Lefebvre saw it as reactionary, the death throes of Romantic egoism, a crisis in the privatised consciousness of the bougeois intellectual – in short, a

neurosis of interiority (*L'Existentialisme*, pp. 227–8). Even those literary critics removed from the excesses of this philosophy of angst
and interiority, took up its essentialist premises. Thus Clifford
Leech suggests that Arthur Miller's *The Death of a Salesman* does
not really qualify for the tragic ticket because in it 'our concern is
sociological rather than with Willie as an *essential* human being: he
is the victim of the American dream rather than of the human condition' (*Tragedy*, p. 38; his italics).

One can see the counterpart of such ideas in the heritage of both
Romanticism and modernism. By making heightened subjectivity
at once self-validating and the state of mind in which 'the types
and symbols of Eternity' were *objectively perceived*, romanticism
incorporated within itself that empiricist problematic against which
it was in part a reaction. But situated thus, the mind of man could
not for long remain exquisitely fitted to the external world. David
Morse has argued persuasively that Romantic discourse in fact dispensed with fixed entities; further, its language 'is plural and per-
spectival; consciousness is dissolved into multiplicity; science
confronts not essences so much as relations. The signature of God
is withdrawn as guarantor of stable and univocal correspondences
and man confronts a shifting and unstable world, in which there is
no longer any one place to begin' (*Perspectives on Romanticism*, p.
101). And yet it is the nihilistic rather than the materialist implications of all this which feed into the 'English' modernist movement.
The relative insularity of that movement from its more radical continental counterparts has many explanations but one reason is
surely a regressive fixation with the essentialist problematic. Thus
Coleridge's 'inanimate cold world' recurs in Keats' 'The weariness,
the fever, and the fret/Here . . .'; Tennyson's 'here . . ./. . . ghastly
thro' the drizzling rain/On the bald street breaks the blank day';
Arnold's 'Dover Beach', and all the other life-denying land and
street scapes through to, and especially including, those of Hardy
and Eliot, Conrad and Beckett. Essentialism in one of its post-
Romantic guises sustains the tragic integrity of those having to
inhabit those alienating spaces. For example, in Hardy's verse, Time
and inanimate nature enervate consciousness with an unhurried
thoroughness: 'Marching Time drew on, and wore me numb' ('A

Broken Appointment'). And yet: so long as that process is acknowledged unflinchingly, consciousness and identity can never be entirely obliterated. A resolve to endure that which cannot be survived, to know it, to set it down in terms of what Hardy called his 'grave, positive, stark, delineations' (Apology to *Late Lyrics*) – this confers on the suffering subject an identity born of stubborn integrity.

The early Eliot goes even further; alienation from the urban landscape is so extreme that consciousness itself fragments: 'The thousand sordid images/Of which your soul was constituted' (*Preludes*). But the unity of the subject is dispersed only to be reconstituted as a disembodied centre of consciousness instantiated by its own suffering, a vulnerability so profoundly redemptive as to enable the subject finally to suffer into truth, moved by 'some infinitely gentle/Infinitely suffering thing'. The subject in Eliot's later verse finds its way back to a 'point of intersection of the timeless/With time', and there achieves a mystical sense of unity not dissimilar to, yet now so much more tentative than, Wordsworth's 'central peace subsisting at the heart of endless agitation'. Others in this tradition have been less successful yet managed nevertheless to vindicate the transcendent subject. It is sustained now by two surrogate universals – the absurdity of the human condition and (once again) consciousness as the grid of a determining absence, the latter now so powerfully conditioning experience and knowledge as to function as a kind of inverted Kantian category of consciousness. Despite this, or maybe because of it, a writer like Beckett (in the words of Edward Bond) 'is said to have made liberal – even capitalist – culture possible. He is said to have shown that however you degrade people an unquenchable spark of humanity remains in them' (*Guardian*, 3. 11. 80, p. 12). Texts like *Waiting for Godot* do indeed sustain those surrogate universals though only by collapsing them almost entirely into the subject where they survive as the forms not of Unchanging Truth but of an etiolated, suffering stasis.

Lawrence, Leavis and Individualism

D. H. Lawrence is a writer-critic seminal in a movement in many ways opposed to both modernism as represented by Hulme and Eliot, and existentialism. Yet he shared with the former at least a dislike of humanism or, more precisely, of democratic humanitarian philosophy. In his essay on Whitman and democracy Lawrence identifies and attacks 'the great ideal of Humanity' (*Selected Essays*, p. 80), an ideal based on a fetishising of 'Average Man' (p. 75). Interestingly Lawrence also attacks the essentialist corollary of humanist ideology proper; he summarises it as follows: 'the Whole is inherent in every fragment . . . every human consciousness has the same intrinsic value . . . because each is an essential part of the Great Consciousness. This is the One Identity which identifies us all' (p. 81). But Lawrence's alternative to this remains within the essentialist problematic. It is an alternative rooted in an uncompromising individualism; for Lawrence 'the Whitman One Identity, the *En Masse*, is a horrible nullification of true identity and being' (p. 85). More generally, when Lawrence asserts that 'once you . . . postulate Universals, you have departed from the creative reality' (p. 88) he articulates an idea which will give impetus to a powerful subsequent movement in literary criticism, one which fetishises the concrete and finds perhaps its most celebrated statement in Leavis' interpretation of Lawrence. It is a movement which is strenuously anti-metaphysical in its polemics, yet which cannot eradicate metaphysics from its own vision. Consider, for example, Lawrence's belief in the creative reality of individuality: 'A man's self is a law unto itself; the living self is 'an unscrutable, unfindable, vivid quick'; it is not, insists Lawrence, *spirit*. On the contrary (and he insists on this too), it is simply there, simply given. We must, he adds, allow 'the soul's own deep desires to come direct, spontaneous into consciousness . . . from the central Mystery into indefinable *presence* . . . The central mystery is no generalised abstraction. It is each man's primal original soul or self, within him' (pp. 89–90). The *transcendent* universal is repudiated only to be collapsed back into its *immanent* counterpart. And teleology is just a few lines further on: 'The living self has one purpose only: to come into its own fullness of being' (p. 91; cf. the reference in *Kangaroo* to the 'absolute . . . the central self, the *isolate, absolute self*', p. 309).

Obviously, there is a sense in which Lawrence's individualism could be positive, in for example his conception of another individual in terms of '*present otherness*' (p. 92). At first this looks like commitment to otherness. Yet, because uniqueness is conceived still as the instantiation of a universal – the 'actual man present before us is an inscrutable and incarnate Mystery' (p. 90) – it works to guard against rather than to comprehend difference. What is foregrounded is not the identity of the other so much as the integrity of the self, the precondition of perceiving this other 'who is himself' being that 'I am my own pure self' (p. 92). Otherness becomes a projection of the self, a foil against which subjective integrity is confirmed. Behind this is a more general concern with 'homogeneous, spontaneous coherence' as against the 'disintegrated amorphousness' which according to Lawrence characterised American life (p. 94; cf. Yeats: 'We Irish, born into that ancient Sect/But thrown upon this filthy modern tide/And by its formless spawning fury wrecked', *Collected Poems*, p. 376).

The 1917–18 essay on Whitman makes explicit the defensive, potentially reactionary nature of Lawrence's individualism; here is an even more urgent affirmation of the soul's integrity: 'the soul wishes to keep clean and whole. The soul's deepest will is to preserve its own integrity, against the mind and the whole mass of disintegrating forces' (p. 274). The unspoken discourse running through this passage is that of power, something which becomes explicit in *Aaron's Rod*: 'yield to the deep power-soul in the individual man, and obey implicitly . . . men must submit to the greater soul in a man. . . and women must submit to the positive power-soul in man, for their being' (p. 347).

Lawrence's fear of the supposedly disintegrative forces in the modern world, especially their effects upon selfhood, is taken up by his most celebrated critic, F. R. Leavis and, more generally, the movement Leavis inspired. He writes of 'the vital intelligence, unthwarted by emotional disorders and divisions in the psyche' which links Lawrence with Blake; there is, says Leavis, no profound emotional disorder in Lawrence, no major disharmony; intelligence is the servant of 'the whole integrated psyche . . . not thwarted or disabled by inner contradictions' (*D. H. Lawrence: Novelist*, pp. 12,

27–8; in fact, the work of recent writers – for example Paul Delany and Kate Millett[12] – suggests rather the opposite). Leavis also finds in Lawrence the familiar universal/essence conjunction: 'the intuition of the oneness of life' which 'expresses itself in an intensity of preoccupation with the individual' (p. 105). This intensity is 'religious' because it moves 'to something transcending the individual' (p. 115), or, reversing the direction of the spiritual metaphor, to a 'depth that involves an impersonal wholeness' (p. 124). What follows is predictable enough: in Lawrence class (for example) is important 'but attention focusses on the *essential humanity*' (p. 88).

Lawrence takes pride of place in the Great Tradition, about which I can only afford the space to remark that what it excludes is the most significant thing about it. Indeed, what is so striking now is just how much not only the Hulme–Eliot but also the Lawrence–Leavis inspired movements wanted to actively exclude and deny; 'tradition', 'essential humanity', 'spontaneous fullness of being', far from being affirmations of 'life' seem now more like a fear of it – in particular a fear of contamination by difference and otherness, a fear of disintegration through democracy and change.

*

Terry Eagleton is surely correct in remarking that since the demise of *Scrutiny* virtually no literary theory of major importance has appeared in Britain ('The Idealism of American Criticism', p. 59). With the significant exception of the cultural materialism of Raymond Williams, it is to America and Europe that we have to look for developments in the post-war period. Yet for all its resourcefulness, American literary theory, as Frank Lentricchia has recently shown, continued the process whereby idealist strategies succeeded one another to keep occluded the historical and material conditions of human existence generally and literary practice specifically. So, for example, Northrop Frye's neo-Kantian reaction to Romantic subjectivism succeeded in recuperating an idealist view of human nature as answering to or evoking the structure of literature, while other critics, influenced now by existentialism, identified the subject in terms of an anguished consciousness situated, in virtue of its capacity to create coherent fictions, in part-transcendence of a chaotic universe. According to Lentricchia, both Frye and the existentialists imply 'a last ditch humanism in which human desire, conscious of itself as "lack", to cite Sartre's term, and conscious of the ontological nothingness of its images, confronts a grim reality which at every point denies us our needs . . . Our "environment" is alien, but . . . its very alien quality beckons forth our creative impulses to make substitutive fictive worlds' (*After the New Criticism*, pp. 33–4; cf. Frank Kermode: 'It is not that we are connoisseurs of chaos, but that we are surrounded by it, and equipped for coexistence with it only by our fictive powers,' *The Sense of an Ending*, p. 64).

The political fatalism among the post-war British intelligentsia has been attributed in part to a form of the same spiritual quietism, one prefigured, argues Edward Thompson, in Auden's verse. If that verse reveals 'a mind in recoil from experiences too difficult and painful to admit of easy solutions', the poet's revision of it indicates a regression to just such a solution, one arguably always latently there in the verse and according to which the traumas of Europe are to be understood not historically but in terms of an underlying human nature and the evil therein (*The Poverty of Theory*, pp. 1–33). William Golding (to take just one other notorious example) has described his novel *Lord of the Flies* as an attempt to trace the defects of society back to the defects of human nature (see the essay 'Fable' in *The Hot Gates*). When existing political conditions are thus thought to be as unalterable as the fixed human condition of which they are, allegedly, only a reflection, then salvation comes, typically, to be located in the pseudo-religious absolute of Personal Integrity (*The Poverty of Theory*, p. 28). Across the years there echoes and re-echoes the disillusion of the radical intelligentsia after the French Revolution: 'from the impulse of a just disdain,/Once more did I retire into myself' (Wordsworth, quoted p. 4 of Thompson). Dressed in existentialist guise it became Colin Wilson's return to religion via the Outsider, a reaffirmation of religion's 'Absolute essential framework', namely that its truth is 'determinable *subjectively* . . . "Truth is subjectivity"' (Kierkegaard)' (*The Outsider*, pp. 284–5).

Such manifestations of essentialism allowed the implications of that uniquely uncompromising exploration of modernist alienation, Conrad's *Nostromo*, to he circumvented. In *Nostromo* we encounter the familiar alienated human condition but in this instance it is devoid even of the attenuated post-Romantic forms of transcendent subjectivity: 'Decoud caught himself entertaining a doubt of his own individuality. It had merged into the world of cloud and water, of natural forces and forms of nature.' Adrift in 'the solitude of the Placid Gulf', and beholding the universe only as 'a succession of incomprehensible images', Decoud shoots himself. The sea into which he falls 'remained untroubled by the fall of his body'; he disappears 'without a trace, swallowed up in the immense indifference of things' (pp. 409, 411–12). Such is the logic of an essentialism finally severed from its absolute counterpart. The absence of that absolute – Coleridge's inanimate cold world, here the immense indifference of things – finally engulfs and dissolves even the petrified subject.

The Decentred Subject

When Lawrence elaborates his philosophy of individualism he reminds us of the derivation of 'individual': that which is not divided, not divisible (*Selected Essays*, p. 86). Materialist analysis tends to avoid the term for just those reasons which led Lawrence to embrace it, preferring instead 'subject'. Because informed by contradictory social and ideological processes, the subject is never an indivisible unity, never an autonomous, self-determining centre of consciousness.

The main historical antecedents of this process of decentring have often been cited: Copernicus displaced man and his planet from their privileged place at the centre of the universe; Darwin showed that the human species is not the *telos* or goal of that universe; Marx displaced man from the centre of history while Freud displaced consciousness as the source of individual autonomy. Foucault adds the decentring effected by the Nietzschean genealogy (an addition which would appropriately challenge the suspiciously sequential coherence of the foregoing 'history' of decentring!): 'What is found at the historical beginning of things is not the inviolable identity of their origin; it is the dissension of other things. It is disparity' (*Language, Counter-Memory, Practice*, p. 142).

Foucault identifies an 'epistemological mutation' of history not yet complete because of the deep resistance to it, a resistance, that is, to 'conceiving of difference, to describing separations and dispersions, to dissociating the reassuring form of the identical' (*Archaeology of Knowledge*, pp. 11–12). He summarises his own task as one of freeing thought from its subjection to transcendence and analysing it 'in the discontinuity that no teleology would reduce in advance; to map it in a dispersion that no pre-established horizon would embrace; to allow it to be deployed in an anonymity on which no transcendental constitution would impose the form of the subject; to open it up to a temporality that would not promise the return of any dawn. My aim was to cleanse it of all transcendental narcissism' (p. 203). Transcendental narcissism validates itself in terms of teleology, the subject, the pre-established horizon; against this Foucault's history charts discontinuity, anonymity, dispersion.

Barthes offers a similar emphasis. To speak positively of the decentred subject is never just to acknowledge his or her contradictions: 'It is a diffraction which is intended, a dispersion of energy in which there remains neither a central core nor a structure of meaning: I am not contradictory, I am dispersed' (*Roland Barthes*, p. 143); 'today the subject apprehends himself *elsewhere*' (p. 168). This entails not only a non-centred conception of identity but, correspondingly, a non-centred form of political awareness: 'According to Freud . . . one touch of difference leads to racism. But a great deal of difference leads away from it, irremediably. To equalize, democratize, homogenize – all such efforts will never manage to expel "the tiniest difference", seed of racial intolerance. For that one must pluralize, refine, continuously' (p. 69). Sexual transgression is affirmed while recognising that it tends to carry within itself a limiting inversion of the normative regime being transgressed (pp. 64–5, 133). The more radical alternative to sexual liberation through transgression is a release of sexuality from meaning. Then there would be, for example, not homosexuality but '*homosexualities*' 'whose plural will baffle any constituted, centred discourse' (p. 69).

This dimension of post-structuralist theory arouses justifiable suspicion for seeming to advance subjective decentring simply in terms of the *idea* of an anarchic refusal adequate unto itself, thereby recuperating anti-humanism in terms of the idealism it rejects and rendering the subject so completely dispersed as to be incapable of acting as any agent, least of all an agent of change. Equally though, this criticism itself runs the risk of disallowing the positive sense of the ideal cited earlier – that which in virtue of its present unreality affirms known potentialities from within existing, stultifying, social realities. Ideologically ratified, those 'realities' become not merely an obstacle to the realisation of potential, to the possibility of social change, but work to make both potential and change literally unthinkable. This is why, quite simply, a vision of decentred subjectivity, like any other vision of liberation, cannot be divorced from a critique of existing social realities and their forms of ideological legitimation. It is here that we might, finally, invoke an earlier emphasis in Barthes' work. In *Mythologies* he reminded us that the myth of the human condition 'consists in placing Nature at the bottom of History'; to thus eternalise the nature of man is to render the destiny of people apparently unalterable. Hence the necessity to reverse the terms, to find history behind nature and thereby reveal nature itself as an ideological construct preempting change (*Mythologies*, p. 101).

Perhaps this remains the most important objective in the decentring of man, one which helps make possible an alternative conception of the relations between history, society and subjectivity, and invites that '*affirmation* which *then determines the noncentre otherwise than as loss of the centre*' (Derrida, *Writing and Difference*, p. 292; his italics). It is a radical alternative which, in the context of materialist analysis, helps vindicate certain objectives: not essence but potential, not the human condition but cultural difference, not destiny but collectively identified goals.

Notes

Chapter 1: Contexts

1. For a brief account of the critical controversies surrounding Webster, see the Critical Bibliography in Jonathan Dollimore and Alan Sinfield, eds, *The Selected Plays of John Webster*.
2. James reigned between 1603 and 1625; for convenience I use 'Jacobean' to denote the drama which appeared from around 1600 to 1625.
3. Hiram Haydn, *The Counter Renaissance*, p. 14.
4. Christopher Hill, *The Intellectual Origins of the English Revolution*; see also Margot Heinemann, *Puritanism and Theatre*.
5. The crucial role played by the bourgeoisie was not to *lead* a revolution so much as to 'sweep away the social and political institutions that had hindered the growth of bourgeois property and the social relations that went with it' (I. Deutscher, *The Unfinished Revolution*, cited on p. 280 of Hill's *Change and Continuity in Seventeenth Century England*).
6. Louis Althusser, *Lenin and Philosophy*, pp. 121–3.
7. See Joel Hurstfield, 'The Politics of Corruption in Shakespeare's England', especially p. 24.
8. These advances make it necessary for us also to analyse the practice of literary criticism; as Pierre Macherey observes, what any text signifies is inseparable from the history of its interpretations: 'Literary works are not only produced, they are constantly reproduced under different conditions – and so they themselves become very different' (*Interview*, p. 6). This point is independent of Macherey's dubious proposition, in the same interview, that 'all the interpretations which have been attached to [works] are finally incorporated into them' (p. 7).
9. It is impossible to summarise adequately the transition in a few words or indeed to mark its parameters, but Brian Easlea begins his recent and intriguing study of 'this dramatic transformation in human thought' as follows: 'In 1500 educated people in western Europe believed themselves living at the centre of a finite cosmos, at the mercy of (supernatural) forces beyond their control, and certainly continually menaced by Satan and his allies. By 1700 educated people in western Europe for the most part believed themselves living in an infinite universe on a tiny planet in (elliptical) orbit about the sun, no longer menaced by Satan, and confident that power over the natural world lay within their grasp' (*Witch Hunting, Magic and the New*

Philosophy, p. 1). Historians often remind us that – in the words of Lawrence Stone – 'the real watershed between medieval and modern England' was the period 1580–1620 (*Crisis of the Aristocracy*, p. 15). On some of the social, economic and political changes of this period see also Conrad Russell, *The Crisis of Parliaments*, especially pp. 195–217.

10. The literature on ideology is immense; the following books make accessible the most important issues: Centre for Contemporary Cultural Studies, *On Ideology*; Jorge Larrain, *The Concept of Ideology*; Göran Therborn, *The Ideology of Power and the Power of Ideology*.

11. This charge of atheism was made against Marlowe the day before he was murdered in May 1593; his accuser was Richard Baines (British Museum: Harleian ms 6848 fol. 185–6). The Baines document is reprinted in C. F. Tucker Brooke's *The Life of Marlowe*, pp. 98-100; the Marx passage is from the introduction to *Contribution to the Critique of Hegel's Philosophy of Right*, and can be found in *Early Writings*, ed. T. B. Bottomore, p. 44.

12. The cognitive conception of ideology is clearly related to the preoccupation in this period with the appearance–reality dichotomy. This preoccupation did not suddenly emerge in the early seventeenth century but the particular form it took at this time does contribute to what Herschel Baker has called 'one of the major revolutions in modem thought: the conviction that the world is not as it seems, and that "truth" lies buried somewhere beneath the swarming, misunderstood presentations of sense' (*The Wars of Truth*, pp. 331–2). Particularly important was the empiricist and materialist emphasis given to this view in the work of Bacon and Hobbes. Distinguishing between appearance and reality becomes a potentially revolutionary strategy for arguing against entrenched systems of belief (see Kathryn Russell, 'Science and Ideology', p. 186).

13. The critique of religion as ideology – in particular its mystification of power relations – is consolidated in the early decades of the seventeenth century; by the time of Winstanley it is uncompromising: 'The former hell of prisons, whips and gallows they [the clergy] preached to keep the people in subjection to the king; but by this divined hell after death they preach to keep both king and people in awe to them, to uphold their trade of tithes and new raised maintenance. And so . . . they become the god that rules.' Winstanley also saw the way dominant power structures remained even after individuals had gone: 'That which is yet wanting on your [i.e., Cromwell's] part to be done is this, to see the oppressor's power to be cast out with his person' (*The Law of Freedom*, pp. 299, 275).

14. For a discussion of this passage and the play as a whole see Margot Heinemann, *Puritanism and Theatre*, pp. 40–3.

15. All of the plays which figure in this study involve some statement of relativism – as indeed do many other texts of the period. Thus Hamlet declares 'there is nothing either good or bad, but thinking makes it so' (II. ii. 249–50); while Donne's 'The Progress of the Soul' concludes with these lines: 'There's nothing simply good, nor ill alone,/Of every quality comparison,/The only measure is, and judge, opinion.' Relativism could be (and

remains) potentially either conservative or radical in its implications. The belief that there is no universal order or ultimate truth can be used to legitimate the status quo: what exists is as valid as anything that might exist. Conversely, relativism can rob that existing order of the ideological legitimation (e.g. the appeal to the authority of the universal) which, historically, it has almost inevitably depended upon. In those plays discussed here it is the second conception which predominates.

16. Throughout I use 'man' not neutrally but as a concept with essentialist implications; where I mean 'people' (women and men) or 'human kind', I try to say so.

17. Throughout I use 'radical' in this second, general, sense; cf. *Webster's Third New International Dictionary* which defines it as 'marked by a considerable departure from the usual or traditional'. It is a use which concurs with that of the editors of a recent *Biographical Dictionary of British Radicals in the Seventeenth Century*, who, 'in the proper etymological sense of the term . . . define radicals as those who sought fundamental change by striking at the very root of contemporary assumptions and institutions' (p. viii). The distinction noted here in relation to Montaigne, the editors invoke in relation to Hobbes; they remark that his inclusion in such a dictionary might seem anomalous but justify it, quite rightly, because 'his influence on the Commonwealth was so critical, his concept of a supremely autonomous sovereign so subversive of conventionally established authority, and his secularist and materialist politics so revolutionary in their implications' (Richard Greaves and Robert Zaller, eds, p. xiii). Michael Walzer in *The Revolution of the Saints* uses 'radical' somewhat more inclusively, identifying in the period 'revolutionary organisation and radical ideology' and also 'the development of a theory of progress' – itself a sign of 'the new political spirit, the new sense of activity and its possibilities, the more radical imagination, that mark the sixteenth and seventeenth centuries' (pp. 1, 12).

18. Quoted in V. C. Gildersleeve, *Government Regulation of the Elizabethan Drama*, p. 101.

19. James I said: 'I mean to make use of all religions to compass my ends' (C. V. Wedgwood, *The Thirty Years War*, pp. 190–1). An intriguing instance of just how blatantly the sermon could be at the service of the state is provided by James's attempt to curb cross-dressing: 'Yesterday the bishop of London called together all his Clergie about this towne, and told them he had expresse commaundment from the King to will them to inveigh vehemently and bitterly in theyre sermons against the insolencie of our women, and theyre wearing of [male attire] . . . by adding withall that yf pulpit admonitions will not reforme them he wold proceed by another course' (*The Letters of John Chamberlain*, II, 286–9; cf. Webster, *The White Devil*, III. ii. 245–9).

20. The apprentices also attacked the theatres themselves although the reasons are not clear. Ann Jennalie Cook argues that this was because the theatres were an expensive pleasure denied the apprentices. The evidence, however, seems inconclusive – see Sara Pearl's review of Cook's *The Privileged Playgoers* in *The Times Literary Supplement*, 29.1.82, p. 100.

21. Alternatively the objection might be that this kind of analysis is too abstract to speak to the 'theatrical experience' of these plays. Arguably, what passes for such experience is itself susceptible to Brecht's famous criticism of 'empathy' (*Einfühlung*; see *Brecht on Theatre*, index). But even taking the objection on its own terms it is misconceived: the antimasque scenes like those discussed in the following section are some of the most rudely theatrical in Jacobean drama; at the same time they are thoroughly subversive in a way which is (let's admit it) intellectual.

22. Stephen Orgel, *The Illusion of Power*; Stuart Clark, 'Inversion, Misrule and the Meaning of Witchcraft'; Louis Montrose, '"Eliza, Queene of Shepheardes" and the Pastoral of Power'.

23. See Peter Burke, *Popular Culture in Modern Europe,* especially chapter 7, 'The World of Carnival'; Natalie Zemon Davis, 'Women on Top: Symbolic Sexual Inversion and Political Disorder in Early Modem Europe'; David Kunzle, 'World Turned Upside Down: The Iconography of a European Broadsheet Type'.

24. Like the play within a play in *The Spanish Tragedy* and *Hamlet*, the antic or antimasque confronts the court with its own corruption.

Chapter 2: Emergence: Marston's *Antonio* Plays and Shakespeare's *Troilus and Cressida*

1. To see it as such is still an orthodoxy: 'Divine vengeance forms the narrative and thematic centre of *each* revenge play' (R. Broude, 'Revenge and Revenge Tragedy in Renaissance England', p. 55; my italics).

2. Compare Montaigne, who says that man is 'fast tied and nailed to the worst, most senselesse, and drooping part of the world' (*Essays*, II, 142).

3. Most notably, of course, in the first book of his *Laws*.

4. This is argued by Williarn R. Elton in 'Shakespeare's Ulysses and the Problem of Value'.

5. This claim is not anachronistic: such a counter-perspective was available in the early seventeenth century – see chapter 15 below.

Chapter 3: Structure: From Resolution to Dislocation

1. For further analyses of this tradition, see Terry Eagleton, *Criticism and Ideology*, especially chapter 1; Terence Hawkes, *Structuralism and Semiotics*, especially chapter 5; Francis Mulherne, *The Moment of Scrutiny*; Frank Lentricchia, *After the New Criticism*.

2. Correspondingly, Walter Benjamin's defence and elucidation of Brechtian epic theatre had its origins in Benjamin's own analysis of German seventeenth-century tragedy. Terry Eagleton makes this point and also usefully explores the relevance of Benjamin's work on the *Trauerspiel* for seventeenth-century English literature (*Walter Benjamin*, chapter 1); for a brief but suggestive application of Benjamin's ideas to Elizabethan drama, see

Charles Rosen's review article (of John Osborne's translation of Benjamin's *The Origin of German Tragic Drama*) 'The Ruins of Walter Benjamin'.

3. This and the next section concentrate on some 'founding fathers' of twentieth-century criticism of Jacobean drama. This is not to imply that their aesthetic and tragic categories have remained unchanged in the work of more recent critics. However, the change that has occurred has often been within the framework of these earlier theorists and, more generally, of philosophical idealism (see, for example, chapter 12). Another tendency has been for the older categories to be obliquely rather than confidently affirmed; here, the virtually complete absence of new theoretical work in this country in the post-war period is an important factor (see chapter 16).

4. This emphasis in Bradley – one which may fairly be described as redemptive – is developed as part of his rejection of a confident Christian providentialism and suggests why it is wrong to assume that the redemptive view of, say, *King Lear* is confined to Christian interpretations (the implication of Michael Long's discussion of the play in *The Unnatural Scene*, especially pp. 186–7).

5. The opposition between coherent fiction and chaotic reality becomes 'one of modernism's characterizing shibboleths' (Lentricchia, *After the New Criticism*, p. 54).

6. Thus Archer complained of Bosola that he was 'full of contradictions', adding: 'there is no difficulty in making a character inconsistent; the task of the artist is to show an underlying harmony between the apparently conflicting elements' (quoted from G. K. and S. K. Hunter, p. 84). For the survival of this view into recent times, see, for example, Wilbur Sanders' claim that 'what made "construction" impossible to Webster was a failure to perceive the human significance of the "characters" he had "introduced" so promisingly. He was unable to discover the question he wanted to put to them' (*Essays in Criticism*, p. 186).

7. Suggestive departures from both perspectives include the following: H. B. Parkes, 'Nature's Diverse Laws: the Double Vision of the Elizabethans'; Una Ellis-Fermor, *The Frontiers of Drama*; Arnold Hauser, *Mannerism: the Crisis of the Renaissance and the Origin of Modern Art*; W. R. Elton, 'Shakespeare and the Thought of His Age'; Stanley Fish, *Self-Consuming Artifacts*; Michael McCanles, *Dialectical Criticism and Renaissance Literature*.

8. Cf. *The Messingkauf Dialogues*: 'true realism has to do more than just make reality recognisable in the theatre. One has to be able to see through it . . . to see the laws that decide how the processes of life develop. These laws can't be spotted by the camera' (p. 27).

9. John Russell Brown, ed., *The Duchess of Malfi*, p. xxiii and Lois Potter, 'Realism and Nightmare: Problems of Staging *The Duchess of Malfi*'.

10. The allusion to Sidney is most obvious in Bosola's remark a few moments later: 'In what a shadow, or deep pit of darkness,/Doth womanish and fearful mankind live' (V. v. 100–1). The source for this is a passage from *Arcadia* – which also includes Bosola's image of the tennis balls: 'In such a shadow or rather pit of darkness the wormish mankind lives, that neither they know how to foresee nor what to fear, and are but like tennis balls, tossed by the

racket *of higher powers*' (p. 817; my italics). In the sentence which precedes this passage Sidney refers also to 'the strange and secret working of justice' thus subordinating the idea to precisely that which Webster uses it to subvert.

11. See also R. B. Parker, 'Dramaturgy in Shakespeare and Brecht'.

12. Roland Barthes' essay 'The Death of the Author' has been at the centre of a new round in the old controversy over authorial intention – a controversy which continues to set up false oppositions. If, as here, our concern is with historical process, and if we allow that this is, with whatever difficulty. retro- spectively accessible, then several kinds of relationship between author and text can be allowed in principle though not necessarily established in prac- tice. The author is never the autonomous source of meaning, but the articu- lation of historical process which may be present in the author's text might well be intentional (in the case of, say, Brecht, it wouldn't make sense to conceive of it otherwise). On the other hand, aspects of that historical process may be unconsciously pulled into focus because, irrespective of intention, it is already there in the language, forms, conventions, genres being used. In this second case the critic will be dis-covering that of which the author is unaware. Yet another kind of analysis may involve bringing a more or less completely effaced history to the text. The question of intention is not irrelevant then, but it does seem less important than the fact that his- torical process is as much there in what we identify as culture, language and art, as in what we identify as overt political process. Presumably no single text can ever adequately address its own historical moment – no more than can the critic. This does not obviate the pressing need to bring history to the text as well as reading history *through* and *in* it. Foucault's essay 'What is an Author?' (in *Language, Counter-Memory, Practice*) is an important contribu- tion to the debate although his emphasis is different from mine. See also Janet Wolff, *The Social Production of Art*, chapter 6.

13. Realist mimesis denotes not a transhistorical reality but, rather, emergent categories of objectivity demonstrably closer to our own than those being displaced. Philosophically, realism has two, virtually opposite, meanings. As contrasted with nominalism, realism is the theory that universals have a reality of their own; as contrasted with idealism, realism affirms the independ- ent existence of the external world. My usage derives from this second sense and overlaps with materialism.

Chapter 4: Renaissance Literary Theory: Two Concepts of Mimesis

1. On the theory, history and development of the concept of mimesis, see Erich Auerbach, *Mimesis*; E. Panofsky, *Idea: A Concept in Art Theory*, especially p. 47; William K. Wimsatt and Cleanth Brooks, *Literary Criticism: A Short History*, especially p. 26; Arnold Hauser, *The Social History of Art: Renaissance, Mannerism and Baroque*, especially p. 2; W. Tatarkiewicz, *History of Aesthetics*, especially I, 144.

2. And, even, in the work of earlier writers; M. A. Quinlan in *Poetic Justice in the Drama* lists, among others, Ascham, Gascoigne and Whetstone as being aware of, and sympathetic to, the idea. Quinlan rightly observes that because of the growing opposition to drama, especially in the form of censorship, 'it was far more necessary for the defenders to justify the drama on the grounds of morality than to show that its chief end was to please' (p. 30).

3. Quoted in Clarence C. Green, *The Neo-Classic Theory of Tragedy in England*, p. 141.

4. Compare F. Patrizi: 'the poet similarly [to the painter] can either paint a likeness, or express fantasies of his own devising, which have no counterpart in the world of art or nature, nor in God's universe' (*Della Poetica*, 1586, p. 91).

5. Sidney also speaks of the 'erected wit' knowing what perfection is but being prevented from reaching unto it by the 'infected will' (p. 101); G. F. Waller finds in this passage a dialectical relation between the Magical tradition (represented by Bruno) which emphasises the power of the mind to aspire and transform, and Calvin's denunciation of man – a relation which created in England in the late sixteenth century 'an intellectual flashpoint of some power' ('This Matching of Contraries: Bruno, Calvin and the Sidney Circle', p. 336).

6. See also p. 55; J. W. H. Atkins offers a similar interpretation in *English Literary Criticism: the Renaissance*, p. 120.

7. The conflict between realism and didacticism which was coming into especial prominence at this time can be seen from Chapman's dedication to *The Revenge of Bussy D'Ambois*: 'For the authentical truth of either person or action, who (worth the respecting) will expect it in a poem, whose subject is not truth, but things like truth? Poor envious souls they are that cavil at truth's want in these natural fictions; material instruction, elegant and sententious excitation to virtue, and deflection from her contrary, being the soul, limbs, and limits of an authentical tragedy.'

8. All references to Bacon are to the one-volume edition of the *Works* (ed. John M. Robertson) although titles of individual works are also given.

9. In *Descriptio Globi Intellectualis* this alignment of philosophy is even more explicit: 'In philosophy the mind is bound to things' (p. 677).

10. That Bacon had this kind of drama in mind is suggested by his remark in *Novum Organum* to the effect that 'stories invented for the stage are more compact and elegant, and more as one would wish them to be, than true stories of history' (p. 270).

11. In *Poems and Dramas of Fulke Greville*, ed. Bullough, vol. I.

12. Cf. stanzas 103 and 110; Greville's view of the painter differs from Sidney's: see *Apology*, p. 102.

13. In fact, Greville's 'images of life' closely resemble the 'images of true matters' which Sidney sees as the historian's rather than the poet's true concern (*Apology*, p. 109).

14. Maclean, 'Greville's Poetic', pp. 170–91 and Sidney, *Apology*, p. 102.

15. Greville thus makes explicit some of the profound intellectual conflicts latent

in the theatre of his day – as Ellis-Fermor argued in *The Jacobean Drama*, chapter 10; see also Paula Bennett, 'Recent Studies in Greville', p. 379.

Chapter 5: The Disintegration of Providentialist Belief

1. See, for example, G. T. Buckley, *Atheism in the English Renaissance*; P. H. Kocher, *Christopher Marlowe: A Study of His Thought, Learning and Character*; E. A. Strathmann, *Sir Walter Raleigh: A Study in Elizabethan Scepticism*; D. C. Allen, *Doubt's Boundless Sea: Scepticism and Faith in the Renaissance*; William R. Elton, *King Lear and the Gods*, especially pp. 42–57; Christopher Hill, *The World Turned Upside Down*, chapter 8. G. E. Aylmer, in a recent survey of the evidence, represents the 'popular scoffers and blasphemers' as not the same as real 'unbelievers' ('Unbelief in Seventeenth Century England', p. 23). This is, surely, to overlook an important point: blasphemy and scoffing were often a refusal of religiously mystified authority – a refusal which attacked the heart of the mystification – and, as such, their potential subversiveness was not neutralised by the fact that the individuals concerned might not be fully committed atheists.

2. The composition of the Elizabethan/Jacobean theatre audiences is still a topic of dispute. Recently Ann Jennalie Cook has argued, convincingly, that more of the privileged attended the theatres than was once thought to be the case (see her *The Privileged Playgoers of Shakespeare's London*). Many of these were the new rich and the upwardly mobile who were likely to be sceptical of traditional forms of ideological legitimation of the dominant order. Although Cook stresses the diversity of occupation and background among these groups, she also implies that their monopoly of land, education and wealth gave them more of a hegemonic unity than in fact was the case. It is worth remembering that there already existed within these groupings some of the conflicts which would generate a civil war.

   Margot Heinemann points out that even in the private theatres the audiences included 'many groups who were interested in new, potentially subversive, thinking and who later provided the nucleus of Parliamentarian criticism and opposition to the Crown – lawyers and law students; gentry up in London on legal or Parliamentary business; richer citizens and merchants; and, among the greater gentry and nobility, some who were sharply critical of the changes at the new Court. It is significant that several of the plays which fell afoul of the Royal censorship in these years (*Eastward Ho, The Isle of Gulls, Philotas*) were written for the private theatres' ('Shakespearean Contradictions and Social Change', p. 11). In some ways the traditional emphasis on the diversity of Shakespeare's audience still holds good, although with the important qualification that (in this study at least) there is no longer a concern to establish its shared sub-stratum of (orthodox) belief. Further, whatever the difficulties of establishing the exact composition of that audience, we can be sure that the theatres were transmitting ideas which had, hitherto, been more or less the property of an intellectual elite. As I indicated earlier, it is this fact of transmission, as well as the nature of the ideas themselves, which made the theatres potentially subversive.

3. See Glynne Wickham, *Early English Stages*, vol. II, part I, pp. 82, 85.

4. On the specifically political exploitation of providentialist ideology, see W. H. Greenleaf, *Order, Empiricism, Politics 1500–1700*, especially chapters 2–7.

5. On *Richard II* see Graham Holderness, 'Shakespeare's History: *Richard II*'.

6. Other critics who have advocated this idea include Willard Thorpe, *The Triumph of Realism in Elizabethan Drama*, pp. 137–8; David Horowitz, *Shakespeare: An Existential View*, p. 125; John Holloway, *The Story of the Night*, pp. 94–5; J. M. R. Margeson, *The Origins of English Tragedy*, pp. 8, 143.

7. For a summary of the diverse senses of nature and natural law in the period, see Haydn, *The Counter-Renaissance*, pp. 461–8.

8. See Williamson, 'Mutability, Decay, and Seventeenth Century Melancholy'; Harris, *All Coherence Gone*; Haydn, *The Counter-Renaissance*, pp. 524–44.

9. See also H. R. Patch, *The Goddess Fortuna in Medieval Literature*.

10. Cosmic decay needs also to be distinguished from the principle of renaissance contrariety which Robert Grudin has explored in *Mighty Opposites: Shakespeare and Renaissance Contrariety*. Grudin shows how Baldassare Castiglione, Paracelsus, Bruno and Montaigne develop the idea of an interaction of contraries as a primary force of experience. Its difference from cosmic decay lies in the fact that this principle was generally conceived as 'positive and regenerative' (p. 3; see also pp. 18, 19–20, 22 and 35).

11. Hakewill's attack on Goodman, entitled *Apologie or Declaration of the Power and Providence of God*, appeared in 1627. For a detailed account of the controversy see Harris, *All Coherence Gone*.

12. John Jonston, *An History of the Constancy of Nature*, 1657, p. 2, quoted on p. 84 of Baker, *The Wars of Truth*.

13. Further see Haydn, *The Counter-Renaissance*, chapter 4; Peter Berger, *The Social Reality of Religion*, pp. 111–13; Charles Webster, ed., *The Intellectual Revolution of the Seventeenth Century*, chapters 16–24.

14. And of course Luther: 'This is the highest degree of faith . . . to believe Him righteous when by His own will He makes us necessarily damnable' (*Luther and Erasmus*, ed. E. G. Rupp, p. 138).

15. There was also a strategic factor at work here; Calvin's writing, because it 'possessed the great political virtue of ambiguity . . . was subject not so much to a private process of internalisation . . . as to a public process of development, accretion, distortion, and use' (Walzer, *The Revolution of the Saints*, p. 23).

16. On Calvin's insistence on taking cognisance of the empirical and phenomenal aspects of existence, see Charles Trinkaus, 'Renaissance Problems in Calvin's Theology', especially pp. 61–2.

Chapter 6: *Dr Faustus*: Subversion Through Transgression

1. This concept, originating in a classification of Benveniste's, is developed by Catherine Belsey in *Critical Practice*, chapter 4.
2. Still important for this perspective is Nicholas Brooke's 1952 article, 'The Moral Tragedy of Doctor Faustus'.
3. The Manichean implications of protestantism are apparent from this assertion of Luther's: 'Christians know there are two kingdoms in the world, which are bitterly opposed to each other. In one of them Satan reigns . . . He holds captive to his will all who are not snatched away from him by the Spirit of Christ . . . In the other Kingdom, Christ reigns, and his kingdom ceaselessly resists and makes war on the kingdom of Satan' (*Luther and Erasmus*, ed. Rupp, pp. 327–8; see also Peter Lake, *Moderate Puritans and the Elizabethan Church*, pp. 144–5). J. P. Brockbank, in a discussion of the Manichean background of *Dr Faustus*, notes similarities between Faustus and the Manichean bishop of the same name mentioned by Augustine in the *Confessions* – himself an adherent of the Manichean faith for nine years; on Manicheanism generally, see also John Hick, *Evil and the God of Love*, chapter 3.
4. Cf. Walzer: 'The imagery of warfare was constant in Calvin's writing'; specifically of course, warfare between God and Satan (*The Revolution of the Saints*, p. 65).
5. Cf. C. Burges, *The First Sermon* (1641): 'A man once married to the Lord by covenant may without arrogancy say: this righteousness is my righteousness . . . this loving kindness, these mercies, this faithfulness, which I see in thee . . . is mine, for my comfort . . . direction, salvation, and what not' (p. 61; quoted from Conrad Russell, *Crisis of Parliaments*, p. 204).
6. Margaret Walters reminds us how Christian iconography came to glorify masochism, especially in its treatment of crucifixion. Adoration is transferred from aggressor to victim, the latter suffering in order to propitiate a vengeful, patriarchal God (*The Nude Male*, p. 10; see also pp. 72–5). Faustus' transgression becomes subversive in being submissive yet the reverse of propitiatory.

Chapter 7: *Mustapha*: Ruined Aesthetic, Ruined Theology

1. Ronald Rebholz argues that Greville probably wrote *Mustapha* between 1594 and 1596 and made his extensive revisions of it around 1607–10 (*Life*, pp. 101–2, n. 42, 329–31). The later version is the text of the editions of both Bullough and Rees, and is the one followed here.
2. On Greville as a radical protestant see Rebholz, chapter 2; Greville's experience of that dilemma led him, argues Rebholz, from 'the optimism of a Protestant humanist to an extreme Christian pessimism' (*Life*, p. xxiv).
3. On Greville's attempts to reconcile stoicism and Christianity, and his difficulty in so doing, see Rebholz, especially pp. 84–5, 104, 219.
4. It has recently been established that this annotation was made by Sir Kenelm

Digby, who may have seen the play through the press – see W. Hilton Kelliher, 'The Warwick Manuscripts of Fulke Greville', pp. 117–18.

5. Compare *Mustapha*, IV. iv. 6: 'Change hath her periods, and is natural'.

6. Quoted from D. P. Walker, *The Decline of Hell*, pp. 57, 200; see also Walker's interesting discussion of Bayle on Manicheanism, pp. 53–8, 178–201.

7. Greville's criticism of the church in this respect was not confined to that of Rome; eventually it was to include his own: see, for example, *Treatise of Religion*, especially stanzas 24, 62–3, 68, 82, 99, 169.

8. On some of the contemporary political implications of Greville's surviving plays see Rebholz (pp. 101–8, 132-6, 200–5), and in particular his argument that Greville's revisions of *Mustapha* make it even more explicitly a critique of James I and his court.

Chapter 8: *Sejanus*: History and *Realpolitik*

1. See, especially, Stephen Greenblatt's discussion of the contradictions in Renaissance providentialist historiography as they affect Raleigh's *History of the World* (*Sir Walter Ralegh*, chapter 5); Peter Burke, *The Renaissance Sense of the Past*; Moody E. Prior, *The Drama of Power: Studies in Shakespeare's History Plays*, chapter 2, 'Ideas of History'.

2. See *History*, p. 80, also Ben Jonson, *Works*, ed. Herford and Simpson, vols. II, 4–5 and IX, 589.

Chapter 9: *The Revenger's Tragedy*: Providence, Parody and Black Camp

1. I am assuming nothing, nor contributing to the debate, about the authorship of this play.

2. Archer, *The Old Drama and the New*, p. 74; John Peter, *Complaint and Satire in Early English Literature*, p. 268. Instead of Archer's indignation, or Peter's rendering of the play respectable, another tradition of critics showed a deep fascination with 'Tourneur's' psychopathology. Thus J. Churton Collins writes that 'Sin and misery, lust and cynicism, fixed their fangs deep in his splendid genius, marring and defacing his art, poisoning and paralysing the artist' (*The Plays and Poems*, p. lvi), while T. S. Eliot, described the motive of the *Revenger's Tragedy* as 'truly the death motive, for it is the loathing and horror of life itself' (*Selected Essays*, p. 190).

3. These arguments are more fully outlined, and contested, in Jonathan Dollimore, 'Two Concepts of Mimesis: Renaissance Literary Theory and *The Revenger's Tragedy*', pp. 38–43.

4. This is, perhaps, the 'pose of indignant morality' that Archer detected (*The Old Drama and the New*, p. 74) but misunderstood. But even Archer had misgivings: 'One cannot, indeed, quite repress a suspicion that Tourneur wrote with his tongue in his cheek' (p. 75). Indeed one cannot!

5. If, as seems probable, *The Revenger's Tragedy* was written after May 1606,

such obliquity may, apart from anything else, have been an effective way of avoiding a tangle with the statute of that month to restrain 'Abuses of Players'. This Act not only forbade the player to 'jestingly or profanely speak or use the holy name of God or of Jesus Christ, or of the Holy Ghost or of the Trinity', but also commanded that the same were not to be spoken of at all 'but with *feare and reverence*' (my italics). It is precisely this kind of 'feare and reverence' which is being parodied. The statute is reprinted in W. C. Hazlitt, *The English Drama and Stage*, p. 42.

6. See also J. M. R. Margeson, *The Origins of English Tragedy*, p. 136; G. Boklund has demonstrated how Webster uses repeated ironic reversals for an entirely different purpose – namely, to demonstrate that it is 'chance, independent of good and evil' which governs events in *The Duchess of Malfi* (*The Duchess of Malfi: Sources, Themes, Characters*, pp. 129–30). Webster's *The Devil's Law-Case* offers an overt parody of peripeteias and providentialist intervention not dissimilar to that found in *The Revenger's Tragedy* (see especially III. ii. 147–58).

7. From R. J. Hollingdale's selection, *Essays and Aphorisms*, pp. 51–4; for a complete edition of *Parerga and Paralipomena*, see E. F. J. Payne's two-volume translation.

8. See *The Works of Cyril Tourneur*, ed. A. Nicoll, pp. 16–18.

9. *Ibid.*, p. 275.

10. Compare Hobbes: 'I put for a general inclination of all mankind, a perpetual and restless desire of power after power, that ceaseth only in death' (*Leviathan*, chapter 11).

11. Compare Shakespeare's *Timon*: 'thou wouldst have plunged thyself/In general riot, *melted* down thy youth/In different beds of lust' (IV. iii. 256–8), and Spenser's Redcrosse, with 'The false Duessa', 'Pourd out in loosnesse on the grassy grownd,/Both carelesse of his health, and of his fame' (*The Faerie Queene*, I. 7. 7).

12. Compare Montaigne: 'Men misacknowledge the naturall infirmatie of their minde. She doth but quest and firret, and vncessantly goeth turning, winding, building and entangling her selfe in hir own worke; as doe our silke-wormes, and therein stiffleth hir self' (*Essays*, III, 325). This image was a popular one, and the Montaigne passage was twice borrowed by Webster (see J. W. Dent, *John Webster's Borrowings*, p. 85).

Chapter 10: Subjectivity and Social Process

1. Instead of a theatre which presents events 'as an inexorable fate, to which the individual is handed over helpless despite the beauty and significance of his reactions', Brecht advocates one in which fate itself is studied closely and shown to be of human contriving (*Brecht on Theatre*, p. 87).

2. *Considerations on Western Marxism*, pp. 59–67; on Althusser, Anderson claims that nearly all his novel concepts were drawn from Spinoza.

3. I should emphasise here that my criticism is, specifically, of humanism in its essentialist manifestations. The significance of any concept or movement in

thought changes across history and essentialist humanism is very different from, say, those humanistic trends in the Renaissance which facilitated real though relative possibilities of intellectual liberation. The validity of other forms of humanism is not my concern here.

4. Compare Conrad Russell: 'The notion of every man in his place was hard to combine with the effect of inflation on the social structure' (*The Crisis of Parliaments*, p. 196).

5. On the concern in Jacobean tragedy with 'the growth and concentration of state power' see J. W. Lever, *The Tragedy of State*, especially p. 4.

6. On the relationship of Renaissance humanism to Christianity see Charles Trinkaus, *In Our Image and Likeness: Humanity and Divinity in Italian Humanist Thought*, and Hiram Haydn, *The Counter-Renaissance*, pp. 27–75.

7. Raymond Williams comments interestingly on this question of anticipation – using Hobbes and Jacobean drama as his examples – in *Politics and Letters*, pp. 161–2.

8. And nominalism, the belief that universals like 'man' have no referents: 'things named are everyone of them singular and individual' (*Leviathan*, chapter 4).

9. On Hobbes see further Christopher Hill, *Puritanism and Revolution*, chapter 9, 'Thomas Hobbes and the Revolution in Political Thought'.

10. See also Anthony Wilden's chapter on Montaigne and the paradoxes of individualism in *System and Structure*, pp. 88–109.

11. Although not fully agreeing with Lawrence Stone's criteria for individualism, I believe his analysis of the phenomenon in the period supports this conclusion. In particular his analysis of the effects on the individual of social mobility, the breakup of hierarchical structures, and puritanism, show how anachronistic are the categories of post-Enlightenment individualism. See *The Crisis of the Aristocracy*, especially pp. 35–6, 579, 584.

12. Lynn White Jr., 'Death and the Devil', contends that the period 1300–1650 'was the most psychically disturbed in European history' for reasons which included rapid cultural change compounded by a series of disasters – famine, pestilence and war. Its manifestations included necrophilia, masochism and sadism. On the basis of the evidence presented, however, White's conclusions remain dubious.

13. Compare Richard Helgerson, who finds in Thomas Lodge 'the mixture of rebellion and submissiveness, so inimical to a stable identity, which he and his contemporaries seemed unable to avoid' (*The Elizabethan Prodigals*, p. 105).

Chapter 11: *Bussy D'Ambois*: A Hero at Court

1. For a diametrically opposed reading of *Bussy* and one firmly within the perspective of essentialist humanism, see Richard S. Ide's *Possessed With Greatness* (1980): 'Bussy does not renounce his heroic conception of self at death. Rather he transcends it by progressing to a higher, more admirable mode of heroism . . . "outward Fortitude" is not rejected, but . . . improved

upon by an inner fortitude equally extraordinary, equally heroic, and in this situation morally superior' (p. 99).

Chapter 12: *King Lear* and Essentialist Humanism

1 Thus Irving Ribner (for example) argues that the play 'affirms justice in the world, which it sees as a harmonious system ruled by a benevolent God' (*Patterns in Shakespearean Tragedy*, p. 117).

2. Other critics who embrace, invoke or imply the categories of essentialist humanism include the following: A. C. Bradley, *Shakespearean Tragedy*, lectures 7 and 8; Israel Knox, *The Aesthetic Theories of Kant, Hegel and Schopenhauer*, p. 117; Robert Ornstein, *The Moral Vision of Jacobean Tragedy*, p. 264; Kenneth Muir, ed., *King Lear*, especially p. lv; Grigori Kozintsev, *King Lear: The Space of Tragedy*, pp. 250–1. For the essentialist view with a pseudo-Nietzschean twist, see Michael Long, *The Unnatural Scene*, pp. 191–3.

Jan Kott suggests the way that the absurdist view exists in the shadow of a failed Christianity and a failed humanism – a sense of paralysis in the face of that failure (*Shakespeare Our Contemporary*, pp. 104, 108, 116–17).

3. Barbara Everett, 'The New King Lear'; William R. Elton, *King Lear and the Gods*; Cedric Watts, 'Shakespearean Themes: The Dying God and the Universal Wolf'.

4. For John Danby, Cordelia is redemption incarnate; but can she really be seen as 'allegorically the root of individual and social sanity; tropologically Charity "that suffereth long and is kind"; analogically the redemptive principle itself? (*Shakespeare's Doctrine of Nature*, p. 125; cf. p. 133).

5. In-form rather than determine: in this play material factors do not determine values in a crude sense; rather, the latter are shown to be dependent upon the former in a way which radically disqualifies the idealist contention that the reverse is true, namely, that these values not only survive the 'evil' but do so in a way which indicates their ultimate independence of it.

6. By contrast compare Derek Traversi who finds in the imagery of this passage a 'sense of value, of richness and fertility . . . an indication of redemption . . . the poetical transformation of natural emotion into its spiritual distillation' (*An Approach to Shakespeare*, II, 164).

Chapter 13: *Antony and Cleopatra*: *Virtus* under Erasure

1. See also Lawrence Stone, *The Crisis of the Aristocracy*, pp. 239–40, 265–7; Ruth Kelso, *The Doctrine of the English Gentleman in the Sixteenth Century*, pp. 11ff.

2. Machiavelli concurs: 'it is impossible that the suspicion aroused in a prince after the victory of one of his generals should not be increased by any arrogance in manner or speech displayed by the man himself' (*Discourses*, p. 181).

3. Compare the dying Bussy: 'Here like a Roman statue; I will stand/Till death hath made me marble' (V. iii. 144–5).
4. See below, chapter 15.
5. In North's Plutarch, Shakespeare's source, we are told that Cleopatra engineered this 'scene' in order to deceive Caesar into thinking she intends to live (*Antony and Cleopatra*, ed. Ridley, p. 276). It is difficult to infer this from the play, but, even if we are inclined to see her anger as feigned, it still presupposes the point being made here, namely that a double standard works for master and servant.

Chapter 14: *Coriolanus*: The Chariot Wheel and its Dust

1. Likewise with Hobbes; in *Leviathan* he posits as mankind's 'general inclination' 'a perpetual and restless desire of power after power' (chapter 11). But this is not so much because man is determined thus by his nature, it is, rather, because of perverse conditions of existence whereby the individual 'cannot assure the power and means to live well, which he hath at present, *without the acquisition of more*' (my italics).
2. Further support for this conclusion comes from Buchanan Sharp's revealing study of social disorder between 1586 and 1660 which concludes: 'the disorders that have been the subject of this work fit within a long tradition of anti-aristocratic and anti-gentry popular rebellion in England . . . the result of social and economic grievances of such intensity that they took expression in violent outbreaks of what can only be called class hatred for the wealthy' (*In Contempt of All Authority*, p. 264). See also E. C. Pettet, '*Coriolanus* and the Midlands Insurrection'.
3. But see also Jonson's *The Devil is an Ass*:

   We see those changes daily: the fair lands
   That were the client's, are the lawyer's now;
   And those rich manors there of goodman Taylor's
   Had once more wood upon them, than the yard
   By which they were measured out for their last purchase.
   Nature hath these vicissitudes. (II. i.)

Chapter 15: *The White Devil*: Transgression Without Virtue

1. In the majority of instances Webster's *sententiae* are what he calls them: 'axioms' (i.e. 'a proposition generally conceded to be true' – *OED*): 'Of all axioms this shall win the prize/'Tis better to be fortunate than wise' (IV. vi. 178–9).
2. Compare *Selimus*: 'nothing is more hurtfull to a Prince/Than to be scrupulous and religious' (ll. 1734–5).
3. Images of poison and disease were, as M. C. Bradbrook points out, 'frequently used as symbols of spiritual decay' (*Themes and Conventions*, p. 190).

But perhaps here the pervasive disease imagery has less to do with the evil of the 'human condition' and more to do with its insecurity – political as well as metaphysical. The association between the *hidden* workings of disease and of policy is made by Donne in the *Devotions*, pp. 51–2.

4. See note 19 to chapter 1.

5. Isabella in Middleton's *Women Beware Women* criticises the willingness of those women who, in relation to men, embrace their subjection so willingly:

> When women have their choices, commonly
> They do but buy their thraldoms, and bring great portions
> To men to keep 'em in subjection.
>
> . . . no misery surmounts a woman's.
> Men buy their slaves, but women buy their masters.
>
> (I. ii. 174–81)

And yet, in her next thought she is made to rationalise this in terms which resemble the very 'false-consciousness' she has just been criticising: 'honesty', 'love' and 'Providence' make everything all right (ll. 182–4). By contrast, the celebrated denunciation of men in *The Roaring Girl* is not amenable to such recuperation; as Simon Shepherd remarks in an interesting discussion of it, 'The play notes corruption at all levels of "normal" society. And it particularly concerns itself with sexual crime. Moll indicts the entire libertine outlook on the world . . . she sees the male exploitation of women, coupled with the insecurities of women's work and the fact that women have no way of expressing or defending themselves' (*Amazons and Warrior Women*, p. 80).

6. See Karl Kautsky, *Thomas More and his Utopia*, pp. 99–100; Christopher Hill, *The World Turned Upside Down*, p. 306.

7. See also Margaret George, 'From "Goodwife" to "Mistress": the Transformation of the Female in Bourgeois Culture', and Lillian S. Robinson, 'Women Under Capitalism' (pp. 150–77 of *Sex, Class and Culture*); Lisa Jardine, *Still Harping on Daughters: Women and Drama in the Age of Shakespeare*.

8. Dusinberre in *Shakespeare and the Nature of Women* claims too much in arguing that 'the drama from 1590 to 1625 is feminist in sympathy', and that the dramatists adopt radical attitudes to women's rights (pp. 5, 11).

9. On the alienated and unemployed intellectual, see also David Aers and Gunther Kress, 'Dark Texts Need Notes: Versions of Self in Donne's Verse Epistles'.

10. For a reading of Webster's plays in terms of essentialist humanism, see Travis Bogard who finds in them no ultimate law, either of God or man, but an affirmation of 'integrity of life' (Dello's words in *The Duchess*). For Bogard 'This defiance, this holding true to one's essential nature' (p. 42) – what he elsewhere calls 'stubborn consistency of self' (p. 55) – 'carries its own protection in its own self-sufficiency. It flourishes in adversity; in the lowest depths it achieves the sublime' (*The Tragic Satire of John Webster*, pp. 42, 55, 145).

11. Quoted from Haskell M. Block and Herman Salingar, eds, *The Creative Vision*, pp. 158–61, Brecht's text is ambiguous and gives rise to significantly

different translations of the penultimate sentence; cf. that of John Willett
and Ralph Manheim in *Collected Plays*, vol. 5, pt. ii, pp. 145–6.

Chapter 16: Beyond Essentialist Humanism

1. For an excellent discussion of this and other forms of individualism, see
   Steven Lukes, *Individualism*.
2. For Brecht and Benjamin see above, chapters 3 and 10, also Terry Eagleton,
   Walter Benjamin, and Susan Buck-Morss, 'Walter Benjamin – Revolutionary
   Writer', parts I and II. In *The Jargon of Authenticity* Adorno offers a powerful
   critique of German existentialism, in which, he argues, 'Man is the ideology
   of dehumanisation' (p. 59; see also pp. 60–76).
3. This perspective does not entail determinism – as Roy Bhaskar's recent
   theory shows. His argument can best be summarised in terms of three of its
   conclusions about society: (i) it 'stands to individuals . . . as something that
   they never make, but that exists only in virtue of their activity'; (ii) it is 'a
   necessary condition for any intentional human act at all'; (iii) it is 'both the
   ever-present *condition* (material cause) and the continually reproduced
   outcome of human agency'. Consequently: 'people, in their conscious
   activity, for the most part unconsciously reproduce (and occasionally transform) the structures governing their substantive activities of production.
   Thus people do not marry to reproduce the nuclear family or work to sustain
   the capitalist economy. Yet it is nevertheless the unintended consequence
   (and inexorable result) of, as it is also a necessary condition for, their activity'
   (*The Possibility of Naturalism*, pp. 42–4). Bhaskar's argument deserves more
   attention than I can give it here. But its importance lies in the fact that it
   shows how purposiveness, intentionality and self-consciousness characterise
   human actions but not necessarily transformations in the social structure; it
   also sustains 'a genuine concept of *change* and hence of *history*' (p. 47). As
   Bhaskar observes (p. 93), his theory is close to Marx's own contention that
   people make their own history but not in conditions of their choosing; to be
   historically positioned is not necessarily to he helplessly determined. Like
   Bhaskar, but from a different position, Anthony Giddens rejects determinism, insisting on the importance for social practice and human agency of
   what he calls *duality of structure*. It entails a view of reason and intention as
   constituted only within the reflexive monitoring of action which in turn presupposes, but also reconstitutes, the institutional organisation of society
   (*Central Problems in Social Theory*, chapters 2 and 3; see also Williams,
   Marxism and Literature, especially pp. 75–83).
4. On some important similarities and differences between cultural materialism,
   structuralism and post-structuralism as they affect English studies, see
   Raymond Williams, 'Crisis in English Studies'. To the extent that psychoanalytic theory still invokes universal categories of psycho-sexual development
   it is incompatible with the materialist perspective outlined here; on this, see
   Stuart Hall, 'Theories of Language and Ideology', especially p. 160.

5. The transcendental pretence is defined by Solomon as the ideological conviction that 'the white middle classes of European descent were the representatives of all humanity, and as human nature is one, so its history must be as well. This transcendental pretence was – and still is – the premise of our thinking about history, "humanity" and human nature' (*History and Human Nature*, p. xii).

6. Compare Macpherson on Locke: 'A market society generates class differentiation in effective rights and rationality, yet requires for its justification a postulate of equal natural rights and rationality. Locke recognised the differentiation in his own society, and read it back into natural society. At the same time he maintained the postulate of equal natural rights and rationality. Most of Locke's theoretical confusions, and most of his practical appeal, can be traced to this ambiguous position' (*The Political Theory of Possessive Individualism*, p. 269). See also Peter Gay, *The Enlightenment: An Interpretation*, II, 167–74.

7. 'Race: A Basic Concept in Education', quoted from p. 14 of Ashley Montagu, *Man's Most Dangerous Myth*.

8. 'The intuition of essence helps set up "essential" hierarchies in which the material and vital values of human life occupy the lowest rank, while the types of the saint, the genius and the hero take first place' (Marcuse, *Negations*, p. 63).

9. Although Hume's belief in universal man represents an important strand in his (an Enlightenment) thinking, it coexists with a strong sense of actual human difference albeit, often, on a superior/inferior model (see D. Forbes, *Hume's Philosophical Politics*, chapter 4). Hume here exemplifies (rather than being responsible for) something which has persisted in western culture: the ideology of 'man' incorporates both a universalist view of human nature as constant, and the view of human nature expressed in terms of cultural difference and diversity: the second has legitimated a superior/inferior classification, the first (in the name of basic sameness) cultural imperialism. A similar point is made, in relation to the history of anthropology, by Edmund Leach in *Social Anthropology*, chapter 2. The racism which this often entails has, of course, found its way into certain strands of modernist literature.

10. M. H. Abrams and, more recently, Jonathan Culler, have pointed to the determinism implicit in the concepts of Romanticism, especially that of organic form which according to Coleridge 'is innate. It shapes as it develops itself from within.' This, as Abrams points out, was merely to substitute for the determinism of mechanistic philosophy its organic – and of course, essentialist – counterpart (see Abrams, *The Mirror and the Lamp*, p. 173; Culler, *The Pursuit of Signs*, chapter 8).

11. Bradley was also closely associated with the neo-Hegelian, T. H. Green; see G. K. Hunter, 'A. C. Bradley's *Shakespearean Tragedy*', in *Dramatic Identities*, pp. 270–85.

12. Kate Millett, *Sexual Politics*; Paul Delany, *D. H. Lawrence's Nightmare*.

Bibliography of Work Cited

* denotes editions of plays used for quotation.

Abrams, M. H., *The Mirror and the Lamp: Romantic Theory and the Critical Tradition*, New York: Norton, 1958.

Adorno, Theodore, *The Jargon of Authenticity*, trans. K. Tarnowski and Frederic Will, London: Routledge, 1973.

Aers, David, and Kress, Gunther, 'Dark Texts Need Notes: Versions of Self in Donne's Verse Epistles', *Literature and History*, 8 (Autumn 1978), 138–58.

Aggeler, G. D., 'Stoicism and Revenge in Marston', *English Studies*, 51 (1970), 1–10.

Allen, D. C., *Doubt's Boundless Sea: Scepticism and Faith in the Renaissance*, Baltimore: Johns Hopkins, 1964.

Althusser, Louis, *For Marx*, London: New Left Books, 1977.

—, *Lenin and Philosophy and Other Essays*, London: New Left Books, 1977.

Anderson, Perry, *Consideration on Western Marxism*, London: Verso, 1979.

Aquinas, *Selected Writings*, ed. M. C. D'Arcy, London: Dent, 1964.

Archer, William, *The Old Drama and the New*, London: Heinemann, 1923.

Arnold, Matthew, *Culture and Anarchy*, London: Smith, Elder, 1891.

Auerbach, Erich, *Mimesis*, trans. Willard R. Trask, Princeton University Press, 1968.

Aylmer, G. E., 'Unbelief in Seventeenth Century England', in *Puritans and Revolutionaries: Essays in Seventeenth Century History Presented to Christopher Hill*, ed. D. H. Pennington, Oxford: Clarendon, 1978.

Babcock, Barbara A., *The Reversible World: Symbolic Inversion in Art and Society*, Ithaca and London: Cornell University Press, 1978.

Bacon, Francis, *Essays*, Introduction by Michael J. Hawkins, London: Dent, 1972.

—, *The Philosophical Works* (one volume), ed. John M. Robertson, London: Routledge, 1905.

—, *Works*, 14 vols, edited by J. Spedding, R. L. Ellis and D. D. Heath, 1857–1861, Stuttgart: Frommann, 1961–3.

Baker, Herschel, *The Image of Man: A Study of the Idea of Human Dignity in Classical Antiquity, the Middle Ages and the Renaissance*, New York: Harper, 1961.

—, *The Wars of Truth: Studies in the Decay of Christian Humanism in the Earlier Seventeenth Century*, London: Staples, 1952.

Baker-Smith, Dominic, 'Religion and John Webster', in *John Webster*, ed. Brian Morris, London: Benn, 1970.

Barber, C. L., *The Idea of Honour in the English Drama 1591–1700*, Gothenburg: Göteborg, 1957.

Barish, J., 'The New Theatre and the Old', in *Reinterpretations of Elizabethan Drama*, ed. N. Rabkin.

Barker, R., ed., *1848: The Sociology of Literature*, Colchester: University of Essex, 1977.

Barthes, Roland, 'The Death of the Author', in *Image, Music, Text*, ed. Stephen Heath, Glasgow: Fontana, 1977.

—, *Mythologies*, trans. Annette Lavers, St Albans: Paladin, 1973.

—, *Roland Barthes*, trans. Richard Howard, London: Macmillan, 1977.

Beard, Thomas, *Theatre of God's Judgement*, London: Adam Islip, 1597.

Beer, Barrett L., and Jack, Sybil M., eds, *The Letters of William, Lord Paget of Beaudesert 1547–63*, Camden Miscellany (xxv), London: Royal Historical Society, 1974.

Beier, A. L., 'Social Problems in Elizabethan London', *Journal of Interdisciplinary History*, 9 (1978–9), 203–22.

Belsey, Catherine, *Critical Practice*, London: Methuen. 1980.

Benjamin, Walter, *Understanding Brecht*, trans. Anna Bostock, London: New Left Books, 1977.

Bennett, Paula, 'Recent Studies in Greville', *English Literary Renaissance*, 2 (1972), 376–82.

Bennett, Tony, *Formalism and Marxism*, London: Methuen, 1979.

Berger, Peter, *The Social Reality of Religion*, London: Faber, 1969.

Bevington, David, *From Mankind to Marlowe: Growth of Structure in the Popular Drama of Stuart England*, Cambridge, Mass.: Harvard University Press, 1962.

Bhaskar, Roy, *The Possibility of Naturalism: A Philosophical Critique of the Contemporary Human Sciences*, Brighton: Harvester Press, 1979.

Bloch, E., et al., *Aesthetics and Politics*, London: New Left Books, 1977.

Block, Haskell M., and Salingar, Herman, eds, *The Creative Vision: Modern European Writers on their Art*, New York: Grove Press, and London: Evergreen Books, 1960.

Bluestone, Max, '*Libido speculandi*: Doctrine and Dramaturgy in Contemporary Interpretations of Marlowe's *Doctor Faustus*', in N. Rabkin, ed., *Reinterpretations of Elizabethan Drama*.

Bogard, Travis, *The Tragic Satire of John Webster*, Berkeley: University of California Press, 1955.

Boklund, G., *The Duchess of Malfi: Sources, Themes, Characters*, Cambridge, Mass.: Harvard University Press, 1962.

Bradbrook, M. C., 'Fate and Chance in *The Duchess of Malfi*', in G. K. and S. K. Hunter, eds, *John Webster: A Critical Anthology*, pp. 132–49.

—, *Themes and Conventions of Elizabethan Tragedy*, Cambridge University Press, 1969.

Bradley, A. C., *Shakespearean Tragedy* (second edition), London: Macmillan, 1905.

—, *Oxford Lectures on Poetry* (second edition), London: Macmillan, 1909.

Bray, Alan, *Homosexuality in Renaissance England*, London: Gay Men's Press, 1982.

Brecht, Bertolt, *Brecht on Theatre*, ed. John Willett, London: Methuen, 1964.

—, *Collected Plays* (vol. 5, part. ii: *Mother Courage and Her Children*), ed. John Willett and Ralph Manheim, London: Methuen, 1980.

—, *The Messingkauf Dialogues*, trans. John Willett, London: Methuen, 1965.

—, *Schriften Zum Theatre*, vol, 7, Frankfurt: Suhrkamp Verlag, 1964.

—, *Gesammelte Werke*, vol. 17, Frankfurt, 1967.

Bridenthal, Renate, and Koonz, Claudia, eds, *Becoming Visible: Women in European History*, Boston: Houghton, Mifflin, 1977.

Brockbank, J. P., *Marlowe: Dr Faustus*, London, Arnold, 1962.

Brockbank, Philip, 'Upon Such Sacrifices', *Proceedings of the British Academy*, 62 (1976), 109–34.

Brooke, C. F. Tucker, *The Life of Marlowe and the Tragedy of Dido Queen of Carthage*, London: Methuen, 1930.

Brooke, Nicholas, *Horrid Laughter in Jacobean Tragedy*, London: Open Books, 1979.

—, 'The Moral Tragedy of Doctor Faustus', *Cambridge Journal*, 5 (August 1952), 662–87.

—, *Shakespeare: King Lear*, London: Arnold, 1963.

Broude, R., 'Revenge and Revenge Tragedy in Renaissance England', *Renaissance Quarterly*, 28 (1975), 38–58.

Browne, Thomas, *Religio Medici, Urn Burial, Christian Morals and Other Essays*, ed. John Addington Symonds, London: Scott, n.d.

Brustein, Robert, '"The Monstrous Regiment of Women": Sources for the Satiric View of the Court Lady in English Drama', in G. R. Hibbard, ed., *Renaissance and Modern Essays*, London: Routledge, 1966.

Buck-Morss, Susan, 'Walter Benjamin – Revolutionary Writer' (two parts), *New Left Review*, 128 (1981), 50–75; 129 (1981), 77–95.

Buckley, G. T., *Atheism in the English Renaissance*, New York: Russell, 1965.

Burckhardt, Jacob, *The Civilization of the Renaissance in Italy*, London: Phaidon, 1965.

Burke, Peter, *Popular Culture in Early Modern Europe*, London: Temple Smith, 1978.

—, *The Renaissance Sense of the Past*, London: Arnold, 1979.

Burton, Robert, *The Anatomy of Melancholy*, ed. Holbrook Jackson, 3 vols, London: Dent, 1932.

Calvin, John, *Institutes*, trans. Henry Beveridge, 2 vols, London: Clarke, 1949.

Camus, Albert, *Selected Essays and Notebooks*, trans. Philip Thody, Harmondsworth: Penguin, 1970.

Carey, John, *John Donne: Life, Mind and Art*, London: Faber, 1981.

Cassirer, Ernst, *The Individual and the Cosmos in Renaissance Philosophy*, Philadelphia: University of Pennsylvania Press, 1973.

—, et al., *The Renaissance Philosophy of Man*, University of Chicago Press, 1948.

Castiglione, Baldassare, *The Book of the Courtier*, trans. Thomas Hoby, London: Dent, 1974.

Castle of Perseverance, in *Four Morality Plays*, ed. Peter Happé, Harmondsworth: Penguin, 1979.

Centre for Contemporary Cultural Studies, *On Ideology*, London: Hutchinson, 1978.

Chamberlain, John, *The Letters*, ed. Norman E. McClure, 2 vols, Philadelphia: American Philosophical Society, 1939.

Chambers, E. K., *The Elizabethan Stage*, 4 vols, Oxford: Clarendon, 1923.

* Chapman, George, *Bussy D'Ambois*, ed. N. S. Brooke, Manchester University Press, 1964.

Clark, Stuart, 'Inversion, Misrule and Witchcraft', *Past and Present*, 87 (1980), 98–127.

Coleridge, Samuel Taylor, *Biographia Literaria*, ed. George Watson, London: Dent, 1965.

—, *Essays and Lectures on Shakespeare*, London: Dent, 1907.

Conrad, Joseph, *Nostromo*, Harmondsworth: Penguin, 1963.

Cook, Ann Jennalie, *The Privileged Playgoers of Shakespeare's London 1576–1642*, Princeton University Press, 1981.

Cousins, A. D., 'The Protean Nature of Man in Marston's Verse Satires', *Journal of English and Germanic Philology*, 79 (1980), pp. 517–29.

Culler, Jonathan, *The Pursuit of Signs: Semiotics, Literature, Deconstruction*, London: Routledge, 1981.

Curreli, Mario, and Martino, Alberto, eds, *Critical Dimensions: English, German and Comparative Literature Essays in Honour of Aurelio Zanco*, Cuneo: Saste, 1978.

Curtis, Mark H., 'The Alienated Intellectuals of Early Stuart England', in Trevor Aston, ed., *Crisis in Europe 1560–1660*, London: Routledge, 1965.

Daiches, David, *Critical Approaches to Literature*, London: Longmans, 1956.

Danby, John, *Shakespeare's Doctrine of Nature*, London: Faber, 1949.

Davies, Sir John, *Nosce Teipsum*, in *Poems*, ed. Robert Krueger, Oxford: Clarendon, 1975.

Davies, Stevie, *Renaissance Views of Man*, Manchester University Press, 1978.

Davis, Natalie Zemon, 'Women on Top: Symbolic Sexual Inversion and Political Disorder in Early Modern Europe', in Babcock, *The Reversible World*.

* Dekker, Thomas, *The Dramatic Works*, ed. Fredson Bowers, 4 vols, Cambridge University Press, 1953–61.

Delany, Paul, *British Autobiography in the Seventeenth Century*, London: Routledge, 1969.

—, *D. H. Lawrence's Nightmare: The Writer and His Circle in the years of the Great War*, Brighton: Harvester, 1979.

Dent, R. W., *John Webster's Borrowings*, Berkeley: University of California Press, 1960.

Derrida, Jacques, *Positions*, trans. Alan Bass, London: Athlone, 1981.

—, *Writing and Difference*, trans. Alan Bass, London: Routledge, 1978.

Descartes, René, *The Philosophical Works*, trans. Elizabeth S. Haldane and G. R. T. Ross, 2 vols, Cambridge University Press, 1931.

Deutscher, L., *The Unfinished Revolution: Russia, 1917–1967*, London: Oxford University Press, 1967.

Dollimore, Jonathan, 'Two Concepts of Mimesis: Renaissance Literary Theory and *The Revenger's Tragedy*', *Themes in Drama*, 2, *Drama and Mimesis*, ed. James Redmond, Cambridge University Press, 1980.

* —, and Alan Sinfield, eds, *The Selected Plays of John Webster*, Cambridge University Press, 1983.

Donne, John, *Biathanatos*, with a bibliographical note by J. William Hebel, New York: The Facsimile Text Society, 1930.

—, *The Complete English Poems*, ed. A. J. Smith, Harmondsworth: Penguin, 1971.

—, *Devotions*, ed. A. Raspa, Montreal: McGill-Queen's University Press, 1975.

—, *Sermons, Complete Poetry and Selected Prose*, ed. John Hayward, London: Nonesuch, 1929.

Dusinberre, Juliet, *Shakespeare and the Nature of Women*, London: Macmillan, 1975.

Eagleton, Terry, *Criticism and Ideology: A Study in Marxist Literary Theory*, London: New Left Books, 1976.

—, 'The Idealism of American Criticism', *New Left Review*, 127 (1981), 53–65.

—, 'Ideology, Fiction, Narrative', *Social Text*, 1 (1979), 62–81.

—, *Walter Benjamin, or Towards a Revolutionary Criticism*, London: Verso, 1981.

Easlea, Brian, *Witch-Hunting, Magic and the New Philosophy: An Introduction to Debates of the Scientific Revolution 1450–1750*, Brighton: Harvester, 1980.

Eliot, T. S., *Selected Essays* (third edition), London: Faber, 1951.

—, 'Ulysses, Order and Myth', reprinted as 'Myth and Literary Classicism' in *The Modern Tradition: Backgrounds of Modern Literature*, ed. Richard Ellmann and Charles Fiedelson, Jr, New York: Oxford University Press.

Ellis-Fermor, Una, *The Frontiers of Drama*, London: Methuen, 1964.

—, *The Jacobean Drama* (fifth edition), London: Methuen, 1965.

Ellrodt, Robert, 'Self-Consciousness in Montaigne and Shakespeare, *Shakespeare Survey*, 28 (1975), 37–50.

Elton, William. R., *King Lear and the Gods*, San Marino: The Huntington Library, 1968.

—, 'Shakespeare and the Thought of His Age', in *A New Companion to Shakespeare Studies*, ed. K. Muir and S. Schoenbaum, Cambridge University Press, 1971.

—, 'Shakespeare's Ulysses and the Problem of Value', *Shakespeare Studies*, 2 (1966), 95–111.

Everett, Barbara, 'The New King Lear', *Critical Quarterly*, 2 (Winter 1960).

* *Everyman*, in *Mediaeval Drama*, ed. David Bevington, Boston: Houghton, Mifflin, 1975.

Farnham, Willard, *The Medieval Heritage of Elizabethan Tragedy*, Oxford: Blackwell, 1936.

Fekete, John, *The Critical Twilight: Explorations in the Ideology of Anglo-American Literary Theory from Eliot to McLuhan*, London: Routledge, 1977.

Ficino, Marcilio, *Commentary on Plato's Symposium*, 1574 edition, trans. G. Neal, in S. Davies, *Renaissance Views of Man*.

—, *Platonic Theology* (Book III, chapter 2), trans. Josephine L. Burroughs, *Journal of the History of Ideas*, 5 (1944), 227–39.

Fish, Stanley, *Self-Consuming Artifacts: The Experience of Seventeenth Century Literature*, Berkeley: University of California Press, 1972.

Fly, Richard D., '"Suited in Like Conditions as Our Argument": Imitative Form in Shakespeare's *Troilus and Cressida*', *Studies in English Literature 1500–1900*, 15 (1975), 273–92.

Forbes, Duncan, *Hume's Philosophical Politics*, Cambridge University Press, 1975.

Foucault, Michel, *Language, Counter-Memory, Practice*, Ithaca and New York: Cornell University Press, 1977.

—, *The Archaeology of Knowledge*, trans. A. M. Sheridan Smith, London: Tavistock, 1974.

—, *The Order of Things: An Archaeology of the Human Sciences*, London: Tavistock, 1970.

—, *Power/Knowledge*, ed. Colin Gordon, Brighton: Harvester, 1980.

Frost, D. L., *The School of Shakespeare*, Cambridge University Press, 1968.

Gay, Peter, *The Enlightenment: An Interpretation*, 2 vols, London: Weidenfeld and Nicolson, 1967–70.

George, Margaret, 'From "Goodwife" to "Mistress": The Transformation of the Female in Bourgeois Culture', *Science and Society*, 37 (1973), 152–77.

Giddens, Anthony, *Central Problems in Social Theory*, London: Macmillan, 1979.

Gierke, Otto von, *Natural Law and the Theory of Society 1500–1800*, trans. Ernest Barker, 2 vols, London: Cambridge University Press, 1934.

Gildersleeve, V. C., *Government Regulation of the Elizabethan Drama*, New York, 1961.

Golding, William, *The Hot Gates and Other Occasional Pieces*, London: Faber, 1965.

Goodman, Godfrey, *The Fall of Man, or the Corruption of Nature, Proved by the Light of Our Natural Reason*, London: Felix Kingston, 1616.

Gramsci, Antonio, *Selections From Prison Notebooks*, ed. and trans. Quintin Hoare and Geoffrey Nowell Smith, London: Lawrence and Wishart, 1971.

Greaves, Richard, and Zaller, Robert, *The Biographical Dictionary of British Radicals in the Seventeenth Century*, vol. 1, Brighton: Harvester, 1982.

Green, Clarence C., *The Neo-Classic Theory of Tragedy During the Eighteenth Century*, New York: Blom, 1966.

Greenblatt, Stephen, *Sir Walter Ralegh: The Renaissance Man and His Roles*, New Haven and London: Yale University Press, 1973.

—, *Renaissance Self-Fashioning*, University of Chicago Press, 1980.

Greenleaf, W. H., *Order, Empiricism, Politics 1500–1700*, London: Oxford University Press, 1964.

Greville, Fulke, *The Life of Sir Philip Sidney*, ed. Nowell Smith, Oxford: Clarendon, 1907.

*—, *Mustapha*, in *Selected Writings*, ed. Joan Rees, London: Athlone, 1973.

—, *The Remains: Being Poems of Monarchy and Religion*, ed. G. A. Wilkes, Oxford University Press, 1965.

—, *Letter to an Honourable Lady*, in *Works*, ed. A. B. Grosart, vol. 4, New York: ASM Press, 1966.

—, *Poems and Dramas*, ed. Geoffrey Bullough, 2 vols, Edinburgh and London: Oliver and Boyd, 1939.

Grudin, Robert, *Mighty Opposites: Shakespeare and Renaissance Contrariety*, Berkeley, Los Angeles and London: University of California Press, 1979.

Gunby, D. C., '*The Duchess of Malfi:* A Theological Approach', in Brian Morris, ed., *John Webster*.

Hakewill, George, *An Apologie or Declaration of the Power and Providence of God*, Oxford: William Turner, 1635.

Hall, Stuart, 'Theories of Language and Ideology', in Stuart Hall, et al., *Culture, Media, Language: Working Papers in Cultural Studies 1972–9*, London: Hutchinson, 1980.

Harris, Victor, *All Coherence Gone: A Study in the Seventeenth Century Controversy Over Disorder and Decay in the Universe*, London: Cass, 1966.

Hauser, Arnold, *Mannerism: The Crisis of the Renaissance and the Origin of Modern Art*, London: Routledge, 1965.

—, *The Social History of Art: Renaissance, Mannerism and Baroque*, London: Routledge, 1962.

Hawkes, Terence, *Structuralism and Semiotics*, London: Methuen, 1977.

Haydn, Hiram, *The Counter-Renaissance*, New York: Charles Scribner, 1950.

Hazlitt, W. C., *The English Drama and Stage*, London: Roxburghe, 1869.

Hegel, G. W. F., *On Tragedy*, ed. Anne and Henry Paolucci, New York: Anchor, 1962.

—, *Philosophy of Mind* (part III of the *Encyclopaedia of the Philosophical Sciences*, 1830), trans. William Wallace, Oxford: Clarendon, 1971.

Heinemann, Margot, *Puritanism and Theatre: Thomas Middleton and Oppositional Drama Under the Early Stuarts*, Cambridge University Press, 1980.

—, 'Shakespearean Contradictions and Social Change', *Science and Society*, 41 (1977), 7–16.

Helgerson, Richard, *The Elizabethan Prodigals*, Berkeley, Los Angeles and London: University of California Press, 1976.

Heywood, Thomas, *An Apology for Actors*, reprinted for the Shakespeare Society, London, 1841.

Hick, John, *Evil and the God of Love*, Glasgow: Collins, The Fontana Library, 1968.

Hill, Christopher, *The Century of Revolution 1603–1714* (second edition), Walton-on-Thames: Nelson, 1980.

—, *Change and Continuity in Seventeenth Century England*, London: Weidenfeld and Nicolson, 1974.

—, *God's Englishman: Oliver Cromwell and the English Revolution*, London: Weidenfeld and Nicolson, 1970.

—, *Intellectual Origins of the English Revolution*, Oxford: Clarendon, 1965.

—, *Puritanism and Revolution: Studies in Interpretation of the English Revolution of the Seventeenth Century*, London: Panther, 1968.

—, *The World Turned Upside Down: Radical Ideas During the English Revolution*, Harmondsworth: Penguin, 1975.

Hobbes, Thomas, *The English Works*, ed. Sir William Molesworth, 11 vols, Aelen: Scientia, 1966.

—, *Leviathan*, ed. Michael Oakeshott, Oxford: Blackwell, 1946.

—, *Man and Citizen* (selected works), ed. Bernard Gert, Brighton: Harvester, 1978.

Holderness, Graham, 'Shakespeare's History: *Richard II*', *Literature and History*, 7 (1981), 2–23.

Holloway, John, *The Story of the Night*, London: Routledge, 1961.

Hooker, Richard, *Of the Laws of Ecclesiastical Polity*, introduction by C. Morris, 2 vols, London: Dent, 1969.

—, 'Of the Certainty and Perpetuity of Faith in the Elect', in *Works*, ed. Rev. J. Keeble, volume III, Oxford University Press, 1845.

Horovitz, David, *Shakespeare: An Existential View*, London: Tavistock, 1965.

Hulme, T. E., *Speculations: Essays on Humanism and the Philosophy of Art*, London: Routledge, 1960.

Hume, David, *An Enquiry Concerning Human Understanding*, L. A. Selby-Bigge (second edition), Oxford: Clarendon, 1962.

—, *Essays, Moral, Political and Literary*, ed. T. H. Green and T. H. Grose, 2 vols, London: Longmans, Green, 1875.

—, *A Treatise of Human Nature*, ed. L. A. Selby-Bigge (second edition), Oxford: Clarendon, 1978.

Hunter, G. K., *Dramatic Identities and Cultural Tradition: Studies in Shakespeare and His Contemporaries*, Liverpool University Press, 1978.

—, and S. K. Hunter, eds, *John Webster: A Critical Anthology*, Harmondsworth: Penguin, 1969.

Hurstfield, Joel, 'The Politics of Corruption in Shakespeare's England', *Shakespeare Survey*, 28 (1975), 15–28.

Ide, Richard S., *Possessed With Greatness: The Heroic Tragedies of Chapman and Shakespeare*, London: Scolar Press, 1980.

James, Mervyn, *English Politics and the Concept of Honour 1485–1642, Past & Present*, Supplement 3 (1978).

Jardine, Lisa, *Still Harping on Daughters: Women and Drama in the Age of Shakespeare*, Brighton: Harvester, 1983.

Johnson, Samuel, *Selected Writings*, ed. R. T. Davies, London: Faber, 1965.

Jonson, Ben, *Discoveries 1641; Conversations 1619*, Bodley Head Quartoes, Edinburgh University Press, 1966.

*—, *Sejanus*, ed. W. F. Bolton, London: Benn, 1966.

—, *Sejanus*, ed. Jonas A. Barish, New Haven and London: Yale University Press, 1965.

—, *Works*, ed. C. H. Herford and Percy Simpson, 11 vols, Oxford: Clarendon, 1922–52.

Kant, Immanuel, *Critique of Pure Reason*, trans. Norman Kemp-Smith, London: Macmillan, 1968.

Kautsky, Karl, *Thomas More and His Utopia*, trans. H. J. Stenning, London: Black, 1927.

Kelliher, W. Hilton, 'The Warwick Manuscripts of Fulke Greville', *The British Museum Quarterly*, 34 (1969), 107–21.

Kelly, H. A., *Divine Providence in the England of Shakespeare's Histories*, Cambridge, Mass.: Harvard University Press, 1970.

Kelly-Gadol, Joan, 'Did Women Have a Renaissance?' in Renate Bridenthal and Claudia Koonz, *Becoming Visible*.

Kelso, Ruth, *The Doctrine of the English Gentleman in the Sixteenth Century*, Urbana, Ill.: University of Illinois Studies in Language and Literature, vol. 14, no. 1–2, 1929.

Kermode, Frank, *The Sense of an Ending*, London: Oxford University Press, 1966.

Kernan, Alvin, *The Cankered Muse: Satire of the English Renaissance*, New Haven: Yale University Press, 1959.

Kitsch, Arthur C., *Jacobean Dramatic Perspectives*, Charlottesville: University Press of Virginia, 1972.

Knight, G. Wilson, *The Imperial Theme*, London: Macmillan, 1965.

Knights, L. C., *Drama and Society in the Age of Jonson*, London: Chatto, 1957.

Knox, Israel, *The Aesthetic Theories of Kant, Hegel and Schopenhauer*, New York: Humanities Press, 1958.

Kocher, P. H., *Christopher Marlowe: A Study of his Thought, Learning and Character*, New York: Russell, 1962.

Kott, Jan, *Shakespeare Our Contemporary*, trans. Boleslaw Taborski, London: Methuen, 1967.

Kozintsev, Grigori, *King Lear: The Space of Tragedy*, trans. Mary Mackintosh, London: Heinemann, 1977.

Krook, Dorothea, *Elements of Tragedy*, New Haven and London: Yale University Press, 1969.

Kunzle, David, 'World Turned Upside Down: The Iconography of a European Broadsheet Type', in Babcock, *The Reversible World*.

* Kyd, Thomas, *The Spanish Tragedy*, ed. Philip Edwards, London: Methuen, 1959.

Lake, Peter, *Moderate Puritans and the Elizabethan Church*, Cambridge University Press, 1982.

La Primaudaye, Peter de, *The French Academy*, Londini: Gorg. Bishop, 1594; London: T. Adams, 1618.

Larrain, Jorge, *The Concept of Ideology*, London: Hutchinson, 1979.

Lawne, William, *An Abridgement of the Institution of Christian Religion*, trans. Christopher Fetherstone, Edinburgh, 1587.

Lawrence, D. H., *Aaron's Rod*, Harmondsworth: Penguin, 1950.

—, *Kangaroo*, Harmondsworth: Penguin, 1950.

—, *Selected Essays*, introduction by Richard Aldington, Harmondsworth: Penguin, 1950.

Leach, Edmund, *Social Anthropology*, Glasgow: Fontana, 1982.

Leech, Clifford, *Shakespeare's Tragedies and Other Studies in Seventeenth Century Drama*, London: Chatto, 1950.

—, *Tragedy*, London: Methuen, 1969.

Lefebvre, Henri, *L'Existentialisme*, Paris: Editions du Sagittaire, 1946.

Lentricchia, Frank, *After the New Criticism*, London: Athlone, 1980.

Lever, J. W., 'Shakespeare and the Ideas of His Time', *Shakespeare Survey*, 29 (1976), 79–91.

—, *The Tragedy of State*, London: Methuen, 1971.

Levin, Richard, *New Reading's vs. Old Plays: Recent Trends in the Reinterpretation of English Renaissance Drama*, University of Chicago Press, 1979.

Levi-Strauss, Claude, *The Savage Mind*, London: Weidenfeld and Nicolson, 1966.

Lisca, Peter, '*The Revenger's Tragedy*: A Study in Irony', *Philological Quarterly*, 38 (1959).

Locke, John, *An Essay Concerning Human Understanding*, ed. Peter H. Nidditch, Oxford: Clarendon, 1975.

—, *Some Thoughts Concerning Education*, in *Educational Writings*, ed. James L. Axtell, Cambridge University Press, 1968.

Long, Michael, *The Unnatural Scene: A Study in Shakespearean Tragedy*, London: Methuen, 1976.

Lovell, Terry, *Pictures of Reality: Aesthetics, Politics, Pleasure*, London: British Film Institute, 1980.

Lukács, Georg, *History and Class Consciousness: Studies in Marxist Dialectics*, trans. Rodney Livingstone, London: Merlin Press, 1971.

Lukes, Steven, *Individualism*, Oxford: Blackwell, 1973.

Luther, Martin, *On the Bondage of the Will*, trans. J. I. Packer and O. R. Johnston, London: Clarke, 1957.

MacCallum, M. W., *Shakespeare's Roman Plays and their Background*, London: Macmillan, 1967.

McCanles, Michael, *Dialectical Criticism and Renaissance Literature*, Berkeley: University of California Press, 1975.

Macherey, Pierre, *Interview, Red Letters*, 5 (1977), 3–9.

—, *A Theory of Literary Production*, trans. Geoffrey Wall, London: Routledge, 1978.

Machiavelli, Niccolò, *The Discourses*, ed. Bernard Crick, Harmondsworth: Penguin, 1970.

—, *The Prince*, trans. George Bull, Harmondsworth: Penguin, 1961.

Maclean, Hugh N., 'Greville's Poetic', *Studies in Philology*, 61 (1964), 170–91.

Macpherson, C. B., *The Political Theory of Possessive Individualism: Hobbes to Locke*, Oxford University Press, 1964.

Mankind, in *English Moral Interludes*, ed. Glynne Wickham, London: Dent, 1976.

Marcuse, Herbert, *Negations: Essays in Critical Theory*, trans. J. Shapiro, London: Allen Lane, the Penguin Press, 1968.

Margeson, J. M. R., *The Origins of English Tragedy*, Oxford: Clarendon, 1967.

Marlowe, Christopher, *Dr Faustus 1604–16, Parallel Texts*, ed. W. W. Greg, Oxford: Clarendon, 1950.

*—, *Dr Faustus*, ed. John Jump, London: Methuen, 1962.

—, *Dr Faustus*, ed. Roma Gill, London: Benn, 1965.

* —, *The Jew of Malta*, ed. T. W. Craik, London: Benn, 1966.

* —, *Tamburlaine*, ed. J. W. Harper, London: Benn, 1971.

Marston, John, 'A Cynicke Satyre', in *Poems*, ed. Arnold Davenport, Liverpool University Press, 1961.

* —, *Antonio and Mellida*, ed. G. K. Hunter, London: Arnold, 1965.

* —, *Antonio's Revenge*, ed. G. K. Hunter, London: Arnold, 1966.

Marx, Karl, *Early Writings*, ed. T. B. Bottomore, London: Watts, 1963.

—, *Selected Works* (one volume), London: Lawrence and Wishart, 1968.

—, *Selected Writings in Sociology and Social Philosophy*, ed. T. B. Bottomore and Maximilien Rubel, Harmondsworth: Penguin, 1963.

Mepham, John, 'The Theory of Ideology in *Capital*', in *Issues in Marxist Philosophy*, vol. 3, ed. John Mepham and D-H. Ruben, Brighton: Harvester, 1979.

Michel, Lawrence, and Sewall, Richard B., *Tragedy: Modern Essays in Criticism*, Westport, Conn.: Greenwood Press, 1963.

* Middleton, Thomas, *Selected Plays*, ed. D. L. Frost, Cambridge University Press, 1978.

Millett, Kate, *Sexual Politics*, London: Hart-Davis, 1971.

Milton, John, *Comus*, Introduction by William Bell, London: Macmillan, 1899.

—, *Paradise Lost*, ed. Alastair Fowler, London: Longman, 1971.

Montagu, Ashley, *Man's Most Dangerous Myth: The Fallacy of Race* (fifth edition), Oxford University Press, 1974.

Montaigne, Michel, *Essays*, trans. John Florio, 3 vols, London: Dent, 1965.

Montrose, Louis, '"Eliza, Queene of Shepheardes" and the Pastoral of Power', *English Literary Renaissance*, 10 (1980), 153–82.

More, St Thomas, *The Complete Works*, vol., 4, ed. J. H. Hexter and E. Surtz, New Haven: Yale University Press, 1965.

—, *Utopia*, ed. Maurice Adams, London: Walter Scott, n.d.

Morris, Brian, ed. *John Webster*, London: Benn, 1970.

Morse, David, *Perspectives on Romanticism: A Transformational Analysis*, London: Macmillan, 1981.

Mulhern, Francis, *The Moment of Scrutiny*, London: New Left Books, 1979.

Munz, Peter, *The Place of Hooker in the History of Thought*, London: Routledge, 1952.

Nashe, Thomas, *The Unfortunate Traveller and other Works*, ed. J. B. Steane, Harmondsworth: Penguin, 1972.

Nietzsche, Friedrich, *The Birth of Tragedy and the Genealogy of Morals*, trans. F. Golding, New York: Doubleday, Anchor, 1956.

—, *The Will to Power*, ed. W. Kaufmann, New York: Vintage Books, 1968.

Orgel, Stephen, *The Illusion of Power: Political Theatre in the English Renaissance*, Berkeley: University of California Press, 1975.

Ornstein, Robert, *The Moral Vision of Jacobean Tragedy*, University of Wisconsin Press, 1965.

Panofsky, E., *Idea: A Concept in Art Theory*, trans. J. S. Peake, Columbia: University of South Carolina Press, 1968.

Parker, R. B., 'Dramaturgy in Shakespeare and Brecht', *University of Toronto Quarterly*, 32 (1963), 230–46.

Parkes, H. B., 'Nature's Diverse Laws: The Double Vision of the Elizabethans', *Sewanee Review*, 58 (1950), 402–18.

Patch, Howard Rollin, *The Goddess Fortuna in Medieval Literature*, London: Cass, 1967.

Pearl, Sara, 'Houses Full of Gentlemen', *Times Literary Supplement*, 29.1.82, p. 100.

Pearl, Valerie, *London and the Outbreak of the Puritan Revolution*, Oxford University Press, 1961.

Perkins, William, *Works*, ed. I. Breward, Abingdon: Sutton Courtenay Press, 1970.

Peter, John, *Complaint and Satire in Early English Literature*, Oxford: Clarendon, 1956.

Pettet, E. C., '*Coriolanus* and the Midlands Insurrection of 1607', *Shakespeare Survey*, 3 (1950), 34–42.

Pico della Mirandola, *Oration: On the Dignity of Man*, in S. Davies, ed., *Renaissance Views of Man*.

Pliny, *The History of the World*, trans. Philemon Holland, selected and edited by Paul Turner, London: Centaur, 1962.

Plutarch, *Morals*, trans. Philemon Holland, London: A. Hatfield, 1603.

Popkin, Richard H., *The High Road to Pyrrhonism*, San Diego: Austin Hill, 1980.

—, *History of Scepticism from Erasmus to Spinoza*, Berkeley, Los Angeles and London: University of California Press, 1979.

Potter, Lois, 'Realism versus Nightmare: Problems of Staging *The Duchess of Malfi*', in *The Triple Bond: Plays, Mainly Shakespearean, in Performance*, ed. Joseph Price, Pennsylvania State University Press, 1975.

Prior, Moody E., *The Drama of Power: Studies in Shakespeare's History Plays*, Evanston, Ill.: Northwestern University Press, 1973.

Prynne, William, *Histriomastix*, preface by Arthur Freeman, New York and London: Garland, 1974.

Quinlan, M. A., *Poetic Justice in the Drama*, Notre Dame: Indiana University Press, 1912.

Raab, Felix, *The English Face of Machiavelli: A Changing Interpretation 1500–1700*, London: Routledge, 1964.

Rabkin, N., *Reinterpretations of Elizabethan Drama*, New York: Columbia University Press, 1969.

Raleigh, Walter, *History of the World*, ed. C. A. Patrides, London: Macmillan, 1971.

Rebholz, Ronald, *The Life of Fulke Greville*, Oxford: Clarendon, 1971.

Ribner, Irving, *Patterns in Shakespearean Tragedy*, London: Methuen, 1960.

Ricks, Christopher, *English Drama to 1710* (vol. 3 of *History of Literature in the English Language*), London: Sphere Books, 1971.

Robbe-Grillet, Alain, 'Nature, Humanism and Tragedy', in *Snapshots and Towards a New Novel*, trans. Barbara Wright, London: Calder and Boyars, 1965.

Robinson, Lillian S., *Sex, Class and Culture*, Bloomington and London: Indiana University Press, 1978.

Rosen, Charles, 'The Ruins of Walter Benjamin', *New York Review of Books*, vol. 24, no. 17, pp. 31–40.

Rossiter, A. P., *Angel With Horns and other Shakespearean Lectures*, ed. Graham Storey, London: Longman, 1961.

Rupp, E. Gordon, ed., *Luther and Erasmus: Free Will and Salvation*, London: SCM, 1969.

Russell, Conrad, *The Crisis of Parliaments*, London: Oxford University Press, 1971.

Russell, Kathryn, 'Science and Ideology', in J. Mepham and D-H. Ruben, eds, *Issues in Marxist Philosophy*.

Rymer, Thomas, *The Critical Works*, ed. Curt A. Zimansky, New Haven: Yale University Press, 1956.

Salingar, L. G., '*The Revenger's Tragedy* and the Morality Tradition', *Scrutiny*, 6, no. 4 (1938), 402–24.

——, *Shakespeare and the Tradition of Comedy*, London: Cambridge University Press, 1974.

Sanders, Wilbur, *The Dramatist and the Received Idea: Studies in the Plays of Marlowe and Shakespeare*, Cambridge University Press, 1968.

——, Review Article, *Essays in Criticism*, 22 (1972), 182–91.

Sartre, Jean-Paul, *Politics and Literature*, trans. J. A. Underwood, London: Calder and Boyars, 1973.

Schopenhauer, Arthur, *Essays and Aphorisms*, trans. R. J. Hollingdale, Harmondsworth: Penguin, 1970.

——, *Parerga and Paralipomena*, trans. E. F. J. Payne, 2 vols, Oxford: Clarendon, 1974.

* *Selimus* (?Robert Greene), Malone Society Reprints, 1908, reprinted Oxford, 1964.

Seneca, Lucius Annaeus, *Letters From a Stoic*, trans. R. Campbell, Harmondsworth: Penguin, 1969.

Shakespeare, William, * *Complete Works*, ed. Peter Alexander, the Tudor Edition, London and Glasgow: Collins, 1951.

——, *Antony and Cleopatra*, ed, M. R. Ridley, London: Methuen, 1965.

——, *Coriolanus*, ed. Philip Brockbank, London: Methuen, 1976.

——, *King Lear*, ed. Kenneth Muir, London: Methuen, 1964.

——, *Richard II*, ed. Peter Ure, London: Methuen, 1966.

Sharp, Buchanan, *In Contempt of All Authority: Rural Artisans and Riots in the West of England 1386–1660*, Berkeley, Los Angeles and London: University of California Press, 1980.

Shepherd, Simon, *Amazons and Warrior Women: Varieties of Feminism in Seventeenth-Century Drama*, Brighton: Harvester, 1981.

Sidney, Sir Philip, *Arcadia*, ed. Maurice Evans, Harmondsworth: Penguin, 1977.

—, *An Apology for Poetry*, ed. Geoffrey Shepherd, Manchester University Press, 1973.

Sinfield, Alan, *Literature in Protestant England 1560–1660*, London: Croom Helm, 1982.

Smith, George Gregory, ed., *Elizabethan Critical Essays*, 2 vols, Oxford: Clarendon, 1904.

Solomon, Robert C., *History and Human Nature*, Brighton: Harvester, 1980.

Spenser, Edmund, *The Faerie Queene*, ed. Thomas P. Roche Jr, Harmondsworth: Penguin, 1978.

Spingarn, J. E., *A History of Literary Criticism in the Renaissance*, New York and London: Columbia University Press, 1908.

Stone, Lawrence, *The Causes of the English Revolution 1529–1642*, London: Routledge, 1972.

—, *The Crisis of the Aristocracy 1558–1641*, Oxford University Press, 1965.

—, 'The Educational Revolution in England 1560–1640', *Past and Present*, 28 (1964), 41–80.

—, Review, *English Historical Review*, 77 (1962), 327–8.

Strathmann, E. A., *Sir Walter Ralegh: A Study in Elizabethan Scepticism*, New York: Columbia University Press, 1951.

Stubbes, Philip, *Anatomy of Melancholy*, ed. Frederick J. Furnivall, London: Trubner, for the New Shakespeare Society, 1877–9.

Tatarkiewicz, W., *History of Aesthetics*, 3 vols, The Hague: Mouton; Warsaw: PWN-Polish Scientific Publishers, 1970.

Therborn, Göran, *The Ideology of Power and the Power of Ideology*, London: Verso, 1980.

Thomas, Keith, *Religion and the Decline of Magic*, Harmondsworth: Penguin, 1978.

Thompson, E. P., *The Poverty of Theory*, London: Merlin, 1978.

Thorpe, Willard, *The Triumph of Realism in Elizabethan Drama 1558–1612*, Princeton University Press, 1928.

Tillyard, E. M. W., *Shakespeare's History Plays*, London: Chatto, 1944.

Tinsley, John, 'Tragedy and Christian Belief', *Theology*, March 1982, pp. 98–105.

Tourneur, Cyril, *Plays and Poems*, ed. J. Churton Collins, 2 vols, London, 1878.

—, *Works*, ed. Allardyce Nicoll, London: The Fanfrolico Press, 1929.

—, *The Revenger's Tragedy*, ed. R. A. Foakes, London: Methuen, 1966.

Traversi, Derek, *An Approach to Shakespeare* (third edition), 2 vols, London: Hollis and Carter, 1969.

Trilling, Lionel, *The Opposing Self*, New York: Viking Press, 1955.

Trinkaus, Charles, *In Our Image and Likeness: Humanity and Divinity in Italian Humanist Thought*, 2 vols, London: Constable, 1970.

—, 'Renaissance Problems in Calvin's Theology', *Studies in the Renaissance*, 1 (1954), 59–80.

Ullmann, Walter, *The Individual and Society in the Middle Ages*, London: Methuen, 1967.

Vickers, Brian, *Shakespeare: Coriolanus*, London: Arnold, 1966.

Waith, Eugene M., *The Herculean Hero in Marlowe, Chapman, Shakespeare and Dryden*, London: Chatto, 1962.

Walker, D. P., *The Decline Of Hell: Seventeenth Century Discussions of Eternal Torment*, London: Routledge, 1964.

Waller, G. F., 'This Matching of Contraries: Bruno, Calvin and the Sidney Circle', *Neophilologus*, 56 (1972), 331–43.

Walter, John, and Wrightson, Keith, 'Dearth and the Social Order in Early Modern England', *Past and Present*, 71 (1976), 22–42.

Walters, Margaret, *The Nude Male: A New Perspective*, New York and London: Paddington Press, 1978.

Walzer, Michael, *The Revolution of the Saints: A Study in the Origins of Radical Politics*, London: Weidenfeld and Nicolson, 1966.

Watts, Cedric, 'Shakespearean Themes: The Dying God and the Universal Wolf', in M. Curreli and A. Martino, eds, *Critical Dimensions*.

Webster, Charles, ed., *The Intellectual Revolution of the Seventeenth Century*, London: Routledge, 1974.

Webster, John, *The White Devil; The Duchess of Malfi*, ed. John Russell Browne, London: Methuen, 1960, 1964.

—, *The Duchess of Malfi, The White Devil*, ed. Elizabeth M. Brennan, London: Benn, 1964, 1966.

* —, *Selected Plays*, ed. Jonathan Dollimore and Alan Sinfield, Cambridge University Press, 1983.

Wedgwood, C. V., *The Thirty Years War*, London: Cape, 1944.

White, Jr., Lynn, 'Death and the Devil', in *The Darker Vision of the Renaissance*, ed. Robert S. Kinsman, Berkeley, Los Angeles, London: University of California Press, 1974.

Wickham, Glynne, *Early English Stages*, vol. II, part 1, London: Routledge, 1963.

Wilden, Anthony, *System and Structure: Essays in Communication and Exchange*, London: Tavistock, 1972.

Williams, R., 'Crisis in English Studies', *New Left Review*, 129 (1981), 51–66.

—, *Culture*, Glasgow: Fontana, 1981.

—, 'Forms of English Fiction in 1848', in *1848: The Sociology of Literature*, ed. F. Barker.

—, *Keywords*, Glasgow: Fontana, 1976.

—, *The Long Revolution*, Harmondsworth: Penguin, 1965.

—, *Marxism and Literature*, Oxford University Press, 1977.

—, *Modern Tragedy*, London: Verso, 1979.

—, *Politics and Letters*, London: New Left Books, 1979.

—, *Problems in Materialism and Culture*, London: Verso, 1980.

Williamson, George, 'Mutability, Decay and Seventeenth Century Melancholy', *English Literary History*, 2 (1935), 121–50.

Wilson, Colin, 'Beyond the Outsider', in *Declaration*, ed. Tom Maschler, London: MacGibbon and Kee, 1957.

Wimsatt, William K, and Brooks, Cleanth, *Literary Criticism: A Short History*, New York: Alfred A. Knopf, 1959.

—, *The Outsider*, with new introduction, London: Pan, 1978.

Winstanley, Gerrard, *The Law of Freedom and Other Writings*, ed. Christopher Hill, Harmondsworth: Penguin, 1973.

Wolff, Janet, *The Social Production of Art*, London: Macmillan, 1981.

Wolff, Robert Paul, *The Poverty of Liberalism*, Boston: Beacon Press, 1968.

Woodbridge, Linda, *Women and the English Renaissance: Literature and the Nature of Womankind 1540–1620*, forthcoming, University of Illinois Press and Brighton: Harvester, 1983.

Wright, Louis B., *Middle Class Culture in Elizabethan England*, London: Methuen, 1964.

Wrightson, Keith, *English Society 1580–1680*, London: Hutchinson, 1982.

Yuill, W. E., *The Art of Vandalism: Bertolt Brecht and the English Drama*, Inaugural Lecture, London: Bedford College, 1977.

Index of Names and Texts

Index of Subjects

312